COMPLETE POEMS

The Other Voice in Early Modern Europe: The Toronto Series, 6

The Other Voice in
Early Modern Europe:
The Toronto Series

SERIES EDITORS Margaret L. King *and* Albert Rabil, Jr.

Recent Publications in the Series

1
MADRE MARÍA ROSA
Journey of Five Capuchin Nuns
Edited and translated by Sarah E. Owens
2009

2
GIOVAN BATTISTA ANDREINI
Love in the Mirror
Edited and translated by Jon R. Snyder
2009

3
RAYMOND DE SABANAC AND SIMONE ZANACCHI
Two Women of the Great Schism: The Revelations *of Constance de Rabastens by Raymond de Sabanac and* Life of the Blessed Ursulina of Parma *by Simone Zanacchi*
Edited and translated by Renate Blumenfeld-Kosinski and Bruce L. Venarde
2010

4
OLIVA SABUCO DE NANTES BARRERA
The True Medicine
Edited and translated by Gianna Pomata
2010

5
LOUISE-GENEVIÈVE GILLOT DE SAINCTONGE
Dramatizing Dido, Circe, and Griselda
Edited and translated by Janet Levarie Smarr
2010

PERNETTE DU GUILLET

Complete Poems

A Bilingual Edition

Edited with introduction and notes by

KAREN SIMROTH JAMES

Poems translated by

MARTA RIJN FINCH

ITER

Iter Inc.
Centre for Reformation and Renaissance Studies
Toronto
2010

Iter: Gateway to the Middle Ages and Renaissance
Tel: 416/978-7074 Fax: 416/971-1399
Email: iter@utoronto.ca Web: www.itergateway.org

CRRS Publications, Centre for Reformation and Renaissance Studies
Victoria University in the University of Toronto
Toronto, Ontario M5S 1K7 Canada
Tel: 416/585-4465 Fax: 416/585-4430
Email: crrs.publications@utoronto.ca Web: www.crrs.ca

Printed in Canada

We thank the Gladys Kriebel Delmas Foundation for a generous grant of start-up funds for The Other Voice, Toronto Series, a portion of which supports the publication of this volume.

Iter and the Centre for Reformation and Renaissance Studies gratefully acknowledge the generous support of James E. Rabil, in memory of Scottie W. Rabil, toward the publication of this book.

Library and Archives Canada Cataloguing in Publication
Du Guillet, Pernette, 1520?-1545
Complete poems : a bilingual edition / Pernette du Guillet ; edited with introduction and notes by Karen Simroth James ; poems translated by Marta Rijn Finch.

(The other voice in early modern Europe : the Toronto series ; 6)
Poems in French and English.
Translation of: Rymes de gentile et vertueuse dame, D. Pernette du Guillet, lyonnoise.
Co-publ. by: Centre for Reformation and Renaissance Studies.
Includes bibliographical references and index.
Issued also in electronic format.
ISBN 978-0-7727-2065-8

I. James, Karen Simroth, 1959- II. Finch, Marta Rijn, 1944- III. Victoria University (Toronto, Ont.). Centre for Reformation and Renaissance Studies IV. Iter Inc V. Title. VI. Series: Other voice in early modern Europe. Toronto series ; 6

PQ1619.D35A25 2010
841'.3 C2010-904323-5

Cover illustration: *Portrait of a Lady* by an unknown artist, ca. 1540, private collection

Cover design: Maureen Morin, Information Technology Services,
University of Toronto Libraries
Typesetting and production: Iter Inc.

A mon Jour
(M. R. F.)

For Stu and Katherine
(K. S. J.)

Contents

Acknowledgments

I am deeply grateful to Mary McKinley for encouraging me to embark on this project, for offering valuable feedback and advice when most needed, and for her wise counsel over the years since my first forays into the *Rymes*. My warm thanks go to Leah Chang, Cathy Yandell, Jeff Persels, Kelly Peebles, Cynthia Skenazi, George Hoffman, Megan Conway, and Kendall Tarte for their helpful comments and suggestions on various portions of the manuscript and on related conference papers along the way. I wish also to thank François Rigolot for the insights gleaned from a Folger Institute Seminar years ago, which helped to focus my early research on the *Rymes*.

I would not have gotten very far in this endeavor without the talented and dedicated collaboration of Marta Finch, from whom I have learned much about poetry and translation. We are both immensely grateful to Al Rabil for his commitment to this series and to publishing this volume, and for his support and guidance through the publication process.

Finally, none of this would have been possible without the encouragement, understanding, and tremendous patience of Stu and Katherine James, to whom I dedicate this volume with love.

Karen Simroth James

My debt to Karen James is impossible to overstate. She pushed me to refine individual words and lines to a level I could not have achieved alone, and my appreciation of this poetry grew with all that I learned through her. I would like also to thank my sister Annie Finch who translated the poems of Louise Labé for another volume in the Other Voice series; without her encouragement, I should never have taken up this task. My poet-mother, Margaret Rockwell Finch, whose experience with her own writing has spanned more than 80 years, was invaluable—especially when my thoughts were so steeped in the French that I had trouble getting a clear view of the English. My two daughters also played a part—artist Christine Lashley who provided sustenance to Karen and me during our last intense work-session, and Rebecca Bondellio, another writer, who, as I labored over two of these epigrams, labored to bring forth a new life. My greatest appreciation, however, is for Charles—my own beloved "Day," whose love and gentle understanding helped me through it all.

Marta Rijn Finch

~

KAREN SIMROTH JAMES teaches and is Language Program Director in the Department of French at the University of Virginia, where she also directs the digital archive, *The Renaissance in Print: Sixteenth-Century French Books in the Douglas H. Gordon Collection.*

MARTA RIJN FINCH is a Vermont poet who wrote her first verse at age five. An early fascination with languages led to the study of French, Latin, Greek, Russian, and Chinese. She lived in France for six years, attended the Sorbonne, and translated the poetry of philosopher Simone Weil during her stay in Lyon.

Pernette du Guillet (ca. 1520–1545)

KAREN SIMROTH JAMES

The Other Voice

Published soon after her death in 1545, the collected poems of Pernette du Guillet—*Rymes de gentile et vertueuse dame D. Pernette du Guillet, Lyonnoise*—evoke a young woman's experiences with love and her birth as speaking and writing subject.[1] The seventy-three poems composed during her short life represent a variety of lyric genres prevalent in the early French Renaissance, including epigrams, songs, verse epistles, and elegies.[2] Du Guillet adopts elements of Italian Neoplatonism and Petrarchan poetics, and responds to the works of other French poets, including Clément Marot and Maurice Scève. Her poems recognize the attraction and force of physical desire, while resolutely upholding the goal of a spiritual and intellectual union with the beloved that will result in reciprocal affection and mutual contentment. The *Rymes* draw the reader into an intimate world of conversational exchanges that echo learned philosophical debates on the nature of love. Du Guillet's poetry encompasses a variety of forms, influences, and rhetorical strategies, conveying a lyric voice quite different from those of her better-known contemporaries in Lyon, Maurice Scève and Louise Labé, who drew from the same pool of literary sources. Pernette du Guillet's unique use of poetic conventions and philosophical models allows her to assert her rights in love and her active role as a writer in an era when a woman's speech exposed her to censure, and silence protected her feminine virtue.

1. The first edition of the *Rymes*, published by Jean de Tournes in Lyon in 1545, includes seventy poems by Du Guillet, a preface by the editor, Antoine du Moulin, a liminary poem by the printer, and four lyric epitaphs in praise of the deceased poet by Maurice Scève and Jean de Vauzelles. In his subsequent 1552 edition, Jean de Tournes added three poems attributed to Du Guillet. For details about the publication history of the *Rymes*, see the section below on the reception of the *Rymes*.

2. Although not true equivalents of the French, we have chosen the closest possible English terms to refer in translation to these genres: *épigrammes*, *chansons*, *épîtres*, and *élégies*. V.-L. Saulnier categorized and numbered the poems by genre in the first important modern study of Du Guillet's work, "Etude sur Pernette du Guillet et ses *Rymes*," in *Bibliothèque d'Humanisme et Renaissance* 4 (1944), 7–119. See the section below on the French text for more about the naming and numbering of the poems.

According to Antoine du Moulin's preface to the first edition of the *Rymes*, the young woman's grieving husband brought her poems to light after her death, providing a socially acceptable context for publishing love poetry by a woman, an otherwise risky venture at that time. Literary tradition has long linked Pernette du Guillet's name with that of Maurice Scève, identifying Du Guillet as the inspiration for Scève's *Délie* (Lyon, 1544). She herself inscribed Scève's name in her verse through anagrams and wordplay, prompting literary historians until the late twentieth century to read her poetry largely in the shadow of Scève's *canzoniere*, focusing undue attention on suppositions pertaining to a Platonic love between the two poets, although we have no external evidence regarding the nature of their relationship.[3]

More recent critical approaches to the *Rymes*, however, have set aside this autobiographical focus to explore the collection in ways that shed light on Du Guillet's poetic techniques in relation to the works of her contemporaries and predecessors.[4] The poems of the *Rymes* engage in intertextual dialogue with the *Délie*, as well as with other important works of poetry and theories of love in circulation in mid-sixteenth-century Lyon, displaying innovative responses to those texts.[5] Pernette du Guillet's literary dialogues with the works of Scève and others—the *Rhétoriqueurs*, Marot, the Petrarchan poets, and the Neoplatonists—reveal a young writer fully aware of her difference from her male counterparts, both contemporary and historical. Within traditions focusing on the experience and voice of

3. Joseph Buche first published this identification of Scève's *Délie* with Pernette du Guillet, based on his reading of the two works. See "Pernette du Guillet et la <<Délie>> de Maurice Scève," in *Mélanges de Philologie offerts à Ferdinand Brunot* (1904; Geneva: Slatkine Reprints, 1972), 33–39. As Floyd Gray notes, however, the appearance of Scève's name in the *Rymes* as anagrams and puns is "flimsy evidence on which to base a claim for anything other than the poetic relationship that is assumed here." *Gender, Rhetoric, and Print Culture in French Renaissance Writing* (Cambridge: Cambridge University Press, 2000), 184.

4. The list of noteworthy studies of the *Rymes* is now (happily) too numerous to fit in one opening footnote. I have indicated particularly relevant publications in the notes to the poems themselves and in corresponding passages of the Introduction. See also the list of resources in the bibliography of this volume.

5. Françoise Charpentier observes that "l'œuvre baigne dans une intertextualité dont Scève est loin d'être la seule composante, tant au niveau du contenu que de la forme" (the work is bathed in an intertextuality of which Scève is far from being the only element, on the level of content as well as of form). "Projet poétique, travail poétique dans les *Rymes* de Pernette du Guillet: Autour de trois quatrains," in *Poétique et Narration: Mélanges offerts à Guy Demerson*, ed. François Marotin and Jacques-Phillippe Saint-Gérand (Paris: Champion, 1993), 146. Unless otherwise indicated, all translations of secondary sources are my own.

the male poet and lover, the female lyric subject of the *Rymes* gently, humorously, yet firmly, asserts her right to speak and be heard.

The variety and complexity of the voices in the collection constitute a particularly compelling feature of the *Rymes*. They extol the beloved's virtues, yet also offer spirited criticism of his behavior. They speak at times in the abstract vocabulary of Neoplatonism, but at other times in a straightforward and often light-hearted tone of common sense that suggests a passing conversation rather than a philosophical discourse on love. The collection as a whole presents the authorial voice of a young female poet who expresses admiration of her beloved's impressive learning and eloquence, but who, beyond that praise, conveys a full range of emotions pertaining to love and to the process of writing. How the poet creates this unique lyric subject within literary traditions, and in a time of social constraints that gave women no voice, remains a central and intriguing aspect of the *Rymes*.

Ce Climat Lyonnois[6]

Pernette du Guillet wrote her poetry in the stimulating intellectual and artistic climate of mid-sixteenth-century Lyon. The city's geographical location at the confluence of the Rhône and Saône rivers and the crossroads of important trade routes between France and Italy favored commerce and promoted the transport and exchange of new ideas. Goods and money flowed particularly freely during the fairs held four times each year in Lyon. The vigorous economy attracted new industry in the first decades of the sixteenth century, including silk and printing. Foreign bankers—many from Florence, Genoa, Lucca, and Milan—contributed to making Lyon one of Europe's most important financial centers. Wealthy merchants joined lawyers and doctors among the city's well-to-do, and its artisan class prospered in the environment of economic growth.[7] The royal court, beginning

6. Du Moulin uses this phrase in his preface, addressed to the "Ladies of Lyon," to emphasize the city's remarkable climate for encouraging learning and fostering literary accomplishments.

7. For a detailed account of the fairs, see Louis Bourgeois, *Quand la cour de France vivait à Lyon, 1494–1551* (Paris: Fayard, 1980), chap. 3 ("Lyon, trône des foires"), 23–44; Marc Brésard, *Les foires de Lyon aux XVe et XVIe siècles* (Paris, A. Picard, 1914). Natalie Zemon Davis outlines the city's tremendous growth between 1530 and 1550, when "its resident population increased by a third, from around 45,000 people to 65,000," and explains the role of the fairs in Lyon's status as a financial and commercial capital of Europe. "The Sacred and the Body Social in Sixteenth-Century Lyon," in *Past and Present* 90 (February 1981), 43. For

with the military campaigns in Milan and Naples, spent lengthy visits in Lyon, many of which were marked by pomp and pageantry,[8] but the elite and ruling classes of the city nevertheless knew a relative autonomy from the seat of royal and state power (the king and *parlement*) and the church authorities (the theologians of the Sorbonne) in Paris.

The cosmopolitan culture of Lyon, with its many wealthy foreign inhabitants, favored the importation and circulation of new literary and artistic models, particularly those of the Italian Neoplatonists and Petrarchan poets, as well as texts associated with the humanist movement in France, and later with the Reform movement.[9] The flow of new ideas and the relatively well-educated population meant a large market in Lyon itself for printed books, including the classics in Greek and Latin, the newer works of Italian poets and philosophers, translations of all those texts into the vernacular, and contemporary French works. The fairs guaranteed a national and international market for the books printed in Lyon. When the magistrates decided to found a new school in 1527—the *Collège de la Trinité*—humanist scholars from elsewhere in France flocked to Lyon to take advantage of the city's open intellectual atmosphere and booming economy.[10]

François Rigolot cites the climate of vigor and astonishing freedom that characterized the world of printing in Lyon as an important factor contributing to the "Louise Labé phenomenon"—referring to the other highly celebrated "Dame de Lyon," whose collected works were published by Jean de Tournes in 1555 and 1556,

---

more details on commerce and on the demographic impact of the city's population growth in the first half of the sixteenth century, see Richard Gascon, *Grand commerce et vie urbaine au XVIe siècle, Lyon et ses marchands*, vol. 1 (Paris: Ecole Pratique des Hautes Etudes and Mouton, 1971).

8. The pageantry associated with royal visits to the city was often commemorated in printed volumes, such as *La Magnificence de la suberbe et triumphante entrée de la noble & antique Cité de Lyon faicte au Treschrestien Roy de France Henry deuxiesme de ce Nom, Et à la Royne Catherine son Espouse le XXIII. de Septembre M.D. XLVIII* (Lyon: Guillaume Rouille, 1549), written by Maurice Scève. See *The entry of Henri II into Lyon: september 1548*, ed. Richard Cooper (Tempe, AZ: Medieval & Renaissance texts and studies, 1997).

9. See Lucien Romier, "Lyons and Cosmopolitanism at the Beginning of the French Renaissance," in *French Humanism, 1470–1600*, ed. Werner L. Gundersheimer (London: Macmillan, 1969), 90–109. For more on the role of Italians in the commerce and culture of Renaissance Lyon, see Jacqueline Boucher, *Présence italienne à Lyon à la Renaissance, du milieu du XVe à la fin du XVIe siècle* (Lyon: Editions LUGD, 1994).

10. L. Gerig refers to Renaissance Lyon as an "earthly paradise" for unhappy scholars. "Le Collège de la Trinité à Lyon avant 1540," in *Revue de la Renaissance* IX (Geneva: Slatkine reprints, 1968), 74.

ten years after his publication of the *Rymes*.[11] In this environment favorable to writers and to printers, Tournes published more than 500 editions before his death in 1564—elegantly printed volumes of the classics and of contemporary works of religion and literature, primarily in the vernacular. He was the first printer in Lyon to publish Dante and Petrarch in Italian; his editions in French include the literary works of Clément Marot, Bonaventure des Périers, Pernette du Guillet, Marguerite de Navarre, Maurice Scève, Jacques Peletier, Louise Labé, and Pontus de Tyard. Astute in business, Jean de Tournes—like many of his fellow printers in Lyon—was also a learned man, steeped in the humanist culture and ideals of the books he printed. He shared his interests and aspirations with a network of writers and scholars in his city, among them his longtime collaborator, Antoine du Moulin.[12] The presence of a liminary poem by the printer to the reader, along with a preface by Du Moulin, situates the *Rymes* in this intellectual network of the world of printing in Renaissance Lyon.[13]

In his prolific career, Jean de Tournes published several successful editions of works by women writers—notably Pernette du Guillet, Louise Labé, and Marguerite de Navarre—along with texts conveying a favorable account of women or discussing the roles of men and women in love. Antoine Héroët's *La parfaicte amye*, for example, published by Jean de Tournes in 1547, was one of the most well-known texts in the Renaissance *querelle des amyes*, part of an ongoing exchange of works defending or condemning female nature, begun in the Middle Ages and known as the *querelle des femmes*.[14] In 1551, Tournes published Pontus de Tyard's French translation of Leone Ebreo's *Dialoghi d'amore*, the

11. As Rigolot suggests, Louise Labé may well have responded to Antoine du Moulin's exhortation to the ladies of Lyon in his preface to the *Rymes*, benefiting from the relatively favorable atmosphere for women writers in Lyon. See *Louise Labé Lyonnaise, ou La Renaissance au féminin* (Paris: Champion, 1997), 15–16.

12. Natalie Zemon Davis explains that Jean de Tournes discussed Italian poetry with Scève, morality with Des Périers, and topics such as physiognomy with Du Moulin. "Le monde de l'imprimerie humaniste: Lyon," in *Histoire de l'édition française*, vol. 1, *Le livre conquérant* (Paris: Promodis, 1983), 265.

13. For a discussion of the role of the printing trade in the literary life of Lyon in the first half of the sixteenth century, see "Le Clos d'un excellent Lyon" in the introduction by Elise Rajchenbach to *Rymes* (Geneva: Droz, 2006), 10–19. See also Henri-Jean Martin, "Les imprimeurs et l'humanisme," in *Lyon, l'humaniste*, ed. Claude Royon (Paris: Editions Autrement, 2004), 67–74.

14. See the series editors' Introduction at www.itergateway.org/iter20.htm, and the notes for poem 39, "Perfect Love" ("Parfaicte amytié").

influential dialogues on love that Pernette du Guillet would have known, perhaps both in the original Italian and in French. The translation, or parts of it, may well have circulated in manuscript form in the literary circles of Lyon before its publication.

Printed music books represented another important component of the book trade in Lyon, encompassing the sacred and the secular, and supplying the local market—including aristocrats and the wealthy merchant class—as well as a national and international market engaged by the fairs. Music flourished in Renaissance Lyon, playing a significant role in the lives and theories of many literary figures in the city, such as Symphorien Champier and Jean Lemaire de Belges, who closely associated music with love and with poetry, as well as Rabelais, Dolet, Des Périers, and Aneau, whose works reflect their musical interests.[15] Two of the three songbooks in which Pernette du Guillet's poems were published during her lifetime were printed in Lyon.[16]

Musical skill was also a valued feminine accomplishment, as Antoine du Moulin tells us in his preface to the *Rymes*, where he praises the poet's mastery of so many musical instruments, including the lute and the spinet, and calls on the ladies of Lyon to follow her example in striving for similar perfection. (As noted above, four of Du Guillet's epigrams were set to music and published in local anthologies as early as 1540 and 1541.) With Du Moulin's praise of the poet's lute playing in mind, we are not surprised to find that instrument evoked within the collection, although the role it plays there is not precisely that which the preface suggests. In the imagined scenario of poem 43, the female speaker fantasizes about seducing and controlling her

15. See Frank Dobbins, "Lyons: Commercial and Cultural Metropolis," in *The Renaissance: From the 1470s to the end of the 16th century*, ed. Iain Fenlon, Man and Music (Englewood Cliffs, NJ: Prentice Hall, 1989), 197–215. Dobbins explains the role of music in literature, at the court, and in the church in Lyon during the sixteenth century. See also Dobbins, *Music in Renaissance Lyon* (Oxford: Clarendon, 1992), and "Recueils collectifs de musique et de poésie," in *Le poète et son œuvre: De la composition à la publication*, ed. Jean-Eudes Girot (Geneva: Droz, 2004), 147–71.

16. The *Second livre contentant xxvii chansons nouvelles a quatre parties en ung volume* (Paris: P. Attaingnant and H. Jullet, 1540) includes poems 52 and 53. These two poems also appear in the same year in Jacques Moderne's *Le parangon des chansons. Sixiesme livre contenant XXV chansons nouvelles au singulier prouffit et delectation des musiciens*, published in Lyon. Poems 12 and 14 were published in *Le parangon des chansons. Neufviesme livre contenant XXXI chansons nouvelles* (Lyon: Jacques Moderne, 1541). Rajchenbach's edition of the *Rymes* (Droz, 2006) reproduces the pages of these and later sixteenth-century "partbooks" for singers in the appendices, along with information on the composers and modern scores for five epigrams based on the Renaissance songbooks.

beloved by jumping nude into the water of the clear fountain pool and playing her lute to lure him closer.[17] Although the sensual wish is not fulfilled, it is doubtful that this scene, however hypothetical, is exactly what Du Moulin had in mind when exhorting the ladies of the city to devote themselves to virtue, following the young poet's example.[18]

In Renaissance poetry, the lute often served as a metaphor for the art and song of the poet. Carla Zecher's study of *Sounding Objects* explores the roles that lutes and other instruments played as physical objects signifying poetic imagination and production in the literature and visual arts of the Renaissance. Musical skill could represent spiritual effort and virtuous accomplishment on the part of a woman, but Zecher shows how the lute itself, with its rounded shape, could also symbolize *voluptas*—both in the positive sense of "honnête volupté" and in the negative connotation of physical gratification and excess—concluding that, "when it came to women's lute playing, the slope leading from desirability to disrepute was a slippery one."[19]

The manner in which the depiction of a lute in a woman's hands could suggest either praiseworthy artistic accomplishment or excessive sensuality serves to illustrate the precarious position of Renaissance women engaged in literary pursuits. On the one hand, Lyon in the middle of the sixteenth century was indeed a milieu relatively favorable to the education of women and their participation in the vibrant cultural and intellectual life of the city. The influence of Italian culture and Neoplatonic theory resulted in a privileged situation for at least a minority of women of means with access to education and

17. Poem 43 is also known as "elegy 2" (élégie II) in the naming and numbering system established by Saulnier in his 1944 study. For more about the two conventions, see the section on the French text in this Introduction. See also the concordance for the two systems at the end of this volume. On the definition of the *élégie* in the Renaissance and the classification of five of Du Guillet's poems as such, see Philip Ford, "A propos des 'élégies' de Pernette Du Guillet," in *Le poète et son œuvre*, 165–67.

18. Cathy Yandell demonstrates the difference in the meanings of the word *vertu* as applied to women and to men in Du Moulin's preface, as well as Pernette du Guillet's particular use of the term in the *Rymes*; see *Carpe Corpus: Time and Gender in Early Modern France* (Newark: University of Delaware Press, 2000), chap. 3. See also Jan Boney's discussion of virtue and virtuosity in the context of the *Rymes* in "'Ardeur de veoir': Reading Knowledge in Pernette du Guillet's *Rymes*," in *Esprit Créateur* 30 (Winter 1990), 49–60.

19. Carla Zecher, *Sounding Objects: Musical Instruments, Poetry, and Art in Renaissance France* (Toronto: University of Toronto Press, 2007), 139. Zecher discusses the lute poems of Louise Labé and Pernette du Guillet on pages 149–52. See also Marcel Tetel, "Le luth et la lyre de l'école lyonnaise," in *Il Rinascimento a Lione*, vol. 2 (Roma: Edizioni dell'Ateneo, 1988), 949–62.

with leisure time for literary activity.[20] On the other hand, Pernette du Guillet, like any educated woman who wished to write, was necessarily bound by social conventions that placed the highest value on a woman's domestic roles, considering her place to be in the home and censuring her appearance and speech in public in order to protect her chastity, her greatest virtue.[21] Rigolot points out that despite the atmosphere of relative intellectual freedom and openness to new ideas that characterized Lyon at the time Jean de Tournes was publishing the works of Pernette du Guillet and Louise Labé, all was not for the best in this seemingly ideal climate: "a woman writer had to defend herself before the court of morality for taking up the pen."[22]

As the series editors' Introduction observes, Renaissance women who chose to pursue literary endeavors faced powerful obstacles from longstanding traditional views regarding the inferior and imperfect nature of the female. Renaissance society—following beliefs

20. Natalie Zemon Davis explains that, "in the first half of the sixteenth century, the wealthy and well-born woman was being encouraged to read and study by the availability to her of printed books; by the strengthening of the image of the learned lady, as the writings of Christine de Pisan and Marguerite de Navarre appeared in print; and by the attitude of some fathers, who took seriously the modest educational programs for women being urged by Christian humanists like Erasmus and Juan Luis Vives." "City Women and Religious Change," chap. 3 in *Society and Culture in Early Modern France* (Stanford: Stanford University Press, 1975), 73. See also Michèle Clément, "Comment un nouveau champ littéraire est créé à Lyon: 'en donnant lieu à la main féminine' (1530–1555)," in *L'émergence littéraire des femmes à Lyon à la Renaissance, 1520–1560*, ed. Michèle Clément and Janine Incardona (Saint-Etienne: Publications de l'Université de Saint-Etienne, 2008), 15–28.

21. See Ann Rosalind Jones, "The Mirror, the Distaff, the Pen: The Ideological Climate of Women's Love Poetry," chap. 1 in *The Currency of Eros: Women's Love Lyric in Europe, 1540–1620* (Bloomington: Indiana University Press, 1990). Popular emblem books expressed and promoted these values in visual and poetic form, highlighting the importance of chastity as the highest of female virtues, the association of a woman's silence with her virtue, and the insistence on her rightful place at home. Several editions of Alciato's widely read emblem books were published in Lyon, including one French translation, *Emblèmes d'Alciat* (Lyon: Guill. Rouille, 1549), in which the image of a statue of Venus with her foot resting on the back of a tortoise illustrates the moral proverb, "Publiée soit de la femme / Non la beaulté, mais bonne fame" (May only the good reputation of a woman be made public, and not her beauty), 244. The admirable tortoise, a mute animal that never leaves its home, is a model for women to emulate. See the facsimile of this edition available in the digital resources of "The Renaissance in Print: Sixteenth-Century French Books in the Douglas Gordon Collection" at the University of Virginia: http://iris.lib.virginia.edu/rmds/gordon/gordonimages/Gordon1548_A54_n1_2/.

22. "…une femme écrivain devait se justifier de prendre la plume devant le tribunal de la morale" (*Louise Labé Lyonnaise*, 20).

transmitted from Antiquity and the Middle Ages—by and large viewed women as inherently irrational, flighty, and deceitful creatures, prone to melancholy, and incapable of controlling their passions. Women were therefore typically excluded from any civic activity and advised against going out in public. Societal constraints and lack of education made it difficult for women to write and even more so to publish their work.[23] These deeply ingrained beliefs and attitudes about women were an integral part of the culture of Renaissance Lyon, where Pernette du Guillet acquired more learning than most of her peers and wrote poetry, publishing several poems during her lifetime, though most of what she wrote was published posthumously. Despite the city's relatively open literary environment, she—as well as her editor and printer—must have faced the inevitable risks that a woman's speech implied, not only for her moral reputation, but also for the commercial success of her published work.

How to Read the Rymes: *the Power of the Paratext*[24]

We know remarkably little about the young poet of the *Rymes*. The biographical sketches that have served to introduce this work in literary anthologies and critical studies relate information gleaned from the original editor's introduction to the volume or inferred from

23. In her study of Castiglione and Ariosto, Valeria Finucci points out that in the Renaissance "any individuality for women would have been the product not only of a social, public self subject to the authority of the ruler/prince but also of a private self subject to the authority of the father/husband in the privacy of the home." *The Lady Vanishes: Subjectivity and Representation in Castiglione and Ariosto* (Stanford: Stanford University Press, 1992), 12. For additional analyses of the social, legal, and literary status of women in the Renaissance, see Evelyne Berriot-Salvadore, *Les femmes dans la société française de la Renaissance* (Geneva: Droz, 1990); Constance Jordan, *Renaissance Feminism: Literary Texts and Political Models* (Ithaca: Cornell University Press, 1990); Ruth Kelso, *Doctrine for the Lady of the Renaissance* (Urbana: University of Illinois Press, 1978); Peter Stallybrass, "Patriarchal Territories: The Body Enclosed," in *Rewriting the Renaissance: The Discourses of Sexual Difference in Early Modern Europe*, ed. Margaret W. Ferguson, Maureen Quilligan, and Nancy J. Vickers (Chicago: University of Chicago Press, 1986), 123–42; Merry E. Wiesner, *Women and Gender in Early Modern France* (Cambridge: Cambridge University Press, 1993).

24. The paratext is the term used to refer to the parts of a published work that accompany the text itself, including the title page, preface, liminary poems, epitaphs, and illustrations. Gérard Genette's canonical study examines this privileged "threshold" between the text and the reader and how it influences the reading and interpretation of the text. See Genette, *Seuils* (Paris: Seuil, 1987) and the English translation, *Paratexts: Thresholds of Interpretation*, trans. Jane E. Lewin (Cambridge: Cambridge University Press, 1997).

the poetry, rather than derived from archival evidence. The editorial preface by Antoine du Moulin and the *épitaphes* by Maurice Scève and Jean de Vauzelles—included in the posthumous first edition of the collection and in all subsequent complete editions—indicate that the young married woman left these poems behind at her death on July 17, 1545. The plague ravaged the city of Lyon in this period, suggesting a possible cause of the poet's demise, but we have no documentary evidence to confirm this or any other hypotheses about her life or her death.[25]

All that we have, then, is the poetry itself and the lyric voice of the *Rymes*, which has long been defined and read as "other." Interpretations of that voice have led to a wide spectrum of accounts of the work and its author. The first published "reading" of the collection is that of Antoine du Moulin, whose editorial remarks prefacing the volume have long shaped the way the poems have been interpreted. For a variety of likely reasons, including the need to promote a positive reception for a work of love poetry by a woman, Du Moulin's preface emphasizes the virtuous character, remarkable spiritual qualities, and intellectual talents of the young female writer, underlining the fact that she was married and that her poetry was a private endeavor until her grieving husband brought forward the "little bundle of rhymes" to be published after her death. Du Moulin presents the poet as an example of virtue—and of learning in service of virtue—for other ladies of Lyon to emulate. Because we have no information about the author outside of what is presented to us in the printed preface by Antoine du Moulin, and what we might infer from the poems themselves and the lyric epitaphs that follow them, over the years the rhetorical strategies of the editor have had a tremendous influence on our understanding and appreciation of this collection.

The absence of external documentation regarding the life and work of Pernette du Guillet is one of several factors leading Mireille Huchon to question the authorship of the *Rymes* in her recent study of Louise Labé's *Euvres*.[26] Huchon's argument that Louise Labé is "une

25. As Saulnier notes, 1520 is the date traditionally given for her birth, although slightly earlier and later dates have been proposed, all based on conjecture. Saulnier suggests the plague as a likely cause of the poet's death; he points to an epidemic of the plague in Lyon in 1544, citing a study by Docteur Jules Guiart, "Pourquoi la peste nous a quittés, histoire de la peste en France du XVIe au XVIIIe siècle," in *Revue de l'Université de Lyon*, vol. VI (1933). "Etude," 8–9.

26. Mireille Huchon, *Louise Labé, une créature du papier* (Geneva: Droz, 2006), 69.

créature de papier," that the *Euvres* were the result of a collaborative effort—a literary hoax—has given rise to an intriguing debate about the identity of that celebrated *dame lyonnoise* and about what Huchon's premise means for other women writers of the same period.[27] Whether or not the reader concurs with Huchon's conclusions, the examination of the literary and historical factors affecting female authorship in Renaissance Lyon contributes valuable insights to our understanding of both the *Rymes* and the *Euvres*, asking us to reconsider how a work of poetry constructs the persona of its author, independent of what we may or may not know about the poet herself.

It is essential to recall, however, that scarcity of archival documentation of a woman's life was the norm in the Renaissance. Young women were taught that silence was a virtue, that a woman's place was in the home, and that her speech—or even her very presence in public—could expose her to censure. By and large, a woman did not have a civic or public role or individual legal status, living under the protection of her father and then of her husband. Lack of archival evidence of her existence, then, is not unexpected. In the case of Pernette du Guillet, her poems were published singly or collected in a variety of books between 1540 and 1561—in Lyon and in Paris—by at least eight different printers, making it all the more difficult, or so it would seem, to maintain the sort of literary hoax that Huchon proposes behind Labé's *Euvres*.[28]

27. Huchon's book has elicited strong responses for and against it, underscoring the degree to which our understanding of authorship and authorial voice affects our reading of lyric poetry. The Société Internationale pour l'Etude des Femmes de l'Ancien Régime has established a website, entitled "Louise Labé attaquée!" (http://www.siefar.org/ActuSIEFAR-Labe.html), with articles on the issue by French scholars and journalists. The debate has intrigued those outside the discipline of French Renaissance studies, making its way into Wikipedia articles, for example. In a blog entry on the topic, Ellen Moody, translator and English professor at George Mason University, writes, "One result of this erasure of Labe's identity [...] is the attempt to deny the existence of Pernette du Guillet too. And where will this stop?" ("Erasing Louise Labé," December 14, 2006; reposted in 2009 at http://www.jimandellen.org/feministblog/562.html). Christine Planté's thoughtful assessment of Huchon's argument reminds us that every writer—no matter what we may know of his/her "real life"—is a construct of paper and ink, existing in the reader's understanding and in literary and cultural tradition. See "Tout.e écrivain.e est 'de papier,'" in *L'émergence littéraire des femmes à Lyon*, 257–72.

28. For details on the sixteenth-century printed works containing poems by Du Guillet, see *Rymes*, ed. C. Barataud and D. Trudeau (Paris: Champion, 2006), 24–26, and 230–31. See also *Rymes*, ed. E. Rajchenbach (Geneva: Droz, 2006), 97–98.

Along with this absence of external biographical documentation, it is important to take into account the role played by literary and rhetorical tradition in constructing the poetic subject in the Renaissance. As Gray explains, "if the private self intrudes into sixteenth-century texts, it is almost always conditioned by rhetorical training as well as contemporary cultural constraints."[29] Despite our understanding of these factors, we nevertheless curiously continue to read the author's life in the *Rymes*. That tendency prompts us to explore the ways in which the work constructs a lyric subject and the nature of the authorial persona conveyed by the poems. An autobiographical reading of the collection reflects in part the extent to which our understanding of the discourse of poetry, after the influence of Romanticism, implies the reader's participation as a "bystander" who overhears the poet's "speech"—often the expression of his or her innermost thoughts. We are well aware that literary voices and the subjects they "represent" are fictional constructs, even when *intended* to be autobiographical, but we are inclined nevertheless to look for unity of voice and subject in the work.[30] This search for unity in the text is one factor that has hindered readers of the *Rymes* from appreciating the dialogic nature of the poetic model and the ideal love that the poems project, and from recognizing the impact of Du Moulin's rhetorical strategies.[31]

29. Gray, *Gender, Rhetoric, and Print Culture*, 64–65.

30. On the link between poetic subjectivity and discourse, see Antony Easthope, *Poetry as Discourse* (London: Methuen, 1983). Easthope concludes: "Subjectivity must be approached not as the point of origin, but as the effect of a poetic discourse" (31). Formulating the issue from the reader's perspective in an influential essay on the notion of authorship, Michel Foucault argues that the attempt to identify the author in the literary work reflects a principle of unity that stems from the reader's desire to reconcile contradictions in a series of texts. "What is an Author?" in *Partisan Review* 4 (1975), trans. James Venit, 603–14. Olivia Holmes traces the emergence of an implied author—"an aggregate of inferences based on the text, primarily on the use of the first person"—to the emergence of author-ordered lyric collections in the thirteenth century, when vernacular poetry shifted from an oral to a written medium; see *Assembling the Lyric Self: Authorship from Troubadour Song to Italian Poetry Book* (Minneapolis: University of Minnesota Press, 2000), 4. Joel Fineman looks at these issues in Shakespeare's sonnets; see *Shakespeare's Perjured Eye: The Invention of Poetic Subjectivity in the Sonnets* (Berkeley: University of California Press, 1986).

31. See Jones's remarks about Du Moulin's preface in *Currency of Eros*, 82–83. Leah Chang's study of the 1546 *Rithmes* (Paris: Jeanne de Marnef) shows to what degree that edition resists an author-centered reading, creating instead a gendered volume of poetry that revolves around the concerns of women in love. See "The Gender of the Book: Jeanne de

Antoine du Moulin's editorial interventions and Jean de Tournes's liminary *huitain* highlight the voice that, in certain poems, appears to sing only praise of the beloved, suggesting the female poet's complete deference to his extensive learning.[32] In his preface to the *Rymes*, Antoine du Moulin praises Du Guillet's poetic accomplishments and emphasizes the association of her learning with virtue. He declares that the *Rymes* should inspire the "Ladies of Lyon" to undertake literary projects and thereby share in the glory of the "Ladies of Italy." A moralizing tone underlies his encouragement. Du Moulin hopes that the women of Lyon will not only benefit from this intellectual and literary model, but that they will also follow the moral and spiritual example of her devotion to virtue. With her poetry, what Du Moulin calls her "little pastime," Pernette du Guillet has shown other women "the path to goodness." Du Moulin also explains that the poet's grieving husband convinced him to make this "little bundle of rhymes" known to the public. The presence of a grief-stricken, devoted husband would effectively forestall critics inclined to spread ugly rumors about a woman writing love poems—however Neoplatonic the context—to a man other than her husband. The editor insists on the confused state of the papers brought to him, surmising that the young woman had not yet felt her poems were ready for publication, and explains that he was persuaded to edit them in order to encourage other women to follow this example of moral virtue combined with learning.[33]

The feelings and qualities that Antoine du Moulin attributes to the poet in this preface have, through time, come to serve as biographical information, since so little is known about her life. More significantly, these attributes have influenced subsequent readings of Du Guillet's poetry. Certain poems of the collection do convey the image of a humble young poet, inspired by Platonic love and awed by the vast erudition and eloquence of her beloved. The poems in which this voice is most evident, however, represent only a part of

---

Marnef Edits Pernette du Guillet," in *Early Modern Women and Transnational Communities of Letters*, ed. Julie D. Campbell and Anne R. Larsen (Aldershot: Ashgate, 2009), 97–120.

32. Genette's study of paratextual "seuils" describes this effect. Paratextual elements that accompany a text, such as the title, preface, or illustrations, "surround and extend it, in order to *present* it, in the usual meaning of that verb, but also in its stronger meaning: to *make it present*, to ensure its presence in the world, its 'reception' and its consumption" (*Seuils*, 7). (Translation mine.)

33. On the poetic tradition of the found manuscript, see Perrine Galand-Hallyn and Fernand Hallyn, "'Recueillir des brouillars': Ethique de la silve et poétique du manuscrit trouvé," in *Le poète et son œuvre*, 9–34.

the collected works. A close study of the entire text reveals a complex series of voices that assert contradictory emotions and proclaim the merits of the speaking, writing woman.

Antoine du Moulin's preface has the effect, intended or not, of masking the complexity and subtleties of these voices in the *Rymes*, an editorial intervention that may have helped to ensure the volume's commercial success by averting the censure of contemporary readers. Du Moulin's emphasis on the moral purity underlying the young poet's intellectual endeavors reflects a concern for social codes in Renaissance France, which questioned the virtue of any woman who entered the public domain through speech or writing. This concern is made explicit toward the end of the preface, when Du Moulin contemplates the possibility of a reader—"some odd fellow"—who would take this work in the wrong light. According to the editor, such a reader of bad faith would be motivated by envy, which always trails virtue. Du Moulin cautions the ladies of Lyon not to heed any such jealous rumors, which might discourage them from seeking the good through literature and learning. He concludes by comparing readers of ill will to "les Asnes"—asses who feed on thistles and can therefore appreciate no finer fare—and affirms that he chose to publish the *Rymes* in order to please the ladies of Lyon, even at the risk of displeasing the malicious. As Anne Larsen points out, a preface serves to promote the book that follows, often declaring an authorial intention; in the *Rymes*, it is the editor, not the author, who declares the work's intention, fulfilling the primary aim of the preface—"to negotiate a place for the work, and its author, in the public realm."[34]

34. Anne R. Larsen, "'Un honneste passetems': Strategies of Legitimation in French Renaissance Women's Prefaces," in *L'Esprit Créateur* 30 (Winter 1990), 12. Informed by investigations into printing history, recent studies have yielded new perspectives on the role of this and other such prefaces in the publication and reception of works by women writers. Leah Chang's study of the complex relationship between printers and female authors in the Renaissance examines Du Moulin's rhetorical strategies and argues that he emphasizes the distinction between author and editor, using gender difference as a tool to define, differentiate, and assign value to those roles in his preface. *Into Print: The Production of Female Authorship in Early Modern France* (Newark: University of Delaware Press, 2009). Elise Rajchenbach considers the preface to the *Rymes* in light of two other works published by Jean de Tournes in 1545: *Panegyric des Damoyselles de Paris* (with the editorial collaboration of Antoine du Moulin) and *Il Petrarca* (the works of Petrarch, preceded by an epistle in Italian by Jean de Tournes to Maurice Scève, recounting the latter's reported discovery of the tomb of Petrarch's Laura in 1533). By comparing the paratextual elements of the three volumes, Rajchenbach finds evidence of a concerted editorial strategy designed to promote Lyon as an important center of poetic renewal and innovation, equal to or

Du Moulin's editorial approach was to have a far-reaching effect on the critical reception of the *Rymes*. Rigolot and Read examine this phenomenon in their study of Renaissance prefaces to the works of women writers, describing the "reductive nature" of any preface that assigns moral intent to a literary text whose very essence is to be open to multiple interpretations.[35] Du Moulin confers extreme humility upon the poet, but of course we can have no way of knowing how she felt about her work, except for opinions expressed in the poetry itself. It should suffice to recall that, despite the editor's implication that Du Guillet did not consider her work worthy of publication, four of her poems appeared in print in her lifetime in popular songbooks.[36] She may have kept the rest of her work unpublished for many reasons: it is certainly possible, for example, that the collection as she envisioned it was not yet complete, or she may simply have wished to protect herself from gossip. That issue appears explicitly in poem 42, where the speaker responds to several malicious accusations, presumably attacks on her virtue. The controversy surrounding the publication of women's writings at the time may indeed explain the editor's caution.[37] This explanation of the one-sided interpretation presented in the preface is further corroborated by Saulnier's observation that Du Moulin's remarks are rather commonplace, and that the same ideas can be found in the prefaces of all the collections published by women poets of the day.[38] Whatever the reason or combination of reasons for the content of the preface, it has undeniably influenced the reception of this poetry.

---

surpassing Italy and—perhaps more importantly—Paris. See "'Tu le pourras clerement icy veoir': les *Rymes* de Pernette Du Guillet, publication vertueuse ou stratégie éditoriale?" in *L'émergence littéraire des femmes à Lyon*, 123–64.

35. "De là le caractère généralement réducteur de toute préface lorsqu'elle assigne une intentionalité morale à un texte littéraire dont l'essence est justement d'être ouvert à la pluralité des interprétations." François Rigolot and Kirk Read, "Discours liminaire et identité littéraire: Remarques sur la préface féminine au XVIe siècle," in *Versants* 15 (1989), 75–76.

36. The poems were published anonymously in the partbooks, as was common for the genre.

37. Larsen reminds us that, however real and autobiographical the topos of authorial humility may seem to be in the works of women writers, we must "remain alert to the depiction of female vulnerability as *poetic strategy*" ("French Renaissance Women's Prefaces," 16). In the case of the *Rymes*, it is the editor who adopts the humility topos as a prefatory strategy to deflect potential critics and win over intended readers. The tone of Du Moulin's preface makes more sense, explains Jones, when we take into account the "social climate in which chastity and silence were enjoined upon women." See "Assimilation with a Difference: Renaissance Women Poets and Literary Influence," in *Yale French Studies* 62 (1981), 138.

38. "Etude," 13.

The liminary verse by Jean de Tournes, "To the Reader from the Printer," echoes and reinforces Antoine du Moulin's "reading" of the *Rymes*. The printer's poem, like the prefatory letter, insists that virtuous, chaste love of the pure, Neoplatonic variety forms the basis of the poems to follow. In his critical edition of the *Rymes* (1968), Victor Graham agrees with this assessment, indicating that Jean de Tournes's "admirable little poem" reveals "a sensitive familiarity with the essence of Pernette's thought."[39] While it is true, as Graham points out, that many of the expressions highlighted by the printer do recur frequently in the *Rymes*, the complex poetic voices of the collection lend nuance to—and sometimes contradict—this Neoplatonic "essence."

In addition to the preface, with its assurance that exemplary virtue accompanied the poet's intellectual achievements, we can reasonably attribute to Antoine du Moulin the organization of the poems into the collection we know today. Du Moulin insists that he has retained the "poor order" of her papers, presenting the poems to us "almost as a copy" ("quasi comme pour copie").[40] To what extent the editor imposed an order on the collection is a matter of speculation, but groupings of poems based loosely on themes such as birth and jealousy do suggest some editorial intervention, whether by Du Guillet herself or by Du Moulin after her death. No matter how it may have been determined, the order has shaped our reading of the *Rymes* in the same manner as the liminary texts. The initial poems of the volume focus on the spiritual birth of the poet's intellect, attributed to the rays of light, love, and learning emanating from her beloved—a noble, learned, and eloquent poet. There is a logic to placing the birth poems at the beginning, of course, but read in conjunction with the prefatory texts, the initial poems highlight a relatively humble voice that appears to echo contemporary patriarchal social ideals and literary discourses. Grouping these poems at the beginning has the

39. Pernette du Guillet, *Rymes*, ed. Victor Graham (Geneva: Droz, 1968), 7. Regarding Jeanne de Marnef's re-use of this liminary poem, and the effects of Marnef's editorial choices on the presentation of the 1546 *Rithmes*, see Chang, "Gender of the Book," 116–17.

40. The layout of the poems on the pages of the first edition, running continuously through the volume with only a minimal visual break between each, and no association of page breaks with the ends or beginnings of poems, is consistent with and even reinforces the notion of an immediate transcription of scattered drafts, rather than a carefully thought-out editorial arrangement.

effect of emphasizing that voice and neglecting others, and of setting up the notion of a life, beginning with this birth.[41]

The full title of the collection, *Rhymes of the Noble and Virtuous Lady [D.] Pernette du Guillet of Lyon*, reinforces with its adjectives the image of the chaste female author.[42] On the other hand, the title—presumably chosen by Antoine du Moulin and Jean de Tournes—also evokes the prestige of Petrarch's *Rime sparse*, suggesting that what follows may be a *canzoniere* in the Petrarchan vein, conveying the extended love experience of an individual who suffers and sings of unrequited love. Rajchenbach notes that the French title, *Rymes*, had no precedent in Lyon, or even in France, and calls to mind the Italian model of collections of love poetry by women, such as the *Rime* of Vittoria Colonna (Parme, 1538).[43] The connotative value of a title like *Rymes (Rime)* may well lead readers to expect coherence and consistency within the collection and to look for similarities of poetic voice rather than to notice differences.

The printer's opening epigram, addressed to the reader, emphasizes the notion that the poems to follow will show how virtue triumphs over desire, even in death. Rounding out the presentation of this poetic "life" are the four epitaphs at the end, describing how the poet's virtue manifested itself even in her death at a young age. We have no way of knowing whether or not—or to what extent—the information and assessments offered in these paratextual additions and editorial interventions correspond closely to a real woman's life and character. We can, however, recognize the impact of these combined elements on our reception of the poems. In a sense, the collection

41. Charpentier points out that finding the poems in poor order ("en asséz povre ordre") does not rule out the scenario in which the husband found the texts, though not yet in a final state, at least in something of a tentative arrangement, demonstrating an early classification (*Projet Poétique*, 145). We have no way of knowing who may have imposed the sequence of the poems as they are presented to us. Regarding what we presume to be Du Moulin's ordering of the poems, Gray observes that "our understanding of the story they seem to relate is predicated on [Du Moulin's], and it is not inconceivable that a different arrangement would produce an entirely different story" (*Gender, Rhetoric, and Print Culture*, 83).

42. *Rymes de gentile, et vertueuse Dame D. Pernette du Guillet Lyonnoise.* The adjective *gentil* could mean both "noble/well-born" and "gentle/gracious" in sixteenth-century usage. See the notes to the preface for further discussion of the title.

43. For Rajchenbach, the title of Du Guillet's collection announces a *Lyonnois* model, capable of rivaling the Italian tradition, as Antoine du Moulin confirms in his preface ("'Tu le pourras clerement icy veoir,'" 124). For more on Petrarch and the lyric subject of his *canzoniere*, see the studies by Balsamo, Bloom, Kennedy, and Mazzotta in the bibliography.

is "marketed" or "packaged" as biographical and autobiographical, as representing an exemplary life and voice from start to finish, with implications in the paratext that we will find in this book a unified and edifying poetic voice and subject, although such a reading glosses over the complexity of the poetic subject and its voices in the *Rymes*.

The Trail of Immortal Concern: Birth, Love, and Learning in the Rymes[44]

Steeped in the influences of the earlier *Rhétoriqueurs*[45] and the increasingly popular Petrarchan and Italian Neoplatonist poetry and theories of love, Pernette du Guillet was likely to have been welcomed in the thriving literary society of Lyon. The young writer nevertheless had no models of a female lyric subject to follow in the process of creating her own poetic voice. The conventions of Neoplatonism and Petrarchism—praising and objectifying the beloved and desired lady—relegated women to silence. In Neoplatonic philosophy, despite an ideal reciprocity of love, the woman and her physical beauty served as a rung in the ladder of man's ascent to the realm of the Idea and the ultimate Good. Similarly, in the Petrarchan tradition the woman remained the silent object of the male gaze. The lover's suffering from the lady's lack of response was a precondition for the act of writing poetry. Even in the first epigrams of the *Rymes*, however (those that most closely match the interpretation offered by Du Moulin), the lyric speaker resists this silent role that literary convention would thrust upon her. She attributes the birth of her self-knowledge, and thus of her self-identity, to the beloved, and she honors his eloquence and learning. The voice that expresses that praise, however, does so in terms that also call attention to the speaking subject's own work as poet.

Critics and literary historians have often pointed to the first epigram of the *Rymes* as an example of Du Guillet's Neoplatonism, typical of her submissive and humble stance vis-à-vis the male

44. See poem 56, lines 51–54.

45. *Rhétoriqueurs* (or *Grand Rhétoriqueurs*) is the term used to refer to many of the French poets writing at the end of the fifteenth century and in the first third of the sixteenth century. Rhyme in verse was considered a type of rhetoric, hence the name given to these poets, who were known for their experimentation with complex rhyme schemes and verbal games. Among the best-known *Rhétoriqueurs* are Jean Molinet, Jean Marot, and Jean Lemaire de Belges.

poet, her beloved "Day."[46] The opening and closing references to the "lofty power from the Stars" ("le hault pouvoir des Astres") and contemplation of "an excellence so long revered" ("si haulte qualité") support this reading. This epigram may have found its way to the head of the collection precisely because of its mention of the poet's birth in the second line. Certainly the abstract nature of the references to the beloved and his virtues is typical of Neoplatonist writers.

The lover remains an abstraction in this epigram—the "one who was to me avowed" ("celuy, qui m'est promis"). At the same time, however, the use of first person forms—subject and object pronouns and the possessive adjective "my"—in six of the ten lines serves to foreground the speaking voice of the woman. The verb tense changes from the past (what happened when she was born) to the present, and in line 5 the speaker shifts the focus to her own sentiments and activity. She explains what happened following the moment of celestial promise at her birth:

> Leaving me numb to life—except for when
> The suffering I feel time and again
> Drives me to engrave my deep impression
> Of cruel love, of passion's sweet progression,
>
> Restee suis sans sentyment de vie,
> Fors le sentir du mal, qui me convie
> A regraver ma dure impression
> D'amour cruelle, et doulce passion, (1:4–7)

A sense of suffering led her then to "engrave" her "deep impression"; the combination of the verb "regraver" and its object, "impression," evokes the material aspect of Pernette du Guillet's work as a writer intending to publish her poetry. In Renaissance France, according to the historical dictionaries of Cotgrave and Huguet, *impression* generally referred to an edition and to the printing process itself.[47] In addition, the verb "regraver" evokes the epigram, a genre from

46. The speaker in many of Du Guillet's poems refers to her learned and eloquent beloved as her "Jour" (Day).

47. Randle Cotgrave, *A Dictionarie of the French and English Tongues* (London: Adam Islip, 1611; reprint, Columbia: University of South Carolina Press, 1950). A searchable version created by Greg Lindahl from scans in the Bibliothèque nationale is available online at http://www.pbm.com/~Elindahl/cotgrave/. See also Edmond Huguet, *Dictionnaire de la langue française du seizième siècle*, 7 vols. (Paris: Champion, 1925–1973); Algirdas Julien

Antiquity that was originally engraved or inscribed in stone. Du Guillet's use of the word here suggests the physical act of inscribing words or images on stone or on a page.[48] Although this poem was published posthumously, Du Guillet's apparent contact with contemporary literary figures in Lyon and the printing of four of her poems in songbooks in 1540 and 1541 lend credence to the interpretation of line 6 as a reference to her literary and publishing activity.[49] This first poem in the collection, while initially appearing to reflect the persona of the virtuous, admiring, humble woman poet—in keeping with the account of the author presented by the preface—also serves to introduce the active role of the woman as speaking and writing subject. She becomes much more than a mere echo of her mentor, and attains a position not generally granted to women in Neoplatonic theory, literary practice, and social conventions.

We observe a similar situation in poem 2, where the rays of dawn bring the Day's illumination to the female speaker's dark and troubling night. In this second birth scenario—at this important moment of her intellectual and spiritual awakening—the arrival of the light of day brings joy and unleashes her own voice:

> But when I saw the dawn's defining glow,
> All serene, with its thousand-colored rays,
> Such joy full suddenly did me amaze
> (Seeing how light already round me swirled),
> That with exalted voice I began to praise
> Him who formed for me such a Morn in the World.

Greimas and Teresa Mary Keane, *Dictionnaire du moyen français: la Renaissance* (Paris: Larousse, 1992).

48. The Neoplatonists, following Plato, theorized that the image of the beloved is engraved on the lover's heart. That image then becomes a mirror in which the beloved sees his own reflection, and which will cause him to love the lover as himself, explaining the reciprocal nature of love. For more on this tradition with regard to this and other poems in the *Rymes*, see the section below on Neoplatonism, as well as the notes to poem 1.

49. Lance Donaldson-Evans makes the important point that the adjective "dure" here recalls the "durs Epigrammes" of Scève's *huitain liminaire*. "The Taming of the Muse: The Female Poetic Voice in Pernette du Guillet's *Rymes*," in *Pre-Pléiade Poetry*, ed. Jerry C. Nash (Lexington, KY: French Forum, 1985), 90. Christine Clark-Evans traces the link between *amour* and *art* in the *Rymes*, finding that, in this collection, pure love leads to the art of poetry. This association reflects the Neoplatonic theory that the purest type of love, detached from physical desire, is a form of divine knowledge, directing the soul toward the ideal beauty it seeks. "L'art et l'amour dans *Les Rymes* (1545) de Pernette du Guillet," in *Le moyen français* 35–36 (1996), 161–73.

> Mais quand je vis que l'aulbe apparoissoit
> En couleurs mille et diverse, et seraine,
> Je me trouvay de liesse si pleine
> (Voyant desjà la clarté à la ronde)
> Que commençay louer à voix haultaine
> Celuy, qui feit pour moy ce Jour au Monde. (2:5–10)

Before this moment, the subject—shrouded in darkness—could not see a thing and presumably remained silent, having nothing to express. The arrival of her Day brings an awareness of self *and* a voice to express that identity along with the praise of her beloved. Colette Winn points to this birth of the lyric speaker's identity—which coincides with the birth of her writing—as the essence and originality of the *Rymes*.[50]

The question of the poet's identity recurs in poem 5, frequently cited as an example of the voice of the admiring female pupil, steeped in Neoplatonism. Here she has inscribed her beloved's name twice in the text in anagrammatic form. By a constant oscillation, however, between first and second person, and by a similar use of possessive adjectives, the focus of the poem shifts from the praise of the other (male poet) to the female subject's own poetic work.[51] She attributes her transformation—from vice and ignorance to goodness and wisdom—to her beloved's desire to transform her. Scève did in fact metamorphose the female object of his love and admiration, the pure and unattainable Délie, in his *canzoniere*. Now Du Guillet will strive to accomplish the same service for her beloved, calling attention to her equality with him as a poet. She will flee ignorance by writing poetry to transform him into an ideal figure, and her powers to do so are inspired by his will and eloquence. The poem may well remind the reader of a constant play of mirrors; the individual poet's identity proves difficult to seize as it is reflected from one surface to another, reinforcing an ideal of reciprocity and exchange, yet undermining the

50. "Le chant de la nouvelle née: Les *Rymes* de Pernette du Guillet," in *Poétique* 78 (April 1989), 212. See also Lawrence Kritzman, *The Rhetoric of Sexuality and the Literature of the French Renaissance* (Cambridge: Cambridge University Press, 1991), chap. 1. Kritzman notes: "If the female figure becomes the spectator of her own pleasure it is because du Guillet's delivery into speech, through the rhythmic movement of a poetic chant, enables her to realize a relation to language that is a projection of creative lucidity" (17).

51. Regarding the rich ambiguity in the first line of this epigram, see Gisèle Mathieu-Castellani, "La Parole chétive: Les *Rymes* de Pernette du Guillet," in *Littérature* 73 (February 1989), 50–51. See the notes for poem 5 for further discussion of the opening lines of this epigram and its anagrams.

stability implied by the Neoplatonic goal of a perfect union in love, or by any one-dimensional account of the poet's persona.

Poem 6 also revolves around the poet's identity and voice. As Saulnier points out, most nineteenth-and early twentieth-century anthologies include this epigram in their limited selection of Du Guillet's poetry as an example of the modest voice of the young poet, student of Scève, largely because of the tone of its opening lines:[52]

> With this dizain I show myself clearly
> Not knowing how to honor all your virtues
> Beyond the will—a weak excuse, merely:
>
> Par ce dizain clerement je m'accuse
> De ne sçavoir tes vertus honnorer,
> Fors du vouloir, qui est bien maigre excuse: (6:1–3)

Even in this humbling comparison, however, the poet distinguishes herself from the lover, insisting on the differences that separate her from his eloquence. Her use of the humility topos allows her simultaneously to proclaim her inadequacies and to suggest quite the opposite. The voice of the young woman explains that she could give him the praise that is his due if she had his power, which comes through learning:

> Lend me, then, your eloquent learning to
> Praise you, in just the same way you praise me.
>
> Preste moy donc ton eloquent sçavoir
> Pour te louer ainsi, que tu me loues. (6:9–10)

Although he infuses her with his knowledge, no poet can sing the admiration of another without an identity and a voice strong enough to offer that praise. Furthermore, these verses call attention to the female poet's need of her beloved's learning in order to speak within a male mode of lyric discourse.[53] He represents the essence of the patriarchal conventions that dominated literary production in France and Italy during the Renaissance. A woman wishing to enter into this

52. "Etude," 111.

53. For further discussion of poem 6, see the section on dialogue and imitation below.

discourse must at least appear to do so within the boundaries of its conventions, or *sçavoir*.[54]

In these first poems of the collection, the lyric speaker displays her share of this learning, effectively asserting her own voice and identity, while at the same time extolling her beloved's intellectual qualities in tones that evoke the chaste and virtuous woman described in the preface. This makes a closer examination of the poetic voices in the remainder of the volume all the more important. What do we make of the conclusion of poem 43, for example, where the female speaker decides not to use her poetic and sensual powers against the lover, because the sacred water of the muses' fountain belongs to all poets? Her decision does not negate the force of her vision of her own powers, so vividly depicted in the elegy; it reminds us, rather, that in the economy of the *Rymes*, dialogue replaces monologue. The speech of one of the lovers does not imply the silence of the other, a fundamental principle of this poetry.[55]

Even when addressing the beloved, the nature of the speaker's voice can differ radically from one poem to the next; she sometimes praises him, but at other times reproaches him for not recognizing and returning her love, or for preferring the company of other women to hers. Although her "Day" has taught her a great deal, her adoration of him does not extend to a master/pupil relationship of a servile nature. Poem 32 indicates that she belongs to him only in the sense that he possesses the other half of this perfect Platonic friendship:

> I've so enjoyed the good and hence
> Feel through his guiding influence
> The strong affection of our hearts
> Held by us both in equal parts:
>
> Du bien j'ay eu la jouyssance,
> Dont il m'a donné congnoissance
> Pour m'asseurer de l'amytié,
> De laquelle il tient la moytié: (32:7–10)

54. Jones examines the various positions of "negotiation" adopted by women poets of the Renaissance (including Pernette du Guillet) to respond to dominant gender ideologies and literary discourses. See in particular the introduction to *Currency of Eros*, 1–10, and "Assimilation with a Difference," 135–53.

55. See the notes for poem 43 for further discussion of this conclusion; see also the section below on dialogue and imitation.

The speaker in poem 30 gently reminds her beloved that if he treats her "rudely," as "master," he will never gain what he seeks. In poem 16, the poet reminds her beloved that if God has given him fine assets, she herself has been given reason's power to judge him, and asks that he behave reasonably.[56] Throughout the collection, the female poet rarely speaks in a voice characterized by servility or absolute humility. Filled with jealousy at the sight of her lover conversing with other women, she does not stand by in any docile manner, but reminds the beloved, through her verse, that she alone is worthy of his eloquent attentions. In poem 41, the speaker claims that she in no way wishes to restrain her beloved's liberty, but then explains that he should prefer her company because the "others"—her rivals—are not as worthy of his "fine conversation" ("sainct entretien") as is her own heart, which belongs to him.

Jealousy does not prevent her from seeing the humor in her own reactions. In a playful tone, poem 49 relates a scene that the speaker observes between her beloved and another woman, and pokes fun at her own ensuing feelings of envy. In this tableau, Cupid (*Amour*) happens upon the seated couple engaged in common flirtation, shoots a few "words"—rather than flaming arrows—in their direction, and departs with a blithe *callimera* (Greek for "have a nice day!"). Jealousy causes the speaker watching the scene to wonder if she has overheard correctly, worrying that perhaps Cupid really proclaimed what she fears most:

> When lo! Cupid burst forth with impish glee,
> Raised his bow, and aimed a fiery dart:
> He let fly four words as he drew apart
> And left the scene: *Catch you later, ciao!*
> But, oh! suspicion shot into ***my*** heart
> A fear that he'd said: *Captivate her, now!*

> Voicy Amour sur eulx gay, et dispos,
> Portant un arc, et traictz à la Gregeoise,
> Lequel lascha deux motz à la Bourgeoise,
> Et au partir luy dit, callimera:
> Lors souspeçon en mon cueur myt grand noise,
> Doubtant qu'il dist d'elle: qu'il l'aymera. (49:5–10)

56. See the section below on Neoplatonism for more about the power of judgment associated with the moon and the poet of the *Rymes*.

The epigram begins with a reference to "my Day," recalling the speaker's praise of her beloved and his virtue in many of the poems, such as poem 8, where "my Day" illuminates the darkness of night. The opening reference to "mon Jour" in poem 49, however, immediately gives way to the suspicions and jealousy of the observer. Watching her Day seated next to another woman, the speaker's tone reflects a good-natured recognition of her own possessiveness.

Here and elsewhere we see that, although the female subject admires her beloved's intellect and eloquence, she does not do so blindly. She questions the strength of his love for her, sometimes suspecting the worst of him. She acknowledges in poem 45 that she is jealous, but insists that no one could persuade her that what she has seen with her own eyes was only a figment of her imagination:

> But who could find the strength of words to flow,
> Convincing me—through argument so keen—
> That what I just, with my own eyes, have seen
> Be but a figment of imagination—
> And thus defective judgment contravene?

> Mais qui pourroit estre en propos si fort,
> Et d'argumentz si vivement pourveu,
> Que ce, que j'ay de mes propres yeulx veu
> Soit une folle imagination,
> Il feit accroire à mon sens despourveu? (45:5–9)

In the first line of poem 35, the speaker announces this same mistrust: "I can't believe your words are true—" ("Je ne croy point ce, que vous deites").

In poem 35, as in 49, the speaker acknowledges that her jealousy springs from her feelings of possessiveness toward the beloved. According to Ficino and the other Renaissance Neoplatonists, the lover, in loving, gives himself to the beloved, who will then cherish him as a possession. Human nature dictates that we love and cherish what we possess, and this "truth" is one of the Neoplatonic proofs of the natural reciprocity of love.[57] Du Guillet's humorous recognition

57. The Italian Neoplatonist, Marsilio Ficino (1433–1499), completed his *In Convivium Platonis sive de Amore* (*Commentary on the Symposium of Plato about Love*) around 1469. Ficino's commentary circulated widely in Europe throughout the sixteenth century in several Latin, Italian, and French editions and had a tremendous influence on the French

of the jealousy associated with her possessiveness serves as a playful reminder of the important ideal of exchange and mutual attraction in love. In poem 23, a similar voice reminds the beloved of her own rights in this reciprocal arrangement. She addresses him directly in this epigram, beginning with a confession of her ignorance, "I did, perhaps—through ignorance—fail" ("Je puis avoir failly par ignorance"), but in ten lines she uses the first person pronouns *je*, *me*, and *moy* a total of twelve times, effectively undermining the Renaissance ideal of woman as silent, passive admirer, and the tone of humility suggested in the opening lines of this poem.[58] The poet emphasizes her role as speaking subject in the process of declaring her rights:

> Certainly, I aspire to have my due,
> Despite what others, in dismay, opine;
> Because—if the power of giving you
> Belongs to Love and Faith, you are all mine.
>
> Bien est il vray, que je tasche à avoir
> Ce, qui m'est deu, quoy qui en ait esmoy:
> Car si Amour, et foy ont ce pouvoir
> De vous donner, vous estes tout à moy. (23:7–10)

The mutuality of this Platonic love becomes a quasi-legal matter in poem 27, where the poet presents her case:

> As much as I am yours (and wish to be),
> Let us present the case that you are mine.

Renaissance poets. I have cited examples from the English translation by Sears Jayne, *Commentary on Plato's* Symposium *on Love* (Woodstock, CT: Spring Publications, 1985). For purposes of comparison with the French verse, readers may also wish to consult the French translation, *Marsile Ficin, Commentaire sur le Banquet de Platon*, ed. and trans. Raymond Marcel (Paris: Les Belles Lettres, 1956). Regarding the link between reciprocity and possession, Ficino explains, "Therefore the same likeness which compels me to love you also forces you to love me. Moreover, the lover removes himself from himself and gives himself to the beloved. Therefore the beloved takes care of him as his own possession. For one's own things are always the dearest to one" (*Commentary*, 57); see also *Commentaire*, 158. The lover's possession and corresponding care of the beloved provide a source of comfort in the conclusion of poem 70, "Solace."

58. Gisèle Mathieu-Castellani's comparison of the poet to the *infans* in the mirror stage seems particularly appropriate here. Caught in the specular game of identity with the other, Pernette as Délie "n'accèdera au statut de sujet que dans la maîtrise du langage" (will attain the status of subject only through the mastery of language). "La Parole Chétive," 49.

> Prenez le cas, que, comme je suis vostre
> (Et estre veulx) vous soyez tout à moy: (27:1–2)

In this courtroom ambiance, Cupid's wandering arrows acquire the force of a law that neither party is free to break. This vision of equality in love has little to do with the Petrarchan Cupid and his blind *erreurs* or with the Neoplatonic account of the reciprocity of love that nevertheless imposed silence on the woman. The epigram presents a hypothetical question, suggesting a departure from convention. The speaker, although implying a judgment or "correct" resolution to the debate, never exits from the hypothesis at the end of the poem, leaving the reader (and the lover) to decide the case.

The application of legal discourse to matters of the heart recalls the popular medieval tradition of the courts of love, with their debates on the nature and laws of love and subsequent judgments handed down by the ladies who ruled them.[59] The particulars of the case presented in Du Guillet's poem, with its reference to "this our common good" ("ce commun bien nostre"), may not reflect precisely the same experience of suffering lovers depicted in many of the medieval debates, but the author of the *Rymes* clearly knows and manipulates the tradition, described aptly by Goodrich as a "casuistic analysis that is intensely personal in its subject matter, yet strikingly legalistic in its procedure and method."[60] Goodrich also notes that the judgment in the court of love is "conceived neither as a war, nor as a power play,—it is a question not of possession, but rather of reciprocal recognition and mutual right."[61] It is not surprising, then, that Pernette du Guillet would choose this literary and legalistic framework in which to present her case for reciprocity in love.

In a similar debate of a hypothetical nature, poem 55 considers the question of which comes first, theory or practice. With humor, the speaker boldly presents her opinion that theory precedes practice in both art and love:

59. The judgments of the courts of love were recorded in Latin in the twelfth century by Andreas Capellanus in his *Tractatus de amore*, and in the fifteenth century by Martial d'Auvergne in his *Arrêts d'Amour*. For an overview of this tradition and examination of the judgments of love in relation to the history of jurisprudence, particularly with regard to legal history and women, see Peter Goodrich, "Law in the Courts of Love: Andreas Capellanus and the Judgments of Love," *Stanford Law Review* 48:3 (February 1996), 633–75.

60. "Law in the Courts of Love," 634.

61. Ibid, 674.

> That art is formed from what is known:
> This point a Sophist easily
> Concedes under a deep sleep's cover.
> For me, I say I quite agree—
> Love came first, before the Lover.
>
> Car, qui feit l'art, jà la sçavoit,
> Qui est un poinct qu'un Sophistique
> Concederoit tout en dormant:
> Quand à moy, je dy pour replique,
> Qu'Amour fut premier, que l'Amant. (55:4–8)

The conclusion reminds the reader that Du Guillet, like her male counterparts, knew art and love, and the theories in both domains.[62] Each poet makes of these what s/he can. The theoretical, yet lighthearted argument reinforces the link between the experience of love and the practice of writing poetry and reminds us that two lovers/poets may have different, even opposing, points of view.

Another such philosophical debate occurs in poem 24, which weighs the relative importance of love and the lady for the lover. The epigram evokes the medieval tradition of the courts of love, still popular in the fifteenth and sixteenth centuries, as well as Ebreo's influential dialogues, in which Philo assures Sophia that, "just as the lover is prior to love, so is the beloved; for if there were not a first lovable person or object, it would be impossible to love, and there

62. Leone Ebreo (Léon Hébreu) presents those theories of art and love in his *Dialoghi d'Amore*. First published in Italian in 1535, the *Dialoghi* was an immensely popular work that circulated widely in numerous editions and several translations over the next twenty years. Pontus de Tyard's French translation of the *Dialogues* was published by Jean de Tournes in Lyon in 1551, and may well have circulated in manuscript form in literary circles prior to its printing. The two characters of Ebreo's dialogues are Filone (Philo, Greek for love) and Sofia (Sophia, Greek for wisdom or science)—who together represent the love of wisdom (i.e., philosophy). On the matter of theory and practice in love, Sophia tells Philo, "you cannot deny that knowledge of the theory should always precede application in practice, as it is reason which rule's Man's actions." *The Philosophy of Love (Dialoghi d'Amore) by Leone Ebreo*, trans. F. Friedeberg-Seeley and Jean H. Barnes (London: The Soncino Press, 1937), 233. I have cited the English translation in the remainder of this volume. For readers interested in the parallels between the French translation by Pontus de Tyard and Pernette du Guillet's verse, I have also indicated the relevant page numbers in the modern critical edition of Tyard's translation: *Dialogues d'amour*, trans. Pontus de Tyard, ed. T. Anthony Perry (Chapel Hill: University of North Carolina Press, 1974). For the French version of the passage noted here, see *Dialogues d'amour*, 178.

would be no love."[63] Infused with Neoplatonic theory, poem 24 resolves the debate in a manner that conveys both personal conviction and universal observation. The first lines present the issue:

> Who deserves more a Lover's obligation—
> Does Love or, in truth, Lady earn this role?
>
> A qui est plus un Amant obligé
> Ou à Amour, ou vrayement à sa Dame? (24:1–2)

The initial question is followed by an allusion to the *service d'amour* central to the medieval tradition of courtly love and a reference to the "honor" and the "good" at the heart of Neoplatonic theories of love. The conclusion projects anything but an uneasy or timid voice:

> Yet here's the point that must not be dismissed,
> Which soothes my mind and calms my thoughts to rest:
> Without the Lady, Love would not exist.
>
> Et toutesfois voicy un tresgrand poinct,
> Lequel me rend ma pensee assouvie,
> C'est que sans Dame Amour ne seroit point. (24:8–10)

The speaker, whose gender is not evident, professes a general truth that applies not only to the female poet, but to all men and women who love. It is important to note also that several poems in the collection convey the voice of a *male* speaker, including "Despair" (poem 69), "Cock-and-Bull Story" (poem 67), and "Mummery: Five Posts of Love" (poem 71), uttered by five of Cupid's messengers. "Solace" (poem 70) projects a voice whose gender is not revealed and who addresses the suffering male lover of the previous elegy ("Despair"), offering a third-party defense of the lady's actions.

Without fully contradicting the interpretation of Du Guillet's poetry offered by Du Moulin's preface and the rest of the paratextual apparatus discussed, the examples cited above reveal a much more complex poetic subject than initially implied. In the case of the *Rymes*, the paratext filters out an array of poetic voices in

63. *Philosophy of Love*, 268; *Dialogues d'amour*, 197. This passage appears at first glance to contradict Sophia's earlier assertion that theory precedes practice in love. Whether Love or the Lover comes first is less important to the author of the *Rymes*, however, than the ultimate conclusion that the Lady comes before both.

the collection that convey alternately—or even simultaneously—sensuality and chastity, independence of spirit and adoration of the beloved's intellectual powers, praise and criticism tempered with humor, desire for spiritual union and a need for distance or difference from the other.

Dialogue, Imitation, and the Lyric Voice

The poet's transformation of a variety of literary conventions contributes to the complexity of voice in the *Rymes*, enriching rather than contradicting the all-encompassing, spiritual union in love that this poetry projects as an ideal. Saulnier's "Etude" examines the many traditions upon which Du Guillet builds her "art of variations": medieval courtly love poetry, verse in the style of Marot and in the Petrarchan mold, and poems inspired by Neoplatonism. To express an ideal of unity, the poet avails herself of multiple lyric traditions, creating a personal style that reinforces her independent identity and voice. Despite her humble claims to the contrary, Du Guillet evidently possessed her share of the extensive knowledge that she attributed to Scève. The multiple and at times contradictory voices in the *Rymes* represent a radical departure from the *Délie*. For Scève, as for Petrarch, the *canzoniere* depends upon the silence of the idealized woman. The lady's unbroken silence and the torment of the lover are the necessary conditions for poetic creation.[64] At the heart of many of Du Guillet's poems, however, is an exchange—of light, of knowledge, or of speech—with the beloved, with other contemporaries, with *Amour* (Cupid), with the reader, or with a combination of interlocutors. Furthermore, many of these texts conclude with the speaker's refusal to reduce her beloved poet to silence. Dialogue represents a central motif of the collection, with numerous poems evoking a conversational exchange between lovers, or at least allowing the reader to "overhear" the speaker's words to another.[65]

64. In both the Petrarchan and the Neoplatonic theories of love, the woman remains the silent object of the male gaze and desire; her silence fuels the speech of the lover, whose poetry expresses the stages and states of his suffering. In the Neoplatonic mode, this situation may permit the lover's ascent to a higher spiritual realm, but in practice this applies only to men.

65. For an examination of the types of linguistic exchanges depicted in the *Rymes* and the lexical markers of dialogue, see Karen Simroth James, "*On veult responce avoir:* Pernette du Guillet's Dialogic Poetics," in *A Dialogue of Voices: Feminist Theory and Bakhtin*, ed. Karen Hohne and Helen Wussow (Minneapolis: University of Minnesota Press, 1994), 171–97,

Dialogue also serves as the foundation of Du Guillet's poetic activity. Like other women writers of the Renaissance, she establishes authorial identity through participation in a community of authorship.[66] This was true for male writers as well, but women who chose to write needed to create their own voices within conventions that otherwise assigned a silent and passive role to women, making their dialogue with textual models all the more fundamental to their literary subjectivity.[67] Du Guillet's use of the traditions available to her reflects key aspects of the Renaissance theory and practice of *imitatio*. For Du Guillet, as for many of her peers, imitation takes the form of an intertextual dialogue through which the writer forges a new poetic identity, while acknowledging both the worth and the difference of the predecessor. The most complex type of imitation practiced in the Renaissance, according to Thomas Greene's influential study of the practice, involves the presence—or even the overt dramatization—of the "intertextual makeup" of a work of literature.[68] Such texts recognize their own historicity and acknowledge the cultural or historical discontinuity that separates them from their models in the past.

---

and particularly pages 175–78. On the theory and practice of dialogue in this period in France, see *The Dialogue in Early Modern France, 1547–1630: Art and Argument*, ed. Colette Winn (Washington, DC: Catholic University Press, 1993); Eva Kushner, *Le dialogue à la Renaissance: Histoire et poétique*, Cahiers d'Humanisme et Renaissance 67 (Geneva: Droz, 2004); Janet Levarie Smarr, *Joining the Conversation: Dialogues by Renaissance Women* (Ann Arbor: University of Michigan Press, 2005). On the dialogue in Italy in the sixteenth century, see Virginia Cox, *The Renaissance Dialogue in its social and political contexts, Castiglione to Galileo* (Cambridge: Cambridge University Press, 1992).

66. Jacqueline Risset comments on this phenomenon and the ways in which it must have affected the young poet of the *Rymes*. See *L'anagramme du désir: Essai sur la* Délie *de Maurice Scève* (Rome: Mario Bulzoni, 1971), 19–21, 58–64. See Jones, *Currency of Eros*, 79–82, for a discussion of the atmosphere of collaboration and exchange in Lyon and the importance of dialogue to the work of the woman poet. See also James, "Pernette du Guillet's Dialogic Poetics," 171–97.

67. This process has been examined by feminist critics seeking to understand the strategies adopted by women writers to overcome "anxiety of authorship." For insightful discussions of this topic with regard to women writers in Renaissance France, see Jones, *Currency of Eros*, chap. 1, and "Surprising Fame: Renaissance Gender Ideologies and Women's Lyric," in *The Poetics of Gender*, ed. Nancy K. Miller (New York: Columbia University Press, 1986), 78–83; Colette Winn, "La femme écrivain au XVIe siècle," in *Poétique* 84 (November 1990), 435–52; Lance K. Donaldson-Evans, "The Taming of the Muse"; Katharina Wilson, ed., Introduction to *Women Writers of the Renaissance and Reformation* (Athens, GA: University of Georgia Press, 1987), x–xl.

68. Thomas Greene, *The Light in Troy: Imitation and Discovery in Renaissance Poetry* (New Haven, CT: Yale University Press, 1982), 17.

Pernette du Guillet's *Rymes* do not register temporal discontinuity as a factor in this process; many of the poems do, however, inscribe an awareness of the difference that separates the woman poet from her beloved and his writing. Early in the collection, following the epigrams that focus on the young woman's intellectual birth, the speaking female voice shifts in poem 5 to a consideration of her own work, albeit in praise of the beloved. Poem 7—the famous "R" epigram—revolves around her own writing and a critical dialogue with the other. Her poems recognize and even emphasize the gap that separates her, the woman poet, from her eloquent beloved, while also providing the opening for her own writing. In his study of "Imitation and Intertextuality in the Renaissance," Jean-Claude Carron describes the process we observe here: "Imitation is understood as the 'dialogical' process of bringing about self-awareness through the experience of the other. Through the mediated appropriation of a linguistic and poetic technique, the imitator finds the means to achieve his own 'formation' or his own 'nature.'"[69]

Because a primary intertext for a number of the poems is a contemporary one, Scève's *Délie*, temporal distance is not an issue. The *Rymes* call attention, however, to the gulf between the two texts and poetic systems, imposed by gender, by literary tradition, by societal mores, and by the very pupil/teacher situation which some of Du Guillet's poems offer as initial justification for the woman's poetic speech. Like the humanist texts described by Greene, the *Rymes* do more than "[maintain] a native contemporary convention."[70] Instead, Du Guillet reaches across the divide she depicts, envisioning and proposing changes and accepting the risks involved. Although upholding the validity of the model, she uses the intertext as the catalyst for change and the development of a new poetics of her own. In seeking to define this "dialectical *imitatio*"—the most complex type—Greene notes that the subtext must be significant, determinant, playing a "constitutive role in a poem's meaning," and that the imitation must involve "a conflict between two *mundi significantes*."[71] This struggle is

69. Jean-Claude Carron, "Imitation and Intertextuality in the Renaissance," *New Literary History* 19:3 (Spring 1988), 572.

70. Greene, *The Light in Troy*, 37.

71. Greene, *The Light in Troy*, 46 and 50. In this type of imitation, the text seeks "to prove its historical courage and artistic good faith by leaving room for a two-way current of mutual criticism between authors and between eras. [...] The text is the locus of a struggle between

a dynamic one, yielding artistic power without silencing the author of the subtext, a process that recurs throughout the *Rymes*.[72]

Pernette du Guillet's poem 13 and *dizain* 136 of Scève's *Délie* embody this conflict or current between two systems of thought, two experiences of love, and two different poetic styles used to express them. Both poems revolve around the duality of happiness and pain in love and the way that the "blind god" (Cupid) unifies the two lovers. Within that thematic framework the final two lines of Scève's *dizain* conclude with the wish that both lovers continue to feel this sweet death *as long as* they breathe life.[73] Scève's poem also highlights the involuntary nature of the experience and the lovers' lack of consent to it.[74] Du Guillet's epigram, on the other hand, emphasizes the honorable nature of love and its effects (line 6) and concludes with a wish that both lovers will have long-lasting satisfaction—the same *contentement* that reappears throughout the *Rymes* as the goal of the two lovers' spiritual union:[75]

> Oh, worthy suffering is this, indeed—
> That from the good you give us, little blind
> God! Please also, then, to us accede
> Long-lasting satisfaction of the mind.
>
> Dieu aveuglé, tu nous as faict avoir
> Du bien le mal en effect honnorable:
> Fais donc aussi, que nous puissions avoir
> En noz espritz contentement durable. (13:5–8)

---

two rhetorical or semiotic systems that are vulnerable to one another and whose conflict cannot easily be resolved," 45–46.

72. Gray observes that imitation for Pernette du Guillet is "a means to self-knowledge rather than a sign of subservience" (*Gender, Rhetoric, and Print Culture*, 77).

73. "Fais que puissions aussi long temps sentir / Si doulx mourir en vie respirable." Maurice Scève, *Délie, object de plus haulte vertu*, vol. 1, ed. Gérard Defaux (Geneva: Droz, 2004), CXXXVI, 65. All quotations from the *Délie* are from this edition.

74. "Sans autrement ensemble consentir," (*Délie*, CXXXVI, 65).

75. Yandell examines the "suspended time" that characterizes the "contentement durable" of Du Guillet's epigram, as opposed to the "temporal contingency" established in Scève's *dizain*. "Carpe Diem, Poetic Immortality, and the Gendered Ideology of Time," in *Renaissance Women Writers: French Texts / American Contexts*, eds. Anne R. Larsen and Colette Winn (Detroit: Wayne State University Press, 1994), 119. See the additional development of this topic in *Carpe Corpus*, chap. 3.

Saulnier's study presents Scève's poem as the model for Du Guillet's epigram; various critics have read poem 13 as a response to *dizain* 136 or vice versa.[76] After outlining convincing reasons to suggest that Du Guillet's poem was the model and Scève's the response, Joyce Miller emphasizes the fundamental point that "reflections on the experience that unites the lovers lead to divergent conclusions."[77] We have no way of knowing which poem may have been composed first; much more significant are the differences in the two texts based on the same point of departure.

Pernette du Guillet's poem 16 and Scève's *dizain* 56 provide another telling example of the conflict between two "signifying worlds" that Greene identifies as the key element of dialectical imitation.[78] In Scève's poem, reason has been enslaved ("asservie") by the enfeebled body and troubled mind and senses. The speaker presents all four—reason, body, mind, and senses—to his beloved lady as his only hope of a cure.[79] Using the same elements, Pernette du Guillet's epigram exudes order and clarity, rather than disorder and trouble. Mind and soul "bedeck" the body, and the will of the Divine gives us sense and intellect with which to discern the good, as ordained and governed by reason. Recognizing the divine gifts possessed by her beloved, the speaker nevertheless reminds him that God has given her reason and its power, which allows her to judge him:

> So if God gave you assets rich and fine,
> He gave me reason to best appreciate
> And judge your knowledge and your happy state.

> Parquoy, si Dieu de telz biens te guerdonne,
> Il m'a donné raison, qui a pouvoir
> De bien juger ton heur, et ton sçavoir. (16:5–7)

76. "Etude," 27. See also Jacqueline Risset, *L'anagramme du désir*, 59–61.

77. Joyce Miller, "In the Margins of Amatory Discourse: The *Responces* of Pernette du Guillet," *Sixteenth Century Journal* 24:2 (Summer 1993), 366. Miller points to Du Guillet's choice of the *huitain* (eight-line poem) as one indication that she was not responding to Scève's *dizain*; neither does Du Guillet's epigram follow the pattern of her other lyric *responce* poems (365–66).

78. Greene, *The Light in Troy*, 46.

79. "En toy des quatre a mis leur guerison," (*Délie*, LVI, 29).

Du Guillet's lyric speaker is not interested in using her powers to rescue her beloved from his troubles or put an end to his suffering in the way that the courtly suitor might wish for his *belle dame* to do; rather, she points to her rational powers to explain her capacity and right to judge him and to ask him to be more reasonable. The male speaker of *dizain* 56 is a troubled soul, acting irrationally and guided by emotions, whereas the female subject of poem 16 speaks rationally of her power of discernment and her ability—guided by reason—to judge her beloved's knowledge and eloquence. She wishes to see him gain control over his troubled mind and senses. Jones notes that this poetic exchange "rewrites" the traditional gender distinctions of the Renaissance: "The male poet invokes the apparatus of Neoplatonic theory in order to confess that it is not operating as it should in this instance; the woman poet responds that it is working perfectly in her case and ought to work better in his."[80]

An intriguing poetic exchange of a different sort revolves around a ring, given by the lady to her beloved.[81] Du Guillet's poem 10 and Scève's *dizains* 347 and 349 are all based on this same scenario, although the language used to convey the meaning of the gift of the ring differs significantly in the works of the two poets. We don't know the order in which the three poems were composed, but Susan Delaney has proposed that Du Guillet's ring poem is a response to *dizain* 347, and that Scève's *dizain* 349 in turn is a response to Du Guillet's epigram.[82] In Pernette du Guillet's poem, the speaker addresses her beloved, not the object itself, and admonishes him for not valuing the ring sufficiently. He should appreciate it more, not for the precious metal of which it is made, but for what the hand—of the poet writing these verses, as well as that of the artisan who joined the diamond to the gold—seeks to affirm through its craft, which is the lady's everlasting love:

80. Jones, *Currency of Eros*, 90. See also Josiane Rieu, "Pernette du Guillet: Poétique et réflexivité dans les *Rymes* (1545)," in *Dans les miroirs de l'écriture: La réflexivité chez les femmes écrivains d'Ancien Régime*, ed. Jean-Philippe Beaulieu and Diane Desrosiers-Bonin, Paragraphes 17 (Montreal: University of Montreal, 1998), 38–39.

81. The topos of a beloved's ring offered as a symbol of undying love was used by many Renaissance writers, including the Italian Petrarchist poet, Serafino dell'Aquila (1466–1500), who wrote four sonnets about a ring given to him by his lady. Pernette du Guillet was undoubtedly familiar with Serafino's sonnets; poem 62—one of her two epigrams in Italian—is a variant or copy of one of his poems.

82. Susan Delaney, "Lyric Dialogue in the 'Ring' Poems of Pernette du Guillet and Maurice Scève," *The French Review* 68:5 (April 1995), 822–29.

But the hand which, to heighten many-fold
Its loyalty toward you, wanted to bind
It with an eternal diamond; there you'll find,
Etched onto its face, a heart's contours,
To show what you must not forget—inclined
As you are to do—her love, which long endures.

Mais pour la main, qui pour plus rendre estable
Sa foy vers toy, te l'a voulu lyer
D'un Dyamant, où tu peulx desplier
Un cueur taillé en face pardurable,
Pour te monstrer, que ne doibs oublier
Comme tu fais, la sienne amour durable. (10:5–10)

The speaker specifically tells her beloved that, if he will only pay attention to it, this ring will show him what he seems to be forgetting—her devotion.

Scève's *dizain* 347 may well have prompted Du Guillet's epigram, given the manner in which the *dizain*'s speaker views the lady's gift. The ring may come from her "sacred finger," but the "holy power" of that hand has rendered him prisoner. Having no beginning or end, the ring to which he addresses his reflections becomes a sign of his everlasting captivity, rather than of her eternal devotion.[83] Scève's second poem on this topic reflects a more positive assessment of the ring, perhaps a revised opinion following receipt of Du Guillet's epigram. Again addressing the object itself and referring to the lady metonymically—by her hand and the "flesh so preciously alive" that the ring has touched—the speaker in *dizain* 349 now views the ring as a remedy for the Petrarchan pain that afflicts him cruelly. Worn daily,

83. For, as I comprehend in turning you around,
Your round form has no beginning
and no end either, which lets me understand
that I am captive without any possibility of liberty.

Car, comme puis en te tournant comprendre,
Ta rondeur n'a aulcun commencement,
Ny fin aussi, qui me donne à entendre,
Que captif suis sans eslargissement. (7–10)
Délie, CCCXLVII, 158.

the ring will remind him perpetually of his lady's devotion, serving as an "eternal relic of her chaste fidelity."[84]

Although "relique," as the last word of Scève's *dizain* 349, implies a more positive interpretation of the ring by evoking the sacred nature of the lady's love and fidelity, the term also defines her devotion as something revered, yet past, or not of this world. The adjective "eternal" specifically qualifies the relic, rather than the lady's pure love. Even this closing line—rehabilitating the ring and revising the speaker's estimation of it—nevertheless objectifies and transforms the love and devotion it was meant to represent into a relic, inspiring veneration, but disassociated from a living and breathing woman. This is the very process by which the beloved lady becomes Délie, "constituée Idole de ma vie" (made the Idol of my life), throughout Scève's *canzoniere*. The ring, which originally touched the lady's precious hand, has here been transformed into a mystical object with curative properties. Wearing and venerating the ring may alleviate the lover's suffering, but in the transformation of ring to relic, the devoted and faithful lady recedes, lifeless, into the shadows.

Poems that appear to respond to or engage in dialogue with Scève's *Délie* often reflect a wider and more general dialogue with traditions known to both poets. Du Guillet's poem 69, "Despair," is based on an unidentified Italian model also imitated by François Ier, but the first two lines of the elegy are also nearly identical to the opening lines of Scève's *dizain* LX:[85]

> Can this be Love that slays me to the bone,
> Who loved so well that hatred was unknown?
>
> Si c'est Amour, Pourquoy m'occist il donc,
> Qui tant aymay, et hayr ne sceuz onc? (69:1–2)
>
> Si c'est Amour, pourquoy m'occit il doncques,
> Qui tant aymay, & oncq ne sceuz hayr? (1–2)
> *Délie*, LX, 31

84. "Tu me feras perpetuellement / De sa foy chaste eternelle relique," (*Délie*, CCCXLIX, 160). On the conclusion of this *dizain*, see Delaney, "Lyric Dialogue," 826.

85. See *Annexe X* of Rajchenbach's edition of the *Rymes* for a transcription of François Ier's prose manuscript (238–39). See also Saulnier, "Etude," 42–44.

Clearly, both Scève and Du Guillet, like the king, knew the same model. They were undoubtedly also familiar with the first line of Petrarch's poem 132 in the *Rime sparse*:

> If it is not love, what then is it that I feel?
> S'amor non è, che dunque è quel ch'io sento? (1)[86]

The "clear fountain pool" of Du Guillet's poem 43 represents another point of literary intersection between the *Rymes*, the *Délie*, and Petrarch's *Rime sparse*. The water of the "clere & heureuse fontaine" of Scève's *dizain* 235, where the beloved lady has washed her hands, will hold the reflection of her beautiful eyes and lips. The suffering lover says he will come to worship more often at the "holy mirror" of the "sacred waves" if they preserve the image of his lady.[87] A momentary touch by the woman—whose finger once wore the ring and whose hands have plunged into this water—turns the pool, like the ring, into an object of veneration representing the absent woman. Such a situation is the complete opposite of the conclusion of Pernette du Guillet's poem 43, in which the female speaker, who briefly imagines enslaving and silencing her beloved with the waters of a "clere fontaine," chooses to bring her fantasy to an end so as not to deprive the world of the other's poetry. The speaker in Du Guillet's elegy opts to guarantee her beloved's *presence*, highlighting her goal of mutual contentment, rather than to predicate her own verse on the beloved's absence—that is, his silence—and this choice turns her mythological allusion to an entirely different end.

Du Guillet's fountain pool in poem 43 is the setting for an Ovidian-inspired scene between the female speaker, comparing herself to Diana, and her beloved, whom she casts in the role of Actaeon. For this reason, the elegy calls to mind Scève's *dizain* 168 and the emblematic woodcut illustration that precedes it, depicting Actaeon at the moment when he is transformed into a stag and chased by his own hounds.[88] The last line of *dizain* 168 repeats the *devise*,

86. *Petrarch's Lyric Poems: The Rime Sparse and Other Lyrics*, ed. and trans. Robert M. Durling (Cambridge, MA: Harvard University Press, 1976), 270–71.

87. "Car plus souuent ie viendroys adorer / Le sainct miroir de voz sacrées undes," (*Délie*, CCXXXV, 109).

88. Ovid recounts the myth of Actaeon who, while hunting in the woods, happens upon the goddess Diana while she is bathing nude in a pool in the company of her nymphs. As punishment for his accidental transgression, Diana throws a handful of water in his face,

or motto, that surrounds the woodcut: "Fortune hunts me with my own."[89] Actaeon's name is not mentioned in the *dizain*, but the emblem that precedes it prompts us to read Scève's poem in the light of the Ovidian myth. Stephen Murphy points out that the final couplet of the *dizain* expresses in outward terms the lover's dark interior state, in which his beloved is only present as a memory of her name.[90] Pierre Martin emphasizes that what provokes the metamorphosis in Scève's *dizain* is the memory of Délie's divine name, not the sight of the beloved bathing nude, surrounded by nymphs, as in the Ovidian tale; Diana/Délie is absent, and this metamorphosis is a spiritual one, brought about by interior contemplation that brings life to the soul, but metaphorical death to the body.[91]

Pernette du Guillet's use of the Ovidian myth departs radically from the model of interior contemplation and metaphorical death in Scève's *dizain* 168. On the surface, the language of Du Guillet's elegy more closely recalls Petrarch's use of this Ovidian tale in poem 23 of the *Rime sparse*. The day is warm; desire is on the move; a woman stands naked in the fountain pool. She throws water in the ardent admirer's face with her hands—water that has the power to punish the lover's transgression by transforming him. In Petrarch's poem, the lover is turned into a stag (*cervo*) and chased by his hounds, as in Ovid's version of the myth.[92] In Du Guillet's elegy, the speaking woman imagines turning her beloved—if he should try to approach her in the fountain pool—not into a stag ("cerf"), but into a loyal servant ("serf" or "serviteur"), basing her important shift in meaning on the homophones, "cerf" and "serf." Despite the similarities on the lexical level, however, Du Guillet's conclusion is diametrically opposed

causing him to be transformed into a stag who is then chased and killed by his own hunting dogs. For an English translation from the Renaissance, see Ovid, *Metamorphoses*, trans. Arthur Golding (London: W. Seres, 1567), book 3, lines 138–231, in the Perseus Digital Library, http://www.perseus.tufts.edu/cgi-bin/ptext?lookup=Ov.+Met.+3.138. See also *Metamorphoses*, trans. A. D. Melville, with introduction and notes by E. J. Kenney (New York: Oxford University Press, 1998), 55–58.

89. "Fortune par les miens me chasse," *Délie*, CLXVIII, 79.

90. Stephen Murphy, "The Death of Actaeon as Petrarchist Topos," in *Comparative Literature Studies* 28:2 (1991), 137–55.

91. Pierre Martin, "De Maurice Scève à Pernette du Guillet, ou le jeu d'Actéon," in *Le mythe de Diane en France au XVIe siècle*, ed. Jean-Raymond Fanlo and Marie-Dominique Legrand, Cahiers D'Aubigné; Albineana 14 (Niort; Paris: Librairie Honoré Champion, 2002), 39–55.

92. See Sara Sturm-Maddox, *Petrarch's Metamorphoses: Text and Subtext in the "Rime Sparse"* (Columbia: University of Missouri Press, 1985).

to Petrarch's. The female speaker concludes in favor of guaranteeing both the beloved's presence and his continued work as a poet in support of their mutual *contentement*, whereas Petrarch's use of the Diana/Actaeon myth ends with the speaker—the suffering lover—transformed into a wandering stag, fleeing his hounds. Scève's *dizain* 168 concludes with the same figure of perpetual suffering.

Du Guillet may well have known the Petrarchan tradition through the Italian poet's work itself, through Scève's adoption of Petrarchan elements in the *Délie*, and through the works of other Italian and French *Pétrarquistes*.[93] Her use of Petrarchan motifs, however, is unique and often at odds with their conventional associations. Poem 8, for example, presents the image of the beloved's sweet rays of light illuminating the female speaker's being, as if bringing bright daylight at midnight:

> Because the sweet light from my Day will soar,
> Enlightening me so, that at midnight
> He helps me to perceive within my mind
> That to which my eyes were ever blind.
>
> Puis que mon Jour par clarté adoulcie
> M'esclaire toute, et tant, qu'à la mynuict
> En mon esprit me faict appercevoir
> Ce, que mes yeulx ne sceurent oncques veoir. (8:5–8)

Du Guillet's epigram recalls a similar image in a sonnet by the Italian Petrarchist poet, Chariteo, who describes his lady's eyes as capable of making midnight into day ("far a mezzanotte il giorno"). Chariteo himself imitates a line in Petrarch's sonnet 160, which evokes the power of the Lady's eyes to make light the night and dark the day ("far chiara la notte, oscuro il giorno").[94] Gillian Jondorf points to this epigram in the *Rymes* as an example of Pernette du Guillet's process of deepening or extending the meaning of a Petrarchan antithesis. As Jondorf explains, this poem "embodies the conventional idea that the absence of the loved one is night, his presence day," but Du Guillet

93. See Gordon Braden, *Petrarchan Love and the Continental Renaissance* (New Haven: Yale University Press, 1999); Jean-Luc Nardone, *Pétrarque et le pétrarquisme* (Paris: Presses Universitaires Françaises, 1998).

94. Cited by Saulnier ("Etude," 47).

also adds the notion "that the loved one's presence brings perception, the ability to see clearly, not just light but enlightenment."[95]

Pernette du Guillet's enrichment of this Petrarchan motif stands in sharp contrast to the conclusion of Scève's *dizain* 92. For the speaker of the *Délie*, the appearance of the sun's bright rays serve as a reminder of the lady's brilliant beauty. Unfortunately, he cannot hear a single sweet word from her ("un seul doulx mot"), and her silence prevents his happiness and guarantees his continued suffering. The sun's rays cannot cheer him in this condition, wherein even noon, the brightest part of the day, is like eternal night for him.[96] The juxtaposition of night and day represents the lover's pain in the *Délie*, whereas Pernette du Guillet uses this same motif—a central metaphor of the *Rymes*—to convey a moment of spiritual illumination that launches an ongoing, positive process of self-knowledge and communication. The Petrarchan and Scèvian topos that concludes with the lady's silence and the poet's expression of his suffering provides an opening for enlightened dialogue in Du Guillet's poetry. The exchange of ideas and words evoked in so many poems of the *Rymes* does not resolve the antithesis in favor of one side or the other, but allows the speaking subject and her beloved to move beyond it.[97]

Scève's *Délie* is the most obvious intertext of this collection, but the *Rymes* establish a number of other important intertextual dialogues. The works of the Italian Neoplatonists served as a significant source of inspiration for Du Guillet's *Rymes*, as discussed later in this Introduction. Her poems display both a debt to and a departure from models provided by Petrarchan tradition, as well as by Clément Marot and his followers and the earlier *Rhétoriqueurs* poets.

Although the *Rhétoriqueurs* of the first part of the sixteenth century may not have heavily influenced Pernette du Guillet, her

95. Gillian Jondorf, "Petrarchan Variations in Pernette du Guillet and Louise Labé," in *The Modern Language Review* 71:4 (October 1976), 767. Regarding Louise Labé's use of Petrarchan tradition, see Deborah Lesko Baker, *The Subject of Desire: Petrarchan Poetics and the Female Voice in Louise Labé* (West Lafayette, IN: Purdue University Press, 1996).

96. "Me pourra donc tel Soleil resjouir, / Quand tout Mydi m'est nuict, voire eternelle?" (*Délie*, XCII, 45). Similarly, in *dizain* 51, despite the lady's brilliant beauty, which casts the sun's light into shadow, the suffering speaker receives no illumination from her, concluding: "Mais quand sa face en son Mydy je voy, / A tous clarté, et à moy rend tenebres" (But when I see her countenance at its most brilliant, to all it gives light, and to me, darkness). *Délie*, LI, 27.

97. See Kritzman, *Rhetoric of Sexuality*, 18–20, regarding Du Guillet's dialogue with and divergence from Neopetrarchan tradition.

poem 60—depicting a debate between friends over the relative merits of Italian and French—is clearly reminiscent of the *Concorde des deux langages* by Jean Lemaire de Belges, first published in 1511.[98] Lemaire's long narrative poem recounts a journey to the temples of Venus and Minerva in search of "concorde" between the two languages and cultures. At the temple of Minerva, the figure of "Labeur Historien" shows the traveling poet a magical mirror reflecting the image of the two languages intertwined in harmony. That vision remains an ideal, however, which the poet can only hope to find some day, after long study, in the temple of Minerva.[99] Pernette du Guillet addresses the relative merits of the two languages also, but her ten-line epigram cuts to the heart of the matter, leaving aside the metaphorical journey, allegorical elements, and imaginary architecture. As with Du Guillet's particular use of Petrarchan antitheses, the two sides of the argument here are allowed to coexist in the end; neither is silenced. The epigram presents an amicable disagreement and discussion—not so much resolved as concluded on an ambiguous note that asks us to continue weighing words and their meanings:

> For fine descriptions, which one makes no matter;
> But, to offer a judgment more insightful:
> The former pales in meaning to the latter.
>
> Je dy, qu'ilz sont tous deux beaux à descrire:
> Mais pour en faire au vray le jugement,
> Celuy depeinct ce, que cestuy veult dire. (60:8–10)

In the sixteenth century, the verb "depeindre" (also spelled "despeindre") had two different and opposite definitions: "to make pale or remove color from" and "to depict or describe in a painterly way." Based on the first of the two meanings, the final line of the poem indicates that the former (Tuscan) renders but a pale version of that

98. Jean Lemaire de Belges, *Concorde des deux langages*, ed. Jean Frappier (Paris: Droz, 1947).

99. Regarding this ideal of exchange and communication between the two cultures and languages, Cynthia Skenazi points out: "les deux langages s'affrontent ainsi sans se confondre et le désir de les harmoniser est surtout enrichissement du répertoire français dans et par le dialogue de deux cultures" (the two languages thus confront each other without merging, and the desire to harmonize them is above all for the enrichment of the French repertoire in and through dialogue between the two cultures). *Le poète architecte en France: Constructions d'un imaginaire monarchique* (Paris: Champion, 2003), 65.

which French expresses. Conversely, if we translate "depeinct" as "depicts," then the epigram ends with a recognition of the equal worth of each language (one depicts what the other means). We have no way of knowing which of these two definitions Pernette du Guillet had in mind for the verb in poem 60. Given the influence of the *Rhétoriqueurs* poets and their wordplay, however, and the lexical ambiguity that surfaces in many poems of the *Rymes*, it is highly likely that Du Guillet intended for her readers to be puzzled by this conclusion, which requires us to continue weighing the merits of each meaning.[100]

Questions of interpretation are the focus of poem 7, where we find another possible influence of Lemaire on Du Guillet's *Rymes*. The entire epigram revolves around the speaker's attempts to discern the meaning of a mysterious letter "R" apparently written on one of her papers, perhaps on the manuscript of a poem:

> For this R, "err" might well be understood,
> Showing error for praise of me applied;
> Or R is nothing, a remainder, set aside.
>
> Car pour errer, R, se peult comprendre.
> Signifiant que le loz, qu'on me preste,
> Soit une erreur, ou que R, est riens, ou reste: (7:4–6)

The questions and doubts that arise, based on the sound of the letter "R" and words it might represent (*errer, erreur, riens, reste, responce*), call to mind a similar poem by Lemaire, based on the letter "M" in "les Regretz de la Dame Infortunée," although the playful tone of Du Guillet's poem is quite different from Lemaire's mournful verses.[101]

The influence of Clément Marot's work on the *Rymes* is more significant, which comes as no surprise, as his poetry was being published with great success in both Lyon and Paris in the 1530s and

100. See the notes to poem 60 for more about the conclusion of this epigram and Finch's alternate translation of the last three lines.

101. Jean Lemaire de Belges, "Les Regretz de la Dame Infortunée, sur le trespas de son trescher frere unique," in *Les Illustrations de Gaule et singularitez de Troye, par Jean le Maire de Belges*, 1507, in vol 3 of *Œuvres*, ed. Auguste Jean Stecher (Louvain: J. Lefever, 1885). Saulnier notes that Pernette du Guillet took from Lemaire neither specific details nor precise formulas, but a particular rhetorical technique ("Etude," 31). Gray points out that, "whereas Jean Lemaire's *M* has mortuary connotations, Pernette's *R* is more ambivalent, allowing her to interrogate its implications, much as a pupil might a pedagogue's, but in playful and parodic fashion" (*Gender, Rhetoric, and Print Culture*, 78).

1540s.[102] Du Guillet's "Coq à l'asne" ("Cock-and-Bull Story," poem 67), for example, was directly inspired by Marot's poems of this type.[103] In his 1548 *Art Poetique Français*, Thomas Sébillet attributed to Marot the invention of this poetic genre, named for "the capricious variety of incoherent statements expressed by the French proverb of the leap from rooster to ass; the vices of all provided its subject matter."[104] Pernette du Guillet's *coq à l'âne* presents a misogynistic rant by a male speaker with little faith in female virtue. Marot's *coq à l'âne* poems combine this theme with jabs at the clergy, government officials, and other civic leaders. Although expressed in a male voice like Marot's models, Du Guillet's poem diverges from his examples by focusing primarily on the topic of female vanity and promiscuity.

Pernette du Guillet's poem 73, "To a Foolish Rhymer," follows the model of Marot's "Epître au roy," built on the same playful variations of rhyme. The inspiration is obvious, but Du Guillet adds new versions of the wordplay and writes her epistle in eight-syllable lines (*vers octosyllabes*), rather than the ten-syllable lines (*vers décasyllabes*) used by Marot.[105] Following the *tradition marotique*, Du Guillet's "Cock-and-Bull Story" and her verse epistle, "To a Foolish Rhymer," project satirical and humorous voices—one male and the other presumably female—who bear no resemblance to the humble, chaste figure of the poet described in Du Moulin's preface and suggested by the opening epigrams. These later poems in the collection remind the reader that Du Guillet responded to more

102. Marot himself participated in the revisions of the 1538 publication of his *Œuvres* in Lyon, considered the definitive edition because it was the last to benefit from the poet's involvement in the editorial process. Posthumous editions of the *Œuvres* were published in Lyon in 1544 (the year of Marot's death) and in 1546 by Jean de Tournes, with a preface by Antoine du Moulin. See the introductions to Clément Marot, *Oeuvres poétiques complètes*, 2 vols., ed. Gérard Defaux (Paris: Bordas, Classiques Garnier, 1990–1993).

103. Cotgrave's dictionary cites the expression, *saulter du coq à l'asne*, meaning, "to digresse from the matter, or, to leape suddainely, and disorderly, from one matter to another." Bernd Renner defines the *coq à l'âne* as "a form of poetry that commented critically on current events behind the protective veil of an allusive style that jumped from topic to topic without any apparent coherence—hence the alternative designation of *non sequitur*," *The Rabelais Encyclopedia*, ed. Elizabeth Chesney Zegura (Westport, CT: Greenwood Press, 2004), 40–41.

104. "... la variété inconstante des non cohérents propos, que les Français expriment par le proverbe du saut du Coq à l'âne. Sa matière sont les vices de chacun." *Traités de poétique et de rhétorique de la Renaissance*, ed. Francis Goyet (Paris: Livre de Poche, 1990), 134–35.

105. See the notes for poem 73 for more on the links between Du Guillet's poem and Marot's model.

than one lyric tradition, displaying her own version of the eloquent learning that she attributes elsewhere to her beloved.

As further evidence that Du Guillet knew and used multiple sources, we return to the intriguing example of poem 6. This epigram, appearing to convey directly the humble voice of the admiring pupil—the persona so often associated with Pernette du Guillet—in fact imitates an earlier *rondeau* by Jeanne Gaillarde, a contemporary of Clément Marot. Gaillarde's *rondeau* was a response to Marot's poem praising her confident eloquence and her "golden pen" ("plume dorée"). She writes to him: "If I were as eloquent and learned / as you say, I would do my duty to pay my debt."[106] Du Guillet addresses a very similar claim to her beloved:

> Not to say, had I such power as you,
> Duty would not make recompense its due—
> At least for all the good you claim to see.
>
> Je ne dy pas, si j'avois ton pouvoir,
> Qu'à m'acquicter ne feisse mon debvoir,
> A tout le moins du bien, que tu m'advoues. (6:6–8)

Yet even as she echoes the earlier lyric exchange between Gaillarde and Marot, Du Guillet evokes her own poetic dialogue with Scève by specifically referring to her poem as "ce dizain"—the verse form used 449 times in the *Délie*—and to his praise of her. The conclusion is typically Pernettian, with its call for reciprocity and exchange:

> Lend me, then, your eloquent learning to
> Praise you, in just the same way you praise me.
>
> Preste moy donc ton eloquent sçavoir
> Pour te louer ainsi, que tu me loues. (6:9–10)

The capacity of this epigram to convey what appears to be an intensely personal and immediate reaction, to invoke intertextual dialogue with more than one model, and to conclude with a wish for reciprocity in both love and writing, embodies the quintessential quality of the *Rymes*.

106. "Si fusse autant éloquente et apprise, / Comme tu dis, je ferais mon devoir de m'acquitter." "Réponse au précédent rondeau, par la dite Jehanne Gaillarde," published in *L'Adolescence clémentine* in 1529. See Marot, *Œuvres poétiques*, vol. 1, 143–44.

Two other epigrams echo, yet transform, poems by Marot's followers published in contemporary songbooks and in an anthology entitled, *La Fleur de Poésie Françoyse* (1543). Several lines of Du Guillet's poem 53 resemble those of a *huitain* later attributed to François Ier that appears in music books and the poetry anthology. Poem 52 represents a lyric response to another anonymous piece in the same publications.[107] More than a borrowing of a first or last line of another poem, the *responce* or *responsif* was, as Miller explains, a poem "linked to a preceding poem (in an anthology) in various ways: citation plus rebuttal, variation or elaboration on a theme, continuation or *récit suivi*."[108] Miller's study focuses on the poems in which the intertextual link is sustained throughout the response poem and examines how Du Guillet's *responces*—including poems 52 and 53—transform the models in keeping with her own poetic strategies and vision of love.

Du Guillet's poem 18 responds to a *huitain* that was first published anonymously in two songbooks in 1538 and 1539 and later appeared in editions of poetry by both Marot and Saint-Gelais.[109] Miller shows how Du Guillet's response poem modifies the model to make a point about reason and love that counters Marot's original rhetorical stance. Without an understanding of the *responce* tradition and the way in which Du Guillet rewrites the model, the meaning of this epigram remains relatively obscure; but, as Miller points out, Du Guillet's contemporaries "would have recognized the skillful manipulation of the device and the intention of its poetic statement."[110]

107. Saulnier identifies these sources ("Etude," 36). For in-depth analysis of Pernette du Guillet's use of these models, see Miller, "In the Margins," 354–59. Miller explains that these two response epigrams by Du Guillet appear to be based on the versions of the model poems in the Parisian songbook of 1538, Pierre Attaingnant's *Second livre contenant XVII Chansons*.

108. "In the Margins," 353–54. See also H. H. Kalweis, "The *Responce* Genre in Early Modern French Renaissance Poetry," in *Bibliothèque d'Humanisme et Renaissance* 65 (1983), 77–86.

109. The authorship of the original poem remains uncertain; it is included in modern editions of both Marot and Saint-Gelais. See Mellin de Saint-Gelais, *Œuvres poétiques françaises*, vol. 2, ed. Donald Stone Jr. (Paris: Société des Textes Français Modernes, 1995), 54; and Clément Marot, *Œuvres poétiques*, vol. 2, ed. Gérard Defaux (Paris: Bordas, 1993), 334. Defaux notes that the poem in question may not be Marot's since it appears in the 1574 edition of the *Œuvres Poëtiques de Mellin de Saint Gelais* (Lyon: Antoine de Harsy, 1574), but also points out that the editions of Saint-Gelais's poetry are not always trustworthy, leaving the question of authorship unresolved (1136).

110. "In the Margins," 361. Du Guillet's *rebours* repeats the last line of the model poem as it appears in the 1538 Paris *chansonnier*, one of multiple editions of this songbook. Miller

Similarly, without an understanding of the models involved or of musical tradition, it is difficult for modern readers to appreciate fully Pernette du Guillet's "Ballad for Adonis" ("Conde Claros de Adonis," poem 64). For the subject, Du Guillet was inspired both by Mellin de Saint-Gelais's "Déploration sur la mort d'Adonis," published by Antoine du Moulin in 1545, and by the work of a Hellenistic poet now known as Pseudo-Theocritus.[111] Mellin de Saint-Gelais's *chanson* imitates the work of another Hellenistic poet, Bion, treating the same theme of Venus's lament following the demise of her beloved Adonis at the tusk of a wild boar. The model for Mellin's poem highlights the goddess's intense grief over the death of her beloved Adonis and her regret for her own immortality. Pernette du Guillet's Greek source, rather than focusing on Venus's violent emotions, recounts the goddess's cool-headed punishment of the contrite boar, an aspect of the tale that Du Guillet develops further.

Both Du Guillet's and Saint-Gelais's poems were published separately in 1545 in Lyon. They then appeared together in numerous collections in the sixteenth century. In the 1546 *Discours du voyage de Constantinople*, Du Guillet's poem followed Mellin's anonymously, with the erroneous subtitle, "suite, prise de l'Espagnol" ("continuation, taken from the Spanish"). Antoine du Moulin corrected that mistake in his 1547 edition of the *Déploration*, where he identifies "Conde Claros de Adonis" as being the "invention" of "D. Pernette du Guillet" and not derived from a Spanish source. The two poems again appeared in subsequent editions of the *Déploration* in the 1540s and 1550s, and were set to music in several sixteenth-century songbooks.[112]

---

explains that the models for poems 18, 52, and 53 appear in close proximity in Attaingnant's 1538 *XXVII Chansons*, suggesting that Du Guillet may have seen or owned a copy of that edition of the songbook and worked from it in writing her response epigrams (359–60). For more on the differences between Du Guillet's poem 18 and the model, see Barataud and Trudeau, *Rymes*, 63–64. See also the notes for poem 18 in this volume.

111. On Pernette du Guillet's "Conde Claros de Adonis," see Perrine Galand-Hallyn's extensive study, "Le latin à la rescousse du français: Trois humanistes autour de Vénus éplorée," in *Lyon et l'illustration de la langue française à la Renaissance*, ed. Gérard Defaux with the collaboration of Bernard Colombat (Lyon: ENS Editions, 2003), 308–43. See also Saulnier, "Etude," 50–53, and "Mellin de Saint-Gelais, Pernette du Guillet et l'air <<Conde Claros>>, in *Bibliothèque d'Humanisme et Renaissance* 32:3 (1970), 525–37; C. Martinez, "Conde Claros de Adonis," in *Il Rinascimento a Lione*, ed. Antonio Possenti and Giulia Mastrangelo (Rome: Edizioni dell'Ateneo, 1988), 683–97.

112. For a complete chronology and bibliography of these various editions, see Galand-Hallyn, "Le latin à la rescousse du français," 330–31.

Galand-Hallyn argues that Du Guillet's *chanson* is a response to Mellin de Saint-Gelais's poem, rather than a *suite*, or continuation of Saint-Gelais's "Déploration," as noted in some of the sixteenth-century editions of the two poems.[113] Du Guillet's choice of a model infused with more humor than the one chosen by Saint-Gelais (whose own poem focuses on the anger and passionate lament of Venus) allows her to emphasize different aspects of the myth and to add elements of her own. For example, she includes the peaceful domestic scene of Cupid and his wife, Psyche, playing chess at home when they hear the cries of the swan bearing the news of Adonis's death. Du Guillet also develops the legalistic aspect of the tale much more fully than does her Greek source, and in a manner that recalls earlier poems in the *Rymes*, where questions of love are presented for debate in the medieval tradition of the courts of love.[114] In this long ballad-like poem, Pernette du Guillet displays the same lyric strategies as elsewhere, using her intertextual models to develop a different poetic voice and sensibility, not openly opposing her sources, but modifying them for her purposes in the tradition of *imitatio*.[115]

The title of this *chanson* points to the importance of music in Pernette du Guillet's works. Even a scholar as erudite as Saulnier first overlooked the meaning of "Conde Claros de Adonis," calling the title obscure; however, he explains in a later article that the expression *conde claros* refers to both a Spanish ballad, or "romance," about the Count Claros of Montalban and, by extension, the well-known tune to

113. "Le latin à la rescousse du français," 315.

114. Galand-Hallyn observes that Du Guillet's development of the judicial metaphor here presents "une parodie de cour d'amour, la nature porcine de l'accusé ne contribuant guère au sérieux de l'affaire" (a parody of a court of love, the porcine nature of the accused hardly contributing to the seriousness of the affair); the boar himself seems first to possess the sort of courtly manners attributed to the ideal lover in Petrarchan poetry, and then finally to display "un repentir presque chrétien" (an almost Christian repentance). "Le latin à la rescousse du français," 317–18.

115. For Galand-Hallyn, the poems by Mellin de Saint-Gelais and Pernette du Guillet, along with a third by the neo-Latin poet, Jean Salmon Macrin, offer an interesting example of the "imitation-emulation around a same theme" typical of the humanist poets, but one that takes on particular interest because of its place in the sixteenth-century "querelle" on the nature of the ode. Galand-Hallyn summarizes the basics of the debate pertaining to the ode, from Sébillet's view that Mellin's poem was a model of the vernacular ode, equaling the works of Pindar and Horace, to Du Bellay, who called Mellin's and Pernette's pieces "chansons vulgaires" (vulgar songs), to Aneau and Des Autels, who defend the merits of both "chansons" about the death of Adonis as valid examples of the French ode. See "Le latin à la rescousse du français," 309–11.

which it was sung.[116] Different versions of the Spanish text circulated in the fifteenth century, and in the sixteenth century a specific melody came to be associated with it. The tune became a "standard," known by most musicians, and therefore subject to variations and improvisation.[117] We do not know if Du Guillet's poem was ever sung to this tune, but the musical tradition was undoubtedly part of her intertextual dialogue in the Renaissance practice of *imitatio*.

Pernette du Guillet's Neoplatonism

Like many of her contemporaries, Pernette du Guillet found a significant source of inspiration in Neoplatonic theory and tradition. As a result of economic and cultural exchange with Italy, she and the other poets of Renaissance Lyon came to know the works of Italian Neoplatonists Ficino, Ebreo, Castiglione and Bembo, and—primarily through them—the dialogues of Plato. The works of all four Italian authors were being translated into French around the time that Pernette du Guillet was composing her *Rymes*.[118] By the mid-sixteenth century, she and her fellow French poets were well acquainted with the Platonic doctrine of love and its principal myths. The Renaissance Neoplatonist vision of ideal love endowed woman with spiritual gifts that could in theory surpass those of man. As Ian Maclean concludes, however, there was "no profound change in attitudes toward the relative position of the sexes in the imperfect, sublunary

116. "Etude," 51; "Pernette du Guillet et l'air 'Conde Claros,'" 525.

117. See Pascale Boquet and Gérard Rebours, *50 Standards, Renaissance & Baroque, avec Variantes, Exemples, & Conseils pour Jouer & Improviser* (Courlay: Editions Fuzeau, 2006), for an explanation and examples of musical standards and improvisation during the Renaissance. See p. 46 for the musical notation of the "Conde Claros / Conteclare" tune and variants.

118. The first complete French translation of Ficino's *Commentaire sur le Banquet de Platon*, by Jean de la Haye, was published in Poitiers in 1546; Jacques Colin d'Auxerre translated Castiglione's *Le Courtesan*, published in Paris in 1537; Jean Martin's translation of Bembo's *Les Asolains* was published in 1545. Ebreo's *Dialogues* were translated by both Pontus de Tyard and Denys Sauvage, with two editions published in Lyon in 1551. Although some of the translations were published after Pernette du Guillet's death, she is very likely to have encountered manuscript and earlier partial versions in print already in circulation in Lyon, along with the original Italian texts. Sears Jayne identifies several paraphrases in French of short passages from Ficino's *De amore* by Champier (1503), Héroët (1536), and Corrozet (1541), and explains that the French translation by De la Haye was completed as early as 1542 (*Commentary*, 21).

world."[119] Despite the theoretical reciprocity of Platonic love, woman's primary role was, by her physical and spiritual beauty, to guide man up the Platonic ladder and to ensure the preservation of the species. Although Neoplatonists like Ebreo and Castiglione created dialogues and discussions on love with women as participants, the female voice was essentially restricted to serving as courtly complement to that of the male, or as a sort of sounding board to reflect the ideas expressed by men.[120] Woman did not ascend the ladder herself, or at least she had no public voice with which to speak of her ascent.

Leone Ebreo's *Dialoghi d'amore*, in particular, deeply influenced the writers—male and female—of Renaissance Lyon. The impact of his version of Platonism, with its focus on the cosmic dimensions of love, is evident in the poetry of both Du Guillet and Scève.[121] Ebreo's text may have been all the more important to Du Guillet as a prototype of a dialogue between a man and a woman about love. Philo and Sophia consider theories of how love functions on a human and cosmic scale, a discussion that takes place within the framework of concerns about the nature of their own love for each other.[122] Sophia raises thoughtful

119. Ian Maclean, *The Renaissance Notion of Woman: A Study in the Fortunes of Scholasticism and Medical Science in European Intellectual Life* (Cambridge: Cambridge University Press, 1980), 25. See also Robert Merrill (with Robert J. Clements), *Platonism in French Renaissance Poetry* (New York: New York University Press, 1957). Merrill's account of the influence of Platonic doctrine in French Renaissance poetry, and notably in the works of the *Pléiade* poets, remains an important study of this topic. In particular, see xi–xii for a discussion of the role played by the Lyonnais poets in the spread of Platonism.

120. See Virginia Cox, "Seen But Not Heard: The Role of Women Speakers in Cinquecento Literary Dialogue," in *Women in Italian Renaissance Culture and Society*, ed. Letizia Panizza (Oxford: European Humanities Research Centre, 2000), 385–400.

121. Regarding Ebreo's impact on Du Guillet's poetry, Saulnier observes a double influence, both formal and philosophical ("Etude," 55). Risset notes that the dialogue between the *Délie* and the *Rymes* reflects and echoes another dialogue, that of Sophie and Philon in Ebreo's *Dialogues d'amour* (*L'anagramme du désir*, 58). See also Robert Cottrell, "Pernette du Guillet's *Rymes*: An Adventure in Ideal Love," in *Bibliothèque d'Humanisme et Renaissance* 31 (1969): 553–71. Cottrell, citing Saulnier, affirms that Ebreo's *Dialoghi* deserve to be called the "breviary of Lyonnais Platonism of the 1540s and 1550s" (557). See above, n62, for details on the modern English and French editions of Ebreo's dialogues. For the original Italian text, see Santino Caramella's critical edition of the *Dialoghi* (Bari: Laterza, 1929), based on the 1535 edition published in Rome.

122. Lawrence Kritzman identifies a parallel between Du Guillet and Ebreo's Sophia. See *Rhetoric of Sexuality*, 13. The lyric subject of the *Rymes*, however, claims a more active role in her dialogue with the beloved and with literary tradition than the more passive role that Ebreo assigns to Sophia.

objections or doubts, to which Philo sometimes reacts with respect and interest. Often, however, he dismisses his beloved lady's point of view, dogmatically presenting a resolution to her doubts before proceeding to the next point. In other passages, he is critical of Sophia's questions and ridicules her inability to understand the concepts he has been explaining.[123] In the *Dialogues*, Sophia's proper role is to listen well and to ask the right questions, to which Philo will supply the answers. In the elaboration and development of theories of love throughout the *Dialogues*, Sophia remains a largely passive character.[124] Her only real power over Philo results from her continued resistance to his protestations of love and his desire for physical "delectation" to accompany their spiritual union. Like the *belle dame sans merci*, she possesses no linguistic, discursive power. Her only hold over him is her silence in response to his pleas that she recognize and compensate him for his devotion.

Despite Sophia's passive role, Ebreo's work represents an essential intertext of the *Rymes*, not only for the premise of dialogue between a man and a woman (however flawed the model), but also because of the Italian text's emphasis on the ideal of mutual affection. Not surprisingly, Du Guillet's *Rymes* highlight the concept of reciprocity in love, perhaps the one aspect of Platonism that seems most favorable to women, at least in theory. Ebreo, like Ficino and the other Neoplatonists, held that human beings naturally love and cherish what they possess, which leads to mutual affection.[125] Numerous poems in the *Rymes* focus on both the possessive and reciprocal nature of virtuous *amytié*.[126] In poem 23, as we have already seen, hesitant humility and the speaker's conflicting emotions render

123. Philo criticizes Sophia's attempt to answer a question, for example: "You know better how to ask than to reply, Sophia" (*The Philosophy of Love*, 268). See also *Dialogues*, 198.

124. Larsen demonstrates the degree to which the female interlocutors in Renaissance dialogues are "learners who direct the discussion (as in Castiglione's *Book of the Courtier*) rather than leaders and teachers," conforming to "acceptable conversational feminine behavior and to the overarching concern of *sermo* (conversation) to maintain decorum and behavior suitable for women." *From Mother and Daughter: Poems, Dialogues, and Letters of Les Dames des Roches*, ed. and trans. Anne R. Larsen, The Other Voice in Early Modern Europe (Chicago: University of Chicago Press, 2006), 182.

125. This reciprocity, however, does not result from equality, but rather from the drive for perfection and unity in the universe, which explains the love between superior (male) and inferior (female) creatures. See Marsilio Ficino, *Commentary*, 57; *Commentaire*, 158.

126. In the context of Du Guillet's poetry (and that of her contemporaries), the term *amytié* refers to chaste love and affection, with *parfaicte amytié* (perfect/pure love) being the goal

all the more forceful her concluding reminder of the rights due her in love. Similarly, the legalistic debate of poem 27 focuses on the lovers' mutual obligations, but signals the fact that such reciprocity remains hypothetical, unrealized. Although a number of poems in the *Rymes* focus on the Platonic goal of union through mutual and chaste affection, the poet frequently reminds her readers, as she does in poem 27, that reality rarely lives up to that ideal vision.

Another aspect of the Neoplatonic vision of love that Du Guillet highlights in the *Rymes*—and which minimizes her risk of censure as a woman writing poetry—is the desire to move beyond the attraction of physical beauty to the love of spiritual virtue. The *Rymes* reflect this aim of progressing beyond the physical to the realm of intellect and the soul. The poet's appreciation of her beloved's knowledge and learning elevates their love to this higher level. She admires his *esprit* (mind/intellect/spirit) and *vertu* (wisdom/moral goodness) and interprets his eloquence as a sign of his learning.[127] In poem 17, the speaker states unequivocally that the lover's virtue and his eloquence—his spoken words—attract her more than does his outer beauty:

> Through his virtues which draw me more than beauty
> To love him; his grace and eloquence abound,
> Making me feel supreme the world around.
>
> Par sa vertu, qui à l'aymer m'attire
> Plus que beaulté: car sa grace, et faconde
> Me font cuyder la premiere du monde. (17:3–5)

Elsewhere the *Rymes* do recognize the powerful attraction of desire, but in poem 19, as in 17, the speaker stresses the passionate effect that the beloved's *virtue* and *knowledge* have on her:

> Therefore, accept this pledge, I do implore,
> From one whose every thought you have enchanted
> With knowledge, grace, and virtues by the score.

---

of love in Neoplatonic theory. See the notes for Du Guillet's poem by that name, "Parfaicte Amytié" (39).

127. In the Renaissance, *vertu* could also mean valor, force, or might, particularly when describing men. In the *Rymes*, the word seems to be used exclusively to convey intellectual prowess or eloquence (yet not excluding moral goodness). See Yandell, *Carpe Corpus*, chap. 3; Boney, "Ardeur de veoir."

> Donc te supply accepter le vouloir,
> De qui tu as la pensee ravie
> Par tes vertus, ta grace, et ton sçavoir. (19:8–10)

Du Guillet's portrayal of the ideal love experience follows Neoplatonic theory in this respect, clearly favoring the intellect and eloquence over beauty. Moreover, she goes one step further, placing knowledge, an asset of the intellect (*esprit*), above spirituality, a quality of the soul (*âme*). Saulnier calls this phenomenon "humanist love."[128]

The first six epigrams of the *Rymes* focus on the beloved's *esprit*, *éloquence*, *vertu*, and *sçavoir*. The opening poems of the collection give the impression, if one reads no further, that Du Guillet favors—perhaps almost exclusively—this vision of love as admiration of the beloved's intellect. Numerous poems that follow, however, comment on or dramatize the conflict between virtuous, spiritual love (*amytié*) and physical desire (*amour*). Although Du Guillet clearly designates *amytié* as an ideal, she understands and acknowledges the power of physical love and its role in the arduous journey to *vertu*.[129]

Poem 12, for example, sets up the dichotomy between the pleasures that *Amour* (Cupid) brings and the need to vanquish this troublesome deity, thereby granting new life to the lovers. The first four lines of the epigram paint the pleasures of physical love in terms that capture the enchantment of the experience. After admitting the attraction and strength of this type of desire, the poet recommends an alternative of a higher order to her reader:

> But if you want to waste his sovereignty,
> You must, above all, this desire forfend:
> You'll see him pinned by his own archery,
> And Lovers' lives augmented in the end.
>
> Mais si tu veulx son pouvoir consommer:
> Fault que par tout tu perdes celle envie:
> Tu le verras de ses traictz se assommer,
> Et aux Amantz accroissement de vie. (12:5–8)

128. "Etude," 65.

129. This aspect of her poetry echoes Castiglione's discussions of the lover's internal conflict between rational choice and sensual appetite. Baldesar Castiglione, *The Book of the Courtier*, trans. Charles S. Singleton (Garden City, NY: Anchor Books, 1959), 337.

The second quatrain reflects the Neoplatonic ideal that pervades much of Du Guillet's poetry and her focus on the struggle to defeat *Amour* by rising above one's physical desires ("celle envie"). When those desires are vanquished, the lovers will move on to a new life together, founded on virtue and learning. The speaker, however, recognizes the power of the pleasure brought by *Amour*, a persistent foe of ideal *amytié*. The voice that describes and dramatizes the conflict understands the complexity of human emotions as well as the philosophical theories and literary conventions that define and depict them.[130]

Ficino and his fellow Neoplatonists comment at length on the Platonic notion of two loves, the celestial and the worldly. In Plato's *Symposium*, Pausanias introduces the notion of two coexisting Venuses, accompanied by two Loves. Ficino elaborates on this duality, explaining that the first Venus shines with the light of the divinity, which she transmits to the second Venus, who passes on the "sparks of that light in the matter of the world."[131] Because of the light transmitted by this second Venus, all bodies reflect in varying degrees the divine beauty, which the human intellect first perceives by sight. For Du Guillet, her beloved Day may have awakened her with his intellectual light, but she in her own right emits the light of "chaste love," as she points out in her questions to the beloved in poem 29:

> When you see that I tend with care
> Chaste love's spark inside to flare
> Anew each morn in full array,
> Will you not say you'll love me one day?
>
> Quand vous voyez, que l'estincelle
> De chaste Amour soubz mon esselle
> Vient tous les jours à s'allumer,
> Ne me debvez vous bien aymer? (29:1–4)

Her "spark" of virtuous affection recalls the sparks of light that the second Venus passes on to the world. We may identify the beloved/male poet with the first Venus, shining with divine light—a role

130. Kritzman explains that "the pleasure associated with libidinal drives is not absent from [Du Guillet's] poetry altogether," citing the example of poem 12, where "sexuality is absorbed into a spirituality that reaches epic proportions and inevitably encompasses the entire universe" (*Rhetoric of Sexuality*, 22).

131. *Commentary*, 54; see also *Commentaire*, 154.

attributed to him in many of the poems—and the speaker/female poet with the second Venus, transmitting that light to the world through her poetry. She indicates, however, that her beloved in turn should be inspired by her chaste spark to return her love.

Just as there are two Venuses and two *Amours*, the human mind also has the double capacity to understand (to receive light from the first Venus) and to engender and create (to pass on the light of divine beauty). Our intelligence, associated with the first Venus, venerates and loves the beauty we see, which is an image of the divinity. From the second Venus, however, comes the power to create and the desire to give birth to something beautiful, to produce a form that resembles divine Beauty.[132] Like Ficino, Ebreo elaborates upon the Platonic concept of the human soul that desires to reproduce an image of beauty; he reiterates that the aim and end of love is the birth and production of beauty.[133]

In the search for an active role in poetic dialogue, Du Guillet turns to this Neoplatonic concept of love as a generative force, which she uses not to perpetuate, but to subvert the polarization that permeates Neoplatonic theory, including Leone Ebreo's dialogues. Plato specifically denies all such intellectual reproduction to woman, and Ebreo implies strongly that such creative intellectual activity is beyond her scope. Du Guillet's female lyric subject, however, experiences love in much the same way as the noble, male soul in Ebreo's dialogues, where the lover is pregnant with an image of beauty engraved on his mind or soul. Philo tells Sophia that her divine beauty has been indelibly engraved on his soul.[134] Ficino, also following Plato, alludes to the image of the beloved imprinted or engraved on the lover's soul.[135] This brings us back to the first epigram of the *Rymes*, which describes the female speaker's frame of mind before and at the moment when she meets her beloved, her "divinité." Even after the preordained meeting, she remained lifeless except for a need to engrave the "deep impression / Of cruel love, of passion's sweet progression." In the process of writing and printing, implied by the terms "engrave" and "deep impression," she perceives the "divinity" that inspires her imagination and her poetry.[136]

132. *Commentary*, 54; see also *Commentaire*, 154–55.

133. *Philosophy of Love*, 440; see also *Dialogues*, 303.

134. *Philosophy of Love*, 199; see also *Dialogues*, 158.

135. *Commentary*, 57; see also *Commentaire*, 158.

136. On this point, see Kritzman, *Rhetoric of Sexuality*, 17–18.

For Ebreo and the Neoplatonists, it is the male drive for perfection in the universe that gives birth to beauty. In one of many analogies between lovers and heavenly planets, Philo explains that the moon, representing the world soul, experiences both female and male types of love, including the male desire to create an image of beauty:

> ...as if the soul were made pregnant of the beauty of the intellect and desired to give birth to it in the corporeal world, or as if it had gathered up the seed of that beauty to implant it in the body, like a craftsman who weaves beautiful patterns in his mind that he may give them proper being in the objects which he fashions.[137]

Philo explains further that the lover longs for eventual union with the beautiful being whose image is engraved on his soul, just as the pregnant woman looks forward to bringing forth into the world the child hidden in her womb.[138] Male desire to create and join with an image of beauty replaces the female, inferior capacity for childbearing with a superior act of generation through the masculine activities of writing, printing, and engraving. For Pernette du Guillet, love is both a physical and a spiritual experience, so it should not surprise us that she adopts this metaphor of beauty imprinted or engraved upon the soul and attributes to her lyric subjects roles similar to that of Leone Ebreo's moon/soul, desiring perfection and unity.

The speaker in poem 41 reproaches her lover's errant flirtations on the grounds that his words—rather than his physical beauty—will not yield the same fertile results in the hearts of other ladies. This acknowledgment of the speaker's participation in the process of generating beauty serves as the primary justification for her reproaches to her lover:

137. *Philosophy of Love*, 227; see also *Dialogues*, 174.

138. In this way, the lover's soul becomes pregnant with an image of beauty and desires to reproduce such an image. The lover, then, is the *mother* of Love, according to the *Dialogues*, and the beloved is the *father*. Ebreo explains this phenomenon in terms that escape the usual gender-associated boundaries and division of roles in his dialogues:

> The beautiful which is the beloved is therefore the father and generator of love, and the mother is the mind of the lover, made pregnant of the seed of the beautiful. And the seed is the pattern of this beauty in the mind of the knower which, being pregnant therewith, desires union with the beautiful and the generation of its kind. *Philosophy of Love*, 372 (See also *Dialogues*, 260).

[...] not that I'd complain,
Or wish the least your freedom to restrain;
But your fine conversation, in my view,
Cannot, in them, your golden words ingrain
So well as in *this* heart—that's owned by you.

Non que de toy je me voulsisse plaindre,
Comme voulant ta liberté contraindre:
Mais advis m'est, que ton sainct entretien
Ne peult si bien en ces autres empraindre
Tes motz dorez, comme au cueur, qui est tien. (41:6–10)

Empraindre, according to Huguet's dictionary, means both *féconder* (make fertile) and *inspirer* (to inspire). The beloved's words will, in essence, not only inspire her, but they will also impregnate her, according to the second Venus's capacity and desire to generate an image of divine beauty. The beloved male poet may have inspired the woman's love, and even given her knowledge of self—as the "birth" poems testify—but she, as poet, also has the desire and the power to engender beauty and eloquence in *her* poetry. The verb *empraindre* also suggests the act of printing, the process of imprinting or engraving images or words of beauty on the page for posterity.[139]

The combination of the verb *empraindre* with the golden words ("motz dorez") in the following line evokes the golden rain with which Jupiter impregnated Danae in classical mythology. The expression also recalls a popular French translation of Cato's sayings, entitled the "golden words": *Les mots dorez du Caton en Latin et en francoys: avec plusieurs bons et tres utiles enseignemens, proverbes, adages, authoritez et dictz moraulx des sages*, published in several editions in Paris, Troyes, and Lyon in the 1530s. Along with this double allusion to fertility and the golden words of literature, Du Guillet's references to immortality elsewhere in the *Rymes* (in poems 56, 63, and 70, for example) reinforce the notion of the female poet using the power and will of the mind to generate not children, but poetry (in print) that will transmit her learning and her image of the good to posterity. Like Ebreo's pregnant lover, this female speaker's soul may be impregnated by her beloved's golden words, as this poem suggests, but in order to *re*produce anything successfully from the seeds implanted in her, she

139. Cotgrave's dictionary translates the verb *empraindre* as "to print, stamp, set, press, or thrust hard in."

herself must possess the ability to generate an image of this beauty and virtue that she contemplates.

Pernette du Guillet certainly does not associate her role in this generative act with silence or passivity. On the contrary, she highlights her attempt to intervene in lines 3–4 of this same poem:

> Don't be surprised to any great degree
> When I, through art and learning, persevere,
> And do my best ensuring you stay clear
> Of seeing others[.]
>
> Ne t'esbahis si point je persevere
> A faire tant par art, et par sçavoir,
> Que tu lairras d'aller les autres veoir[.] (41:3–5)

In order to produce an image of virtue inspired by her beloved and his words, she too must exercise the *art* and ***sçavoir*** of the lover's disourse. This subverts the notion expressed in Plato's *Symposium*, and reiterated by the Italian Neoplatonists, that the nobler sort of creative generation is reserved for the souls of men.[140]

The Neoplatonic motif of the generative force of love and the reproductive drive of the lover permits the female poet to ground her unconventional acquisition of speech in a conventional aspect of a theory that otherwise assigned silence and passivity to women. Du Guillet refuses to play the silent role of Délie in Scève's *canzoniere*. There, Délie is an ideal image of the beloved lady that the poet holds in his mind and creates through his own "durs Epigrammes."[141] Du Guillet maintains the importance of the image of beauty in the mind and soul of the lover, recognizing that the lover's words and poetic works shape

140. The love of man for woman is necessary for the generation of the species, but that type of desire produces an offspring less noble than that which the souls of creative men conceive. As the wise woman, Diotima, explains to Socrates: "Everyone would prefer for himself to have had such children as these, rather than the human kind, and they look to Homer and Hesiod and the rest of our good poets and envy offspring of the sort they left behind, offspring which, being such themselves, provide immortal fame and remembrance." *The Dialogues of Plato*, Vol. 2, *The Symposium*, trans. R. E. Allen (New Haven: Yale University Press, 1991), 154 (209c–d).

141. Thomas Hunkeler explains that the lady becomes "Délie" only when she is transformed into "une image gravée dans le coeur de l'amant" (an image engraved in the heart of the lover) or, more precisely, when that internal image is transposed in writing by the lover. *Le vif du sens: Corps et poésie selon Maurice Scève* (Geneva: Droz, 2003), 234.

and modify that image, making of it a new artistic entity. She too enters into this poetic process, however, when desire urges her, as in poem 1, to "engrave the deep impression," and when she acknowledges here in poem 41 that the beloved's golden words are ingrained in and imprinted on her heart with *re*productive results.

Throughout her work—along with occasional accusations of fickleness—Du Guillet's lyric speaker stresses repeatedly that her beloved's knowledge, virtue and eloquence inspire her to cultivate the same qualities, to "praise you, in just the same way you praise me," as she writes in poem 6. Virtue united with love engenders an image of virtue, giving rise to desire of a higher order, as poem 56 reminds us:

> There, the good engenders
> An ardent longing to see,
> Whereby the heart surrenders
> To learning of high degree.
>
> Car il luy engendre
> Une ardeur de veoir,
> Et tousjours apprendre
> Quelque hault sçavoir. (56:31–34)

Work plays an important role in this process, allowing the speaking subject to acquire knowledge, a "minister" of Virtue (line 35).[142] Here the voice of the poet links the pursuit of noble, virtuous love with concerns of immortality—not to be achieved through the intervention of a divinity, but through work:

> And that, in this travail,
> I always may discern
> And stick close to the trail
> Of immortal concern.
>
> Et que tousjours voye,
> Travaillant ainsi,
> Tenir droict la voye
> D'immortel soucy. (56:51–54)

142. See poem 56, n237, for a discussion of the various meanings associated with the words *travail* and *travailler* in the Middle French of the sixteenth century.

Poem 63 also makes reference to the poet's labors in its juxtaposition of the darkness of night (before seeing her beloved) and the brightness of the beloved Day's life-giving intellectual light:

> An idleness is bred
> By night, which so pollutes us;
> By daylight we are led
> To labor that well suits us.
>
> La nuict la paresse
> Nourrit, qui tant nuit:
> Et le jour nous dresse
> Au travail, qui duit [.] (63:31–34)

These lines add significant nuance to the importance attributed to the inspiring light of the Day, the beloved male poet. While he may have awakened her intellectual desires, Du Guillet explains the benefits of the labor that must follow this inspiration. Daylight represents the beloved's learning, which shines brightly like the first Venus with the light of divine Beauty. The poet of the *Rymes* must let her light shine too, however, like the second Venus, engendering and refining her own image of beauty through her work, inspired by her beloved. The plural *nous* (us) of line 33 indicates that this process applies to all poets, putting Du Guillet on equal footing with the figure of the master poet.

Similarly, in the Neoplatonic cosmos, the bright rays of the sun are countered by the moon's more moderate glow, shining in the darkness of night, reflecting the sun's rays; the light from both sun and moon is vital to the proper functioning of the universe. In contrast to her beloved (her Day, whom she compares to the sun), the speaking voice in the *Rymes* often associates herself with the roles and qualities assigned to the Neoplatonic moon—moving in and out of light and shadow, influenced by both the divine sun's enlightenment and the pull of earthly desires. Scève's use of the moon as a figure to represent Délie in his *canzoniere* makes Du Guillet's alignment of her female speaking subject with lunar qualities all the more intriguing. The female "I" of the *Rymes* never overtly refers to herself as the moon, but in poem 70 ("Solace") the unidentified speaker tells the suffering, complaining lover that he should appreciate his situation in a different light. In lines 76–77, the speaker reminds the lover that, because of placing trust in the lady, "you have reached heights far beyond the Moon, / With praise, and fame, and honorable renown" ("Tu es venu trop plus hault, que la Lune, / En loz, et bruict, et honorable fame"). What at first may seem a humbling association becomes much more ambiguous—and strikingly assertive—when we consider the moon's role in Neoplatonic theory.

Ficino explains that the sun as provider—receiving no light from anyone else and giving to all—is male. Earth, which receives the light of the sun and the moon but returns it to no one, is feminine because of her passivity. The moon, however, both receiving and reflecting the sun's light, belongs to the androgynous race.[143] In Leone Ebreo's account, the sun reigns supreme among the heavenly planets, associated with the divine intellect and with the heart because of its active, central role in the cosmos. The moon represents the brain of this universe, and, with its activity similar to that of the sun's divine intellect, displays an essentially male quality.[144] Located farthest from the sun, the passive, female earth receives all light from the heavenly planets, assembling those rays in her center, with no capacity to return or reflect spiritual or intellectual light. Pernette du Guillet rejects the passivity attributed to the female earth in the Neoplatonic cosmos—and to women by literary and social convention—by adapting and transforming elements of this polarized universe to create a female voice that participates actively in the male-centered discourses of the Renaissance. Just as the androgynous moon—the mind of the cosmos—both receives and reflects the light of the sun, the lyric subject of the *Rymes* receives, returns, and passes on the light of learning and true love.

Ficino emphasizes the lunar capacity for reasoned judgment, a quality he, like Plato, attributes to the masculine half of the moon's androgynous nature. Like the moon, the speaking/writing woman of the *Rymes* possesses the capacity to judge the actions and words of others, including those of her beloved. In poem 16, Du Guillet's lyric speaker reminds her beloved that, although God may have given him many fine assets, she herself has been given reason, "to best appreciate / and judge your knowledge and your happy state." She proclaims her power and right to judge him, and asks that he be guided by reason. Here and elsewhere, we see that the young poet's admiration for her beloved's intellect and eloquence is not blind. She recognizes her own

143. *Commentary*, 78; see also *Commentaire*, 174.

144. *Philosophy of Love*, 227; see also *Dialogues*, 174.

jealousy and questions his fidelity in poem 45, placing her trust in what she herself has seen, rather than the words others might use to try to convince her that she is imagining things. Poem 35 opens with an echo of this mistrust, and reflects the speaker's critical assessment, "I can't believe your words are true." The legalistic discourse of poem 27 highlights the speaker's powers of reason and judgment. The lyric speaker frequently judges her beloved and reminds him of her right and power to do so, offering gentle admonishments to a lover who often falls short of her ideal.

Although direct, her judgments, reproaches, and reminders are always humorous and light-hearted, reflecting the courtly tone that Castiglione prescribes for the *cortegiana's* speech. The introduction of parenthetical asides in the epigrams often adds a conversational, rather than philosophical, tone to a debate, as in line 6 of poem 55, where the speaker remarks that even a Sophist would concede the point in his sleep. Robert Cottrell notes this informal tone even in the first epigram, where the speaker's reference to her birth ("Quand je nasquis"), conveys a "curiously parenthetical quality, as if it were an aside uttered in the course of a casual conversation."[145] Such an aside in line 9 of poem 24 ("which soothes my mind and calms my thoughts to rest") lends a personal, even intimate, tone to the speaker's otherwise bold assertion regarding the relative importance of the "Lady" over "Love." In a similar manner, the parenthetical remark in line 4 of poem 45 adds a humorous personal reflection evocative not only of the playful tone of the *tradition marotique*, but also of courtly banter:

> They will say it's only jealousy
> That causes me distress (as I well know).
>
> On me dira, que c'est la jalousie
> (Je le sçay bien) qui faict sur moy effort. (45:3–4)

Such apparently casual comments maintain a tone of courtly conversation for debates about matters central to Neoplatonist discourse, following Castiglione's recommendations regarding the Court Lady's speech.

145. "An Adventure in Ideal Love," 559. Rieu notes a similar effect in the opening question of poem 20, where the familiar, conversational tone of the question reintroduces the psychological reality of the woman in love who wishes to see her beloved ("Poétique et réflexivité," 37).

Whereas Castiglione's participants in the discussions at Urbino have different opinions of women's intellectual powers, those at the court agree on the purpose of the lady's knowledge and speech: to complement (and compliment) the Courtier's talents by engaging him in conversations that please and divert him. The participants in this debate also agree on the vulnerability of the woman who assumes a speaking role, however limited, at the court. The Magnifico warns against this danger, with advice on how to avoid it:

> She must be more circumspect, and more careful not to give occasion for evil being said of her, and conduct herself so that she may not only escape being sullied by guilt but even by the suspicion of it, for a woman has not so many ways of defending herself against false calumnies as a man has.[146]

The only solution for the Court Lady is to strive continually to maintain a balance between affability and vivacity, on the one hand, and a chaste and prudent demeanor on the other.[147] The women present never voice opinions on their fate in the Neoplatonic theory of love. Valeria Finucci argues that they do not actually contribute to the discussion: "Positioned as the subject of a discourse but not as the speaking 'I,' the court lady finds herself presiding mutely over the circuitous demise of her subjectivity."[148]

Pernette du Guillet clearly understands this vulnerability as a woman speaking and writing for a public audience; she adopts a playful, courtly tone when most appropriate, particularly when offering reproaches. In poem 42, she openly addresses the same concerns described by the courtly gathering at Urbino. The speaker in this poem denies a series of slanderous accusations, or *calomnies*, and proclaims her innocence:

> If they say upon more than one
> I must depend to have my fun,
> Chasing pleasures to and fro—
> Worse than that I do not know.

146. *The Book of the Courtier*, 206.

147. *The Book of the Courtier*, 207.

148. *The Lady Vanishes*, 18.

Qui dira, qu'à plusieurs je tens
Pour en avoir mon passetemps,
Prenant mon plaisir çà, et là:
Je ne sçay rien moins, que celà. (42:5–8)

The first four stanzas of this poem refute charges that may already have been made by malicious gossips, recalling Castiglione's description of the Court Lady's vulnerability. Because of her participation in a public dialogue—and because she speaks of love—the female poet faces the danger of false calumnies, against which she is virtually defenseless.[149] Offering a theoretical defense through the very poetic medium that exposes her to those dangers, Du Guillet infuses humor into this scene by multiplying the possible suspicions of her detractors and refuting each charge with the same refrain. To avoid the silence imposed upon women in the Renaissance and the censure of those who break that silence, Du Guillet evokes the context of courtly dialogue reminiscent of Philo and Sophia's conversations and those of the Court Lady in Castiglione's *Courtier*. She departs, however, from the passive, non-judgmental roles of the women participants in those texts.

Evidently well aware of the risks involved in overstepping the limits placed on a woman's speech, Du Guillet situates her own poetic discourse in a context approved by noble society—that of conversation with a courtly admirer.[150] Against this backdrop, she adapts the conventions of Neoplatonism, a profoundly patriarchal discourse, to create an active female poetic voice. She replaces the silent and at best noncommittal female figure of Neoplatonic tradition with a confident voice, ready to engage in debate and assert her own rights.[151] That voice claims a vital, reproductive role in dialogue and in the generation of beauty and poetry. Du Guillet replaces the image of the silent lady, object of veneration and source of suffering in Scève's

149. Du Moulin recognizes this potential problem in his preface when he refers to readers of bad faith—those small minds who might choose to take the work in the wrong light.

150. Larsen highlights the importance to the female interlocutors in Renaissance dialogues of *sermo* (conversation) for maintaining decorum (*From Mother and Daughter*, 182). Concerning the various strategies adopted by women writers seeking to avoid censorship, Jones points out that most Renaissance women poets avoided open challenges to the ideal of the silent woman, preferring instead to "[work] their ways into [public discourse] more by indirection than by confrontation" ("Surprising Fame," 80).

151. For more about women writers' adaptation of Neoplatonism to affirm and authenticate their literary voices, see Elisabeth Caron, "Les femmes et la politique du Néo-Platonisme: Les enjeux à la Renaissance d'un baiser de Platon," *Etudes littéraires* 27:2 (1994), 97–109.

Délie, with the figure of the active, speaking, writing poet who reflects and admires, but also judges the sun.

The many examples cited above illustrate the extent to which the *Rymes* construct intertextual dialogues—not only with Scève's *Délie*, but also with other French poets and with the works of Italian Petrarchist poets and Neoplatonists. Du Guillet acknowledges the discontinuity that separates her poetry from its intertexts, and she builds an innovative poetics on that difference. She cannot follow the literary models available to her without changing them, because those models make no provision for women's speech—not even for a female subject truly engaged in dialogue. She does not wholly reject the subtexts of patriarchal literary tradition, but chooses to create her own poetry in a manner consistent with the Renaissance mode of imitation, which recognizes that the writer is always a rewriter. The imitative challenge, for Du Guillet and other women poets of the Renaissance, must have been particularly daunting, however, because the "reconstruction" process required the invention and addition of the female voice.

The interpretation of that voice naturally evolves according to the interests that readers bring to the text. Nothing external to the work has changed much since the sixteenth century. We have no new information about the person who penned these poems; we have only changes in the physical format in which they appear to us, minimal changes having more to do with typographical conventions than anything else. Huchon's controversial question regarding authorship of this collection along with Labé's urges us, whether or not we agree with the conclusions of the study, to read, interpret, and appreciate from a healthy critical distance the poetic subject that emerges from the *Rymes*. Stripping away presuppositions about the author's life—and recognizing the ways in which elements of the collection itself shape our reading of the authorial voice—enables us to appreciate more fully the unique lyric subject that speaks to us across so many centuries. Despite the mystery of how the poems actually came to the editor and printer and the lack of biographical information—perhaps even *because* of those very uncertainties—Du Guillet's *Rymes* highlight the issues of poetic voice and subjectivity at the heart of all lyric poetry, guaranteeing their relevance and interest for readers of any era.

The Reception of the Rymes

Based on the publication of four editions of the *Rymes* between 1545 and 1552 by successful printers in Lyon and Paris, and the appearance in contemporary songbooks of at least six of the poems (four during the poet's life), we can reasonably assume that Pernette du Guillet's poetry was well received by Renaissance readers, particularly in the decades of the 1540s and 1550s.[152] During the long period from the end of the sixteenth century to the early nineteenth century, the *Rymes*—along with the works of many Renaissance poets—fell into obscurity. Three nineteenth-century editions and a nearly complete edition included in the Pléïade volume of *Poètes du XVIe siècle* (1953) revived the text, although this poetry remained largely unexplored by scholars until the middle of the twentieth century. In his erudite "Etude des *Rymes*," published in 1944, V.-L. Saulnier explored Du Guillet's innovative use of literary traditions and sources, bringing details of the collection to the attention of modern academic readers after a long period of neglect. The publication of Victor Graham's 1968 critical edition provided a valuable tool to late twentieth-century scholars seeking to study the *Rymes*, which were of particular interest after feminist critics drew needed attention to the works of long-forgotten women writers.[153]

Pernette du Guillet's *Rymes* have undergone a renaissance of sorts in the late twentieth and early twenty-first century, as the bibliography of secondary studies shows. Along with feminist criticism, studies of Renaissance theories of imitation and dialogue have enhanced our understanding of how sixteenth-century poets, male and female, created unique authorial voices from and within prevailing literary traditions. Research on the history of the book and the printing trades continues to yield valuable insights pertaining to works published by, for, and about women, as well as printed music books. The year 2006 saw the publication of two new and excellent critical editions

152. See the Editor's Bibliography for details on the editions of the *Rymes*. For more on the 1546–47 Parisian editions published by Jeanne de Marnef, see Chang, *Into Print*, chap. 1, and "Gender of the Book."

153. Françoise Charpentier's inclusion of Pernette du Guillet's poems in the same volume with Louise Labé's poetry and a selection of *Blasons du corps féminin* made all three works more accessible for general readers and classroom use, along with an insightful preface covering essential elements of each of the texts. Louise Labé, *Œuvres poétiques, précédées des Rymes de Pernette du Guillet, avec un choix de Blasons du Corps féminin*, ed. Françoise Charpentier (Paris: Gallimard, 1983).

of the *Rymes*, each with extensive documentation and valuable reference materials.[154] The heightened interest in Pernette du Guillet's poetry, combined with a recognition of the linguistic difficulties that the original French poems represent for many readers (for English speakers who do not read French, certainly, or those unfamiliar with sixteenth-century French and its poetic conventions), led to our desire to provide a bilingual edition of the complete collection. It is our hope that presenting the entire volume in translation, with English versions of the poems side-by-side with the originals, will open the text to non -specialist readers and offer a new avenue of exploration for those already familiar with this poetry in French.[155]

The French Text

The French text of the *Rymes* is based on the first edition, published in 1545 in Lyon by Jean de Tournes.[156] We have included three poems

154. Elise Rajchenbach's edition (Droz 2006) includes a substantial introduction and provides a wealth of documentation of textual sources and allusions, along with valuable reference materials in the appendices, particularly with regard to music. The critical apparatus of the new Champion edition (2006) by Christian Barataud and Danielle Trudeau also includes extensive notes, with a focus on versification and on linguistic difficulties and interpretive challenges in the poems. Although the text of the poetry is essentially the same in both editions (with the exception of minor spelling differences due to slightly different editorial principles), there is remarkably little duplication of information in the critical information provided in each volume. The availability of these two valuable scholarly tools will undoubtedly encourage and aid further study of the *Rymes*.

155. Ann Rosalind Jones's verse translations of fourteen of the poems appear in Katharina Wilson's anthology, *Women Writers of the Renaissance and Reformation* (Athens: University of Georgia Press, 1987), 219–31. Partial or full translations in verse and in prose of several other poems appear in various scholarly studies. See in particular the works by Jones, Yandell, and Miller in the bibliography. Very recently, Norman Shapiro has published verse translations in English of a selection of poems by Pernette du Guillet in his monumental volume, *French Women of Nine Centuries: The Distaff and the Pen* (Baltimore: The Johns Hopkins University Press, 2008), 120–31. Most of the poems in the *Rymes* have never been translated into English until now.

156. For those who wish to see the collection in its original format, two copies of the first edition are available in electronic image [pdf] format on the Gallica website (*La bibliothèque numérique de la Bibliothèque nationale de France*). Those electronic facsimiles were produced from microfilms of two copies of the 1545 *Rymes*—one housed in the Bibliothèque nationale de France in Paris (http://gallica2.bnf.fr/ark:/12148/bpt6k70127q) and the other in the Bibliothèque municipale de Lyon (http://gallica.bnf.fr/ark:/12148/bpt6k791376). For full bibliographic descriptions of three copies of the *editio princeps* in French libraries, as well as detailed descriptions of the other sixteenth-century editions, see *Rymes*, ed. Rajchenbach,

attributed to Pernette du Guillet that were added to the *Rymes* in Jean de Tournes's 1552 Lyon edition. Because these three additional poems are widely accepted as Du Guillet's, we have placed them after her other poems in the text and *before* the epitaphs written at the time of her death by Maurice Scève and Jean de Vauzelles. Footnotes in the text remind the reader of this addition.[157]

For this edition, we have used *u/v* and *i/j* according to modern standards and have reversed the typographical conventions of the 1545 edition pertaining to *a* and *à*, putting the *accent grave* on the preposition *à* and not on the third-person singular form of the verb *avoir*. In the first edition, as in many printed books of the era, the *accent grave* is not used to distinguish between *ou* (the conjunction, "or") and *où* (the relative pronoun, "where/when"). We have added the accent on *où* when needed, to avoid confusion, and made note of the one instance, in poem 26, where *ou* may be read as either conjunction or relative pronoun, leading to two slightly different interpretations of the final line of the poem. For the sake of readability, we have added apostrophes in a few instances where none appear in the original text, converting "lon," for example, to "l'on." We have opted to correct a small number of obvious typographical errors in the *editio princeps*, all of which were corrected in subsequent sixteenth-century and modern editions.[158] Where those small corrections might affect meaning, we have explained the change in a note. We have chosen not to add the *accent aigu* on past participles and certain adjectives, or to remove accents from words no longer accented in modern usage. Other than in the limited categories cited here, we have chosen not to modernize spelling, wishing to present a French text that is accessible, but remains faithful to the original sixteenth-century edition. The English translation on the facing page will help readers unfamiliar with spelling and punctuation in *moyen*

89–91. See also the extensive bibliographical information in the edition by Barataud and Trudeau, 24–26.

157. We have used the text of these three poems as they appear in Victor Graham's 1968 edition, verified in the new critical editions by Barataud/Trudeau and Rajchenbach. Barataud and Trudeau also have inserted the additional poems before the *épitaphes* in their edition. For more about the three poems added in 1552 and their atttribution to Pernette du Guillet, see Rajchenbach's introduction, *Rymes*, 92–95.

158. We have only noted variants from later editions that may affect the meaning of a line or interpretation of a poem. For a list of all variants, see the comprehensive textual documentation in the critical editions of the *Rymes* by Rajchenbach and by Barataud and Trudeau.

français (Middle French), and readers interested in viewing the text in its first edition may do so online, as noted above.

The 1545 edition of the *Rymes* includes very few titles for individual poems and no identifying numbers. Saulnier's influential study groups the poems by genre and numbers them consecutively within each. This system of reference was adopted by Graham in his 1968 edition and has been used in all subsequent editions and studies except the recent Droz critical edition (2006). The editor of that volume, Elise Rajchenbach, chose to number the poems consecutively throughout the volume, eliminating the generic titles and retaining only the titles from the original edition. Believing that approach to reflect the sound practice of bringing the text closer to its original form, we have chosen to follow Rajchenbach's lead, numbering the poems consecutively. We have opted to use Roman numerals for the French poems and Arabic numerals for the English poems, both for ease of reference and to distinguish the two versions visually on the page. We have retained all original poem titles. At the risk of needlessly confusing readers who are encountering the *Rymes* for the first time, we have also chosen to include the generic poem title and number from the Graham edition in brackets under the poem number.[159] We intend for the additional information to be helpful to those already familiar with the *Rymes* in earlier editions and to those consulting the many studies that refer to the poems using the system proposed by Saulnier and adopted by Graham. A table at the end of this edition presents a concordance of the consecutive numbering system with the names and numbers used by Saulnier and Graham.

Introducing the Rymes *in English*

As I began to contemplate work on a bilingual edition of the *Rymes*, I considered the relative merits of different models of translation. Although a direct, prosaic translation of the poems could be helpful to scholars, and free verse might easily appeal to modern ears, I felt that such approaches would not do justice to or convey the essential qualities of the original poetry to today's readers. Those methods may serve well for brief selections in scholarly articles or in broad-

159. For the sake of consistency, we have included the generic name and number with the English poems as well, despite the difficulty of translating the terms *épître* and *chanson* into modern English. "Epistle" (i.e., verse epistle) and "song" do not convey precisely the same expectations of genre, but they are the best approximations available.

ranging anthologies, but the entire collection called for an approach designed to translate both form and content for a twenty-first-century readership. Above all, I knew I would need to find a poet collaborator. Fortunately, Marta Rijn Finch was drawn to this poetry, intrigued and undaunted by the challenge of crafting English poems that would not only be faithful to the meaning of the original text, but would also maintain the same rhyme scheme and a parallel versification in English, with results that capture the rhythm, tone, and subtleties of meaning of the originals, effectively "transmuting" Pernette du Guillet's poems into a new language and time.

Naturally, because of the decision to provide English translations that are successful poems in their own right, there are times when the precise meaning of the English must diverge slightly from the French. These occasional points of *décalage* open a fascinating space for re-examining the ways in which we read and interpret the original verse. The notes to the poems highlight these most interesting words and lines, often pointing to important ambiguities in the original text. Where the French expression or line of verse encompasses more than one meaning or nuance that had to be resolved one way or the other in the English, we have indicated the options considered and explained the rationale behind the choice, hoping to draw the reader's attention to the layers of possible meaning woven into the original poem.

Finch's English verse succeeds remarkably in capturing the original ambiguities and the multiple levels of meaning characteristic of Pernette du Guillet's lexical choices. Poem 38, for example, presented the thorny problem of how precisely to translate *appetisser*, a word with apparently contradictory meanings in sixteenth-century French. (See the notes to poem 38 for more details.) Finch has circumvented the impasse, choosing the expression, "to trifle with the feelings," to aptly characterize Cupid's meddling with the lovers' hearts. The words *honte* and *honteux/honteuse* provide another example of coexisting, yet contradictory meanings, as explained below in the context of poem 68, "The Night." Similar challenges arose throughout the process, due in large part to the evolution of the French language in this period from its medieval forms and meanings toward the more standardized language of the seventeenth century. French—like other vernacular languages—emerged from the shadow of the Latin tongue in the Renaissance and by the middle of the sixteenth century was widely used in published works of literature, but with its meanings, written forms, and spelling conventions still in flux. In this period of transition, many words were used both in their late medieval context and with new connotations that would eventually replace the old in modern French. One such word is *travail*, which originally meant trouble, pain, or care, including the pain and fatigue of childbirth, then labor, or toil that caused pain and trouble, then finally came to refer to intellectual work, as well as manual and physical labor. Du Guillet's use of the word appears to encompass the notions of trouble, toil, and labor, as well as of her work as a writer, a rich range of meaning that Finch handles sensitively in poems 56, 63, and 70.

Elsewhere, ambiguity derives from Du Guillet's use of syntax, requiring the reader to consider more than one interpretation or shade of meaning. In poem 25, for example, the speaker poses a cryptic question: "Now whoever has, or wants to have, two— / Can anyone bring two Loves into being?" ("Or qui en a, ou en veult avoir deux, / Comment peult il faire deux Amours naistre?") The question could imply the prospect of the beloved causing two women to admire him, or that he inspires two types of love, physical and spiritual, in the speaker herself. The English lines maintain that ambiguity, while conveying the underlying essential issue of how one heart can possibly pursue two loves (or two different types of love) satisfactorily. Unclear pronoun references leave the door open to interesting variant readings of certain lines, as explained in the notes for poems 14, 43, and 44. Line four of poem 23, "que dessus vous je m'osasse avancer," remains somewhat ambiguous in the original, encompassing both the idea that the speaker might presume to equal her beloved, *or* to outdo him, with the manner of acting on this audacious and imagined presumption left unspoken. Finch's decision to translate this hypothetical transgressive movement into the realm of the poet's vocation—"and through my work dare rival your success"—echoes the speaking subject's self-conscious references to her work and writing elsewhere in the collection, including poems 1, 2, 5, 6, 7, 56, and 63.

In her translation of poem 68, "The Night," Finch recreates the complex threads of the original poem, which echo multiple literary, philosophical, and theological traditions, in a way that also preserves the poet's awareness of her own role and voice. The translation of lines 179–80—"Always eager, through myth or allegory, / To all alone invent our own perdition"— deftly combines the notion of humanity inventing or forging its own ruin with the idea that our "rash fancy" becomes our "one true science," from the previous lines. Finch's addition of the phrase, "through myth or allegory," reflects and pays homage to Du

Guillet's own use of allegorical techniques in the elegy, and her limited, yet vital use of classical mythology in the *Rymes.*[160]

This elegy also presented the challenge of how to interpret and to translate the problematic adjective, *honteuse,* which in the sixteenth century had both positive and negative connotations, meaning either "bashful / modest / shamefast" or "shameful / dishonorable / disgraceful." The notes for this poem explore the complex nature of the "Dame honteuse" herself. To avoid choosing one interpretation over the other in the English version, Finch has chosen to refer to this figure as the "Masked Lady," an expression that matches the description and role of the allegorical lady in the poem and maintains the rich ambiguity of the original.

Regarding my translation of Antoine du Moulin's preface, I am deeply grateful to Leah Chang for sharing the portions of the preface translated in her book on printers, editors, and female authors, to Cathy Yandell for important insights, and to Marta Finch for her many valuable suggestions, which were particularly helpful in creating a more readable English translation than I would have been able to produce without her wise input. I have tried to strike a balance between providing a faithful translation, close to the original in style and meaning, and an accessible text in English. For the most part, I have retained the long sentences with their multiple clauses, but have chosen to introduce sentence breaks in the longest of those, for the sake of clarity, and to add paragraph breaks at logical points in the preface.

Finally, I wish to express my gratitude to Marta Finch for bringing her many talents and positive energy to this most challenging of projects. I deeply appreciate her willingness to discuss and revisit countless times the most enigmatic poems, including 54, whose "quartan fever" nearly got the best of us. I am also thankful for her

160. Finch was also inspired by a possible allusion to Plato's "allegory of the cave" in book 7 of *The Republic*, in which prisoners see only shadows and hear only echoes of real objects and voices on the wall of the cave where they are chained. According to Plato, what we perceive to be real is in fact an illusion, an imperfect representation, just as the monsters in "The Night" haunt humanity, although they are merely products of our imagination. In the end, the lyric subject of Du Guillet's elegy welcomes the rays of daylight to chase away the troubling illusions and to bring her knowledge of the beloved as well as of herself. For Plato, too, the sun serves as metaphor for intellectual and spiritual illumination, allowing human beings—through reason—to observe things clearly. See Plato, *The Republic*, book 7, in *The Portable Plato*, ed. Scott Buchanan, trans. Benjamin Jowett (New York: Penguin Books, 1977), 546–51.

patience with my dogged adherence to particular readings of some of the lines or poems as a whole, and with my general tendency to focus on *what* is being said more than on *how* it is being said. From her I have learned much about the art and craft of translation, giving me new insights into how we read the *Rymes* and, indeed, all poetry—in French and in English. Our collaboration has been a fruitful process that has naturally raised many intriguing questions of interpretation along the way and reinforced for us the extent to which subjectivity is a construct of language. We hope that this attempt to render a fascinating lyric subject and its voices into another language and time will both engage newcomers to the *Rymes* and inspire additional paths of inquiry for readers already acquainted with this remarkable poetry.

Translator's Note

MARTA RIJN FINCH

Some time ago, just back from several years in Lyon, I was persuaded by my philosopher-father, before his death, to translate for him the poems of a twentieth-century French philosopher he was concentrating on at the time—Simone Weil. We spent hours together going over lines and individual words, trying to understand fully the meaning of each poem, often abstruse and elusive from so great a thinker.

When the opportunity arose to translate Pernette du Guillet's poetry, I was delighted. I thought of the simplicity of lilting Renaissance phrases, replete with Neoplatonic allusions and Petrarchan words of love—ha! I found lovely words and phrases aplenty, but they were hardly less abstruse than those of Simone Weil, with the added challenge of a vocabulary from half-a-millennium ago. (Du Guillet seems to have enjoyed deliberately seeking out those words undergoing change in her time—using them with echoes of their old definitions, sometimes the very opposite of themselves.) I found myself wondering, when I reached poem 45, whether "If I want to rid my imagination of this pain" and "If I want to rid myself of imagined suffering" meant the same thing (becoming "If I want my fancy to be free" as the first line); then, in poem 14, whether "but not without delay" was too far removed from "if it is not quickly" (see line 7).

I should never have been able to accomplish it on my own. Karen Simroth James, who had been studying the work of Du Guillet for many years and grappling with the multifarious meanings of words in this transitional period of the French language, was looking for someone to render the poetry into English verse. During the transformation process, she labored patiently over each poem in its sixteenth-century version before sending me the annotated poems, at which time, after further scrutiny, I translated them into something close to their present state. Then she and I went over them again together, carefully, line by line.

Since this was to be the first appearance in English for most of these poems,[161] it seemed essential to follow strictly Pernette du Guillet's

161. Perhaps two-dozen had been translated into a variety of verse styles, or into prose for scholarly journals, over the last quarter-century—notably by Ann R. Jones, Joyce Miller, and Cathy Yandell. See the selection of fourteen poems translated by Jones in *Women Writers*

meter and rhyme scheme. I held steadfastly to this rule, although other intentions soon fell by the wayside: to adhere to the exact number of syllables; to eschew all use of contractions and vocabulary from a later period; to confine all words to the lines in which they had initially appeared; and to translate a particular French word consistently, using always the same word in English.

Guidelines such as these are easily made, of course, but in the end the poems themselves dictate where they want to go. I soon found that the strict syllable count and absence of contractions were making the lines sound forced. Contractions started to slip in—to help the meter or allow for a better word choice—and seemed to suit the informal, conversational tone of much of the original work. (Indeed, given the frequent use of elision in the French language, it didn't seem too great an imposition.) Certain lines flowed more smoothly into English than did others, where a convoluted syntax required switching them around; however, it was not always preferable to make the poems easily understandable. In Pernette du Guillet's poetry, there is a delicious ambiguity—often from words with several different nuances—that *should* be left intact. (To choose a single meaning for a word which was supposed to carry two or more was one of the most painful decisions that had to be made.) But when the sense of a poem is abstruse and full of ambiguity, if the translator cannot first understand the precise meaning, the work can hardly be rendered into another tongue. Perhaps that, more than anything else, was what led Robert Frost to say that poetry is what gets lost in translation.

One of the words James and I had wanted to be consistent in translating was *Jour*, used by Du Guillet when referring to her special male mentor, her "beloved." The lovely round vowel sounds in the second epigram (poem 2), however, impressed me, and I was wondering what English words could be found to echo them, when "Morn" presented itself to accompany the other "m" and "o" sounds in the last line. Should I ruin the line's flow and use "Day," or risk losing the important connection with other references to *Jour*? It might not have mattered for just a few of the poems appearing in isolation, but in the process of translating the entire collection over the next eighteen months, I saw that this was a decision not to be taken lightly.

---

of the Renaissance and Reformation, ed. Katherina Wilson (Athens: University of Georgia Press, 1987), 219–31. See also Norman Shapiro's recently published verse translations of nine of Du Guillet's poems in *French Women Poets of Nine Centuries: The Distaff and the Pen* (Baltimore: Johns Hopkins University Press, 2008), 120–33.

(In the end, what won out was the sound of the word for the English version.) ***Sçavoir*** was another frequently-recurring word with a special significance throughout the poems, usually translating neatly into "knowledge" or "learning"; in poem 41, however, there is perhaps a suggestion that the speaker might be resorting to feminine wiles. Indeed, Cotgrave's French-English Dictionary of 1611 gives "cunning" as an alternate definition for both *art* and *sçavoir*, (along with "subtiltie, deceit, guile" for the former). Thus, it was tempting to use "arts and savvy" in line 4, but this time I stuck to the more traditional choice, maintaining continuity with the whole.

As for vocabulary, a problem cropped up at the end of line 7 in the second elegy (poem 43), where the word "chaperone" seemed to fit the context perfectly, but did sound a bit Victorian; happily, I found an alternative. Another word, "blight," had been rejected for one of the epigrams, as it did not appear until the seventeenth century. Later, reaching the difficult poem 66, I saw that it would serve admirably there, and succumbed.

Although hesitating to introduce any new words or metaphors, occasionally I saw no way out. And there was always the tone of the poem to be considered. In the fourth elegy (poem 69), I couldn't resist inserting the word "bone" in the first line, though it was not in the French. Interestingly, the next eighteen lines were the easiest of any in the book; for a few days I had the supreme pleasure of thinking I had passed some kind of milestone and was getting the hang of it at last. There was nothing easy about the rest of that poem, however, and the next soon had me tearing out my hair in frustration—like the old crone in the final elegy (poem 68)—over four lines that just would not resolve. Then I recalled a portrait by Leonardo da Vinci, showing numerous knots on the sleeves and bodice of Cecelia Gallerani. Suddenly it made sense: with so many knots adorning a costume, unless new cord or new ribbon was used each time, old knots must have had to be successfully untied and straightened before they could be tied again to hold securely. It turned out to be a wonderful metaphor for the lines themselves, which had to be twisted and reworked before *they* made sense. (See poem 70, lines 23–26.)

Knowing that any current-day rendition of these poems would itself sound old-fashioned in a few years, I courted a slightly old-world tone—hoping for an elegance that was not too stiff, a formality not too awkward. I had already determined that meter and rhyme-pattern were essential in providing the truest echo of the original.

Even a prose translation, constrained as it must be by the syntax and vocabulary of a new language, can only come so close in meaning, and loses a great deal by forfeiting the tempo and the repetition of sounds at line-ends.[162] I felt fortunate that the majority of these poems had been written in ten-syllable lines and made the transition comfortably into English iambic pentameter. But adhering to the exact number of syllables proved restrictive, and the syllabic meter natural to French is not so successfully detected by an English ear; hence, I opted for an accentual-syllabic meter (even using what I have come to call "packed pentameter"). The longest poem in the collection, *Conde Claros de Adonis* (poem 64), provides an interesting example, where the seven syllables in each line might have fit into English iambic trimeter or tetrameter. Using four stresses would loosen the lines a little, allowing more freedom to move the words about, but having all the lines in tetrameter sounded a bit stilted. Since so many elements associated with the English ballad were present (narrative, dialogue, sudden scene shifts, etc.), I followed that form, combining the two meters. This meant that a pair of lines totaling fourteen syllables in the French would now be rendered by two lines in English totaling seven stresses—a satisfying solution. Here I made frequent use of the allowed metrical variation, substituting anapests in the iambic lines.

One advantage of adhering to a formal pattern was that I took extra care researching each word, including its root (assisted by Karen James's invaluable notes) and all synonyms, attempting to find the best rhyme for a line. Sometimes the challenge seemed almost insurmountable, as in two of the songs: one with twenty-four lines centered on only three rhymes (poem 26); the other, twenty lines on two rhymes (poem 29)—though refrains did help somewhat in both of these poems. French prosody of the time had allowed rhymes considered unacceptable in English—*rime riche*—not only homonyms, but compounds of a word (such as *venir* with *parvenir* and *souvenir*), and even the same word if used as a different part of speech. (See poem 71, where *court* is used four times in a short 8-line poem, or *huitain.*) In two places I made an exception and left such a rhyme from the French: *temps / passetemps* became "time" / "pastime" in the first of the songs mentioned above,

162. "Translators who translate poems that rhyme into poems that don't rhyme solely because they claim keeping the rhyme is impossible without doing violence to the poem have done violence to the poem." A. E. Stallings, "Presto Manifesto," *Poetry* (February 2009), 451. This article has also been published online by "Poetry Foundation," http://www.poetryfoundation.org/journal/article.html?id=182841.

and in poem 8, *nuict / mynuict* became "night" / "midnight"—in both cases reducing the number from the original three appearances in the French. (Also, "severe" gave cause for special exceptions—see poems 40 and 41.)

Conde Claros de Adonis (poem 64) presented me with the opposite problem, its 188 lines requiring 94 rhymes—every one different from the others. I managed all but two (and, yes, a few imperfect ones here as well—"lament" / "portent"; "window" / "below"; "mistress" / "distress"). Other difficulties arose: could the Empyrean—almost impossible to rhyme—be considered a sphere? With apologies to Alexander Pope, I decided it could not. Clearly, the Empyrean was a space apart, *beyond* all the others—a realm of fire, residence of the angels: I settled for "gleam." (Later research made me realize that such a statement ought not be made so precipitously, but I had already used the rhyme elsewhere.)[163] *Escarlate* posed another problem—representing not just the color red, but a type of apple—was this an example of the young author's humor, an allusion to roast pig with an apple in its mouth? I had a rhyme for "Pippin" all set to use, then discovered that a pippin apple is green!

La Nuict (poem 68), the 187-line *terza rima*, was one of the most challenging of all the poems, calling for 61 different triple rhymes and two doubles. Given the complexity of their interweaving pattern (aba, bcb, cdc, ded, efe, fgf, . . .) and the difficulty of the subject matter, I found myself resorting to a color-code to keep track of all the rhyming lines. (When I reached the "quartan-fever" epigram [poem 54], I couldn't help thinking that it might have some connection with this pattern of threes: loathing one, loving two, and always the odd fourth to take into account—that is, the new rhyme—which she wanted to quit, having escaped the three!) Some of the easiest rhymes in the book occurred here—right out of the French: "confusion" / "illusion"; "malicious" / "ambitious"; "number" / "encumber." Notice, however, that the third words did not transfer. "Queen" / "serene" / "Machine" was an easy trio, but their French counterparts did not rhyme—*Royne / sereine / Machine*—forcing me to juggle a line.

In fact, an easy transfer happens less frequently than one might expect, for often a word that looks similar in French turns out to be a "false friend," and a dead giveaway that the poem is a translation. (*Triumphant*, in poem 64, line 112, comes to mind.) Since one of the pleasures of working with Pernette du Guillet's poetry was the rich

163. S. K. Henninger, Jr. *Touches of Sweet Harmony: Pythagorean Cosmology and Renaissance Poetics*. (San Marino, CA: The Huntington Library, 1974), 120–24.

ambiguity of the words she chose, it is fortunate that so many of our words *do* have common cognates that have retained their multiple connotations in both languages. The word *vain*, for example, in *La Nuict*, encompasses our meanings of empty, conceited, and futile. In several places here I kept such a word from the French, sacrificing a proper rhyme to maintain the feel or sense of the original—*concupiscence*, *essence*, and *science* (also *condition* and *perdition*); but usually I had to choose just one of the definitions, especially when having to turn to the use of a synonym. Even pronouns that contributed to the ambiguity in French often had to be translated differently in English, as at the end of the second elegy (poem 43), or in poem 48.

Coq à l'asne (poem 67) is an informal, playful piece, based on a sequence of non sequiturs strung together, encouraging creative rhymes like "courtesan" with "sort is an," and "donor" with "shown her," in keeping with the silly, nonsensical mood of the poem. (Despite this mood, there are still a few threads running through the seemingly-illogical whole.) *A un sot rimeur*, the last of Du Guillet's poems in the collection (poem 73), is of interest for having the word *rime* or some variation appear in twenty out of its twenty-four lines—sometimes more than once. I did not attempt to echo this pattern in my version, though it left me free to repeat the word "rhyme" more than I might have done otherwise.

The second elegy (poem 43), probably the best known of these poems, and the most often discussed, presented me with numerous opportunities to deviate from self-imposed restrictions. Wanting to keep "Actaeon" at the end of a line for emphasis, I settled for "leapt upon" as a near rhyme, and several times used *enjambement*—not unheard of *chez* Pernette (see poem 33, lines 11–12, for example), but still not used very often. I placed "eject" at line's end with "it" carried over to the following line, which Karen James flagged, saying it seemed "out of place." I was pleased, for that was exactly what that little splash *would* be in such a serene setting—with all the subsequent trouble caused, as the speaker imagines it. The final lines of this elegy presented James and me with many hours of discussion, but I was never able to satisfactorily resolve my own poetic sense of what Du Guillet might have been intending to say with the words themselves. There seems a deliberate glossing of the pronouns here, confusing—or fusing—Apollo and her beloved (as she had elsewhere openly linked them); there is a strong hint of *divinus furor*; and *susciter* is the word used in the French Bible for 'resurrect.' I wanted it to be saying "I am letting him go, against my will, so that he will one day go forth, filled with divine force, to raise up the entire waiting world through his poetry and we all will be content—a sort of peace-on-earth finale. (It is not impossible—though of course we can never know it—that she was working on these very lines when death seized her at such a young age.)

Revision is everything. I spent at least as much time rewriting as I had spent on the initial draft of a poem. The words had to be lived with for a while before they were totally acceptable—like a forgery, sometimes they would begin to *feel* wrong. Occasionally, I would replace a word, forgetting that the reason I had chosen it in the first place was its connection with the original French. I then had to choose between the two: one for authenticity, the other for sound. I would wrap my mind around an idea, a phrase, choices of words, until I was dizzy. It is heartbreaking to have to throw out a good line, a word, a rhyme—especially if it's the third, fourth, seventh, tenth—with so much effort invested in the others. I would hold all the possibilities in my head—working and re-working different combinations, often just on the edge of understanding. Of course, when the "best" one was found, the others all had to be discarded. I noticed that a sort of post-partum blues set in following a particularly long time spent on a passage. Having made elaborate lists of possible words, rhymes, or phrases from the French, I ended up necessarily throwing out more than half of them, then realized that my delight with the progress had been in the thought of using them *all*—what a wonderful poem they would have made.

One late wintry afternoon, while I sat writing in the garden room, in an antique chair brought back from Lyon, a storm was raging outside the window, and the electricity went out. As the dampness began seeping into the house, I lit two candles, placed a wool throw over my knees, and continued to work long after darkness surrounded me and the books spread out on the terra-cotta tile floor. Despite the telephone in the next room and the sound of distant cars muffled by the storm, I suddenly felt a deep affinity with my French poet—her words teeming through my head as I put them down on paper in their new form. Though centuries removed, inside we have not changed so very much, and my feelings were close to what I could imagine hers. I hope that in the poems recorded here some of those feelings shine through.

PERNETTE DU GUILLET

Complete Poems
A Bilingual Edition

ANTOINE DU MOULIN

AUX DAMES LYONNOISES

Comme ainsi soit que l'inclination, laquelle naturellement nous avons à noz semblables, nous face esmouvoir selon le bon, ou maulvais accident advenu à ceulx de nostre complexion, je ne doubteray point que la plus part de vous, Dames vertueuses, ne soit assés marrie de soy mesmes du trespas de celle vertueuse, gentile, et toute spirituelle Dame D. Pernette du Guillet, sans d'avantage par ce petit recueil sien vous renouveller la douleur, qui encor vous saingne au cueur (mesmement à vous, qui de plus privee frequentation l'avez congneue) pour l'oultrage faict n'a guieres par la Mort à elle et à vous, comme envyeuse de nostre bien. Mais les instantes, et affectionnées remonstrances de son dolent mary m'ont persuadé, comme luy, à vous vouloir plus tost desplaire pour un peu, vous renouvellant vostre particulier regret, que de voulour generalement priver toutes celles, qui ne la congneurent onc de face, de ce petit amas de rymes, lesquelles elle nous laissa pour tesmoingnage de la dexterité de son divin esprit, et lequel, en le lisant, sera suffisant (j'en suis tout asseuré) de la faire regretter non seulement à ses accointées, mais aussi à toutes personnes de vertu avec une perpetuelle hayne contre la Mort, qui nous a privez de la consummation, que par cest heureux commancement la felicité de son celeste engin nous promettoit.

Car, veu le peu de temps, que les Cieulx l'ont laissée entre nous, il est quasi incroyable comme elle a peu avoir le loysir, je ne dy seulement de se rendre si parfaictement asseurée en tous instrumentz musiquaulx, soit au Luth, Espinette, et autres, lesquelz de soy requierent une bien longue vie à se y rendre parfaictz, comme elle estoit, et tellement, que la promptitude, qu'elle y avoit, donnoit cause d'esbahissement aux plus experimentez : mais encores à si bien dispencer le reste de ses bonnes heures, quelle l'aye employé à toutes bonnes lettres, par lequelles elle avoit eu premierement entiere et familiere congnoissance des plus louables vulgaires (oultre le sien) comme du Thuscan, et Castillan, tant, que sa plume en pouvoit faire foy: et apres avoit jà bien avant passé les rudimentz de la langue Latine aspirant à La Grecque (si la Lampe de sa vie eust peu veiller jusques au soir de son eage) quand les Cieulx nous enviantz tel heur la nous ravirent, ô Dames Lyonnoises, pour vous laisser achever ce, qu'elle avoit si heureusement commencé: c'est à sçavoir de vous

TO THE LADIES OF LYON[1]

As we all have a natural inclination toward others like ourselves, and are moved by what good or evil befalls those of a similar disposition,[2] I have no doubt whatsoever that most of you, virtuous Ladies, are already sufficiently afflicted by the passing of that virtuous, noble, and most spiritual Lady, [D.] Pernette du Guillet,[3] without the addition of this little collection of hers to renew the pain that still bleeds in your hearts (especially those of you who knew her well personally) from the outrage committed recently against both her and you by Death, as if envious of our good fortune. Nevertheless, the insistent and affectionate pleas of her grieving husband moved me to believe, as he did, that it would be preferable to displease you a little, renewing your private sorrow, than to universally deprive all ladies who never met her of this little bundle of rhymes,[4] which she left us as evidence of the dexterity of her divine mind. Once read, they will surely cause her loss to be lamented, not only by those of her acquaintance,[5] but by all persons of virtue who hold Death in perpetual contempt for preventing us from enjoying what the felicity of her celestial intellect promised with this fortunate beginning.[6]

Seeing the short time that the Heavens allowed her to remain among us, it is almost impossible to believe that she was able to find the time,[7] not only to become such an accomplished player of all musical instruments, including the Lute,[8] Spinet, and others, which by themselves require a long life at which to become as perfectly proficient as she was (so much so that her quick aptitude for them astonished the most experienced of musicians), but also to spend the rest of her precious hours so well, using them for literature and all good learning.[9] In that way she gained, first and foremost, complete familiarity with and knowledge of the most noteworthy vernacular languages besides her own, including Italian and Spanish, to which her pen attested.[10] She had already gone well beyond the rudiments of the Latin tongue, aspiring to learn Greek[11] (if only the Lamp of her life had been able to shine until the evening of her age), when the Heavens, envying our good fortune, snatched her away from us. O Ladies of Lyon, you are left now to finish what she so felicitously began—that is, to devote yourselves as she did to virtue, and in such a way that, if she has shown you the path to goodness with this little

excerciter, comme elle, à la vertu, et tellement, que, si par ce sien petit passetemps elle vous a monstré le chemin à bien, vous la puissiez si glorieusement ensuyvre, que la memoire de vous puisse testifier à la posterité de la docilité et vivacité des bons espritz, qu'en tous artz ce Climat Lyonnois a tousjours produict en tous sexes, voire assés plus copieusement, que guere autre, que l'on sache.

Qui est la cause, qui m'a meu, entre les autres persuasions, à vous communiquer ce peu de commencement, que son affectionné mary a trouvé parmy ses brouillars en assés povre ordre, comme celle, qui n'estimoit sa facture estre encor digne de lumiere jusques a ce, que le temps la luy eust par frequent estude et estendue, et lymée. Et pource en la mesme sorte que luy, et moy avons trouvé Epygrammes, Chansons, et autres diverses matieres de divers lieux, et plusieurs papiers confusément extraictz, les vous avons icy, quasi comme pour copie, mis en evidence, tant pour satisfaire à ceulx, à qui privément en maintes bonnes compaignies elle les recitoit à propos, comme la plus part faictz à leur occasion, que aussi pour ne vouloir perdre soubz silence d'eternel oubly chose, qui vous peust non seulement recreer, mais faire honneur à vous, Dames Lyonnoises, et vous faire priser en maintes contrees toutes les fois, que ces petites, et louables jeunesses siennes seront en grande admiration leues de tous.

Et quand ce ne seroit, quelles pourront inciter quelcune de vous, ou d'ailleurs, et l'animer aux lettres, pour participer de ce grand et immortel los, que les Dames d'Italie se sont aujourdhuy acquis, et tellement, que par leurs divins escriptz elles ternissent le lustre de maintz hommes doctz, et comme en France semblablement tant de honnestes et vertueuses Dames, et Damoiselles s'y adonnent avec une grande expectation de leur perpetuelle renommée au grand honneur, et louange de tout ce Royaulme: et quand ce ne seroit (rediray je) que pour toutes ces justes, et louables occasions, ne devrois je estre jugé ingrat, et oultrageux à vous toutes, si, ayant cecy entre mains, je vous eusse celé ce petit esguillon de vous poulser à plus hault bien en perpetuelle recommandation de vostre renommee? Certainement il n'est celuy (pour depravé jugement, qu'il aye) qui ne m'en deust à bonne occasion blasmer, comme larron de l'honneur, et publicque louange de vostre sexe.

Et si d'avanture se trouve quelque bigerre cerveau (comme communement la vertu ne va jamais seule sans envie) qui vueille prendre cecy en maulvaise part, pour n'en sçavoir autant faire, ny en approcher cent lieues pres, je vous supply croire, que toute personne

pastime of hers, you may be able to follow in her steps so gloriously that the remembrance of you may bear witness to posterity of the vivacity and aptitude for learning of the fine minds that, in all the arts, the Climate here in Lyon has always produced in both sexes—surely much more abundantly than in any other city known.

That reason (among others) moved me to share with you this meager beginning that her devoted husband found in rather poor order among her scattered papers, as of one who did not yet consider her work to be worthy of publication,[12] until time and frequent study would have expanded and polished it. And because he and I, in the same manner, found Epigrams, Songs, and other sundry writings in various places,[13] and numerous pages pulled together haphazardly,[14] we have put them forth for you here, almost as a copy. We have done so as much to satisfy those to whom she recited them whenever the occasion arose in many a private gathering of good company (for which purpose most were composed),[15] as from a desire not to lose in the eternal silence of oblivion something that could not only delight you,[16] but also honor you, Ladies of Lyon, and bring you esteem in many lands every time these little, yet praiseworthy, youthful works of hers are read and greatly admired by all.

Even were that not to be the case, they may inspire one among you here—or elsewhere—and encourage her to take up literary pursuits in order to share in the great and immortal fame that the Ladies of Italy have acquired in our time.[17] By their divine writings, they tarnish the luster of many a learned man; in like manner, here in France so many honorable and virtuous Ladies and Gentlewomen devote themselves to such pursuits with a great expectation of their eternal renown, to the great honor and glory of this entire kingdom. And even were it not, I repeat, for all these right and commendable reasons, should I not be judged ungrateful and injurious to you all, if, having it in my hands, I hid from you this modest incentive to push you toward a higher good in perpetual consideration of your reputation? Certainly there is no one (no matter how depraved his judgment may be) who would not then have good reason to condemn me as a thief of the honor and public acclaim of your sex.

And if, by chance, there be some odd fellow[18] (as envy commonly accompanies virtue)[19] who would wish to take this[20] the wrong way, for not knowing how to do as much, nor even how to come close to it by 100 leagues,[21] I beseech you to trust in what everyone of good, sound judgment knows quite well—that just as each person naturally judges

de bon, et sain entendement sçait tres bien, que, tout ainsi que naturellement chascun de soy juge les autres, les bons, comme vous, Dames bonnes, et vertueuses, feront tousjours bien leur prouffit en tout, et par tout: car il n'est si petite, ne si meschante chose, dont on ne puisse tirer quelque peu de bien, et utilité, qui l'y vouldra chercher, et le prendre en bonne intention. Et pource, quand vous orrez detracter l'envie pour vous descourager, et destourner de bien faire, souvienne vous, qu'il fault necessairement: que les Asnes voisent tousjours à leurs chardons, et à Dieu mes Dames, en grace de qui j'ay mieulx aymé desplaire aux malingz, que, en leur complaisant, vous faire tort.

De Lyon ce XIIII. d'Aoust, 1545.

others by his own nature, good souls (like you, honest and virtuous Ladies) will always find benefit everywhere and in everything; for there is nothing so petty or mean from which there can't be drawn a little something good and useful, by one who will look for it and take it with good intentions. Therefore, when you hear envy's disparaging insinuations, attempting to discourage and distract you from doing what is right, remember this—that Asses always feed upon their thistles.[22] So Adieu, my Ladies, for whose good graces I preferred to displease the malicious than, by pleasing them, to cause you any harm.

From Lyon, this 14th day of August, 1545.

L'imprimeur au lecteur

Quelle puissance Amytié puisse avoir,
Quand la vertu y est au vif empraincte,
Tu le pourras clerement icy veoir,
Appercevant une affection saincte
De chaste amour si haultement attaincte
En foy loyalle, et si bien poursuyvie,
Qu'elle peult cy, sans aucune contraincte,
(Maulgré la Mort) faire taire l'Envie.

To the Reader from the Printer[23]

What power fond affection finds to wield,
With virtue set and vividly engrained,
You can observe now clearly here revealed,
And glimpse a noble friendship long sustained
By a chaste love, so loftily attained—
Through faith pursued, and known to never tire—
That it can in this case, all unconstrained,
    And despite even Death, silence Desire.

I

[Epigramme I]

Le hault pouvoir des Astres a permis
(Quand je nasquis) d'estre heureuse et servie:
Dont congnoissant celuy, qui m'est promis,
Restee suis sans sentyment de vie,
Fors le sentir du mal, qui me convie
A regraver ma dure impression
D'amour cruelle, et doulce passion,
Où s'apparut celle divinité,
Qui me cause l'imagination
A contempler si haulte qualité.

II

[Epigramme II]

La nuict estoit pour moy si tresobscure,
Que Terre, et Ciel elle m'obscurissoit,
Tant, qu'à Midy de discerner figure
N'avois pouvoir, qui fort me marrissoit:
    Mais quand je vis que l'aulbe apparoissoit
En couleurs mille et diverse, et seraine,
Je me trouvay de liesse si pleine
(Voyant desjà la clarté à la ronde)
Que commençay louer à voix haultaine
Celuy, qui feit pour moy ce Jour au Monde.

1
[Epigram 1][24]

As lofty power from the Stars allowed,
I was happy at birth, well served; but then[25]
I met the one who was to me avowed,[26]
Leaving me numb to life—except for when
The suffering I feel time and again
Drives me to engrave my deep impression[27]
Of cruel love, of passion's sweet progression,[28]
Where that divinity at first appeared,[29]
Leading my mind to muse, in quiet session,
Upon an excellence so long revered.[30]

~

2
[Epigram 2]

How terrible—the darkness of my night
Which so obscured Heaven, and Earth below,
That at Midday there was too little light
For discerning shapes. It troubled me so;[31]
    But when I saw the dawn's defining glow,
All serene, with its thousand-colored rays,
Such joy full suddenly did me amaze
(Seeing how light already round me swirled),
That with exalted voice I began to praise[32]
Him who formed for me such a Morn in the World.[33]

~

III

[Epigramme III]

Ce grand renom de ton meslé sçavoir
Demonstre bien, que tu es l'excellence
De toute grace exquise pour avoir
Tous dons des Cieulx en pleine jouyssance.
    Peu de sçavoir, que tu fais grand nuysance
A mon esprit, qui n'a la promptitude
De mercier les Cieulx pour l'habitude
De celuy là, où les trois Graces prinses
Contentes sont de telle servitude
Par les vertus, qui en luy sont comprinses.

IV

[Epigramme IV]

Esprit celeste, et des Dieux transformé
En corps mortel transmis en ce bas Monde,
A Apollo peulx estre conformé
Pour la vertu, dont es la source, et l'onde.
Ton eloquence, avecques ta faconde,
Et hault sçavoir, auquel tu es appris,
Demonstre assez le bien en toy compris:
Car en doulceur ta plume tant fluante
A merité d'emporter gloire, et prys,
Voyant ta veine en hault stille affluante.

3

[Epigram 3]

A wide renown of learning so diverse[34]
As yours well demonstrates your excellence
In all the rare graces the Heavens disburse,[35]
The full enjoyment that their gift presents.
    But oh! dearth of learning, how you incense
These thoughts of mine, which lack the agility
To thank the Heavens for that facility
Of mind where—captive—the three Graces
Are serving now in sweet tranquility,[36]
Among the virtues such a one embraces.[37]

~

4

[Epigram 4]

Celestial spirit, transformed by Gods and sent[38]
In mortal body to the World below:
Fashioned on Apollo, it is evident,[39]
You are virtue's source and all its flow.[40]
Your eloquence, beyond surcease, and so
Supreme a breadth of knowledge now attained
Well demonstrate your good as unrestrained;[41]
Your sweet pen gently pouring forth the while
Deserves all of the praise and glory gained
From riches seen to stream in noble style.[42]

~

V
[Epigramme V]

Puis qu'il t'a pleu de me faire congnoistre,
Et par ta main, le VICE A SE MUER,
Je tascheray faire en moy ce bien croistre,
Qui seul en toy me pourra transmuer:
C'est asçavoir de tant m'esvertuer
Que congnoistras, que par esgal office
Je fuiray loing d'ignorance le vice,
Puis que desir de me transmuer as
De noire en blanche, et par si hault service
En mon erreur CE VICE MUERAS.

~

VI
[Epigramme VI]

Par ce dizain clerement je m'accuse
De ne sçavoir tes vertus honnorer,
Fors du vouloir, qui est bien maigre excuse:
Mais qui pourroit par escript decorer
Ce, qui de soy se peult faire adorer?
    Je ne dy pas, si j'avois ton pouvoir,
Qu'à m'acquicter ne feisse mon debvoir,
A tout le moins du bien, que tu m'advoues.
    Preste moy donc ton eloquent sçavoir
Pour te louer ainsi, que tu me loues.

~

5
[Epigram 5]

Because it has pleased you to show me how[43]
To cause my vice to change through your review,[44]
I'll try to see this good grows in me now,
For it alone can change me into you:[45]
That is, I will so strive, that after due
Exertion on my part, you'll come to see[46]
How far from the vice of ignorance I flee—
Because your desire to change me arrays
My dark with light: your service so nobly[47]
Causing my vice to change wherein it strays.[48]

6
[Epigram 6]

With this dizain I show myself clearly[49]
Not knowing how to honor all your virtues
Beyond the will—a weak excuse, merely:[50]
For can one's pen embellish or enthuse
Where awe already by itself accrues?
    Not to say, had I such power as you,
Duty would not make recompense its due—
At least for all the good you claim to see.[51]
    Lend me, then, your eloquent learning to
Praise you, in just the same way you praise me.[52]

VII
[Epigramme VII]

R, au dizain toute seule soubmise
M'a, à bon droict, en grand doubtance mise
De mal, ou bien, que par R, on peult prendre.
Car pour errer, R, se peult comprendre.
Signifiant que le loz, qu'on me preste,
Soit une erreur, ou que R, est riens, ou reste:
Mais si par R, on veult responce avoir,
Je dy, combien que n'aye le sçavoir,
Ne les vertus, que ton R, m'advoue,
Qu'errer je fais tout homme, qui me loue.

VIII
[Epigramme VIII]

Jà n'est besoing que plus je me soucie,
Si le jour fault, ou que vienne la nuict,
Nuict hyvernale, et sans Lune obscurcie:
Car tout cela certes riens ne me nuit,
Puis que mon Jour par clarté adoulcie
M'esclaire toute, et tant, qu'à la mynuict
En mon esprit me faict appercevoir
Ce, que mes yeulx ne sceurent oncques veoir.

7
[Epigram 7]

R, by itself, sent with this dizain,[53]
Has rightly caused great doubt in me: I strain
Over whether the R means bad or good.
For this R, "err" might well be understood,[54]
Showing error for praise of me applied;
Or R is nothing, a remainder, set aside.
But if R denotes a response is sought,[55]
I'll say how much there is I've not been taught;
Lacking those virtues your R seems to infer,
I cause each man who praises me to err.[56]

8
[Epigram 8]

I do not need to worry, any more,
At end of day or coming on of night—[57]
A moonless, wintry night, dark to the core;
Surely, henceforth, no harm can give me fright,
Because the sweet light from my Day will soar,
Enlightening me so, that at midnight
He helps me to perceive within my mind
That to which my eyes were ever blind.[58]

IX
[Epigramme IX]

Plus je desire, et la fortune adverse
Moins me permect, que puisse celuy veoir,
A qui elle eust par mainte controverse
Faict mainct ennuy, si ne fust son sçavoir,
Qui des Cieulx a ce tant heureux pouvoir
De parvenir tousjours à son entente:
Dont avec luy ce soulas puis avoir,
Que, luy content, je demeure contente.

X
[Epigramme X]

Si tu ne veulx l'anneau tant estimer,
Que d'un baiser il te soit racheptable:
Tu ne doibs pas, au moins si peu l'aymer,
Qu'il ne te soit, non pour l'or acceptable,
Mais pour la main, qui pour plus rendre estable
Sa foy vers toy, te l'a voulu lyer
D'un Dyamant, où tu peulx desplier
Un cueur taillé en face pardurable,
Pour te monstrer, que ne doibs oublier
Comme tu fais, la sienne amour durable.

9
[Epigram 9]

Desiring the more, the less I am allowed
To see him—by Fortune's adverse design
Which would, through constant troubles, his life cloud
In torrents of dispute, but for his fine
Learning—that favored attribute Divine—[59]
Whereby he finds success in every aim.
And so, with him, I find this solace mine:
That as he is content, I am the same.[60]

10
[Epigram 10][61]

If you will not this ring so much esteem
That it be worth your kiss to free its hold,[62]
Just don't dislike it so that you can't deem
The ring acceptable—not for the gold,
But the hand which, to heighten many-fold
Its loyalty toward you, wanted to bind
It with an eternal diamond; there you'll find,
Etched onto its face, a heart's contours,
To show what you must not forget—inclined
As you are to do—her love, which long endures.[63]

XI
[Epigramme XI]

Comme le corps ne permect point de veoir,
A son esprit, ny sçavoir sa puissance:
Ainsi l'erreur, qui tant me faict avoir
Devant les yeulx le bandeau d'ignorance,
Ne m'a permis d'avoir la congnoissance
De celuy là, que pour près le chercher
Les Dieux avoient voulu le m'approcher:
Mais si hault bien ne m'a sceu apparoistre.
  Parquoy à droict l'on me peult reprocher,
Que plus l'ay veu, et moins l'ay sceu congnoistre.

~

XII
[Epigramme XII]

Le Corps ravy, l'Ame s'en esmerveille
Du grand plaisir, qui me vient entamer,
Me ravissant d'Amour, qui tout esveille
Par ce seul bien, qui le faict Dieu nommer.
  Mais si tu veulx son pouvoir consommer:
Fault que par tout tu perdes celle envie:
Tu le verras de ses traictz se assommer,
Et aux Amantz accroissement de vie.

~

11
[Epigram 11]

Just as the body does not permit the mind
To see—nor its own power realize—
So, error, which keeps me sore confined
(The blindfold of ignorance before my eyes),[64]
Has not permitted me to recognize
The one the gods had willed to come to me,
That I might find him—sweet proximity!
No, such pure good was not meant for my view;[65]
    Thus can I be reproached most fittingly:
The more I saw, the less of him I knew.[66]

12
[Epigram 12]

How my soul marvels at the body's thrall
From this great pleasure that comes over me,
Enraptures me through Love who arouses all,
By that sole good which names him Deity.[67]
    But if you want to waste his sovereignty,
You must, above all, this desire forfend:
You'll see him pinned by his own archery,
And Lovers' lives augmented in the end.[68]

XIII
[Epigramme XIII]

L'heur de mon mal, enflammant le desir
Feit distiller deux cueurs en un debvoir:
Dont l'un est vif pour le doulx desplaisir,
Qui faict que Mort tient l'autre en son pouvoir.
    Dieu aveuglé, tu nous as faict avoir
Du bien le mal en effect honnorable:
Fais donc aussi, que nous puissions avoir
En noz espritz contentement durable.

XIV
[Epigramme XIV]

Le grand desir du plaisir admirable
Se doit nourrir par un contentement
De souhaicter chose tant agreable,
Que tout esprit peult ravir doulcement.
    O que le faict doit estre grandement
Remply de bien, quand pour la grand envie
On veult mourir, s'on ne l'a promptement:
Mais ce mourir engendre une autre vie.

13
[Epigram 13][69]

Happy my pain, inflaming desire's measure:
Two hearts distilled into a single heed—[70]
Where one breathes in the air of sweet displeasure
That puts the other in power of Death's greed.
    Oh, worthy suffering is this, indeed—
That from the good you give us, little blind
God! Please also, then, to us accede
Long-lasting satisfaction of the mind.[71]

14
[Epigram 14]

Such intense desire for glorious pleasure
Must thrive on satisfaction in the way
It longs for some delight beyond all measure
To sweetly lure the entire mind astray.
    Oh, how fully must the event convey
The good, when, upon that peak of splendor,[72]
One longs for death—though not without delay;[73]
And this death will another life engender.[74]

XV
[Epigramme XV]

Pour contenter celuy, qui me tourmente,
Chercher ne veulx remede à mon tourment:
Car en mon mal voyant qu'il se contente,
Contente suis de son contentement.

XVI
[Epigramme XVI]

L'ame, et l'esprit sont pour le corps orner,
Quand le vouloir de l'Eternel nous donne
Sens, et sçavoir pour pouvoir discerner
Le bien du bien, que la raison ordonne:
    Parquoy, si Dieu de telz biens te guerdonne,
Il m'a donné raison, qui a pouvoir
De bien juger ton heur, et ton sçavoir.
    Ne trouve donc chose si admirable,
Si à bon droict te desirent de veoir
Le Corps, l'Esprit, et l'Ame raisonnable.

15
[Epigram 15][75]

To make content the one who gives me torment,
I seek no remedy for such torment;
For seeing in my pain that he's content,
I am content, then, in his contentment.[76]

~

16
[Epigram 16]

The body is with mind and soul bedecked
When we are given, by will of the Divine,
Sense and knowledge so that we can detect
The highest good which reason can assign.[77]
    So if God gave you assets rich and fine,
He gave me reason to best appreciate
And judge your knowledge and your happy state.[78]
    Hence, think it not so very strange a thing
If Body, Mind, and Soul rightly await
To see you make full use of reasoning.[79]

~

XVII
[Epigramme XVII]

Je suis tant bien, que je ne le puis dire,
Ayant sondé son amytié profonde
Par sa vertu, qui à l'aymer m'attire
Plus que beaulté: car sa grace, et faconde
Me font cuyder la premiere du monde.

XVIII
[Epigramme XVIII]

Que d'avoir mal pour chose si louable,
Comme à chascun son grand contentement,
Tout bon esprit (tant soit peu raisonnable)
Le pourra croire, et par bon jugement.
Mais si voulez congnoistre clerement,
Lequel des deux a sur plaisir puissance,
Fauldra gouster d'un meur entendement
L'heur, et malheur de vostre congnoissance.

17

[Epigram 17]

I am so favored, words won't come to me,
Having fathomed his sentiments profound,
Through his virtues which draw me more than beauty[80]
To love him; his grace and eloquence abound,
Making me feel supreme the world around.[81]

18

[Epigram 18][82]

That suffering for so worthy a thing
Great contentment to every one presents,
Any good mind, even ill-reasoning,
Can well believe, to judge with common sense.[83]
    But should you wish to know, with confidence,
Which of these has power over pleasure:[84]
You must partake, from your own acquaintance,
Of Happiness and Pain—with studied measure.[85]

XIX
[Epigramme XIX]

Je te promis au soir, que pour ce jour
Je m'en irois à ton instance grande
Faire chés toy quelque peu de sejour:
Mais je ne puis: parquoy me recommande,
Te promectant m'acquicter pour l'amande,
Non d'un seul jour, mais de toute ma vie,
Ayant tousjours de te complaire envie.
Donc te supply accepter le vouloir,
De qui tu as la pensee ravie
Par tes vertus, ta grace, et ton sçavoir.

XX
[Epigramme XX]

Sçais tu pourquoy de te veoir j'euz envie:
C'est pour ayder à l'ouvrier qui cessa,
Lors, qu'assembla en me donnant la vie,
Les differentz, où après me laissa.
    Car m'esbauchant Nature s'efforça
D'entendre, et veoir pour nouvelle ordonnance
Ton hault sçavoir, qui m'accroist l'esperance
Des Cieulx promise, ainsi que je me fonde,
Que me feras avoir la congnoissance
De ton esprit, qui esbahit le Monde.

19
[Epigram 19]

I promised you last evening, I admit
(With many fond entreaties on your side),
To come today and stay with you a bit.[86]
I cannot now; but this to you confide:
I'll make amends—a promise to provide
My whole life for this one day supplanted,
My wish of pleasing you forever granted.
Therefore, accept this pledge, I do implore,
From one whose every thought you have enchanted
With knowledge, grace, and virtues by the score.[87]

20
[Epigram 20]

I desired to see you—do you know why?[88]
To aid the maker with work that was suspended
In giving me life, trying to ally
Diverse parts of me, left unamended.[89]
    Leaving me rough-hewn, Nature intended,
With your learning, to set a higher scale—
Ensuring thus that my hopes *would* prevail,
As Heaven promised—if only you'd be so kind,
As to make the introduction it would entail,
So I can know what astounds the World: your mind.[90]

XXI
[Epigramme XXI]

Si le servir merite recompense,
Et recompense est la fin du desir,
Tousjours vouldrois server plus, qu'on ne pense,
Pour non venir au bout de mon plaisir.

XXII
[Epigramme XXII]

En Daulphiné Ceres faisoit encor moisson,
Estant à Millery Bacchus en sa boisson:
Parquoy je puis juger, voyantz les vins si vertz,
Que Venus sera froide encor ces deux hyverz.

XXIII
[Epigramme XXIII]

Je puis avoir failly par ignorance,
Celà me fault, maulgré moy, confesser:
Mais que je prenne en moy telle arrogance,
Que dessus vous je m'osasse avancer:
Je vous supply ne me vouloir penser
Si indiscrette à faire mon debvoir.
Bien est il vray, que je tasche à avoir
Ce, qui m'est deu, quoy qui en ait esmoy:
Car si Amour, et foy ont ce pouvoir
De vous donner, vous estes tout à moy.

21
[Epigram 21]

If the act of serving merits reward,[91]
And if reward be desire's end,[92]
Always would I serve, though thought untoward,[93]
So as to thus my pleasure long extend.

22
[Epigram 22]

In Dauphiné, Ceres gathers the harvest still,
While Bacchus, over in Millery, drinks his fill;[94]
Thus I can predict, seeing the wine so green,[95]
Through two more winters yet, a Venus cold and lean.[96]

23
[Epigram 23]

I did, perhaps—through ignorance—fail:
I really must, despite myself, confess;
But that I would let arrogance prevail
To such extent that I would so transgress
And through my work dare rival your success?—[97]
Please do not think of me that this is true.
    Certainly, I aspire to have my due,[98]
Despite what others, in dismay, opine;[99]
Because—if the power of giving you
Belongs to Love and Faith, you are all mine.[100]

XXIV
[Epigramme XXIV]

A qui est plus un Amant obligé
Ou à Amour, ou vrayement à sa Dame?
Car son service est par eulx redigé
Au ranc de ceulx, qui ayment los, et fame.
  A luy il doibt le cueur, à elle l'Ame,
Qui est autant, comme à tous deux la vie:
L'un à l'honneur, l'autre à bien le convie:
Et toutesfois voicy un tresgrand poinct,
Lequel me rend ma pensee assouvie,
C'est que sans Dame Amour ne seroit point.

XXV
[Epigramme XXV]

Or qui en a, ou en veult avoir deux,
Comment peult il faire deux Amours naistre?
Je ne dy pas, que ne puisse bien estre
Un cueur plus grand, que croire je ne veulx:
Mais que tout seul il satisfeit à eulx,
Celà n'a point de resolution,
Qui sceust absouldre, ou clorre ma demande:
  Et toutesfois ainsi qu'affection
Croist le desir, telle obligation
Peult Dame avoir à la Vertu si grande,
Que de l'Amant la qualité demande
Double merite, ou double passion.

24
[Epigram 24]

Who deserves more a Lover's obligation—
Does Love or, in truth, Lady earn this role?[101]
For both reduce his service to that of one
Where love of praise and glory takes control.
    To him he owes his heart, to her his soul—[102]
Which for them both is like to life's own zest;
By one toward honor, one toward good, he's pressed.
Yet here's the point that must not be dismissed,
Which soothes my mind and calms my thoughts to rest:
Without the Lady, Love would not exist.

25
[Epigram 25]

Now whoever has, or wants to have, two—
Can anyone bring two Loves into being?[103]
I don't say I'm wholly disagreeing
That some heart could be larger than I knew;
But whether one alone can both pursue
With satisfaction, is not at all sure,
And cannot serve to end my agitation.
    Yet in the way affection can secure
Increased desire, so great virtue can lure
A Lady to owe such an obligation
That the Lover's worth demands oblation:
And double passion, double worth, endure.[104]

XXVI
[Chanson I]

J'ay esté par un long temps
Deceue de l'esperance:
Et si encor point n'attens
D'elle plus grand' asseurance,
Que celle là, que ma foy
Me peult promettre de soy.

Je voy les uns fort contents,
Les autres pleins de souffrance:
De ceulx là les rys j'entens,
De ceulx cy la douleance:
Ces passions j'apperçoy
Regner toutes deux en moy.

Je rys du bien, où je tens
En tresgrand' resjouyssance:
Et pleure, que je pretens
Qu'un autre en ayt jouyssance:
Ce que de mes yeulx je voy,
Et à grand peine le croy.

Toutesfois tel passetemps
Me donne encor confiance,
Qu'un jour je verray le temps,
Que cil fera la vengeance
Du mal, qu'il m'a faict de soy
Au bien, où je me deçoy.

26
[Song 1]

I was deceived a long time[105]
By hope's indifference;
Expecting, with that as paradigm,
No comfort therein, I hence
Now turn to my own fealty
For promised harmony.

Some I see have joys sublime,
Others, pain intense;
I hear from the former laughter chime,
From the latter, deep laments.
These two passions, in full degree,
Control me currently.[106]

I laugh with the good that I hold prime,
In utmost jubilance;
And cry at rivals, believing I'm
Losing my influence:
Even what my own eyes see
Holds little credulity.[107]

Nevertheless, this pastime
Still gives me confidence
That someday soon, in better clime,
He'll afford me recompense—[108]
Turning the pain he's caused in me
To the good I'm deceived there be.[109]

XXVII
[Epigramme XXVI]

Prenez le cas, que, comme je suis vostre
(Et estre veulx) vous soyez tout à moy:
Certainement par ce commun bien nostre
Vous me debvriez tel droict, que je vous doy.
Et si Amour vouloit rompre sa Loy,
Il ne pourroit l'un de nous dispencer,
S'il ne vouloit contrevenir à soy,
Et vous, et moy, et les Dieux offencer.

XXVIII
[Epigramme XXVII]

Soit que par esgalle puissance
L'affection, et le desir
Debattent de la jouyssance
Du bien, dont se veulent saisir:
    Si vous voulez leur droict choisir,
Vous trouverez sans fiction,
Que le desir en tout plaisir
Suyvra tousjours l'affection

27
[Epigram 26]

As much as I am yours (and wish to be),
Let us present the case that you are mine.[110]
By this our common good now, certainly,
We could, by one, the other's rights define;
And Love, if wanting to break or to resign
His law, could not exempt either of us,[111]
Without his own self having to realign—
And you, and me, and the gods, offending thus.

~

28
[Epigram 27]

One day, with equal power in store,
Affection and desire came,
Debating the good, and which had more
Enjoyment of its worth to claim;[112]
    In judging the winner of this game,
You'll find in truth, without objection,[113]
Desire—whatever pleasure's name—
Always follows after affection.[114]

~

XXIX
[Chanson II]

Quand vous voyez, que l'estincelle
De chaste Amour soubz mon esselle
Vient tous les jours à s'allumer,
Ne me debvez vous bien aymer?

Quand vous me voyez tousjours celle,
Qui pour vous souffre, et son mal cele,
Me laissant par luy consumer,
Ne me debvez vous bien aymer?

Quand vous voyez, que pour moins belle
Je ne prens contre vous querelle,
Mais pour mien vous veulx reclamer,
Ne me debvez vous bien aymer?

Quand pour quelque autre amour nouvelle
Jamais ne vous seray cruelle,
Sans aucune plaincte former,
Ne me debvrez vous bien aymer?

Quand vous verrez, que sans cautelle
Tousjours vous seray esté telle,
Que le temps pourra affermer,
Ne me debvrez vous bien aymer?

29
[Song 2][115]

When you see that I tend with care
Chaste love's spark inside to flare
Anew each morn in full array,[116]
Will you not say you'll love me one day?[117]

When you see with what calm I bear
The suffering and long despair
Wasting me slowly thus away,
Will you not say you'll love me one day?

When you see that for one less fair
I let no quarrel trouble the air,
Just my own claim of you betray,[118]
Will you not say you'll love me one day?

When some other new love you share,
And I don't complain, although aware,
Nor yet lash out in cruel display,[119]
Will you not say you'll love me one day?

When you can see that I forswear
Ruse and stratagem, yet declare
With you, through time, I choose to stay,[120]
Will you not say you'll love me one day?

XXX
[Epigramme XXVIII]

Si je ne suis telle, que soulois estre,
Prenez vous en au temps, qui m'a appris,
Qu'en me traictant rudement, comme maistre,
Jamais sur moy ne gaignerez le prys.
    Et toutesfois vous voyant tousjours pris
En mon endroit, vostre ardeur me convye
Par ce hault bien, que de vous j'ay compris,
A demeurer vostre toute ma vie.

XXXI
[Epigramme XXIX]

Si je n'ay peu, comme voulois,
Vous reciter au long, et dire
Ce, dequoy tant je me doulois,
Imputez le à mon cueur plein d'ire,
Pour n'avoir peu ouyr mesdire
Du bien, que je doibs estimer,
Et pour qui on debvroit mauldire
Tous ceulx, qui m'en veulent blasmer.

30
[Epigram 28]

If I am not what I once used to be,
Go blame time who made me understand[121]
That if, as master, you should treat me rudely,
You'd never succeed in gaining the upper hand.[122]
    And yet I see always in you a grand
Concern for me, an ardor that portrays
Your noble good to sway me and to brand
Me yours to stay the rest of all my days.[123]

31
[Epigram 29]

If I could not, as I had thought,
Recount at length and thus explain
To you how much I've been distraught,
Accuse my heart, so filled with pain
From hearing clamors of disdain[124]
Against the good I hold so dear:
For that, one ought to curse the bane
Of those whose blame of me I hear.[125]

XXXII
[Chanson III]

O vraye amour, dont je suis prise,
Comment m'as tu si bien apprise,
Que de mon Jour tant me contente,
Que je n'en espere autre attente,
Que celle de ce doulx amer,
Pour me guerir du mal d'aymer.

Du bien j'ay eu la jouyssance,
Dont il m'a donné congnoissance
Pour m'asseurer de l'amytié,
De laquelle il tient la moytié:
Doncques est il plus doulx, qu'amer,
Pour me guerir du mal d'aymer.

Helas amy, en ton absence
Je ne puis avoir asseurance
Que celle, dont (pour son plaisir)
Amour cault me vient dessaisir
Pour me surprendre, et desarmer:
Gueris moy donc du mal d'aymer.

32
[Song 3]

O true love, you've trapped me now!
I'm so well trained; please tell me how
My Day can bring me such content
That I not ask him to present
More than this sweet bitterness
To cure me of love's dark duress.[126]

I've so enjoyed the good and hence
Feel through his guiding influence[127]
The strong affection of our hearts
Held by us both in equal parts:[128]
More sweet, then, is this bitterness,
To cure me of love's dark duress.[129]

Alas, beloved, when you must go,
My confidence departs also—
For artful Love comes (all in jest)
To snatch it from me, does his best
To surprise and leave me powerless:
Cure me, then, of love's dark duress.[130]

XXXIII
[Chanson IV]

La fortune envieuse
Voyant mon Jour passer,
De la nuict est joyeuse
Pour me faire penser,
Vray ce, que le Ciel dict,
Pour se mettre en credit.

Mais sçavoir n'ay envie
Des Planettes le cours
Pour congnoistre ma vie,
Ayant autre discours:
Car tant que je verray
Mon Jour, je ne mourray.

Ne trouves point estrange,
Si, quand ne le puis veoir,
Je me trouble, et me change,
Tant, qu'il me fault douloir
Du mal, que mon cueur sent,
Quand de moy est absent.

Ce que j'y suis tenue,
Ne me faict tant l'aymer,
Que sa vertu congneue
Me contrainct l'estimer
Par son loz tant requis,
Qui m'est honneur acquis.

Sa grace accompaignee
Plus, qu'à nul, j'ay peu veoir:
Parquoy pour luy suis nee,
D'autre je n'ay vouloir:
Les Dieux pour moy l'ont mis
Au bout des vrays amys.

33
[Song 4]

How envious Fortune,
  Seeing my Day advance,
  Is happy when night comes soon,
  To give my thoughts the chance
  Of seeing the Sky's true sense
  And start its influence.[131]

But I wish left unknown
  The charted planets' course;
  For to understand my own,
  I seek another source:
  So long as I espy
  My Day, I shall not die.[132]

Do not then think it strange,
  When he is out of sight,
  If I grow troubled, and change,
  Fearing the way he might
  Cause pain within my heart—
  As when we are apart.[133]

Dependence on him brews
  Not my love so well
  As his renowned virtues
  All my esteem compel:
  His fame, so much admired,
  Is honor for me acquired.

Accompanied graces adorn
  Him more than I've ever seen.
  He is why I was born—
  And now wish no other mien!—
  The Gods placed him for me
  In deepest intimacy.[134]

O amytié bien prise,
Que j'ay voulu choisir
Par vraye foy promise,
Qui mon cueur vint saisir,
Quand honneur s'allia
Au bien, qui nous lia.

Ma fortune accomplie
En mon heureux sejour
De plaisir fut remplie,
Quand j'apperceu mon Jour:
Qui bien congneu l'aura,
Mon amy aymera.

Heureuse destinee
En mon heur apparoit,
Ne sçaichant femme nee
Qui peult, ne qui sçauroit
Eviter la moytié
De sa noble amytié.

D'estre d'autres requise,
N'y vueillez point venir:
Car je suis tant apprise,
Que j'ay pour souvenir
La grandeur de son cueur
Estre du mien vainqueur.

Et si je n'ay la grace
Pour meriter d'avoir
Ce bien, et qu'on pourchasse
De le me decevoir,
Ma fermeté fera,
Qu'il se contentera.

Oh, valued friendship this,[135]
    Which I expressly chose[136]
    Through a true faith's promise
    That broke my heart's repose:
    Honor found in tether
    With good links us together.

My fortune, now fulfilled
    In my most happy stay,
    Was with pleasure thrilled,
    As I first glimpsed my Day:[137]
    Those who to him attend
    All love my beloved friend.

O happy Fate! to appear
    And make my fortune good—
    Knowing that in his sphere
    No woman living could
    Resist a mere half-share
    Of such noble care.[138]

So sought by others' demand[139]
    (Don't wish to go there, please!),
    How well I understand—
    For I have memories:
    His heart, so grand, so fine,
    Vanquishing over mine.

And if I have not the grace
    To merit the good I find,[140]
    Or anyone tries to chase
    His influence from my mind,
    My refusal to relent
    Shall make him well content.[141]

XXXIV
[Epigramme XXX]

Ma voulenté plus grande, que l'effect,
Si elle estoit justement mesuree,
Rendre ne peult mon desir si parfaict,
Qu'elle ne soit en luy demesuree.
    Et toutesfois s'estant avanturee
De tout en tout son pouvoir mesurer,
Oncques n'a peu seulement endurer
Son moindre effort: que seroit du surplus?
    Pour autant donc ne s'ose avanturer
De plus vouloir ce, qu'elle veult le plus.

~

XXXV
[Epigramme XXXI]

Je ne croy point ce, que vous deites,
Que tant de bien me desiriez,
Comme à celle, pour qui vous feites
Ce, que pour vous faire debvriez.
    Mais quelle plus estimeriez,
Ou celle, qui d'un cueur tremblant,
N'ose dire ce, que vouldriez:
Ou qui le dict d'un faulx semblant?

~

34
[Epigram 30]

My will, greater than what it can procure
(If *any* measure could be genuine),
Cannot render my desire so pure
That it be but superfluous therein.[142]
 Although my will did venture to begin
Testing to see what strength its power bore,[143]
It never could firmly hold ground before
The least thrust—and what would the rest bring?
 So now my will dare not seek anymore
What once it wanted more than anything.[144]

35
[Epigram 31]

I can't believe your words are true—
That you desire such good for me
As her for whom the things you do[145]
Are those which for yourself should be.[146]
 But which one is more worthy: she
Who, with a heart in turbulence,
Dares *not* say words of flattery—
Or she who says them, in pretense?[147]

XXXVI
[Epigramme XXXII]

L'une vous ayme, et si ne peult sçavoir
Qu'Amour luy soit ou propice, ou contraire:
L'autre envers vous faict si bien son debvoir,
Que plus ne sçait, où vous doibve complaire.
    Or je demande en si doubteux affaire
A quelle plus debvez estre tenu?
Car celle là d'un cueur simplement nu
Pour vous se oublie, et pour soy pensive est:
Et ceste cy, taschant par le menu
A vous gaigner, de son bien se desvest.

XXXVII
[Epigramme XXXIII]

Or bien, puis qu'ainsi le voulez,
Soit faict, sans y contrevenir:
Mais si au ranc des desolez
Il me fault par ce point venir,
Je vous supply vous souvenir
De regarder plus amplement,
Que tel en son dire ample ment,
Comme contre moy remply d'ire,
Et qu'il ne dict rien simplement,
Que je n'entende, qu'il veult dire.

36
[Epigram 32]

One can love you even without knowing
If Love look well upon her cause or nay;
The other, out of duty, all bestowing,
Knows not how to please another way.[148]
So now I wonder with whom you will stay
The longer, in such a dubious affair?[149]
The former, with heart artlessly laid bare,
Forgets herself for you in reverie;
The latter, to gain you, takes the utmost care,
Losing her best, shed—oh, so cleverly.[150]

37
[Epigram 33]

Since this is how you'd have it be,
So be it then, and no debate;
But if the matter must bring me
To suffer in this wretched state,
I beg you, do not hesitate—
Consider closely in what way
Such types as he will so inveigh
Against me in lies of smooth-tongued ire:
There's nothing so simple he can say
That I not know his meaning's dire.[151]

XXXVIII
[Chanson V]

Dames, s'il est permis,
Que l'amour appetisse
Entre deux cueurs promis,
Faisons pareil office:
Lors la legereté
Prendra sa fermeté.

S'ilz nous disent volages
Pour nous en divertir:
Asseurons noz courages
De ne nous repentir,
Puis que leur amytié
Est moins, que de moytié.

Se voulantz excuser,
Que leur moytié perdue
Peult ainsi abuser
Tant, qu'elle soit rendue:
La loy pour nous fut faicte
Empruntant leur deffaicte.

Si j'eusse esté apprise,
Comme il failloit aymer,
Je n'eusse esté reprise
Du feu trop allumer,
Qu'estaindre j'ay bien sceu,
Quand je l'ay apperceu.

Ne nous esbahissons
Si le vouloir nous change:
Car d'eulx nous congnoissons
La vie tant estrange,
Qu'elle nous a permis
Infinité d'amis.

38
[Song 5]

Ladies, if Love's allowed
To trifle with the feelings[152]
Between two hearts avowed,
Let's trace his double-dealings:
Thus will flirtation
Receive validation.[153]

If men call us erratic,
To scuttle our intent,
Let us remain emphatic,
Refusing to repent—
For affections they bear
Are less than half-share.[154]

They'll put forth the excuse
That this half they now lack
Constitutes an abuse
Until it be paid back—
But the law is on our side:
The default justified.[155]

If only I'd been taught
More of what Love requires,
I would not have been caught
Stoking too high the fires—
But know how, at first sight,
To extinguish them outright.[156]

Let us not show surprise
If desire makes us change;
From them we realize
Life's so very strange,
And that it does permit
Us choices infinite.[157]

Mais puis qu'occasion
Nous a esté donnee,
Que nostre passion
Soit à eulx adonnee:
Amour nous vengera,
Quand foy les rengera.

But since this chance right now
To each of us is given,
Let our passions somehow
Direct to them be driven:
Love will avenge us all
When faith holds *them* in thrall.[158]

XXXIX
[Elégie I]

Parfaicte amytié

Quand est d'Amour, je croy, que c'est un songe,
Ou fiction, qui se paist de mensonge,
Tant que celuy, qui peult plus faire encroire
Sa grand faintise, en acquiert plus de gloire.
Car l'un faindra de desirer la grace,
De qui soubdain vouldra changer la place:
L'autre fera mainte plaincte à sa guise,
Portant tousjours l'amour en sa devise,
Estimant moins toute perfection,
Que le plaisir de folle affection:
Aussi jamais ne s'en trouve un content,
Fuyant le bien, où tout bon cueur pretent.
Et tout celà vient de la nourriture
Du bas sçavoir, que tient la creature.
Mais l'amytié, que les Dieux m'ont donnee,
Est à l'honneur toute tant adonnee
Que le moins seur de mon affection
Est asseuré de toute infection
De Faulx semblant, Danger, et Changement,
Estant fondé sur si sain jugement,
Que, qui verra mon amy apparoistre,
Jamais fasché ne le pourra congnoistre:
Pource qu'il est tousjours à son plaisir
Autant content, que contient mon desir.
Et si voulez sçavoir, ô Amoureux,
Comment il est en ses amours heureux:
C'est que de moy tant bien il se contente,
Qu'il n'en vouldroit esperer autre attente,
Que celle là, qui ne finit jamais,

39
[Elegy 1]

Perfect Love[159]

As for Love, I'm convinced it's just a dream,
Or fable, that feeds upon a steady stream[160]
Of lies—so long as he, who can inflame
Belief, still, in its ruse, wins further fame.[161]
For one man feigns desire to gain the graces
Of someone whom he very soon displaces;
Another, groaning disavowals his mode,
Inscribes true love into his chosen code,[162]
Having less esteem for real perfection
Than pleasures found in uncontrolled affection;
No, never will a man who is content
Flee from the good—a pure heart's natural bent:[163]
And this all comes from nourishing with care
That baser knowledge which all creatures share.
But the love the Gods to me have given[164]
Is toward honor so completely driven
That he who is least sure of my affection
Can rest assured he's free of all infection
From False Appearance, Danger, Alteration—[165]
With such sound judgment used in its foundation.
Catching sight of my beloved friend,
One would never know him to offend:
Since his content achieves the fullest measure
With my desire included in his pleasure.
And O, Lovers!—if you wish to know
How, in love, his happiness does grow,
It's that he is so satisfied with me
That he hopes for no other surety
Than one that will continue to endure

Et que j'espere asseurer desormais
Par la vertu en moy tant esprouvee,
Qu'il la dira es plus haultz Cieulx trouvee.
    Parquoy, luy seur de ma ferme asseurance,
M'asseureray de craincte, et ignorance.

And which I hope henceforward to ensure
By this so sorely-tested virtue—mine,
That he will say comes from the great Divine:
    With him thus certain of my confidence,
I'm free, myself, from fear and ignorance.[166]

XL
[Chanson VI]

Sans congnoissance aucune en mon Printemps j'estois:
Alors aucun souspir encor point ne gectois
Libre sans liberté: car rien ne regrectois
En ma vague pensee
De molz, et vains desirs follement dispensee.

Mais Amour tout jaloux du commun bien des Dieux
Se voulant rendre à moy, comme à maintz odieux,
Me vint escarmoucher par faulx alarmes d'yeulx,
Mais je veis sa fallace:
Parquoy me retiray, et luy quictay la place.

Je vous laisse penser, s'il fut alors fasché:
Car depuis en maintz lieux il s'est tousjours caché,
Et, quand à descouvert m'a veue, m'a lasché
Maintz traictz à la volee:
Mais onc ne m'en sentis autrement affolee.

A la fin congnoissant, qu'il n'avoit la puissance
De me contraindre en rien luy faire obeissance,
Tascha le plus, qu'il peult, d'avoir la congnoissance
Des Archiers de Vertu,
Par qui mon cueur forcé fut soubdain abbatu.

Mais elle ne permit qu'on me feist autre oultrage,
Fors seulement blesser chastement mon courage,
Dont Amour escumoit et d'envie, et de rage:
O bien heureuse envie,
Qui pour un si hault bien m'a hors de moy ravie.

40
[Song 6]

In my Spring, I had not any knowledge yet:
And so I had no cause to utter sighs, or fret—
Free without freedom, I had nothing to regret
From my thoughts that wandered
Into silly, idle yearnings, foolishly squandered.[167]

Then Love, jealous of the good held by Divine allies,
Wanting to make me join the others who despise
Him, lured me to a skirmish with falsely-flashing eyes.
But I saw through his trick
And drew far back, abandoning him to his bailiwick.[168]

I leave you to imagine how angry he became,
For after that he'd hide, as if it were a game,
Then burst into my view—arrows without aim
In all directions reeling!
(Though I never suffered any change of feeling.)

Realizing in the end, that he had not the might
To force me to obey him in any way, he quite
Outdid himself to gain that knowledge and insight
The Archers of Virtue held—
By which my battered heart was, in an instant, felled.[169]

However, that allowed not any other abuse
Than to shake my resolve chastely; whereby obtuse
Love foamed forth in rage from all his desires let loose—
Ah, sweet the desire that could
Transport me beyond myself for such a noble good.

Ne pleures plus, Amour: car à toy suis tenue,
Veu que par ton moyen Vertu chassa la nue,
Qui me garda long temps de me congnoistre nue,
Et frustree du bien,
Lequel, en le goustant, j'ayme Dieu sçait combien.

Ainsi toute aveuglee en tes lyens je vins,
Et tu me mis es mains, où heureuse devins,
D'un qui est haultement en ses escriptz divins,
Comme de nom, severe,
Et chaste tellement, que chascun l'en revere.

Si mainte Dame veult son amytié avoir,
Voulant participer de son heureux sçavoir,
Et que par tout il tasche acquicter son debvoir,
Ses vertus j'en accuse
Plus puissantes, que luy, et tant que je l'excuse.

XLI
[Epigramme XXXIV]

Puis que de nom, et de faict trop severe
En mon endroict te puis appercevoir,
Ne t'esbahis si point je persevere
A faire tant par art, et par sçavoir,
Que tu lairras d'aller les autres veoir:
Non que de toy je me voulsisse plaindre,
Comme voulant ta liberté contraindre:
    Mais advis m'est, que ton sainct entretien
Ne peult si bien en ces autres empraindre
Tes motz dorez, comme au cueur, qui est tien.

Love, now I am yours. Please, cry no more aloud:
Through your methods, Virtue chased away the cloud
That held my natural self within a sort of shroud
And kept the good from me—
Which tasting now I love—God knows to what degree.

Completely blinded into your fold I had come,
And you placed me in the hands (oh, sweet delirium)
Of one who is—from fine and noble words as from,
Indeed, his name—severe,
And of such pure demeanor that all around revere.[170]

If his affections now have so many Ladies yearning
To participate in his vast and fortunate learning,
And he, to do what's right, in every way is turning,
I blame those virtues
Much too strong for him—whom I must then excuse.[171]

41
[Epigram 34]

Because, in name and action, I can see
That toward me you are truly too severe,[172]
Don't be surprised to any great degree[173]
When I, through art and learning, persevere,
And do my best ensuring you stay clear
Of seeing others—not that I'd complain,
Or wish the least your freedom to restrain;[174]
    But your fine conversation, in my view,[175]
Cannot, in them, your golden words ingrain
So well as in *this* heart—that's owned by you.[176]

XLII
[Chanson VII]

Qui dira ma robe fourree
De la belle pluye doree,
Qui Daphnes enclose esbranla:
Je ne sçay rien moins, que celà.

Qui dira, qu'à plusieurs je tens
Pour en avoir mon passetemps,
Prenant mon plaisir çà, et là:
Je ne sçay rien moins, que celà.

Qui dira, que t'ay revelé
Le feu long temps en moy celé
Pour en toy veoir si force il a:
Je ne sçay rien moins, que celà.

Qui dira, que d'ardeur commune,
Qui les Jeunes gentz importune,
De toy je veulx, et puis holà:
Je ne sçay rien moins, que celà.

Mais qui dira, que la Vertu,
Dont tu es richement vestu,
En ton amour m'estincellà:
Je ne sçay rien mieulx, que celà.

Mais qui dira, que d'amour saincte
Chastement au cueur suis attaincte,
Qui mon honneur onc ne foulà:
Je ne sçay rien mieulx, que celà.

Poem 42
[Song 7]

If they say my dress is pelted
With lovely golden rain, as melted
Into captive Daphne trembling low—[177]
Worse than that I do not know.[178]

If they say upon more than one
I must depend to have my fun,
Chasing pleasures to and fro—
Worse than that I do not know.

If they say to you I've revealed
Fires in me, long concealed,
To see if force in you would flow—
Worse than that I do not know.

If they say it's the common thrill
Pressing youth to seek their fill
I want from you, to then cry, *Whoa!*—
Worse than that I do not know.

But if they say the lasting Virtue
That so richly clads and girds you
Kindled your love in me to glow—
Better than that I do not know.

And if they say that perfect love—
My heart so chastely touched thereof—
Can never my honor overthrow—
Better than that I do not know.[179]

XLIII
[Elégie II]

Combien de fois ay je en moy souhaicté
Me rencontrer sur la chaleur d'esté
Tout au plus pres de la clere fontaine,
Où mon desir avec cil se pourmaine,
Qui exercite en sa philosophie
Son gent esprit, duquel tant je me fie,
Que ne craindrois, sans aucune maignie,
De me trouver seule en sa compaignie:
Que dy je seule? ains bien accompaignee
D'honnesteté, que Vertu a gaignee
A Apollo, Muses, et Nymphes maintes,
Ne s'adonnantz qu'à toutes œuvres sainctes:
Là quand j'aurois bien au long veu son cours,
Je le lairrois faire appart ses discours:
Puis peu à peu de luy m'escarterois,
Et toute nue en l'eau me gecterois:
Mais je vouldrois lors quant, et quant avoir
Mon petit Luth accordé au debvoir,
Duquel ayant congneu, et pris le son,
J'entonnerois sur luy une chanson
Pour un peu veoir, quelz gestes il tiendroit:
Mais si vers moy il s'en venoit tout droict,
Je le lairrois hardyment approcher:
Et s'il vouloit, tant soit peu, me toucher,
Lui gecterois (pour le moins) ma main pleine
De la pure eau de la clere fontaine,
Lui gectant droict aux yeulx, ou à la face.
Ò qu'alors eust l'onde telle efficace
De le pouvoir en Acteon muer,
Non toutesfois pour le faire tuer,
Et devorer à ses chiens, comme Cerf:
Mais que de moy se sensist estre serf,
Et serviteur transformé tellement,
Qu'ainsi cuydast en son entendement,

43
[Elegy 2][180]

Oh, how often have I longed to find
Myself, when summer's heat is most unkind,
At the edge of a clear fountain pool—there[181]
My fancy takes me strolling, all aware
Of one who's focused on philosophy:
A gentle mind I trust to such degree
As not to fear—even on my own—[182]
To be with him, in that far place, alone.
What do I mean, alone? Rather, escorted
By Integrity—which Virtue from assorted
Nymphs, from Apollo, and the Muses won—
Devoted now to noble works, or none.[183]
I'd watch awhile the progress of his walking;
I'd see him move aside and keep on talking,
While I would inch away, some distance keep,
Then full-naked into the water leap.
Oh, yes, and I should like to have close by
My precious Lute, well tuned to gratify:
Familiar with its sounds, I would erelong
Begin to sing for him a tender song—[184]
To see, in part, what his response might be,
And if he made a beeline straight toward me,
Boldly, I would allow him to draw near;
But if he seemed to desire even a mere
Touch of me—for a start, I'd fling at him
A handful of pure, clear water from the brim
Of the spring—into his face, his eyes, eject
It! Oh, if that splash could have the effect
Of transforming him into Actaeon!
Not, however, that he be leapt upon
As a stag—killed and devoured by his own hounds,
But that he feel, through me, within those bounds,
So changed—like a dear and loyal servant—
And hold that conviction in thought so fervent,

Tant que Dyane en eust sur moy envie,
De luy avoir sa puissance ravie.
    Combien heureuse, et grande me dirois!
Certes Deesse estre me cuyderois.
Mais pour me veoir contente à mon desir,
Vouldrois je bien faire un tel desplaisir
A Apollo, et aussi à ses Muses
De les laisser privees, et confuses
D'un, qui les peult toutes servir à gré,
Et faire honneur à leur hault chœur sacré?
    Ostez, ostez, mes souhaitz, si hault poinct
D'avecques vous, il ne m'appartient point.
Laissez le aller les neuf Muses servir,
Sans se vouloir dessoubz moy asservir,
Soubz moy, qui suis sans grace, et sans merite.
    Laissez le aller, qu'Apollo je ne irrite
Le remplissant de Deité profonde,
Pour contre moy susciter tout le Monde,
Lequel un jour par ses escriptz s'attend
D'estre avec moy et heureux, et content.

That Diana would know how envy devours,
Feeling I'd deprived her of her powers.[185]
  How happy I would think myself, how fine!—
Surely, I might call myself Divine—
A goddess! But for my wish to reach full measure
Would I want, really, to cause such displeasure
To Apollo? also to his Muses, left
Confounded with uncertainty—bereft
Of one who'd gladly serve them for all time,
Honoring their sacred chorus, so sublime?[186]
  Away! away! O lofty longings, fall
Away from me—he's not mine, after all.
Let him go to the nine Muses deferring,
Not some service under me preferring—
Under me, of grace and merit hollow.[187]
  Let him go, lest I provoke Apollo,
Filling him with Divinity unfurled,
To raise against me the entire World[188]
That expects one day, through his works, as meant,
To be, with me, both happy and content.

XLIV
[Epigramme XXXV]

Si j'ayme cil, que je debvrois hayr,
Et hais celuy, que je devrois aymer,
L'on ne s'en doit autrement esbayr,
Et ne m'en deult aucun en rien blasmer.
    Car de celuy le bien dois estimer,
Et si me fuict, comme sa non semblable:
Mais de cestuy le plaisir trop damnable
M'oste le droict par la Loy maintenu.
    Voila pourquoy je me sens redevable
A celuy là, qui m'est le moins tenu.

XLV
[Epigramme XXXVI]

Si descharger je veulx ma fantasie
Du mal, que j'ay, et qui me presse fort,
On me dira, que c'est la jalousie
(Je le sçay bien) qui faict sur moy effort.
    Mais qui pourroit estre en propos si fort,
Et d'argumentz si vivement pourveu,
Que ce, que j'ay de mes propres yeulx veu,
Soit une folle imagination,
Il feit accroire à mon sens despourveu?
Il me feroit grand' consolation.

44
[Epigram 35]

If the one whom I should hate I love,
And the one whom I should love I hate,
One must not wonder overly thereof—
Nor any blame against me generate:[189]
 For the good of one I must appreciate,
Though, seeing me so unlike him, he flee;[190]
While the other's pleasure, perniciously,
Deprives me of my right on legal ground.[191]
 Thus I feel more indebted, as you see,
Toward him who is to me less closely bound.[192]

45
[Epigram 36]

If I want my fancy to be free,
And tell of pain that weighs upon me so,
They will say it's only jealousy
That causes me distress (as I well know).[193]
 But who could find the strength of words to flow,
Convincing me—through argument so keen—
That what I just, with my own eyes, have seen
Be but a figment of imagination—
And thus defective judgment contravene?
Oh, *he* would bring me great consolation.[194]

XLVI
[Epigramme XXXVII]

Ne vous faschez, si à vous je me plaings,
Que congnoissez raison mieulx, que celuy,
Pour qui souvent par motz de courroux pleins
Donner vous puis, en m'escoutant, ennuy.
Je ne le fais pour me plaindre de luy,
Qu'une autre en aye au vray la jouyssance:
Mais certes j'ay grand crainte, et desplaisance,
Quand j'apperçoy vostre amytié desjoindre,
Prenant sur luy esgard, et congnoissance,
Qu'il me delaisse, encor pour une moindre.

XLVII
[Epigramme XXXVIII]

Plus ne m'en chault, la congnoissant à l'œil,
Comme chascun, non plus belle, que bonne:
Mais ce, qui plus m'est grief soubz le Soleil,
Et qui mon ame esbahit, et estonne,
C'est que par tout j'oy un bruict, qui resonne,
De quelque eclipse à mon Jour survenu,
Mais bien à moy: car il m'a prevenu,
Tesmoing n'en veulx, que la perseverance,
Par qui il est tant allé, et venu,
Où moins doubtois en ma foible asseurance.

46
[Epigram 37]

Don't be annoyed if I complain to you,
As more inclined toward reason than is he,
Over whom, often, angry words ensue
That give you sadness, hearing them from me.[195]
  I do it not to blame him that I see
Another one enjoys his full dimension;[196]
But I am filled with grief and apprehension
To see your bonds of friendship come untied
As you observe him, knowing his intention:
To cast me—for a lesser one—aside.

47
[Epigram 38]

It's nothing to me now. Like everyone,
I see she's no more fair than good; and yet,[197]
My greatest source of grief beneath the Sun—
The jolt by which my startled soul's beset—
Are rumors on all sides, where echoes let
Me hear that some eclipse has touched my Day.[198]
It's good for me, for hints he did betray—[199]
With no more need of proof than that he must,
Once he'd arrived, so often slip away—
And I less doubtful then—weak, blinding trust!

XLVIII
[Epigramme XXXIX]

Comme mon Jour, il peult par tout aller
Par une mode au Soleil coustumiere:
Lequel l'on voit monter, et devaller,
Tournant reveoir sa region premiere.
Car de ses rayz à toutes faict lumiere,
Veu qu'elles ont d'ignorance la nuict:
Mais il y est, comme au feu la fumiere,
Plus elle est noire, et plus fort il reluict.

XLIX
[Epigramme XL]

Mon Jour estoit assis tout aupres d'une,
L'entretenant à l'aise, et à repos,
D'affection non autre, que commune,
Mais comme on vient d'un à autre propos.
Voicy Amour sur eulx gay, et dispos,
Portant un arc, et traictz à la Gregeoise,
Lequel lascha deux motz à la Bourgeoise,
Et au partir luy dit, callimera:
Lors souspeçon en mon cueur myt grand noise,
Doubtant qu'il dist d'elle: qu'il l'aymera.

48

[Epigram 39]

Look how my Day can travel to all places
In the manner the Sun is accustomed to—
We watch how it ascends, then downward races,
Turning again to gaze on its first view.[200]
As in all places where the rays embue
Enlightenment in night's dark ignorance,[201]
So here, as in the smoke when fire shines through—[202]
Light glows most brightly where the dark's most dense.[203]

49

[Epigram 40]

Seated close to another was my Day,
Conversing with her calmly, fancy free,
On diverse subjects—with no real display
Of uncommon affection I could see;
When lo! Cupid burst forth with impish glee,
Raised his bow, and aimed a fiery dart:[204]
He let fly four words as he drew apart[205]
And left the scene: *Catch you later, ciao!*[206]
But, oh! suspicion shot into ***my*** heart
A fear that he'd said: *Captivate her, now!*[207]

L
[Epigramme XLI]

Je le devois prendre à augure,
Que plus, qu'elle, il m'estimera,
Et pour ma bonne avanture,
Mesmes qu'il est mon Imera:
Comme disant qu'il m'aymera,
Et que le verray enflammer,
Ainsi que cil, qui premier a
Mon cueur enflammé à aymer.

LI
[Epigramme XLII]

C'est une ardeur d'autant plus violente,
Qu'elle ne peult par Mort, ny temps perir:
Car la vertu est d'une action lente,
Qui tant plus va, plus vient à se nourrir.
    Mais bien d'Amour la flamme on voit mourir
Aussi soubdain, qu'on la voit allumee,
Pource qu'elle est tousjours accoustumee,
Comme le feu, à force, et vehemence:
Et celle là n'est jamais consumee:
Car sa vigueur s'augmente en sa clemence.

50
[Epigram 41][208]

I should have taken it for a sign:
From me to her he'd not deign stray—
That on my head good luck would shine;
And even as he is my Day,[209]
With the words *Captivate* ***me***, I may[210]
See him inflamed the equal of
The time when one first found a way[211]
To set *my* heart aflame with love.

51
[Epigram 42][212]

It is an ardor all the more intense
That neither Death nor Time can mortify:
For Virtue moves with patient reticence,
And lasting longer is nourished more thereby.
    Full many a flame of Love do we see die
As suddenly as it begins to flare,
Being always accustomed to the glare
Of force, and violence—like fire driven.
But never is the former consumed, for there,
The vigor grows with each indulgence given.[213]

LII
[Epigramme XLIII]

Je n'oserois le penser veritable,
Si ce n'estoit pour un contentement,
Qui faict sentir, et veoir ce bien durable
Par la doulceur, qui en sort seulement.
De tous les heurs c'est le commencement:
J'en fais tesmoing le sçavoir estimable.
Est ce le bien qu'on dict tant incroyable?
Je ne le croy, et le sçay seurement.

LIII
[Epigramme XLIV]

En lieu du bien, que deux souloient pretendre,
Je veulx le mal toute seule porter:
Puis que malheur ainsi me veult surprendre,
Il est besoing qu'aprenne à supporter.
O foy, amour, plaisir, se contenter,
Ce n'est moyen de mon mal subvertir.
Helas j'ay bien cause de regrecter
Ce, qui souloit en deux se despartir.

52

[Epigram 43][214]

I would not even dare to think it real,[215]
If not for a contentment, nothing less:
This lasting good it makes me see and feel,
Through sweet delight it can alone express.
  This is the beginning of all happiness:
As proof, I bring high learning for appeal.
Is this the doubted good deemed too ideal?
I believe it not and yet its truth profess.[216]

~

53

[Epigram 44][217]

Instead of the good that two routinely courted,
Give me the ill to shoulder all alone;[218]
For since mischance may choose to leave me thwarted,
I must then learn to bear it on my own.
  Oh! faith, contentment, love, and pleasure known—
This is no way to banish my despair;
Alas, I have good reason to bemoan
The loss of what two people used to share.[219]

~

LIV
[Epigramme XLV]

Un seul je hais, qui deux me faict aymer
Plus par pitié d'aveuglee jeunesse,
Qui trouve doulx ce, que je trouve amer,
Que par instinct d'amoureuse destresse,
Laquelle toute au quatriesme m'adresse,
Le voyant tout en moy se iniquiter.
    Parquoy, voulant envers tous m'acquicter,
Contraincte suis (à fin que ne m'escarte)
Fuyant les trois, le quatriesme quicter,
Pour non trembler si grosse fievre quarte.

~

LV
[Epigramme XLVI]

Aucuns ont dict la Theorique
Estre devant, que la Practicque:
Ce que bien nyer on pouvoit.
    Car, qui feit l'art, jà la sçavoit,
Qui est un poinct qu'un Sophistique
Concederoit tout en dormant:
Quand à moy, je dy pour replique,
Qu'Amour fut premier, que l'Amant.

~

54

[Epigram 45][220]

Just one I loathe, who dictates I love two,
From sympathy for youth who cannot see—
Who takes as sweet what's bitter in my view—[221]
More than impulse for amorous agony
Which straight toward the fourth addresses me,
Seeing such wrong in me by him committed.[222]
　　So, wanting from them all to be acquitted,[223]
I am compelled (or risk myself forsaking)[224]
To quit the fourth—having the three now flitted—[225]
Or lie in dreadful quartan fever shaking.[226]

55

[Epigram 46]

Now some have said that Theory
Comes before Practice—which could be[227]
Well argued, for it has been shown
　　That art is formed from what is known:
This point a Sophist easily[228]
Concedes while under deep sleep's cover.
For me, I say I quite agree—
Love came first, before the Lover.[229]

LVI
[Chanson VIII]

Heureuse est la peine
De qui le plaisir
A sur foy certaine
Assis son desir.

L'on peult assés en servant requerir,
Sans toutesfois par souffrir acquerir
Ce, que l'on pourchasse
Par trop desirer,
Dont en male grace
Se fault retirer.

Car un tel service
Ne pretend qu'au poinct,
Qui par commun vice
L'honneur picque, et poinct.

Et ce travail en fumee devient
Toutes les fois, que la raison survient,
Qui tousjours domine
Tout cueur noble, et hault,
Et peu à peu mine
Le plaisir, qui fault.

Mais l'attente mienne
Est le desir sien,
D'estre toute sienne,
Comme il sera mien.

Car quand Amour à Vertu est uny,
Le cueur conçoit un desir infiny,
Qui tousjours desire
Tout bien hault, et sainct,
Qui de doulx martire
L'environne, et ceinct.

56
[Song 8][230]

Happy is the pain
If one's desire be
Set by pleasure's gain
On true fidelity.[231]

One may seek, in constant service straining,
Without, at last, through such duress obtaining
The thing that one chases
With excess desire—
And then, in bad graces,
Be forced to retire.

From such devoted care,
Just one end can ensue:
For common vice won't spare,
But pierces honor through.[232]

And all that tiresome work like smoke grows thin
Every time that Reason enters in—[233]
Which rules without lapse
All hearts, noble, exalted;
And so slowly saps
The pleasure, defaulted.

But my only goal is
To be his alone,
As I wish it were his
To be my very own.

For Love united with Virtue as counterpart
Conceives Eternal Desire within the heart
That always wants the sum
Of all good—lofty, pure—
That in sweet martyrdom
It girds round fast and sure.

Car il luy engendre
Une ardeur de veoir,
Et tousjours apprendre
Quelque hault sçavoir.

Le sçavoir est ministre de Vertu,
Par qui Amour vicieux est batu,
Et qui le corrige,
Quand dessus le cueur
Par trop il se erige
Pour estre vainqueur.

C'est pourquoy travaille
En moy cest espoir,
Qui desir me baille
Et veoir, et sçavoir.

Estant ainsi mon espoir asseuré,
Je ne crains point, qu'il soit demesuré:
Mais veulx bien qu'il croisse
De plus en plus fort,
A fin qu'apparoisse
Mon cueur ferme, et fort.

Et que tousjours voye,
Travaillant ainsi,
Tenir droict la voye
D'immortel soucy.

Si donc il veult en si hault lieu monter,
Qu'il puisse Amour, et la Mort surmonter,
Sa caducque vie
Devra soulager
D'une chaste envie
Pour l'accourager.

There, the good engenders
An ardent longing to see,
Whereby the heart surrenders
To learning of high degree.[234]

Knowledge is the minister—Virtue's own,
By which all vicious Love is overthrown:[235]
Correcting it whenever
Above the heart it flies
Too high in its endeavor
To gain the victor's prize.

And so, with this hope
Nourishing my yearning,
In great travail I grope,
Toward seeing, toward learning.

And with this hope so securely grounded
I have no fear that it will be unbounded;
But the wish is sincere
That my heart grow steadfast,
So its strength will appear
Resolute, unsurpassed.[236]

And that, in this travail,
I always may discern
And stick close to the trail
Of immortal concern.[237]

Then if toward such a height it seek ascent
That Love and Death will be themselves outspent,
In the frailty of life
It should feel itself braced
And relieved of all strife
From longings so chaste.

Ainsi m'accompaigne
Un si hault desir
Que pour luy n'espargne
Moy, ne mon plaisir.

Since pure desire's treasure
Fills my every limb,
I need not stint my pleasure,
Nor yet myself, for him.[238]

LVII
[Epigramme XLVII]

C'est un grand mal se sentir offensé,
Et ne s'oser, ou sçavoir à qui plaindre:
C'est un grand mal, voire trop incensé,
Que d'aspirer, où l'on ne peult attaindre:
C'est un grand mal, que de son cueur contraindre,
Oultre son gré, et à subjection:
C'est un grand mal, qu'ardente affection,
Sans esperer de son mal allegeance:
Mais c'est grand bien, quand à sa passion
Un doulx languir sert d'honneste vengeance.

LVIII
[Epigramme XLVIII]

Non que je vueille oster la liberté
A qui est né pour estre sur moy maistre:
Non que je vueille abuser de fierté,
Qui à luy humble, et à tous devrois estre:
Non que je vueille à dextre, et à senestre
Le gouverner, et faire à mon plaisir:
Mais je vouldrois pour noz deux cueurs repaistre,
Que son vouloir fust joinct à mon desir.

57

[Epigram 47][239]

It's terrible to feel such an offense
And not to dare nor know where to complain;
It's terrible—surely, it makes no sense
To long for something one cannot attain;
It's terrible—the way one's heart must strain
To serve against one's will in full defeat;
It's terrible—affection's ardent heat,
Bereft of hope of pain's alleviation;[240]
But it's wonderful, indeed, when a sweet
Languor serves passion in true vindication.[241]

58

[Epigram 48]

Not that I would like freedom denied
To someone born to master over me;[242]
Not that I would like to swell with pride—
I who meek to him, to all, ought be;
Not that I would like, each turn, that he
Be governed by my rule to serve my pleasure;
But I *should* like, to enrich our hearts, to see
His will aligned with my desire's measure.[243]

LIX
[Epigramme XLIX]

Point ne se fault sur Amour excuser,
Comme croyant qu'il ait forme, et substance
Pour nous pouvoir contraindre, et amuser,
Voire forcer à son obeissance:
    Mais accuser nostre folle plaisance
Pouvons nous bien, et à la verité,
Par qui un cueur plein de legereté
Se laisse vaincre, ou à gaing, ou à perte,
Esperant plus, que n'aura merité
Son amytié de raison moins experte.

LX
[Epigramme L]

Deux amys joinctz par estroicte amytié
Eurent, sans plus, une dissention:
L'un soubstenoit (par raison la moytié)
Que le Thuscan a plus d'affection:
L'aultre disoit par resolution,
Que le François parle plus proprement.
    Pour les vouloir mettre d'appointement,
Je dy, qu'ilz sont tous deux beaux à descrire:
Mais pour en faire au vray le jugement,
Celuy depeinct ce, que cestuy veult dire.

59

[Epigram 49][244]

One must never use Love as an excuse,
Believing there is form and substance to him
That detains us, dallies with us, to induce—
Yea, force us to obey his every whim.[245]
    But our mad pleasures filled up to the brim
Are what in truth we really ought to blame,
Whereby a heart comes frivolous and tame
To be vanquished. Toward gain or loss it swerves,
Always hoping there will be more to claim
Than senseless affection ever well deserves.

~

60

[Epigram 50][246]

Two, joined in friendship of the closest kind,
Were having no more than a light dispute:
One of the two (and thus a half) opined
That liveliness was a Tuscan attribute;
The other said—in terms quite resolute—
Precision renders French speech more delightful.
    I say, hoping to keep their views less spiteful:
For fine descriptions, which one makes no matter;
But, to offer a judgment more insightful:
The former pales in meaning to the latter.[247]

~

LXI

[Epigramme LI]

Vidi d'intorno del Parnaso fonte
Per gratia di colei, che nulla asconde,
Di gente piena tutto el piano e'l monte:
E piu vidi un, ch'en le sacrate sponde
Stava de l'acque, e tre ghirlande assonte
Havea d'un Lauro, ch'ombregiava l'onde:
Tal ch'Apollo disse, come dir' suole,
Questo sara l'honor mio gran sê vuole.

LXII

[Epigramme LII]

Colpa ne sei, Amor, se troppo volsi
Aggiongendo alla tua la bocca mia:
Ma se punir'mi vuoi di quel, che tolsi,
Fà che concesso il replicar mi sia:
Che tal dolcezza in le tuoi labbia accolsi,
Che fu lo spirto per partirsi via:
Sò ch'al secondo bascio uscira fuora:
Bascia me adunque, se tu vuoi ch'imuora.

61
[Epigram 51][248]

By the spring at Parnassus I could see[249]
(Thanks to her who leaves no detail dim),
With throngs of people on the ridge, the lea,
A man emerging at the sacred rim—[250]
Bearing three wreaths from a Laurel tree[251]
That cast its shade on waters at the brim.
There, Apollo said—his very phrase:
This one, if he's inclined, shall bring me praise.[252]

~

62
[Epigram 52][253]

It's your fault, Love, if I presumed too much,[254]
Adjoining my lips just now onto your own;
But should you wish to punish that wrong touch,
Please let it not be made to stand alone;
The sweetness gathered at your mouth was such
That from myself my soul had nearly flown;
I know a second kiss will let it fly—
Come kiss me then, if you want me to die.

~

LXIII
[Chanson IX]

Je suis la Journee,
Vous, Amy, le Jour,
Qui m'a destournee
De fascheux sejour.

D'aymer la Nuict certes je ne veulx point,
Pource qu'à vice elle vient toute appoint:
Mais à vous toute estre
Certes je veulx bien,
Pource qu'en vostre estre
Ne gist, que tout bien.

Là où en tenebres
On ne peult rien veoir,
Que choses funebres,
Qui font peur avoir.

On peult de nuict encor se resjouyr,
De leurs amours faisant amantz jouyr:
Mais la jouyssance
De folle pitié
N'a point de puissance
Sur nostre amytié.

Veu qu'elle est fondee
En prosperité
Sur Vertu sondee
De toute equité.

La nuict ne peult un meurtre declarer,
Comme le jour, qui vient à esclairer
Ce, que la nuict cache,
Faisant mille maulx,
Et ne veult qu'on sache
Ses tours fins, et caultz.

63
[Song 9]

Beloved, you are the Day
And I the Reflection;[255]
You've turned me away
From a time of dejection.

Hardly could I love the Night wherein
All is open to villainy and sin;[256]
But had I what I would,
I'd be yours through and through,
For only all good
Is residing in you.

There, in shadows dim,
No thing appears
But the doleful and grim,
The cause of our fears.

Still, in night, much pleasure can be found,
As lovers make of love their joy unbound—
Though thrills ensuing from
Such shame uncontrolled
Cannot overcome
Affections we hold:[257]

They clearly rest
On abundance we see
Passing Virtue's test
So equitably.[258]

A murder cannot be revealed by night,
As by the day, which brings forth into light
What night will not show:
Its myriad ills—
So we cannot know
Its sly, evil skills.

La nuict la paresse
Nourrit, qui tant nuit:
Et le jour nous dresse
Au travail, qui duit,

O heureux jour, bien te doit estimer
Celle, qu'ainsi as voulu allumer,
Prenant tousjours cure
Reduire à clarté
Ceulx, que nuict obscure
Avoit escarté.

Ainsi esclairee
De si heureux jour,
Seray asseuree
De plaisant sejour.

An idleness is bred
By night, which so pollutes us;
By daylight we are led
To labor that well suits us.[259]

O happy day! Oh, you she must admire
Whom you desired so to set afire.[260]
Toward light, without fail,
You guide carefully back
Those who, under veil
Of night, have strayed off track.[261]

With such illumination
From this glorious day,[262]
I've sure anticipation
Of a pleasant stay.

LXIV
[Chanson X]

Conde Claros de Adonis

Amour avecques Psiches,
Qu'il tenoit à sa plaisance,
Jouoit ensemble aux eschetz
En tresgrand resjouyssance.

Mais bien tost il a ouy
Bien loing lamenter un Cygne,
Dequoy peu s'est resjouy,
Et l'a prins pour maulvais signe.

Laissons le jeu, je vous pry,
Dict il d'une voix amere
Et allons ouyr le cry
Du messager de ma mere.

Lors tous deux s'en vont bouter
A la prochaine fenestre,
Et leur veue droict gecter
Là, où l'Oyseau pouvoit estre.

Si ont veu sur un estang
Long et grand, comme une Mer,
Un beau Cygne pur et blanc,
Qui chantoit un chant amer.

O Deesse, disoit-il,
Regnant au ciel Empiree,
Par ton engin trop subtil
Nostre joye est empiree.

Puis que par ta grand envie
Au malheureux Adonis
Tu as abregé la vie,
Et sont ses beaulx jours finiz.

64

[Song 10][263]

Ballad for Adonis[264]

Cupid lately was engrossed
With Psyche—all his pleasure—
Playing a game of chess in most
Enjoyable sweet leisure.[265]

All at once he thought he heard
A Swan's far-off lament—[266]
But no joy within him stirred,
For it seemed of ill-portent.

Oh please, we must this game adjourn,
He said (his voice was wary);
Let us go hear what we can learn
From my mother's emissary.

So they both jumped up, distraught,
Ran to the nearest window,
And stared intently where they thought
The Bird was, far below.[267]

There on the lake they looked upon
(As wide as a sea and long)
Sailed a handsome pure-white Swan,
Chanting a mournful song.

O Goddess, you who reign, he wailed,
In the Empyreal Gleam,
Our sweet joy has been assailed
Through your too-subtle scheme.[268]

When you turned your jealous gaze
On Adonis, ill-fated,
You put an end to his fine days
And thus his life abated.

Et nostre povre Maistresse
Seule au boys il a laissee
De douleur, et de destresse
Mortellement offencee.

Tant que plus ne veult porter
Ny le vert, ny couleur gaye:
Mais pour se reconforter
A la mort en vain s'essaye.

Lors l'Enfant à ces nouvelles
Son espouse a accollee,
Et esbranlant ses deux esles
En l'air a prins sa volee.

Lequel tant il a fendu,
Traversant mainte contree,
Qu'aupres il s'est descendu
De sa mere rencontree.

Comme luy, sont arrivez
Les Graces, et ses deux freres
De toute joye privez,
Et de tristesse confreres.

Qui pour donner allegeance
A la Deesse dolente,
Ont tous juré la vengeance
De la beste violente.

Parquoy entrant dans le boys
Chascun desploye sa Trousse,
Mettant les chiens aux abboys
Pour donner au Porc la trousse.

Mais si bien ont pourchassé,
Et continué leur suicte,
Que le Sanglier tout lassé
N'a sceu, où prendre la fuicte.

In the woods, our poor mistress[269]
By Adonis, alone, was left
With the pain of her distress—
Mortally wounded, bereft.

She wants no longer to be wrapped
In her preferred bright green;[270]
Now, for comfort, she is apt
To seek, in vain, death's sheen.

Her child then, hearing of her plight,
Embraced his spouse with care,
And spreading forth broad wings for flight,
Lifted into the air—[271]

Cleaving through it in such haste,
Cross countries far and wide,
That he, in his descent, was placed
Close to his mother's side.

After him, the Graces arrived—
Along with both his brothers;[272]
Of all their joy they were deprived;
In woe, kin to the others.

Wanting to show veneration
For the goddess forlorn,
A swift and full retaliation
On the violent beast was sworn.

So in the woods, each one, that day,
Spread out his quiver before
The eager dogs, to scent their prey,
Then chase and entrap the Boar.

Their pursuit was so steadfast—
Prolonged so relentlessly—
That the poor Boar, worn out at last,
No longer knew where to flee.

Parquoy toute la cohorte
S'est estendue à l'entour,
Et d'une corde bien forte
Au col luy ont faict maint tour.

L'un le traynoit par la corde,
L'esguillonnant, et hurtant,
L'autre sans misericorde
De son arc l'alloit battant.

Ainsi prins l'ont amené
Devant Venus esplouree,
Qui pour luy a demené
Complaincte desesperee.

Et tant de luy se douloit,
Que sans plus vouloir attendre,
Tout soubdain elle vouloit
L'estrangler de sa main tendre.

Mais les Graces luy ont dict,
Qu'elle se feroit oultrage,
A fin qu'à ce contredict
Elle appaisast son courage.

Qui eust veu alors la beste,
Comme morte elle sembloit,
Humblement baissoit la teste,
Tant de peur elle trembloit.

Adonc soubz un arbre espais
Venus de douleur troublee
A commandé faire paix
A toute celle assemblee.

As tu, dict elle au Sanglier,
(Qui estoit mal asseuré,)
Osé ainsi desplier
Ton courroux demesuré?

At this point the entire troop,
With a rope both long and stout,
Surrounded him, formed a loop,
And circled his neck about.

One tugged the rope in front for those
Who poked him to stay on course;
The beating, the slapping, from their bows,
Was endless, with no remorse.

In this way they delivered him
To Venus, sadly weeping:
Every desperate breath was grim
With her lament still keeping.[273]

Her fierce pain was all her cause:
Yielding to grief's demands,
She said she could—without a pause—
Choke him with tender hands.

But the Graces all retorted
She'd only invite more harm;
To insure that it be thwarted,
She must her zeal disarm.

Who then saw the beast would find
How dead he did appear,
How humbly stood, with head declined,
All trembling in fear.

And underneath an ancient oak,
A Venus with voice less shrill
Faced the assembled throng and spoke,
Commanding them to be still.[274]

Turning her head, she then addressed
The Boar—most ill-at-ease:
O you, with anger thus expressed,
How dared you so displease?

Qui t'a meu, beste incensee,
D'avoir mon amy oultré?
Et ce dict, comme offencee,
Adonis luy a monstré,

Qui gisoit tout estendu,
La face descoulouree,
Dont maint souspir a rendu
La povre Amante esploree.

Alors le Sanglier honteux
S'est prosterné à genoulx,
Et d'un son doulx, et piteux
S'est excusé devant tous.

Disant: Deesse honnoree,
Pardonne moy ce meffaict:
Car d'ire deliberee
Ne t'ay cest oultrage faict.

Bien est vray, que quand jc vis
La forme du Jeune enfant,
Certes il me fut advis
De veoir un Dieu triumphant.

Tant me donnoit grand merveille
Sa chair blanche, et delicate,
Et sa bouche plus vermeille,
Que n'est aucune Escarlate.

Parquoy d'une ardeur surpris
Je me laissay approcher,
Me semblant un trop grand prys,
Si je le pouvois toucher.

Dont au contour d'une branche
Pour mon ardeur appaiser,
Descouvrant sa cuisse blanche,
Je la luy vouluz baiser.

Who induced you, senseless beast,
To pierce my beloved friend?
She touched Adonis as she ceased,
As if her heart would rend:

He lay stretched out in his demise,
His face of color robbed.
Overcome with heavy sighs,
The stricken lover sobbed.

Then the Boar, in all his shame,
Dropped to his knees in thrall,
And in soft tones, nearly tame,
Apologized before all:

O honored Goddess, he began,
Please pardon this grievous fault.
I did not by deliberate plan
Against you cause assault.

I admit that when I saw
The form of this fine youth,[275]
He seemed to me, as I looked with awe,
A glorious God, in truth.

I marveled then to such length
At his white skin, so tender—
At his mouth, more red in strength
Than any apple's splendor—[276]

That I let myself approach,
Surprised by zeal for such
A great reward—ah, to encroach,
And manage one mere touch!

So I took to a branch, not high,
To cool my ardor a bit;
Then, perceiving his white thigh,
How I wanted to kiss it!

Mais luy trop chault et ardent,
Suivant sa course adressee,
Se va gecter sur ma dent,
Que je tenois abaissee.

Et tellement luy mescheut,
Qu'à celle heure trop perverse
Au plus pres de moy il cheut,
Tout sanglant à la renverse.

Mais j'atteste tous les Dieux,
Juges de mon innocence,
Que sur moy j'eusse trop mieulx
Desiré si grand offence.

Et pource que la dent feit
Si oultrageux malefice,
Et que tant vers vous meffeit
Je veulx bien qu'on la punisse.

Voicy la dent, et la hurc,
Qui ont causé tel esmoy:
Las, de leur male avanture
Prenez vengeance sur moy.

Ainsi de l'offence grande
Le povre Porc s'excusoit:
Et toutesfois pour l'amande
A la mort il s'accusoit.

Si grande estoit la douleur,
Et le regret, qu'il souffroit,
(Comme cause du malheur)
Qu'à tout tourment il s'offroit.

Parquoy toute l'assistence
Vont à Venus supplier
De mitiguer sa sentence,
Et son courroux oublier.

But such a fervid course he kept,
All burning for the chase,
That on my tusk he fairly leapt,
Despite my averted face.

His misfortune seemed to swell
In the moments succeeding:
O perversity! he fell
Backwards, profusely bleeding.

But I swear before the gods
Who will judge my innocence,
I'd rather this wound on ***me*** *the odds*
Had chosen to dispense.

Since unto my tusk is due
This heinous deed profane—
Cause of such offense to you—
Please, punishment ordain.

Here you see the source of gloom:
My head, and offending tusk;
Alas for their impending doom—
Make your vengeance brusque.

And so it was the poor wild Brute
Apologized, caught his breath,
And mindful of his crime, made suit
For the penalty of death.

Such pain that time cannot assuage,
A regret so cumbersome:
To be the cause of such outrage—
To torture he'd succumb.

On hearing this, each observer[277]
To Venus gave petition
To forget her angry fervor
And grant the Boar remission.

Desliez le donc, dict elle,
Puis que pour mon Amy mort
Il s'accuse à mort cruelle,
Ayant de son faict remord.

Mais qu'il jure, qu'es forestz
Jamais plus il n'entrera:
Ains qu'en boues, et marestz,
Tousjours il se veaultrera.

Et à fin que desormais
Se souvienne du meffaict,
Je veulx qu'il porte à jamais
Une marcque de son faict.

C'est qu'en terre l'estendrez,
Et pour reparer l'injure
Les piedz autant luy fendrez
Que la playe a d'ouverture.

A fin que par ce moyen
Ceulx, qui le rencontreront,
Entendent le malheur mien,
Dont, peult estre, pleureront.

De Venus ce mot sacré
Ne fut point hors de sa bouche,
Que la beste de son gré
Dessus la terre se couche.

Et souffrit patiemment
Executer la sentence:
Puis, debout bien humblement
Remercia l'assistence.

Then, release his bonds, she said,
Since sorry for his act
Toward my beloved friend—now dead—
He chooses death's cruel pact.

Let him swear to not again
Seek forest paths to follow,
But in the muck of marsh and fen
Be now content to wallow;[278]

And let his misdeed be retained
In minds for all of time;
And let him always hold ingrained
The mark of his foul crime.

Stretch him out upon the ground
And to amend the wrong,
Cleave his feet as you have found
The wound—as deep, as long.

In this way, all those who cross
The tracks where he appears
Will understand my own sad loss
And shed, perhaps, their tears.[279]

These sacred words were only just
From Venus' mouth outpoured,
When the Boar dropped to the dust,
Quite of his own accord.

He waited—patient and discreet—
For the sentence to be done;
Then, he humbly, on his feet,
Thanked each and every one.

Et pour montrer qu'il vouloit,
Que l'on sceust sa desplaisance,
N'a depuis, comme il souloit,
Aux boys faict sa demeurance.

As for his grief—to show how well
He wished it understood,
He never went again to dwell,
As he had, within the wood.

~

LXV
[Epigramme LIII]

Toute personne assés Jeune, et moins docte,
Qu'il ne fauldroit pour se experimenter
Par une mode ignorante, et sotte
Vouldra tousjours son pareil frequenter:
    Mais un cueur hault taschera de hanter,
Où il verra sa perfection pleine,
A celle fin, que, pour se contenter,
Tout bien luy soit usure de sa peine.

LXVI
[Epigramme LIV]

Celle clarté mouvante sans umbrage,
Qui m'esclarcit en mes tenebreux jours,
De sa lueur esblouit l'œil volage
A l'inconstant pour ne veoir mes sejours:
Car, me voyant, m'eust consommé tousjours
Par les erreurs de son errante fleche.
    Parquoy l'esprit, qui desir chaste cherche,
En lieu de mort a eu nouvelle vie,
Faillant aux yeulx (dont le corps souffrant seche)
De mes plaisirs la memoire ravie.

65
[Epigram 53]

All those more under-schooled in early youth
Than necessary to an adventurous mind
Will, in a manner foolish and uncouth,
Always prefer frequenting their own kind.[280]
    But one of noble heart is more inclined
To seek perfection in others—and remain
Where, in the end, he's satisfied to find
All good accrue as profit for his pain.[281]

~

66
[Epigram 54][282]

This light that moves—no darkness yet to render,[283]
That in my days of gloom enlightens me—
Dazzles the errant one's fickle eye with splendor,
So he can't see where I have come to be—
Or I would be consumed eternally[284]
Through errors left where straying arrows light;[285]
    And so my mind, with chaste desire in sight,
Instead of death takes on a new life's measure,[286]
While from my eyes (whence all flesh suffers blight)
Effacing rapturous memories of my pleasure.[287]

~

LXVII
[Epître I]

Coq à l'asne

Amy je n'ay Lacquais, ny Page,
Qui bien sceust faire son message,
Ne telle chose raconter,
Que me sens au cerveau monter
En ceste plaine, et bel espace.
    Mon Dieu, comme le monde passe
En oysiveté par simplesse!
Ne voit on point tant de sagesse,
Que le plus fol demeure maistre?
Il n'y a rien si beau, que d'estre
Aupres de quelque beau donneur.
    Seroit ce pas grand deshonneur
De la laisser ainsi pucelle?
Je ne dy pas, que ce fust celle,
Qui m'a donné l'occasion.
    Cherchons autre occupation
Pour parvenir à la legere:
Car voulentiers une estrangere
Sera tousjours la mieulx venue,
Pour autant, que, quand elle est nue,
Elle change d'accoustrement:
Comme celluy, qui point ne ment,
Quand il s'excuse sur un compte.
    Nul n'est tenu de rendre compte
(Apres la paye) du receu.
Ò qu'il est bien pris, et deceu
Le doulx Pigeon aux Tourterelles,
    Laissons celà: ce sont querelles,
Que les Grecz eurent aux Troyens.
On ne veit onc tant de moyens
Despuis que le tabourin sonne.
    Qui sçauroit comme l'eau de Saone
Faict le beau tainct aux Damoiselles,
Tant de peine ne prendroient celles

67
[Epistle 1]

Cock-and-Bull Story[288]

Dear Friend, I've neither Page nor Lackey
To take a message down exactly
Or recount things that make me feel
My head to rush, my senses reel
In this beautiful, big, wide space.
Heavens! the world moves on apace—
Toward sloth, as ignorant thoughts endure;
Don't we often see wisdom so pure
That the greatest fool has the upper hand?[289]
Indeed, no company's quite so grand
As that of some fine, handsome donor.[290]
But wouldn't it mean dishonor shown her
To leave her thus a maid, unclaimed?
Now, I'm not saying she should be blamed
For giving rise to the situation;
Let's seek in some other preoccupation
Success—the easiest we've had yet.
For it's often the female you haven't met[291]
Who proves more welcome than anyone knows;
Especially since she wears no clothes,
When changing out of her attire.[292]
Like the fellow, hardly a liar,
When he excuses his own account.
No one's obliged for any amount
After payment, when it's received.
Oh, how trapped and sadly deceived
Is the meek Pigeon with Turtledoves now![293]
Let's leave it there—the sort of row
The Trojans suffered under the Greeks.[294]
Why, no one has used such techniques[295]
Ever since the drum's been known.[296]
Who could know how the river Soane[297]
So beautifies maidens' complexions
That they'd take pains (and no objections)

A distiller pour se noircir,
(Je voulois dire à s'esclarcir)
Leur blanche, et delicate peau.
    A mal juger ne fault appeau:
Puis qu'on n'en paye, que l'amande:
Celuy, qui me doibt, me demande.
    Mais c'est chose par trop notoire,
Que l'on ne peult bien faire croire,
Qu'une robe faicte à l'antique
Ne monstre le corps si ethique,
Bien qu'il soit un petit trop juste
Pour courtisaner à la buste.
    Mais j'en croirois plus tost la preuve
De son amy, quand il la treuve
Sur le faict de la pipperie.
    C'est ce, qui perd la confrerie
De sainct Amour, qui nous surprent,
Puis qu'en lieu de donner on prent.
    Or à Dieu donc, lasche journee,
Puis qu'elle est jà tant sejournee,
Que l'on n'cn corne plus la prise:
Tant y va le pot, qu'il se brise,
Qui nous faict apres bon mestier.
    S'elle sçavoit bien le mestier,
On ne craindroit point le danger
De ce plaidoyeur estrangier:
Mais qu'on le plume sans mentir
Avant qu'il le puisse sentir.

Distilling to give a darker hue—
Whoops! I meant to say *lighter*—to
Their delicate skin, so white, ideal.
    Judging badly needs no appeal:
There's only a fine to be paid, and then
The one who owes me borrows again.[298]
    But it is so well manifest
(We might believe it with all the rest)
That a dress made in a mode outworn[299]
Shows not a body thin, oh, scorn!—[300]
Though a bit tight, that sort is an
Out-dated style for a courtesan.[301]
    I'd sooner believe what proof unfolds
From her special friend, when he beholds
She's at a point to give him the slip.
    That's how we lose the comradeship
Of saintly Love, to our great wonder—
Instead of giving, we seize and plunder.
    So Adieu to a day no longer strong,
For she by now has tarried too long;[302]
The horn from the hunt already ceases,[303]
Like the well-used pot, smashed to pieces,[304]
Creating need for itself when it fell.[305]
    If she knew her trade really well,
We would not have to feel in danger
From that one giving suit—a stranger;
Let us give him an honest fleecing
Before he is able to feel a thing.

LXVIII
[Elégie III]

La Nuict

La nuict estoit obscure, triste, et sombre,
Toute tranquille, et preste à malefice,
Tous animaulx reposantz soubz son umbre:
Mais mon esprit, tresprompt à son office,
Ne permettoit au corps de sommeiller
Un tant soit peu pour chose, que je feisse.
Parquoy contraincte en mon lict de veiller,
Entray si fort en contemplation,
Qu'on ne m'eust sceu en veillant resveiller:
Lors travaillant l'imagination
Je discourois plus avant, que les Cieulx,
Avecques doulce, et longue passion.
Advis m'estoit qu'en lieu delicieux
Je me trouvois avec un si grand aise,
Que souhaicter je n'eusse sceu de mieulx.
Car en ce lieu tout bruict, tout cry s'appaise,
Et n'oit on rien, dont fort je m'esbahis,
Qui me donna quelque peu de malaise.
Pour m'enquerir descouvrois le pais,
Et ne voyois que figures horribles,
Monstres du monde et de mon Jour hais.
Comment, ô Dieux, ces bestes tant terribles
Peuvent, disois je, icy vivre en silence?
Choses de croire à moy trop impossibles.
Car elles sont aptes à violence,
Et à les veoir ennemyes de paix
Les jugeriez par leur impatience.
Ainsi long temps d'envie je me pais,
Et de desir d'entendre un peu leur estre,
Dont à present, pour un peu, je me tais.
Car je voy là venir à main senestre
Une grand Dame, à qui font reverence
Maint Laboureur, Noble, Marchant et Prebstre.

68

[Elegy 3]

The Night[306]

The night was somber, filled with silent woes,[307]
Poised for evil in tranquility—
Within its shadows all things found repose;
And yet my mind, alert to its facility,
Forbid the sleep my body coveted—
My least effort exceeding all ability.[308]
Forced thus to lie awake upon my bed,
I entered into such deep contemplation,
That none could rouse me as my vigil spread:
Through the workings of my imagination,
I rambled to the Heavens, and on apace,
With passion gentle and of long duration.[309]
I came to what seemed a delightful space
And found therein such ease unparalleled
That I could not have wished a better place.[310]
There, every cry, every noise, was quelled:
One heard nothing and I stood, in surprise,
My sense of ease now partially dispelled,
Searching the land for things new to my eyes.
Horrible forms were all I could detect—
Monsters my Day and all the World despise.
Ye gods! How could such beasts live here unchecked,
I asked myself, *most dreadful in this silence!?*
Impossible things my mind had to reject—
For they are capable of violence,
And you would call them enemies of peace,
To see and judge their fierce intolerance.[311]
For quite a while I let a desire increase
In me: a wish to know more of their being;
Then I held still—all sounds from me to cease.
Entering from the left, I was seeing
A Great Lady, before whom there bowed
Workers, Nobles, Merchants, Priests. All keying

Car elle estoit de si belle apparence,
Que, pour pouvoir à elle parvenir,
L'un ne faisoit à l'autre difference.
Mais bien voyois de tous costez venir
Un si grand peuple, et gentz à si grand nombre.
Que de leurs noms ne me puis souvenir.
Et tant estoient, qu'ilz se faisoient encombre
Pour celle Dame attoucher, et puis suyvre,
Comme captifz, et joyeux de son umbre.
Plus la suyvoient, plus la vouloient poursuyvre,
Son seul regard si fort les delectoit,
Qu'ilz ne pouvoient, sans elle, une heure vivre.
Une grande Royne à son costé estoit
(Deux, ou trois pas toutesfois plus arriere)
Qui sceptre d'or, et couronne portoit.
Mais elle alloit d'une mode si fiere,
Et d'un orgueil si roguement enflee,
Que de parler d'elle donnoit matiere.
Et toutesfois la plus part à l'emblee
Des poursuyvantz à la Dame adressoit:
Parquoy vers elle accouroit l'assemblee.
Le plus souvent pour eulx elle oppressoit
Tous ceulx, qui d'elle au fort ne faisoient compte,
Et au besoing appart les delaissoit.
Mais au contraire elle estoit si tresprompte,
Pour avancer tous ses favorisez,
Qu'elle faisoit à tous les autres honte.
Parquoy les siens, estans ainsi prisez,
Ne craignoyent point souvent à repoulser
Ceulx, qui n'estoyent par elle autorisez.
Dont en peu d'heure elle vint à haulser,
Et tellement son grand pouvoir estendre,
Que les plus loings craignoyent la courroucer.
Et mesmement qu'elle faisoit entendre
A la grand Dame, à croire trop facile,
Qu'elle pouvoit sur les Roys entreprendre.
Et qu'il n'estoit chose tant difficile,
N'engin si dur reduict soubz son pouvoir,
Qui ne devint incontinent docile.

On her great beauty, not a one allowed
Any other to have a better claim,
In approaching her from out among the crowd.
I saw clearly, from all sides they came—
So many groups in crushing overflow
That now I can't recall a single name.
Such crowding made it difficult to go.
Up close, to touch the Lady, they'd contrive
To linger—captives, joyous in her shadow;
The more they followed, the harder they would strive:
Her glance alone brought such delight untold
That none without her an hour could survive.
A Great Queen stayed near her as she strolled[312]
(Though lagging two or three paces behind);
She bore a crown and scepter of pure gold,
But strutted forth in pompous pride combined
With such a boastful haughtiness of style,
That speaking of her strained a cunning mind.[313]
Still, toward her, the hangers-on would file
In throngs—for to the Lady, in private session,
She'd lead the ones whom she deemed worth her while.
Often it was for them—her oppression[314]
Of those not holding her in high regard,
Whom she'd forsake to dearth and dispossession.
She eagerly pushed her favorites so hard
Toward advancement, on the other hand,
That the former all drew back, their honor scarred.
And then her own, seeing *their* worth expand,
Were often not at all afraid to spurn
The ones not sanctioned under her command.
Before too long a time, she came to learn
The heights and breadths that power's greatness brings,
Till distant lands feared where her wrath might turn.[315]
She led the Great Lady—above all things—
To understand (oh, easy to believe!)
That she could then usurp the power of Kings;[316]
And there was nothing she could not achieve,
Of all the challenges she might incur—
No tangle she, with ease, could not unweave.

Or la grand Dame (à parler au devoir)
Estoit aveugle en sa mescongnoissance,
Et ne vouloit ses faultes point sçavoir:
Et pour autant en sa grande puissance
Se reposoit sur ceste avare Royne,
Remettant toute en elle sa fiance:
Qui par sa face attrayante, et seraine
Dessus la terre, et la ronde Machine
En peu de temps la rendit souveraine:
Veu qu'une Vieille hydeuse, et qui rechine
Tousjours des dentz de ses mains embridez.
Seche, et jaulnatre, à courbe, et longue eschine,
Joue enfoncee, yeulx rouges tous ridez,
Ce neantmoins songneuse, et diligente
A appeller les plus oultrecuydez,
Pour sa moytié estoit demy Regente
Pour ceste Royne au besoing soulager,
Car à servir ne fut onc negligente.
Ceste en ce point venoit accourager
Ceulx de sa sorte, et si bien leur aydoit,
Qu'ilz venoient tous de haine à enrager.
Tout chascun (presque) à les ensuyvre ardoit:
Mais à l'escart seoit une autre Dame,
Qui les mieulx nez gentement retardoit.
La face avoit rouge, comme une flamme,
Et toutesfois d'une masque couverte,
Se tenant loing de celle gent infame:
En faictz discrete, et en parler diserte,
Sur la grand Dame ayant tousjours l'œil droict,
Maulgré la Royne à l'avarice experte:
Ceulx, qui fuyoient le faulx, aymant le droict,
La suyvoient tous, et la tenoient de pres,
Dont ilz estoient louez en maint endroit:
Bien que souvent par les malings d'aupres
Fussent mocquez secrettement apart,
Et en public par motz, et signe expres:
Mais la grand Dame allant en mainte part,
Tousjours tournoit sa veue çà, et là,
Dont ilz avoient, maulgré la Royne, part.

But that Great Lady (one must here aver)
Was blinded by not seeing what she must—
In *wanting* not to know what her faults were;
And, in fact, for all her power's thrust,
She leaned upon that avaricious Queen,
Placing into her keeping total trust.
And for her face so lovely, so serene,
The Queen soon set her up as Sovereign
Over all the lands and the round Machine.[317]
Then appeared a Crone, with hideous grin[318]
Of yellowed teeth, whose wrinkled eyes flashed scarlet;
Whose frown was surly, cheeks all sunken in—
With bony hands and spine by age beset,
She took the utmost care in her intent,
Recruiting the most arrogant she could get.
She acted out the part of half-Regent
To that Queen, lessening her load,
And never in her service was delinquent.
Meanwhile, she came to bolster and to goad
The ones of her own sort she'd groomed until
All their hatred into madness flowed.
Everyone, almost, burned to follow still;
But another Lady sat apart, sedate,[319]
Detaining the better-born with gentle skill:
Face flushed, as if from flames that radiate
A rosy glow, and masked, thus to recede
And from that villainous crowd to separate.
All eloquent of speech, discreet in deed,
She kept her eye on the Great Lady always—
Despite the Queen, so expert in her greed.
Lovers of Justice fled from false displays
And followed, staying close within her Sphere—
Which, in many places, earned them praise;
Often, though, the malicious ones most near
Made fun of them secretly, turning aside,
Or chose a public place to rant and jeer.
Still the Great Lady roamed, far and wide,
Constantly turning her gaze hither and yon,
So that she could, despite the Queen, provide

Et tellement, qu'elle, voyant celà,
Pour les ouyr les faisoit approcher:
Car onc à nul elle ne se cela.
Quand quelqu'un d'eulx la pouvoit attoucher,
Et bien au long son vouloir luy deduire,
Elle l'avoit plus, que les autres, cher:
Tant qu'ilz venoient par sa clarté à luyre
Par dessus tous, veu qu'elle les voyoit
Ne la vouloir par les autres seduire.
Aussi desjà trop elle s'ennuyoit
Des importuns, et de leur grand audace,
Parquoy le plus elle les r'envoyoit.
Lors voyoit on chascun leur faire place,
Bien que par fois les plus malicieux
Les empeschoient par faict, ou par menace:
Et cà, et là couroient ambitieux,
Qui machinantz d'un accord se rangeoient,
Contre les bons, avec les envyeux:
Mais à la fin de despit enrageoient:
Car où la Dame honteuse s'approuchoit,
Comme confus, par les siens s'estrangeoient.
La Vieille alors ses cheveulx arrachoit
De grand douleur, et de fine destresse,
Et à gaigner contre eulx elle tachoit.
En telle foule, et si confuse presse
D'elles chacune à son prouffit regarde,
Mais complaisant tousjours à sa Maistresse.
Tant les suyvis, qu'en fin je me pris garde
De Monstres maintz horribles, et difformes,
Que la grand Dame avoit là pour sa garde:
Lesquelz, combien que de diverses formes
Ilz fussent tous, et sans estre semblables,
Si estoient ilz à malfaire conformes.
M'esbahyssant que ces gentz miserables
N'avoient horreur pour un si vain desir,
De frequenter à l'entour de ces Dyables.
Si m'en enquis au long, et à loisir,
D'un poursuyvant, qui d'ardeur perissoit
Pour parvenir au but de son plaisir.

Permission to each one she looked upon
To come approach her closely and be heard—
For she never hid herself from anyone.[320]
If some, to gain her touch, were not deterred—
Regaling her in making their hopes known—
She would hold them above the rest, preferred.
In this way, above all others, they shone
Through her light, as she saw they'd deplore
Having her be seduced by another's tone.
She had already been annoyed before
By the troublesome ones—their audacity
Causing her to banish them more and more.
Each made way within his own capacity;
Although, occasionally, the most malicious
Hindered them—with threats or real tenacity.
Running all around, the most ambitious
Conspired against the good of her retinue,
In league with those whose envy made them vicious.
Finally, overcome with rage to view
The Masked Lady's approach, they, in a ream[321]
Of mass confusion, into themselves withdrew.
Then the Crone would tear her hair in extreme
Distress and agony—yet remain strong,
To vanquish them and show herself supreme.
Thus, each Lady in this tumultuous throng
Pandered to her chosen dignitary,
While seeking her own advantage all along.
With so many followers I grew wary,[322]
At last, of all those hideous, malformed Brutes—
The Great Lady's attendants-in-ordinary:
However dissimilar their attributes,
And functioning on many different levels,
They all were formed alike for foul pursuits.
I was amazed that in their empty revels
Those wretched folk weren't shocked beyond all measure
To find themselves cavorting with such Devils;
So, I questioned fully and at leisure[323]
One of the band perishing from the zeal
Of seeking to attain the end of pleasure.

Mais la clarté qui tant plaisante yssoit
(Ce me dit il) des yeulx de la Princesse,
Tous poursuyvantz en sorte esblouissoit,
Que plus suoyent, et travailloient sans cesse,
Plus ce travail leur estoit grand repos,
Et tout tourment leur servoit de lyesse:
Encor que point n'eussent à tous propos
Si bon aspect d'elle, qu'ilz esperoient,
Si n'estoient ilz pour celà moins dispos:
Ains que tousjours apres ilz tascheroient,
Sans regarder que leur destruction,
Et temps perdu les desespereroient.
Parquoy, voyant leur grand confusion,
Je ne me peux tenir alors de rire,
Bien que sentisse estre une illusion:
Et d'une joye entremeslee d'ire
Non seulement me prins à detester
Ces Monstres vains, mais tresbien les mauldire:
Veu qu'ilz venoient le monde inquieter,
Et si ne sont d'eulx mesmes moins, qu'une umbre
Qui le cerveau nous vient à hebeter,
Au libre arbitre estant fascheux encombre
Pour coulourer nostre concupiscence,
Noz vains desirs, et folies sans nombre.
Et nonobstant qu'ilz n'ayent aucune essence,
Par une folle imagination
Nous en faisons nostre vraye science.
Ò miserable est la condition
De nous humains, laquelle est tousjours prompte
A inventer nostre perdition.
Mais sur ce point je voy l'aulbe, qui monte
Chassant bien loing cette tourbe nuisante
De Vaine gloire, Ambition, et Honte:
Si m'esjouys en la clarté plaisante
De mon cler Jour, que je veis apparoistre,
Pour esclarcir ma nuict tresmal plaisante,
Comme il se faict assez de soy congnoistre.

The light, he told me, which held such appeal,
  Shining forth from the eyes of the Princess,
  Blinded the followers so that they could feel
That the more their labor dragged on, limitless,
  The more their work became a form of rest,
  With each torment affording joyousness.[324]
Even though they never had the best
  (That hoped-for view of her, beyond the rare),
  They never shirked from meeting her behest.
So on they strove, with very little care
  Whether their own ruin—by exclusion
  Or lost time—would cause them all despair.
That was the reason—seeing their confusion—
  My show of self-restraint then came to naught:
  I laughed out loud at what seemed an illusion;
But mirth soon mixed with anger. All distraught,[325]
  And loathing now those sham Monsters, I hurled
  My curses on them in sudden onslaught,
Seeing how they came to disturb the world:
  Mere shadows of themselves, yet they all lumber
  Forth into our minds to come unfurled.
Our free will they grievously encumber
  As they color our concupiscence,
  Futile longings, and follies without number.
Notwithstanding their utter lack of essence,
  Rash fancy feeds our predisposition
  To make of them our one true science.[326]
Ah! miserable is the human condition:
  Always eager, through myth or allegory,
  To all alone invent our own perdition.[327]
But here the dawn rises, palliatory,
  To hide that noisome rabble from my sight:
  Of Shame, and Ambition, and Vainglory.[328]
I rejoice now in the pleasant morning light
  And see appearing my beloved friend,
  My Day, to illuminate this awful night;[329]
  It is enough—one's self to comprehend.[330]

LXIX
[Elégie IV]

Desespoir traduict de la prose du parangon italien

Si c'est Amour, Pourquoy m'occist il donc,
Qui tant aymay, et hayr ne sceuz onc?
Et s'il m'occist, pourquoy plus oultre vis?
Et si je vis, pourquoy sont mes devis
De desespoir, et de plainctz tous confus?
Meilleur m'estoit, soubdain que né je fus,
De mourir tost, que de tant vivre, mesmes,
Que mortel suis ennemy de moymesmes:
Et ne puis, las, et ne puis vouloir bien,
Ne voulant celle, en qui gist l'espoir mien:
Et ne puis rien fors ce, que veult la dame
De qui suis serf de cueur, de corps, et d'ame.
    Estre ne peult mon mal tant lamenté,
Que de plus grand ne soye tourmenté:
Et ne pourrois monstrer si grand douleur,
Qu'encor plus grand ne celast mon malheur.
    Las je ne suis prisonnier, ny delivre:
Et ne me tient en espoir, ny delivre
Mon bien servir, qui de mort prent envie.
    Je ne suis mort, ny je ne suis en vie,
Me contraingnant à plaindre mon mal aise:
Et raison veult toutesfois que me taise
Pour n'offencer ce, que servir desire,
Qui mon vouloir en mille partz dessire.
    L'ame congnoit, que de si tres bas lieux,
Dont mes grandz pleurs montent jusques aux yeulx,
Jamais les voix ne peuvent estre ouyes,
Ny en haulteur si grande resjouyes:
Car ce mien feu, qui peu à peu me fond,
Est dans mon cueur allumé si profond,
Qu'il ne peult pas, bien qu'il soit grand, reluire
Devant les yeulx, qui pour mal me conduire
Font le Soleil de grand honte retraire:
Ainsi je meurs, estant contrainct me taire.

69
[Elegy 4]

Despair, translated from an Italian prose model[331]

Can this be Love that slays me to the bone,[332]
Who loved so well that hatred was unknown?
And if I'm slain, why do I still live on?
And if I live, why have my thoughts all gone
Into confusion, played out in moans forlorn?
Better for me, the moment I was born,
To have died at once and not survived to be,
As now, my own most mortal enemy.
For I cannot, alas, completely quell
Desire for her upon whom my hopes dwell,
And I cannot but fill my Lady's role—
To be her slave in body, heart, and soul.[333]
    This pain cannot give so to lamentation
That I not know a greater tribulation;
And no amount of grief can I reveal
That does not greater misery conceal.
    Alas, I'm not imprisoned, nor am free:
Permitted neither hope nor liberty
To serve my good—now envious of death.
    That I'm not dead nor yet enjoy life's breath
Compels me to bewail this state so bleak;
Yet reason wishes for me not to speak
Lest my desire to serve offend the one
Who shreds my will in a thousand parts, undone.
    The soul knows that from such a place so low,
Whence tears mount toward my eyes to overflow,
Voices are impossible to hear—[334]
Nor at so great a height can they find cheer;
For this my fire, consuming me part by part,
Is lit so deeply down within my heart
That it cannot, though raging large inside me,
Shine forth before those eyes that, to misguide me,
Make the Sun retreat, its honor crushed:[335]
Thus am I dying, forced into silence, hushed.

Pour moy ne voy remede suffisant,
Ne pour ma peine aucun moyen duisant:
Car mon desir a peur de desirer:
Qui tant plus croict, tant plus faict empirer
Ce mien espoir, qui peu à peu me fault:
Et toutesfois en moy point ne deffault,
N'y s'amoindrit ma grande passion:
Mais tousjours croict par obstination.
La Mort me suit, non pour paix me donner,
Mais seulement pour ne m'abandonner:
Aussi celle est, qui pallie, et adumbre
De mes travaulx un non guieres grand nombre:
Parquoy je dy (sans ailleurs recourir)
Qu'on peult trouver plus grand mal, que mourir:
Mais bien meilleur est mourir à qui ayme
En grand douleur, et peine tant extresme:
Car, vivant, fault (miserable) qu'il sente
Les grandz douleurs de la peine presente,
Ayant tousjours du passé souvenir:
La craincte aussi de celles à venir
Incessamment luy redouble sa peine:
Parquoy sa foy est en espoir bien vaine.
Chetifz Amantz: aucun ne deubt s'offrir
A telle ardeur, peine à douleur souffrir
En un espoir (plus vain, que l'on ne pense)
D'une, peult estre, ingrate recompense:
Car de l'amour la force tant aigue
Pour bien servir ne peult estre vaincue.
Et plusieurs fois (et à la verité)
On voit celuy, qui a moins merité,
Estre, pour vray, le mieulx recompensé,
Qui ne deubt estre à tel bien dispensé.
En telle guerre, où vertu sert de vice,
Ne vault avoir ferme foy, ny service.
Puis donc qu'on m'oste, et denye victoire,
Qui m'estoit deue, il est par trop notoire,
Que là, où meurt, et où gloire desvie,
C'est gloire aussi que tost meure la vie.

For me I see no likely anodyne—
No proper means to ease this pain of mine.
Fearful of desiring my desire is:
The more it grows, the more it diminishes
This—my hope, within me, slowly failing;
And yet there is a portion still prevailing
To stem the dwindling of my grand passion,
As on it grows in most persistent fashion.
Pursuing me, Death does not offer peace
And yet seems not to want to give release.
Indeed, death's ability to cast a pall
Over my suffering is hardly much at all;[336]
And so I say (without elsewhere applying)
That one may find a greater pain than dying.
Far better is dying for a lover fraught
With greatest pain, in sorrow all distraught;
For he must feel (poor wretch) while he is living
The anguish that his present pain is giving,
While having still the memory of those past;
And from the ones to come more fear is cast,
Redoubling constantly for him the pain:
That's why his faith in hope is quite in vain.
Forlorn Lovers, to such ardor surrender[337]
Not the self, under pain of woe—in slender
Hope (more vain always than in the mind)
Of compensation that may prove unkind.
The force of love, at once so sharp, so shrewd,
In serving well might yet not be subdued;[338]
For time and time again (to here confess)
One sees a person who, deserving less,
Is best rewarded—one who really should
Have been denied receipt of such a good.[339]
In this fight, where virtue serves as vice,
Loyalty and service can't keep their price.[340]
With victory denied, and so much meant
For me past due, it's all too evident
That there where glory dies and goes astray
It's noble that life end before its day.

Aussi, ô Dieux, avec ceste mort mienne
Mourront mes maulx, et ma playe ancienne,
Mon esperance, et desir obstiné,
Et mon arbitre en mal predestiné,
Mon mal, ma peine avec mes fascheries,
Amour aussi avec ses tromperies.

And so indeed, O Gods, through my demise,
Along with grief, my old wound also dies—
My hopes and my desires, so long sustained,
My will also—toward anguish preordained;[341]
My ills, my pains, together with my cares,
And love, as well, with its deceitful snares.[342]

LXX
[Elégie V]

Confort

Si l'on pouvoit par un repentir cher
Donner remede, et quelque exploict chercher
Aux maulx receuz, et dommages passez,
Certainement j'en demourrois assez
Au dict de ceulx, qui sont perseverantz
En leur amour, sans sortir hors des rancz:
Et qui (vrayement) sont de telle excellence,
Qu'en eulx vertu par longue patience
S'esvertuant plus fort se glorifie:
Nature aussi du tout s'y fortifie,
Et tellement, que dessus eulx Fortune
N'a nul pouvoir, et n'a puissance aucune,
Sinon d'autant, que le veult, et commande
L'injuste Amour, qui raison ne demande.
    Mais que te vault? Tu descharges ta Dame
En l'accusant: et en luy donnant blasme
L'honnores mieulx: Vituperant la loues:
La denyant plus fort tu la te advoues.
Et si tu veulx, comme dure, et cruelle
La blasonner, par raison naturelle
Tu la viendras, comme juste, adorer,
Et en ton cueur sa vertu odorer.
    Car ce, qui deubt le noud lyer, le soult:
Ce, qui devroit bien fort contraindre, absoult:
Et ce, que plus on destrainct, et deslye,
C'est ce, qui plus eternellement lye.
    La haulteur sienne, où son cueur se pourmaine,
(Qui la demonstre estre doulce, et humaine)
La contrainct estre en voulenté tresrude,
Comme confite en toute ingratitude:
    Mais elle fainct, contre le sien vouloir,
D'avoir d'amour un constant nonchalloir:
Car son desir, et la crainte d'injure
Vainct ton servir, qui à t'aymer l'adjure.

70
[Elegy 5]

Solace[343]

If one, by paying dearly with remorse,
Could give redress, and seek out some recourse
For insults of the past, for pain incurred,
Then would I dwell at length on every word,
Referring to the ones who persevere
In love and stray not from their own sphere;
For they are of such excellence, it's true—
That through long-standing patience, their virtue
Forever toward a greater glory strives.
Thence Nature, also, a deeper strength derives—
To such extent, that Fortune's priority
Has, over them, no more authority,
Except as much as wrongful love assumes—
Who asks not what is right, but just presumes.[344]
So, what is this to you? You acquit the ways[345]
Of your lady, accusing her; give praise
When finding fault; and by assigning blame,
You honor her. Denial is your best claim.[346]
And if you should wish to depict her still
As harsh and cruel, by natural right you will[347]
Come to adore her, play your proper part,
As her sweet virtue wafts into your heart.[348]
For he who ties the knot must free it first;
And for release, it must be well coerced:
That which is firmly seized to be set free,
Is that which binds the more, eternally.[349]
The lofty place her heart is wont to stroll
(Where she appears in soft and kindly role)
Impels her toward a heartless state—imbued,
It almost seems, with full ingratitude.
But she pretends, against her secret wants,
To have for love a constant nonchalance.
Fear that her desire be treated wrongly
Defeats your care which bids her love you strongly:[350]

Parquoy ces partz, qui en toy sont amables
D'honnesteté, se font desraisonnables.
Et son amour tressaige contredict
A ton vouloir de raison interdict.
Son sens aigu, son meur entendement
Congnoit assez valeur apertement,
Et qui l'incite, et jour et nuict convie
A te vouloir bien, et heureuse vie,
Et s'il n'estoit honte, qui la revocque,
Elle useroit d'une amour reciproque,
Mais quoy? Raison a sus elle pouvoir,
La destournant de faire son debvoir,
Et la retient à non te satisfaire
Combien qu'elle eust voulenté de ce faire.
Ainsi tu peulx en ton ardeur choisir
Et joye, et dueil, plaisir, et desplaisir,
Doulx, et amer, faveur, et deffaveur,
Desapetit, revoquee saveur.
Donc, ô Amant, prens en toy reconfort,
Et contre Amour vueilles toy monstrer fort.
Ne permetz point que desespoir dispute
Contre ton sens: Mais à guerdon repute,
Voire à tresgrande, et juste recompense,
Qu'il luy desplait toutesfois qu'elle pense,
Que tu n'as mal, que pour luy vouloir bien,
Dont tu ne peulx guerir sans son moyen.
Resjouys toy, et vueilles t'estimer,
Veu que de toy elle se souffre aymer,
T'ayant tousjours au devant de ses yeulx,
Et que de cueur plus triste, que joyeux,
Tes plainctes voit, et sans desdain les lise,
D'elles aussi les piteux motz eslise,
Et que pour toy elle a daigné mouvoir
La sienne main à te faire sçavoir
Sa tendre en toy, et grand compassion
Te declarant par son affection
Chose à autruy non jamais accordee,
Ny par fortune en discord recordee.

Those qualities in you the most endearing
Are, when viewed through virtue, most worth fearing.
And her love, so discreet, now contradicts
The desire in you propriety restricts.[351]
    Her quick, sharp wit and ready intellect
Can easily a worth like yours detect;
And thus stirred up, both day and night she's driven
To hope that unto you life's joys be given.
And if shame didn't cause her hesitation,
She might enjoy a love's reciprocation—[352]
But, what?! No, reason's power to restore
Returns her to her duty as before;
It hinders her attempts at satisfying
You—with whom she would not mind the trying.[353]
    So, in your ardor, you can take the measure
Of joy, of grief, of gain—or loss—of pleasure;
The sweet, the bitter, in and out of favor;
Sickness of heart, memories to savor.[354]
    Now then, Lover, let solace take you far:
Come demonstrate to love how strong you are;
Do not allow despair to argue toward
Subduing sense. Deem this as reward—
Indeed, recompense of enormous kind,
Which gives her grief when she calls it to mind:
For her good, only, is your pain endured;
And by her means, alone, can it be cured.
    Rejoice! Gain self-esteem to see whereof
It is for you she bears the strains of love—
With heart more full of sadness than delight
For having you, always, within her sight.
She sees your lamentations. Without scorn,
She reads them, then selects the words forlorn,
And deigns set down for you with her own hand,
In hopes that you will thereby understand,
The compassion that she feels—so great, so tender—
Declaring, through the means affections lend her,
Those things never to another accorded;
Nor even yet, by chance discord, reported.[355]

Or considere en oultre, que depuis,
Que tu as mis sus elle tes appuyz
Et desdié ta totale fortune,
Tu es venu trop plus hault, que la Lune,
En loz, et bruict, et honorable fame,
Et tu te veulx laisser cheoir en diffame!
Va, remercie, et te prosterne en face
Devant les Cieulx, qui t'ont faict ceste grace
D'estre venu en ce temps pour la veoir
Telle, où Nature a mis tout son sçavoir:
Telle pour qui, pour non la veoir, plaindront
Tous Siecles sainctz, qui apres toy viendront.
Ne cherche point remede à prendre fin,
N'à te priver de sa presence, à fin
Que de ta mort la nouvelle piteuse
Ne luy causast douleur, et vie honteuse.
S'elle te veult avec pitié pourveoir,
Ne dois tu point plus tost desirer veoir
La tienne mort avec le sien honneur,
Que veoir sa coulpe, et ta vie en bon heur?
Et si elle est pour ta douleur en peine,
Ou en soucy, tien pour chose certaine,
Que son vouloir raisonnable conteste
A satisfaire à ton vouloir moleste.
Ayes douleur de sa peine et misere,
La deschargeant de coulpe si legere:
Prefere aussi sa saincte renommee
A vie estant de toy tant peu aymee.
Conforte toy, qu'elle est seule la cause
De ton travail, qui ne peult trouver pause.
Conforte toy par propos immortel,
Que de ton mal le fondement est tel,
Que seulement pour avoir mis si hault
Le tien desir, et l'espoir, qui te fault,
Celà te donne assez de recompence
De ton travail. Pour autant doncques pence
Qu'en ceste soif, et alteration,
Tu peulx avoir refrigeration.

Moreover, now consider, as you must,
Since you have placed upon her all your trust—
Your lot, devotedly, before her strewn—
That you have reached heights far beyond the Moon,[356]
With praise, and fame, and honorable renown:
And now you'd let dishonor bring you down?!
Go! give thanks—oh, fall upon your knees
Before the heavens who have allowed, with ease,
Your coming here, well blessed, to see in time
This vision—Nature's skillful paradigm.
All those denied her shall complain, be glum,
Throughout the centuries left till Kingdom Come.
Seek no ready remedy to deprive
You of her presence, make the end arrive,
Letting the wretched tidings of your death
Cause her life shame and grief with every breath.
But if, from pity, she desires to be
Your provider, would you not rather see
Your own death, together with her honor—
Than your success, inflicting shame upon her?[357]
And if, for your anguish, she is aching,
And grows anxious, there is no mistaking
That her sensible will must deny her
Fulfilling your disagreeable desire.
Ache with sorrow for her pain's oppression!
Acquit her of so minor a transgression;
And her holy renown prefer instead—
Not life by you so little coveted.
Take comfort knowing she alone creates
Your suffering—that never yet abates.
Take comfort through words of immortal touch,
Because the basis of your pain is such
That, placing your desires and all your hope—
So necessary to you—beyond your scope,
You now are given ample recompense
For all your toil. Just think, in consequence:
In your weak state, with thirst unsatisfied,
A cool relief can cause it to subside.[358]

    Car le tourment, que tu souffres pour elle,
Estre te doit joye continuelle
A ton esprit, et doulx contentement,
Et au travail tresgrand allegement.
Car il n'est rien, tant soit grand, en ce monde,
Qui vaille autant, que ce mal, qui te abonde.
    Or te soit donc triumphante victoire
D'estre vaincu d'elle, qui est ta gloire.
    S'elle te tient, et vainc pour son captif,
Son cueur sera au tien plus intentif.
    S'elle te tient soubz condition serve,
A quelque fin, peult estre, te reserve.
Laisse luy donc, toy estant sien, la cure
De ce, qu'elle a, et à soy se procure:
Laisse luy donc le soing, et pensement
De ce, qu'est sien: Car naturellement
On ne veult point veoir la perdition
De ce, qu'on a en sa possession.

For this torment that you for her endure
Must render joy, continuous and pure,
Unto your mind—a sweet contentedness,[359]
To make your labor seem so much the less.
For nothing is so great, this whole world through,
To equal the grief that now abounds in you.
Triumphant victory it must be, thus,
That she—your glory—be victorious;
And if she holds you captive, there's incentive:
Her heart will be toward you the more attentive.
Perhaps, if she holds you in bondage serving,
There is some plan for you she is reserving.[360]
So, being hers, leave to her care alone
What she's procured unto her very own:
And leave to her the gentle, careful heed
Of tending what is hers; because, indeed—
One never wants to see what one has taken
Unto one's own be utterly forsaken.[361]

LXXI
[Epigrammes LV-LIX]

Mommerie de cinq postes d'Amour

Le premier poste

Amour, craingnant qu'ayez abandonné
Lui et son train, en eslongnant sa Court,
Soudainement m'ha ce paquet donné,
Me commandant par le chemin plus court
Vous faire entendre, ainsi que le bruit court,
Qu'il n'y aura de vous belle, ny laide
(Si ainsi est) qu'il ne laisse tout court
Plorer en vain son secours, et son ayde.

Le second

J'ay depesché hastivement
Ce Courrier, pour tant seulement
Vous aller deux petis mots dire,
Que je n'ay eu loisir d'escrire.
Si lui donnez creance et foy,
Comme vous voudriez faire à moy
    Par celuy, qui dessouz ses aelles
    Renge les cœurs des Damoiselles.

Le tiers

Amour, qui au vif m'ha tasté
Du hault renom de voz louenges,
M'ha de si loing, et tant, hasté,
Que, sans craindre chemin gasté
De tant de pluies, et de fanges,
Et sans dormir que tout basté,
Suis venu voir voz faces d'Anges,
Que je trouverois bien estranges,
Si, apres avoir tant couru,
Je n'estois de vous secouru.

71

[Epigrams 55–59][362]

Mummery: The Five Posts of Love[363]

The First Post

Love, fearing you had abandoned him
And all his retinue, leaving his court,
Gave me this packet (almost as if by whim)
And ordered me to choose the path most short
To let you know—as rumors make report—
That not one of you, whether fair or plain
(If any be), would he be quick to thwart—
To make you beg relief or help in vain.

The Second

I dispatched in haste to you[364]
This messenger, in order to
Say just two little words, for I
Had not the time to write them by:
So you'd best trust him faithfully,
The same as you would do for me—
    By one who underneath each wing
    Has maidens' hearts he's harboring.[365]

The Third

Love, who reached my inner core
With praises of your well known graces,
Rushed me so, that long I tore,
Risking roads with holes galore
(Destroyed by rain, with mud-pocked spaces),
And saddle-sleeping, too, I bore—
To come see your angelic faces:
Where I'd find rudeness if the case is
That after running all this distance,
I not be helped by your assistance.

Le quart

Si vous voulez, qu'Amour, ce puissant Dieu,
Aye chez vous tant soit petite place:
Certes il veult loger tout au milieu,
Et plus hault lieu de vostre bonne grace.
Si le voulez, je vous puis dire en face,
Que, nonobstant que je sois son Courrier,
Si veult il bien que tant vers vous je face,
Que je lui serve à present de fourrier.

Le cinquieme

Ce petit Dieu, qui s'est fait maistre
Des tendres cœurs des Damoiselles,
M'ha fait, je ne say comment, naistre
Un doux espoir plein d'estincelles,
Que, qui court pour Dames si belles,
Ne souffre travail, ny esmoy.
S'il est vray, je ne veux pour elles
Espargner mon cheval, ny moy.

The Fourth

If unto Love—that God whose powers are great—
You grant even the slightest space among you,
He's sure to want to lodge within your gate:
In good favor, to inmost parts break through;
And though I'm just his messenger, it's true,
I still can tell you, if you like, straight out:
There's so much for you he would have me do,
That I now serve him as his forward scout.[366]

The Fifth

This little God, who is master now
Over tender hearts of Damozels,[367]
Has caused in me to grow, somehow,
A hope that sweetly, sparkling, swells:
That whoever runs for such fair belles
Will from suffering cares be freed.[368]
If this be true, no wish compels
My sparing, for them, my self or steed.

LXXII
[Epigramme LX]

Pour une anathomie

Qui bien voudra contempler l'Univers,
Où du grand Dieu le grand pouvoir abonde
En elements, et animaux divers,
En Ciel, et Terre, et Mer large et profonde,
Vienne voir l'homme, où la Machine ronde
Est toute enclose, et plus, qui bien le prend.
Car pour soy seul, en ce sien petit monde
Ha tout comprins celui, qui tout comprend.

72
[Epigram 60]

Anatomy Lesson[369]

If one would know the Universe, and sense
How the great power of God overflows
In all its diverse beasts and elements—
Of Land and Sky, the wide Sea's deep repose—
Let him view man, within whose confine shows[370]
The round Machine, and more, for those who see—[371]
Since this, for him alone, did He enclose[372]
In his small world—all, comprehensively.

~

LXXIII
[Epître II]

A un sot rimeur, qui trop l'importunoit d'aymer

Tu te plains, que plus ne rimasse,
Bien qu'un temps fut que plus aymasse
A estendre vers rimassez,
Que d'avoir biens sans rime assez:
Mais je voy, que qui trop rimoye,
Sus ses vieux jours en fin larmoye.
Car qui s'amuse à rimacher,
A la fin n'ha rien à mascher.
Et pource donq rime, rimache,
Rimone tant, et rime hache,
Qu'avecques toute ta rimaille
N'ayes, dont tu sois marri, maille:
Et tu verras qu'à ta rimasse
Comme moy feras la grimace,
Maudisant et blasmant la rime,
Et le rimasseur, qui la rime,
Et le premier, qui rimona,
Pour le grand bien, qu'en rime on ha.
Et tu veux qu'à ta rimaillerie
Celui, qui n'aura maille, rie?
Je te quitte, maistre rimeur,
Et qui plus ha en sa rime heur,
En rime los, en rime honneurs,
Ensemble tous telz rimonneurs.

73
[Epistle 2]

To a Foolish Rhymer, Pestering Too Much For Love[373]

You complain: I've ceased my little rhymes;
Sure, I loved more in former times
Displaying many a rhyming verse
Than having no rhymes and ample purse.[374]
But too much rhyming through the years,
I see, brings old age on with tears.
Those amused by verse creation
Leave no room for rumination;
Composing ditties more and more—
Gnawing, hacking—what's it for?
That you have not, with rhymes so many,
Oh, vexation!—half a penny.
With paltry meter, you will see,
You'll make wry faces, just like me;
Blame the meter, rail in curses
At the rhymer and the verses;
At him whom meter first enchanted—
And all the good it ever granted.
You think that at such rhyming chaff
The penniless will ever laugh?
O, Master Rhymester, I leave you here,
And all who, rhyming, get more cheer—
And fame, and praise—mere social climbers,
The lot of you, such petty rhymers.[375]

Epitaphes de la gentile et spirituelle
Dame Pernette du Guillet
dicte cousine, trespassee
L'an M. D. XXXXV.
Le XVII. de
Juillet.

M. Sc.

L'heureuse cendre aultresfois composee
En un corps chaste, où Vertu reposa,
Est en ce lieu par les Graces posee
Parmy ses os, que Beaulté composa.
　　Ô Terre indigne: en toy son repos a
Le riche Estuy de celle Ame gentile
En tout sçavoir sur toute aultre subtile,
Tant que les Cieulx, par leur trop grand envie,
Avant ses jours l'ont d'entre nous ravie
Pour s'enrichir d'un tel bien mescongneu:
Au Monde ingrat laissant honteuse vie,
Et longue mort à ceulx, qui l'ont congneu.

Epitaphs of the noble, spiritual
Lady Pernette du Guillet,
called cousin, deceased
in the year 1545,
the 17th of
July.

M. Sc.[376]

These fortunate ashes that made up a chaste
Body in times now past—where Virtue stayed
Awhile—on this spot by the Graces are placed,
Among her bones that Beauty once arrayed.
    O undeserving Earth! In you is laid
This rich casing of a gentle Soul, whose quest[377]
For learning extended far beyond the rest;
So that the Heavens, envious, time not come,
Stole her from our midst to enrich their sum
With such a bounty, rarely known—leaving
The harsh World to a life of opprobrium
And all who knew her to a long death, grieving.

Aultre

Beaulté mortelle icy en vain souspire,
Puis que la Mort le corps soubdain ravit.
Mais Vertu vive, et qui jamais n'empire,
Comme l'Esprit au Ciel, en Terre vit.

Si grand Esprit se sentant à malaise
D'estre en son corps estroictement enclos,
Comme un gros feu en estroicte fournaise,
Ne peut durer longuement en son clos.
    Aussi à fin que plus ne fust forclos
De sa celeste, et eternelle envie,
Laissa son Nom avec immortel los
Vivre pour luy ceste caducque vie.

Another[378]

Mortal beauty here breathes but in vain:[379]
The flesh through thieving Death is swiftly gone;
But Virtue, yet alive, to never wane—
Just like the Soul in Heaven, on Earth lives on.

~

So immense a Soul, feeling out of place
To be thus in her body close, confined—
Like great fire in a narrow oven space—
Could not endure for long within its bind.
Ah, to be no more exiled! Still pined
The Soul for things eternal, heavenly,
And left her Name in immortal praise behind,
Having lived in her this life—frail brevity.

~

D. V. Z.

Onc Perle nette en vif, et petit monde
Son per n'eut tant en sçavoir, et faconde,
Que ceste n'ayt amoindry, qui gist cy:
De qui l'esprit par Mort non obscurcy
Demonstra bien, durant sa maladie,
Quelz sainctz propos, sçavoirs, et melodie
Elle avoit sceu, et apprins de soymesmes,
Tant qu'à sa fin proposa si haultz thesmes,
Qu'on la disoit, comme le mourant Cygne,
Se sentir jà immortelle, et voysine
Des bienheureux: si vertu, et sçavoir
Font aux humains la place aux Cieulx avoir.

J. D. V.

Une en son per nette, cousine, et sœur
De tout hault bien, suyvant le chemin seur,
Merite los par l'esprit d'elle veu
De tant de biens, et de sçavoirs pourveu,
Qu'on l'estimoit (en l'estat des Bourgeoises)
Un parangon entre les Lyonnoises.
    Sa maladie onc ne la peut grever:
Car on la veit si haultement resver
En sainctz propos, et tresplaisantz devis,
Qu'en se mourant, comme les Sainctz ravis,
Feit telle fin, que malingz souhaitterent
Ainsi mourir, et les bons desirerent
Telle vertu, et tel sçavoir ensuyvre,
Qui l'Ame au Ciel, et son Nom faict cy vivre.

R. I. P.

D. V. Z.[380]

Never in this small world lived Pearl so pure—
Matched in learning and eloquent allure—[381]
That could outshine the one now resting here:
Whose soul, undiminished within Death's sphere,
Showed so well, beset by malady's cares,
What saintly words of wisdom, what sweet airs,
She knew—and which continued, themselves, to extend:
Reaching such lofty discourse in the end,
That it was said, she—like the dying Swan—
Felt herself immortal, nearly gone
To the chosen ones. A wise and virtuous mind
Thus paves the way to Heaven for humankind.[382]

J. D. V.[383]

Cousin, sister, one in her pairing pure,[384]
Choosing the path of the highest good most sure,
Merits praise for her mind seen to be
Full of goodness and learning, so that she,
Of all the citizenry, was looked upon
By the ladies of Lyon as paragon.[385]
    Her illness never could aggrieve her mind
For she revealed, in reverie refined,
Such sacred words and pleasing thoughts recalled
That in her dying, like the Saints enthralled,
She achieved such end that wicked ones aspired
To die in just that way and the good desired
To follow her in virtue and great learning—
Her soul to Heaven, her Name to life returning.[386]

R. I. P.[387]

Translation Notes

"ANTOINE DU MOULIN TO THE LADIES OF LYON"

1. From 1544 until his death in 1551, Antoine du Moulin was editor, collaborator and translator for Jean de Tournes in Lyon. For a biography of Du Moulin, see Alfred Cartier and Adolphe Chenevière, "Antoine Du Moulin, Valet de chambre de la Reine de Navarre," *Revue d'histoire littéraire de la France* 2 (1895), 469–90. For comments on the collaboration between Du Moulin and the printer, see Davis, "Le monde de l'imprimerie humaniste: Lyon," 266. On the complex relationships between printer, editor, and female author, see Chang, *Into Print*, chap. 1. On the editorial strategies of Jean de Tournes and Antoine du Moulin with regard to this and other books they published in 1545, see Rajchenbach, "'Tu le pourras clerement icy veoir'," 123–35.

From the very beginning of his prefatory letter, Du Moulin defines a target audience: the ladies of Lyon, particularly the "virtuous Ladies" ("Dames vertueuses")—worthy readers who will recognize, value, and emulate the good in this collection and the virtues of its deceased author.

As was typical in books printed in this era, Du Moulin's preface appears without any paragraph divisions in the 1545 edition. I have added paragraph breaks and sentence divisions where they seemed logical, in order to make the text more accessible to modern readers.

2. Du Moulin's opening remarks reflect not only a timeless observation on human nature, but also the popular Renaissance Neoplatonist notion that like souls are attracted to one another. For more about this concept, see n280 for poem 65.

3. Although *vertu* in Du Guillet's poetry is associated with learning, eloquence, and intellectual merit, Du Moulin uses the term to refer to the moral qualities of purity and chastity prescribed for women. See Yandell, *Carpe Corpus*, chap. 3, and Jones, *Currency of Eros*, chap. 3. See also Jan Boney's discussion of virtue and virtuosity in the *Rymes* ("Ardeur de veoir"). The adjective *gentil*, sometimes meaning mild and gracious, was also used in titles to indicate the elevated social status of the bearer, as in the case of *Gentilhomme*, or Gentleman. The two meanings are not mutually exclusive; here each would serve the purpose of the editor's description of the young female poet, both noble and gracious. The third adjective attributed to the poet, *spirituelle*, did not have a decidedly religious connotation in the mid-sixteenth century, representing characteristics linked to the *esprit* (of the spirit, but also of the mind, including wit, and intellectual vivacity), as opposed to corporeal or worldly qualities. The initial "D" that appears before the poet's name here—and in the title of the volume—remains a mystery. It could perhaps simply stand for "Dame" (Lady), but that word is already included in full, so the addition of the initial would be redundant. In the extensive bibliography of his edition of Scève's *Délie*, Gérard Defaux suggests the initial "D" may refer to a given name that perhaps the poet or her editor did not wish to reveal, or to the figure of Délie, object of desire in Scève's *canzoniere*. See *Délie*, ccii–cciii.

4. The expression, "petit amas de rymes," establishes dual and conflicting associations. On the one hand, as Sébillet explains in his 1548 *Art poétique françois*, the terms *rimes* and *rimeurs* refer to the works of lesser writers, whereas *poètes* and *poèmes* are the appropriate terms for those whose eloquence in French warrants the more prestigious label (*Traités de poétiques et de rhétorique de la Renaissance*, 56). Du Guillet's poem 73, entitled "To a Foolish Rhymer" ("A un sot rimeur"), plays on this pejorative terminology, as inspired by Marot. The phrase "petit amas" (little bundle, pile, or gathering) presents the collected poems in a belittling light, diminishing their worth. The word *Rymes* itself, however, chosen as title of the collection, also carries with it the prestige of Petrarch's popular and influential *canzoniere* of love poetry, the *Rime sparse*. (See the Introduction to this volume for more comments on this association.) Throughout his preface, Du Moulin presents a conflicting view of the poems to follow. On the one hand, they are unpolished and unfinished—a modest beginning. On the other hand, they show tremendous potential, reflecting a "celeste engin" (celestial mind/spirit/wisdom) with the power to inspire other women to literary pursuits and devotion to virtue.

5. *ses accointées*: The feminine plural form reminds us that Du Moulin addresses in particular the ladies of Lyon—those who knew the poet personally (in private company), and those who never had that chance, but who will benefit from reading her poetry.

6. In this passage, I was inspired by several "felicitous" phrases in Cathy Yandell's partial translation of Du Moulin's preface (*Carpe Corpus*, 91).

7. The editor expresses his amazement at how much the young poet was able to accomplish in her short life. For an analysis of the role and meaning of time, both in Du Moulin's preface and in the *Rymes*, see Yandell, *Carpe Corpus*, chap. 3, and "Carpe Diem, Poetic Immortality."

8. Music was an important accomplishment for educated upper class women and men, and four of Pernette du Guillet's poems were published in songbooks in Paris and Lyon in her lifetime. The lute, in particular, was associated with poets and the art of poetry, and this instrument plays a role in Du Guillet's poem 43. See the notes for poem 43 and the introduction for more on the lute as metaphor for the poet's art.

9. "Literature and all good learning" is an approximate rendition of the original expression, "les bonnes lettres," which Huguet defines as "lettres, littérature, science," citing numerous examples from such sixteenth-century authors as Rabelais, Du Bellay, and Montaigne. Cotgrave defines the expression simply and broadly as "learning." Philippe Caron explains that the term "bonnes lettres" represents a concept unique to the Renaissance, encompassing the rediscovered and renewed texts of the classics, pagan and Christian authors, and literature, philosophy, and theology. All of this learning reflected the "good" in humanity and was "good" for those who studied it. See Caron, *Des <<belles lettres>> à la <<littérature>>, une archéologie des signes du savoir profane en langue française (1680–1760)* (Louvain: Diffusion Peeters, 1992), 152–53. Marie-Madeleine de la Garanderie elaborates: "Les lettres sont bonnes, c'est-à-dire précieuses, importantes, utiles, bénéfiques. […] Elles sont la culture unique et totale, la nourriture complète de l'esprit: science et sagesse,

éloquence et poésie" (Letters are good, that is to say precious, important, useful, beneficial. [...] They are the unique and total culture, the complete nourishment of the mind/soul: science/knowledge and wisdom, eloquence and poetry). *Christianisme et lettres profanes: Essai sur l'Humanisme français (1515–1535) et sur la pensée de Guillaume de Budé* (Paris: Champion, 1995), 32–33. See both of these studies for a discussion of the transition in the seventeenth century to the concept of *belles lettres.*

10. The "Thuscan" (or Tuscan) language—that of Dante and Petrarch—was both a model and a rival with French in this period, as humanists sought to create a literature in the vernacular to equal that of the ancients. Because of its geographical location and financial situation, Lyon was home to many wealthy merchants and bankers from Italy, and the Italian language and culture had a significant impact on the city's artistic and literary elite. Two epigrams in Italian in the *Rymes* offer evidence of Du Guillet's command of the language. As for Spanish ("Castillan"), we have no way of knowing whether Pernette du Guillet spoke the language, or to what degree. The title of poem 64, "Conde Claros," refers to a Spanish romance, or to the well-known tune associated with it, but the reference is probably to the melody and the musical tradition, rather than to the romance itself, since Du Guillet's topic is the classical myth of Adonis's death, inspired by French and Greek models.

11. The poems themselves give no direct indication of the poet's knowledge of Latin, but the language of ancient Rome was central to humanist education in the Renaissance. If Pernette du Guillet received the type of education implied in Du Moulin's preface, Latin would have been part of it. The primary source of inspiration for "Conde Claros de Adonis" (poem 64) is a Greek text. Wordplay in two of her epigrams is based on Greek words: *callimera* ("bonjour"/hello) in poem 49, and *imera* ("jour"/day) in poem 50.

12. *digne de lumière*: worthy of being brought to light, i.e., of publication.

13. *de divers lieux*: in different places, perhaps in different rooms of the house.

14. *confusément extraits*: This phrase is difficult to translate. It could mean either "written/ copied out in a confused manner" or "drawn out/taken/culled" (from among the many papers) in no apparent order or with difficulty. I have chosen to use the phrase "pulled together haphazardly" to convey the confused state of the poet's papers as found by her grieving husband and the editor. The "rather poor order" of her scattered papers and drafts ("broullars"), mentioned a few lines earlier, may refer as much to the state of completion of the works as to their arrangement, particularly since the conclusion of that sentence observes that the poet must not have felt her works were polished enough to be ready for publication. Barataud and Trudeau suggest in their edition that, "par 'ordre' il faut entendre, le polissage, la dernière main, plutôt que la disposition des pièces" (by order we must understand refinement, the final touch of the poet's hand, rather than the disposition of the pieces). *Rymes*, 33. In any case, the overall message is clear: the papers, appearing to be drafts, possibly hastily written, were found scattered in different places or rooms of the house, with no apparent organization. For more on the poetic tradition of the discovered manuscript, see Perrine Galand-Hallyn and Fernand Hallyn, "'Recueillir des brouillars': Ethique de la silve et poétique du manuscrit trouvé," in *Le poète et son œuvre,* 9–34.

15. Du Moulin stresses here that this poetry was composed and recited for friends in private company.

16. *recréer*: to delight or please, and also to give comfort or solace. Both shades of meaning apply in this context, given the earlier mention of the grief suffered by the deceased poet's friends and by those who would know her only through her poetry.

17. When referring to the celebrated "Ladies of Italy," Du Moulin may have been thinking of Vittoria Colonna (ca. 1490–1547) and Veronica Gambara (1485–1550), both well-born women whose works include poetry in the Petrarchan tradition.

18. *quelque bigerre cerveau*: Cotgrave defines "bigearre, or bigerre" as "odde, humorous, fantasticall;" the Larousse *Dictionnaire du moyen français* defines this adjective as "qui s'écarte des usages reçus; singulier, extravagant" (that which deviates from normal usage; singular/odd, extravagant). "Cerveau" literally means "brain," but Cotgrave's dictionary gives several uses of the word used in pejorative expressions to refer to individuals (lawyers, monks, etc.), which led to the choice of "some odd fellow" for this translation.

19. Here and in the concluding passage, Du Moulin recognizes the danger and harmful impact of readers of bad faith—those who may be motivated by envy to take this poetry the wrong way. These are perhaps the same readers to whose slander or false accusations the poet responds in poem 42.

20. *cecy*: The pronoun refers to "this work/collection/book" (i.e., this "little bundle of rhymes") and therefore, by extension, "these poems."

21. According to the first edition of the *Dictionnaire de l'Académie française* (1694), the expression, "En estre à cent lieuës-, n'en approcher pas de cent lieuës," was used to indicate that what a person thinks or proposes is far removed from reality or the facts.

22. *Les Asnes voisent tousjours à leurs chardons:* Cotgrave's dictionary cites the proverb, "Laissons aux asnes les chardons," meaning, "Let Asses feed on thistles; leave unto poorer spirits dull conceits." The idea is similar here, that asses will always be drawn to or seek out their thistles; they cannot appreciate any finer fare.

"TO THE READER FROM THE PRINTER"

23. This liminary poem by the printer, Jean de Tournes, echoes the points made by Antoine du Moulin in his preface, emphasizing that virtuous, chaste love forms the basis of the poems to follow. See the Introduction for more comments on these paratextual elements.

POEM 1

24. This epigram clearly associates the speaker's happy destiny with the higher powers of the heavenly planets. The age-old belief that events in the heavens affect those on earth came

to the Renaissance from Aristotle and other classical philosophers. European writers of this era saw no inherent contradiction between Christian revelation and the prediction of events through astrology. The fifteenth-century Italian Neoplatonist, Marsilio Ficino, for example, published a commentary on Plato's dialogue on love, the *Symposium*, and a treatise entitled, *On Christian Religion*. Another of Ficino's works, *Platonic Theology*, demonstrates the unity between classical ideas and Christian beliefs concerning the immortality of the soul. (See the Introduction for a discussion of the influence of Ficino and the Italian Neoplatonists on Pernette du Guillet's vision of love in the cosmos.) Note that in poem 33, however, the speaking subject appears to reject astrological divination in favor of truths revealed through her beloved's enlightening presence.

25. The expression "well served" ("servie") reflects the concept of *service d'amour*, the devotion demonstrated by the beloved for his lady in the medieval tradition of courtly love.

26. *dont*: Cotgrave's dictionary indicates that in sixteenth-century usage, the word "dont" could mean "whence," "whereby," or "whereupon." The word is frequently used in this sense in the *Rymes*.

27. This line highlights the physical act of inscribing or printing words and images on a page. The verb "regraver" expresses the technical process of engraving, as well as the suggested repetition of that activity. As noted in the Introduction, the term "impression" refers to an edition and to the printing process itself. The adjective "dure," meaning both physically hard and intellectually difficult, recalls the "durs Epygrammes" of Maurice Scève's opening *huitain* to his *Délie*. Reflecting the origin of the epigram in Antiquity, the phrase "deep impression" in English evokes the words and images engraved deeply and with difficulty into metal or stone, suggesting the intensity of the poet's work, and the effort required by the reader seeking to discern the truth therein. For further commentary on this poem and the verb "regraver," see Jones, *Currency*, 88.

28. The juxtaposition of "passion's sweet progression" and "cruel love" echoes the traditional antithesis of Petrarchan love poetry. Here, however, we learn that the speaker will rise above the Petrarchan suffering by contemplating the noble qualities of the beloved who has inspired her.

29. In line 8, the somewhat ambiguous "where" ("où") denotes the speaker's lifeless state before her beloved's arrival, but it also refers to the "dure impression" of line 6, where "that divinity" makes frequent appearances, that is to say in her (printed) poems.

30. The use of the adjective "hault" in both the first and last lines of the epigram points to the importance of the noble and lofty qualities attributed to the beloved male poet. The term "qualité" in the sixteenth century encompassed the notions of goodness and nobility that many of the poems in the *Rymes* associate with the beloved. Cotgrave's dictionary also indicates "calling" as a contemporary meaning of "qualité," which would suggest that Du Guillet describes not only her beloved's noble virtues, but also his poetic vocation, which she now contemplates as her own. The combination of "divinité" (line 8) and the verb

"contempler" (line 10) underscores the speaker's attitude of reverence toward her beloved and his virtues.

POEM 2

31. Darkness (of night or at midday) is a recurring metaphor in the *Rymes* for the state of the poet's mind and spirit before the illumination brought to her by the eloquence and learning of her beloved. See the Introduction for a discussion of this motif in the Petrarchan tradition.

32. The dawn's illumination—rays of light from her beloved—disperse the troubling darkness of ignorance, allowing the speaker not only to *see* the colors around her, but also to begin to *speak*. Her first words, proclaimed aloud, are of praise for her beloved. The phrase "à voix haultaine" can mean simply, "in a loud voice; loudly," but the adjective "haultaine" also suggests the lofty and exalted nature of the subject's new-found voice.

33. In numerous poems in the collection, the speaker identifies her beloved as her Day ("Jour"), bringing enlightenment to her through love and—more importantly—through his writing and his learned eloquence. This epigram focuses on the moment of dawn, when light and love appear on the horizon—what poetic tradition calls the *innamoramento*. The pronoun "Him" ("Celuy") is somewhat ambiguous in the context of the last line, leaving room for two different (and complementary) interpretations. The pronoun may refer to the beloved male poet himself, with the "Morn" ("ce Jour") indicating the daylight and enlightenment the beloved brings to the speaker at the moment her love and voice are awakened. Alternately, "Him" ("Celuy") may refer to a Divine Maker—the God who created this Day for the speaker, making her moment of awakening possible. This Creator God is associated with the celestial promise evoked in the first epigram. See the Translator's Note for Finch's reflections on this line in the French and in the English.

POEM 3

34. Here, as elsewhere, the speaker praises her beloved's *sçavoir* (his learning, knowledge, and erudition), which she associates with light and with virtue.

35. The reference to the Heavens ("les Cieux"), here and in line 7, echoes the belief that events in the cosmos affect events on earth, an element of classical philosophy that the Renaissance Neoplatonists reconciled with Christian teachings. See above, n24.

36. In Greek mythology, the three Graces—Aglaia, Euphrosyne, and Thalia—were daughters of Zeus, and the sea-nymph Eurynome. These three goddesses of joy, charm, and beauty, attendants of Aphrodite, joined with the Muses to sing for the gods and dance to music played by Apollo on his lyre. It was believed that the Graces, along with the Muses, bestowed the ability to create beauty in art and poetry. It is not surprising to find them associated in this epigram with the beloved, whom the poet elsewhere compares to Apollo (notably in poems 4, 43, and 61). Here, the three Graces are held in happy servitude to the male poet

because of his great virtue and learning. Scève, too, used the image of the Graces encircling or embracing his lady's many virtues: "l'Ame, où Graces tiennent ceinctes / Mille Vertus" (the Soul, where Graces hold enclosed / a Thousand Virtues). *Délie*, CXXVII, 61.

The description of the Graces serving the beloved calls to mind not only the Greek goddesses' attendance on Apollo in classical mythology, but also the rapport of the lover with his lady in the courtly love and Petrarchan poetic traditions. Here, however, it is the divine ladies—the Graces—who are content in their *servitude* to the beloved, because of the many gifts of virtue and learning he possesses. If the goddesses are so captivated, then the reader may be able to comprehend and appreciate the lament of the speaker, who claims *not* to possess the knowledge or quickness of mind to thank the Heavens properly for her beloved's immense talents. In this lament, as we see repeatedly in the *Rymes*, the poem itself reveals anything but a "dearth of learning" on the part of the young poet.

37. With regard to women in the Renaissance, the word *vertu* generally referred to chastity, as is the case in Antoine du Moulin's preface. When applied to men, the term typically encompassed both physical and moral force. The virtues attributed to the beloved in the *Rymes*, however, are his learning and eloquence. As Jan Boney explains, "In du Guillet's poetry *vertu* undergoes an amazing shift, referring to the beloved's poetry as it takes on a meaning most nearly rendered in English by 'virtuosity,' a meaning that was closer to the Italian adjective 'virtuoso.' *Vertu* refers to her beloved's intelligence and to his writing" ("Ardeur de veoir," 54). See also Yandell's study of the concept of *vertu* in the *Rymes* in *Carpe Corpus*, chap. 3.

POEM 4

38. In the French of this period, and in the context of the *Rymes*, *esprit*—"spirit"—refers to the mind and intellect, rather than the soul ("âme").

39. In the *Rymes*, the beloved male poet is often compared to Apollo—Greek and Roman god of poetry and music—whose divinity is linked with the light of the Sun.

40. The association of "source" and "flow" ("onde") with learned virtue evokes the mythological Castalian spring on Mount Parnassus, sacred to Apollo and the Muses and source of poetic inspiration. In this epigram, the beloved—compared to Apollo—*is* the source and the flow of virtue and learning. In line 8, the beloved's pen is characterized as pouring forth its eloquence.

41. *le bien*: The good is an important element in Pernette du Guillet's poetry, founded primarily on the Neoplatonic notion of the ideal Good and also encompassing the more general meaning of goodness and virtue.

42. The epigram concludes with yet another association of the beloved's eloquent writing with the flowing stream of poetic inspiration evoked in lines 4 and 8. The word "style" ("stille") referred to a manner of speaking or writing, with "hault stille" indicating the noblest type of written expression. The word derives etymologically from the *stylus*, a pointed object used for writing or engraving words on waxed tablets in late Antiquity and

the Middle Ages. The "riches seen to stream in noble style" of line 10 echo and reinforce the image of the "sweet pen gently pouring forth" in line 8, and the notion of the "source" and "flow" of virtue in line 4. Citing the conclusion of this epigram, Jan Boney argues that the verb "to see" ("veoir") may often be glossed as "to read" ("lire") in the *Rymes* ("Ardeur de veoir," 57). Josiane Rieu notes that it is the beloved's poetry above all—his "vertus poétiques"—that inspire the speaker's love and words of praise ("Poétique et réflexivité," 34).

POEM 5

43. Gisèle Mathieu-Castellani points out the ambiguity in the first line of this epigram, which could mean "you've made me known" ("tu m'as fait connaître") or "you've taught me to transform vice into virtue" ("tu m'as appris à muer vice en vertu") or "you've given me knowledge of myself" ("tu m'as donné connaissance de moi-même"). "La Parole chétive," 50. Finch's translation of this problematic line is based on the second of the variants noted by Mathieu-Castellani, which also encompasses the notion of self-knowledge. These various interpretations are not mutually exclusive, for the entire poem blurs the boundaries between the male poet's transformation of the woman and her own poetic efforts, her self-knowledge, and her identity as poet.

44. Du Guillet has inscribed Maurice Scève's name twice in this epigram in anagrammatic form, openly framing her lyric subjectivity in relationship to the other poet and identifying Scève as the beloved who inspires her. Even if other models and inspirations take precedence elsewhere in the collection, the epigrams grouped at the beginning of the volume project what Françoise Charpentier calls the "antithesis of night-Pernette-ignorance and day-Lover-knowledge," culminating in this epigram, which reveals the identity of the beloved ("Projet poétique," 147). The capital letters of the anagram in the French draw attention both to Scève's name—easily decipherable to Renaissance readers, familiar with this type of wordplay—and to the idea of transformation for the better. Finch has approximated the original anagrams, maintaining sounds and meaning very close to the French. Because the English versions are not exact anagrams, however, and because presenting them in capital letters would shift emphasis away from the notion of transformation and change (*se muer/mueras*) included in the originals, we used lower case letters in these lines in English. For more about the original French anagrams, see the notes by Barataud and Trudeau for this epigram (*Rymes*, 41–42).

45. This line reflects the popular Neoplatonic idea that virtuous, reciprocal love results in the spiritual union of two lovers—a union in which each soul becomes identical to the other and the two become one. Barataud and Trudeau suggest that, in this case, the movement is one-way, and it is the student who wishes to become the teacher (*Rymes*, 41). The original line may instead imply that this good ("ce bien") that has the power to transform her rests "solely" ("seul") in him, her beloved. In any case, the syntax of the line strongly suggests the theory of the transformation of the two lovers' souls into one, as elaborated by Ebreo and the other Italian Neoplatonists.

46. By her "due exertion"—her efforts to fulfill her duty in a manner equal to his ("par esgal office")—the speaker will flee ignorance in accordance with her beloved's transformative desires.

47. The phrase, "de noir en blanche," is translated here with the contrast of "dark" and "light," in keeping with the central metaphor of darkness and light in the *Rymes*. Boney notes that "this transformation, loaded with the conventional connotation of a change from evil to good, is a reversal (yet a recollection) of the poet's usual inky transformation of the white page" ("Ardeur de veoir," 53). Barataud and Trudeau suggest a possible musical interpretation of this line—that "une note blanche vaut deux noires" (one white note is worth two black), indicating perhaps an increase of value resulting from the process (*Rymes*, 42). Rajchenbach's edition proposes that the change from black to white may refer to the alchemical transformation of a lesser metal into silver, a metal associated with the moon and the feminine (*Rymes*, 122).

The notion of "service" (service, attendance, duty) in love recalls the second line of poem 1, and line 9 of poem 3, and recurs many times throughout the collection. Poem 43 bases an entire imaginary scene of seduction on the idea of *servitude*.

48. Petrarch describes his *giovenile errore* ("youthful error") in the opening sonnet of the *Rime sparse* (*Petrarch's Lyric Poems*, 37). The poet's *erreurs* represent a recurring topos in Petrarchan poetry, indicating both the imperfect work of the inexperienced poet *and* his youthful wanderings, before being struck by love and taken captive by Cupid's arrows. The first poems of Scève's *Délie* convey both meanings of the word. In the preliminary *huitain*, "A sa Délie," Scève acknowledges that the reader will find "mainte erreur, mesme en si durs Epygrammes" (many an error, even in such hard Epigrams). The first *dizain* of the *canzoniere* evokes "L'Œil trop ardent en mes jeunes erreurs" (The too ardent Eye, in my youthful wanderings), *Délie*, I, 4–5. In Du Guillet's poem 5, however, the *erreur* appears to refer primarily to the unpolished, youthful quality of her writing, which the light of the beloved's intellect has begun to transform. Along with gratitude for the beloved's transformative powers, Du Guillet's epigram recognizes the role her own efforts will play in the ongoing process of changing vice into virtue. The concept of *erreur* appears again in poems 7, 11, and 66. See François Rigolot's analysis of poems 5, 7, and 11 in *L'erreur de la Renaissance: Perspectives littéraires* (Paris: Champion, 2002), 80–86.

POEM 6

49. As Saulnier points out, this epigram was inspired by Jeanne Gaillarde's response to a *rondeau* by Clément Marot, first published in Marot's *L'adolescence clémentine* in 1529 (*Etude*, 37). In the "Responce au precedent rondeau, par la dicte Jehanne Gaillarde," the female speaker tells the male poet that if she were as eloquent and learned as he says she is, she would do her duty to pay her debt: "Si fusse autant eloquente, et apprise, / Comme tu dys, je feroys mon debvoir / De m'acquiter" (*Œuvres poétiques*, vol. 1, 143–44). Moreover, Du Guillet's pointed reference to her own ten-line *dizain* evokes Scève's use of the poetic form in his *Délie*. To counter the temptation to read the epigrams of the *Rymes* in a narrow autobiographical mode, it is helpful to remark the degree to which poems like this reflect an intertextual dialogue with numerous poets of the French and Italian Renaissance. See the Introduction for more on this aspect of Du Guillet's poetry.

50. The speaker insists, perhaps ironically, on her inability to do justice in her own verse to her beloved's virtues and extensive learning. Despite her apparent modesty, the poet

proceeds to display her skill at the task disclaimed. Du Guillet's stance of humility here recalls the classical *recusatio*, as it developed in late Antiquity and the Middle Ages, from a rhetorical device with political overtones to a more general lament of the poet's "feelings of inadequacy to celebrate the character and deeds of a *contemporary* political or cultural hero—the modest disclaimer characteristically serving as a pretext for doing the thing disclaimed." Joan G. Haahr, "Justifying Love: The Classical *Recusatio* in Medieval Love Literature," in *Desiring Discourses: The Literature of Love, Ovid through Chaucer*, ed. James J. Paxson and Cynthia Gravlee (Selinsgrove, PA: Susquehanna University Press, 1998), 41. *Recusatio* came to refer to poems on any subject, including love, in which the speaker expresses reluctance to write in a particular style, often based on a claim of inadequacy. Haahr explains that Ovid used the *recusatio* to elevate his love poetry to the same level of importance as epic poetry, a model that deeply influenced Renaissance poets (42).

51. As indicated in Greimas and Keane's *Dictionnaire du moyen français* (Larousse, 1992), the expression *a(d)vouer qqch à qqn* means "reconnaître que la chose est attribuable à" (to recognize that the thing/quality is attributable to someone). In other contexts, the verb *a(d) vouer* reflected its use in medieval feudal society, meaning to recognize someone as protégé and, conversely, to revere someone as lord and master. The relational overtones associated with this verb in this poem fascinated Finch, especially in light of Du Guillet's reference to her beloved as "maître" (meaning both teacher and master) in poems 30 and 58.

52. The poem's conclusion calls attention to the female writer's need for male learning (*sçavoir*) in order to praise her beloved within traditional patriarchal modes of discourse. For more comments on this epigram, see Jones, *Currency of Eros*, 85. Rieu points to this poem as an example of the way in which "games of symmetry" serve to reveal difference, highlighting a gap that invites readers to reflect on identity and the relationship between the self and the other at the heart of the *Rymes* ("Poétique et réflexivité," 35–36).

POEM 7

53. The letter "R" written somewhere on a ten-line *dizain*—perhaps in the margin—puzzles the speaker, who examines the possible meanings of this cryptic sign. Terms such as "comprendre" (to understand), "signifiant" (signifying), and "responce" (answer) highlight the process of interpretation and dialogue at the heart of this epigram.

54. "Errer" (line 4) and "erreur" (line 6) convey the related meanings of "to err" and "error," indicating that the "R"—which echoes the initial sound of both words in French—may imply praise mistakenly given to the speaker. The use of "errer" in line 10 encompasses both meanings of the verb; the speaker suggests that she will cause any man who praises her to err and/or to wander astray. In line 6, the speaker wonders if the letter "R" indicates "rien" (nothing) or "reste" (remainder). The entire epigram revolves around wordplay associated with the letter "R" and questions with humor the role of *erreurs* in love poetry and the entire Petrarchan tradition. For Gisèle Mathieu-Castellani, this poem represents the moment of emancipation of the student from the teacher ("La Parole chétive," 55). A possible source of inspiration for this epigram is a long poem by Jean Lemaire de Belges, entitled, "Ce sont les regretz de la dame infortunee, sur le trespas de son trescher frere unique," in which fifteen

lines are devoted to the associations of words beginning with the letter "M." Liliane Izzi identifies François Villon as another source because of his play on the sound of the letter "R" in the "Ballade à s'amie" and his rejection of the courtly tradition ("Lecture d'un dizain de Pernette du Guillet," in *Courrier du Centre international d'études poétiques*, 200 [October-November 1993], 15–41).

55. Uncertainty reigns as to the meaning of the "R," but the speaker eventually proposes a hypothetical resolution in the last line of the epigram, based on a possible interpretation that attributes power to herself (and to her poetry), and one that belies the tentative tone leading up to the conclusion.

56. The speaker's boast in the closing line includes a subtle reminder that she herself has provoked a problem of interpretation. Regarding the poet's use of "erreur" here, Rigolot concludes, "Pernette a beau jouer les modestes et avouer l'insuffisance de son «sçavoir» (v. 8), elle y met tant de talent qu'on finit par admirer ses artifices" (In vain Pernette feigns modesty and claims the inadequacy of her learning; she does so with such talent that we end up admiring the subtleties of her art). *L'erreur*, 86.

POEM 8

57. Epigram 8 returns to the fundamental juxtaposition of the troubling dark night of ignorance with the sweet light brought by her Day's love and learning. Whereas poem 2 describes the darkness (as if it were night at midday) that shrouded the speaker's life before the arrival of her beloved's light and love, poem 8 depicts a different experience. Even in the darkest night, the sweet light of her Day illuminates her world, allowing her mind/spirit (*esprit*) to perceive that which she could never see with her eyes. See also poem 68, "The Night," where the speaker gives full rein to the troubling darkness of night and ignorance, before the eventual arrival of the beloved Day with light to chase away the monsters of the night.

58. See the Introduction for a discussion of how Du Guillet deepens and moves beyond the Petrarchan antithesis (Day/Night) in this epigram, departing from the models available to her, including Scève's *Délie*.

POEM 9

59. A similar phrase, "du Ciel ce tant heureux povoir," appears in Scève's *dizain* 127 (*Délie*, 61) to indicate his lady's divinely inspired capacity to enrich the soul through the mind ("l'esprit"). For more on *dizain* 127 and Du Guillet's poem 9, see Yandell, *Carpe Corpus*, 103–105.

60. The beloved's extensive learning (a divine gift) allows him to succeed—to reach his aim—despite the troubles and adversity that Fortune brings his way. His knowledge, erudition, and eloquence constitute the virtue that allows him to come out on top in many a dispute or controversy. This poem tells us that as long as her beloved is content—having

surmounted adversity—then the speaker, too, will be content. The notion of mutual contentment through the exercise of learning is a leitmotif of the *Rymes*.

POEM 10

61. The ring offered as a sign of love was a familiar topos in Petrarchist poetry of the Italian and French Renaissance. See the Introduction for more about this tradition and a discussion of Du Guillet's epigram in relation to Scève's *dizains* 347 and 349, which share the theme of a ring given by the lady to her beloved. Du Guillet's poem 10 is addressed to the beloved, however, not to the ring itself, as are Scève's *dizains*. Susan Delaney points out that Scève addresses his lady, "Délie," only metonymically, through her finger and hand, in a "type of representational violence" that dehumanizes its object ("Lyric Dialogue," 823). The tradition of the poetic *blason* and *contreblason* provides another example of this "representational violence" that, even when ostensibly praising the lady or some part of her body, effectively dehumanizes the female object, substituting an isolated part for the whole, which subsequently recedes or disappears. (Scève himself contributed a winning *blason* on the eyebrow to a competition launched by Clément Marot.) Scève's *dizain* 347 addresses the ring, speaking of its connection with the finger that once wore it, on the hand that gave it to him. For the *dizain's* speaker, the ring serves as a sign of his everlasting captivity, rather than of his lady's eternal devotion. If Pernette du Guillet's poem is a response to Scève's *dizain*, the response includes a refusal to enter into the process of objectification through metonymy, choosing instead to address words of reproach and advice directly to the beloved. While participating in the lyric exchange, however, Du Guillet's ring poem displays no overt linguistic signs of the speaker's gender, nor of the beloved's, lending a universal perspective to the epigram when read on its own.

62. *racheptable*: Cotgrave translates this adjective as "redeemable, ransomable, recoverable for money." The word conveys both spiritual and commercial connotations in the original—a perfect choice for this context, in which the speaker admonishes her beloved to esteem the ring, *not* for the precious gold of which it is made, but for what the ring and its diamond will tell him about her enduring love.

63. The speaker's concluding explanation of the importance that the ring should have for her beloved—and her reproach to him for his inclination to forget her devotion—responds to Scève's *dizain*, which presents the lady's hand and the ring as a weapon that imprisons him. Delaney points out that Du Guillet's epigram "re-humanizes" the hand and redeems "its loving intentions" ("Lyric Dialogue," 825).

POEM 11

64. The opening lines of this epigram recognize the power of the body over the mind; physical desires blind the mind, keeping it from seeing or realizing the power of reason. "Error" has blindfolded her; she cannot see what matters because of the distractions of physical desire. On the use of *erreur* in this epigram, as well as in poems 5, 7, and 11, see Rigolot, *L'erreur*, 80–86.

65. "Such pure good" ("Si hault bien") encompasses the beloved's goodness and virtue, including his learning, which the speaker cannot see because of the blindfold of ignorance she wears. Poem 13 invokes the "Dieu aveuglé"—the blind god, Cupid, who is often depicted as wearing a blindfold—but in this poem it is the speaker who cannot see, emphasizing the dangerous effects of physical attraction. The conflict of physical desire and a nobler type of love is also the topic of poem 12.

66. The conclusion of the epigram differentiates between seeing (through physical vision) and knowing (understanding with the insights of reason and learning), recalling poem 8, which praises the Day's sweet light and its capacity to allow the lady's mind and spirit to perceive that which she could never see with her eyes. Poem 11 appears to evoke a time when the speaker was blinded, presumably by desire, to the beloved's goodness and learned virtue. Although her eyes could see him, she did not know his true nature.

POEM 12

67. The first *quatrain* paints the pleasure that fills the speaker as she is overcome with physical desire, governed by the god of Love.

68. The second *quatrain* offers advice on how to vanquish this *Amour*. Leaving behind or passing beyond physical desire ("celle envie") will destroy Cupid's power, causing him to attack himself with his own arrows. This will destroy the baser sort of love he causes and bring new life to the Lovers, whose love will now move on to a purer level of spirit and intellect.

POEM 13

69. This poem and *dizain* 136 of Scève's *Délie* both evoke the duality of happiness and pain in love and the way that love, inflicted by the "blind god" Cupid, unifies the two lovers in their experience. Within the shared thematic and lexical framework, Scève's *dizain* concludes with the wish that both lovers continue to feel this sweet death as long as they breathe, emphasizing the involuntary nature of the experience. Du Guillet's epigram, however, focuses on the honorable nature of love and its effects, concluding with a wish that both lovers will have long-lasting contentment. See the Introduction for further discussion of the intertextual dialogue between these two poems.

70. The flames of love distill the two hearts into one "heed" or duty ("devoir"). The image of flames distilling a substance into its purest essence evokes the medieval tradition of alchemy. For other examples of this image in sixteenth-century poetry, see Barataud and Trudeau, *Rymes*, 127. Duty as the distilled essence of the love experience is a unique characteristic of Pernette du Guillet's philosophy and poetics of love.

71. The blind god Cupid ("Dieu aveuglé") wounds the lovers, but their suffering is "worthy" in the love esthetic of the *Rymes*. Cottrell observes that Du Guillet's epigram includes three expressions that do not appear in Scève's *dizain* 136: "devoir," "honnorable" and "contentement durable" ("An Adventure in Ideal Love," 569). Jones demonstrates that

"it is precisely through deviations in their use of a common vocabulary that each writer establishes a distinct textual identity" (*Currency of Eros*, 91). Yandell points out that Pernette du Guillet's reference to "noz espritz" in the last line of this poem further emphasizes "the spiritual union of the lovers and not simply their common condition" ("Carpe Diem," 119).

POEM 14

72. The sublimation of desire must be accompanied by spiritual love. In Neoplatonic theory, physical love is important for the generation of the species, whereas spiritual love leads the lovers to a nobler union of spirit and intellect. See the Introduction for a discussion of this aspect of Neoplatonism.

73. Finch bases her translation of line 7, "One longs for death—though not without delay," on a reading of the object pronoun, "l'" (it), as referring to the desired death ("on veult mourir") at the beginning of the line. The speaker might long for death, but it should not come too quickly, so as to prolong the pleasure of the moment and its "splendor." Victor Graham seems to have read this conclusion to the poem in the same light, explaining the last line as a reference to "l'extase éprouvée dans la consommation de l'amour" (the ecstasy experienced in the consummation of love). *Rymes* (Geneva: Droz, 1968), 22. Alternately, if the pronoun, "l'" (it) in line 7 refers back to "le faict" (the event) in line 5 (or even to the "bien"—the good that must be part of the event in line 6), then the speaker would *not* want any delay in obtaining it. In this variant reading, one would wish to die if one could not promptly have the desired "event" that conveys the good. The clause, "s'on ne l'a promptement," represents a prime example of the syntactical ambiguity that renders some lines in the collection highly enigmatic, often yielding more than one possible interpretation or nuance of meaning.

74. Barataud and Trudeau emphasize the orientation of desire in a spiritual direction here, and suggest that the allusion of a transition through death to another life echoes evangelical thought and discourse in the Renaissance (*Rymes*, 58). Elisabeth Caron interprets the final *quatrain* as an expression of the student's frustration in the face of a mentor/lover who follows Neoplatonic theory too strictly, denying her the "grand plaisir" described and resigning her to the secondary "contentement." See "Les femmes et la politique du Néo-Platonisme: Les enjeux à la Renaissance d'un baiser de Platon," *Etudes Littéraires* 27:2 (1994), 102–104.

POEM 15

75. Chantal Grimm has recorded this epigram with musical accompaniment in *Les poétesses de la Renaissance, ballades des belles rebelles*, EPM Musique, 2002.

76. Short poems like this, based on wordplay and repetition, were made popular by the *Rhétoriqueurs*, as well as by Clément Marot and his followers. François Ier and Antoine Héroët both included the juxtaposition of "tourment/tourmenter" and "contentement/contenter" in their poetry. A *quatrain* of this type, later attributed to François Ier, appears in *Les fleurs de poesie françoyse*, first published in 1534. See *Les fleurs de poesie françoyse*;

Hécatomphile, ed. Gérard Defaux (Paris: STFM, 2002), 79. See Héroët's *La parfaicte amye*, lines 237–38, regarding the lover's torment and contentment, and line 282 on discretion vs. "contentement" (9–10). For a study of how the rhyme itself serves as the "matière première" of this poem, creating a litany of its key words, "torment" and "content," see Françoise Charpentier, *Projet poétique*, 151–52. Charpentier makes the important point that recent critical fascination with "the poetics of constraint" have allowed us to reevaluate in a more positive light an esthetic that earlier critics viewed unfavorably as limited or impoverished. Several of the poems in the *Rymes* feature the theme of contentment, including poems 9, 12, and 43. Yandell explains that, "in both the philosophical and etymological senses, then, *contentement* involves the notion of quid pro quo, maintenance or exchange" (*Carpe Corpus*, 103).

POEM 16

77. For Pernette du Guillet, sense and knowledge, which are gifts from the divine will, allow us to detect the highest good ("le bien du bien"), ordained and ordered by reason. Du Guillet's characteristic emphasis on the role of reason in her poetics of love reflects the Neoplatonic principle that the mind and intellect—superior to the body and its passions—compel us to seek the supreme good.

78. The beloved's eloquence and learning are gifts from God, as is the speaker's own capacity for reason and judgment. This assertion of her God-given ability to judge the beloved reflects the juridical tone that appears elsewhere, including poems 24, 27, and 64.

79. The last line of Du Guillet's epigram echoes yet reverses the meaning of the last line of Scève's *dizain* 56.

POEM 17

80. The beloved's eloquence, goodness, and grace—his "vertu" and *not* his "beaulté"—attract and inspire the speaker. Although numerous poems in the collection (11, 12, and 14, for example) acknowledge the force of physical attraction, the speaker here delights in her beloved's spiritual and intellectual qualities. As we have seen, *vertu* in the *Rymes* refers to the poet's learning and intellectual valor. The focus on the spiritual over the physical not only reflects Neoplatonic theories of ideal love, but also undoubtedly helped to avert society's censure of a woman writing about love. See below, n87, and the Introduction to this volume for more on the concept of *vertu* in the *Rymes*.

81. *Cuyder*: The French verb comes from the Latin, *cogitare* (to think, to imagine). Modified by the adjectives "faux" or "fol," the term "cuyder" conveyed the notion of a false belief or an allusion (as in the "Fable du Faulx Cuyder" by Marguerite de Navarre). There is perhaps a suggestion of irony here, an impression that her feeling of elation may be temporary or stem from a false belief. Without ruling out that possible nuance in the work of a poet who knew well how to exploit ambiguity, the verb by itself generally meant "to believe," "to think," or "to suppose."

POEM 18

82. Pernette du Guillet's epigram is a lyric *responce* to a poem that has been attributed to both Clément Marot and Mellin de Saint-Gelais, as Joyce Miller explains ("In the Margins," 359). Miller demonstrates that Du Guillet based her response epigram on the text of a model *huitain* that first appeared in two songbooks in 1538. "In the Margins," 354 and 360. The first *quatrain* of the model epigram conveys the idea that the lover is so confused by the conflicting emotions caused by love—both happiness and pain—that he is incapable of judging them, or of knowing which one is the more powerful. The second *quatrain* of the source poem focuses on those contradictory emotions: happiness that turns into suffering if it does not last, and unhappiness or suffering that becomes happiness when endured for something so praiseworthy.

83. Following the convention of the *rebours*, a type of response poem, Du Guillet's epigram begins with the final line of the model poem. Her first *quatrain* focuses on the second of the dual emotions presented by the model. For the speaker of poem 18, the fact that suffering for something so praiseworthy constitutes contentment is a universal truth and should be obvious to anyone with good judgment, thereby mocking the confusion of the speaker in the model poem. "Chascun," in line 2, could also be translated as "each one," meaning "each person." The choice of "every one" in English avoids the implication that the speaker is refering to two lovers in particular and emphasizes the collective truth presented here.

84. Further distancing herself from the doubt and confusion of the lover in the source text, Du Guillet's speaker tells her readers precisely how "to know with confidence / Which of these has power over pleasure." That may mean knowing which emotion will triumph over and restrain pleasure *or* which one will govern and bring access to pleasure—or both.

85. Du Guillet's lyric speaker explains in no uncertain terms that the lover must experience (partake of, or taste)—with "studied measure" from mature understanding—*both* the happiness and the pain of love's acquaintance in order to understand the rapport of those emotions to pleasure. Du Guillet's epigram does not deny the conflicting emotions that come with love. Rather than dwelling on confusion and doubt, however, she expresses her belief in the power of reason and mature understanding, gained through experience, to guide the lover's judgment. In poem 70 ("Solace"), the lady's "meur entendement" (line 39)—the same phrase as in line 7 of this epigram—allows her to detect her lover's worthy qualities, but her wisdom and understanding also encompass a rational adherence to duty. Throughout the *Rymes*, reason serves as a powerful way to understand and to rise above the compelling urges of physical desire.

POEM 19

86. This is the first of the poems in the collection to open on a decidedly conversational note. Others have included an address to the beloved as "tu," but here the topic of a missed engagement carries a down-to-earth tone of everyday concerns. The amends proposed for

the slight to the beloved, however, bring the discourse back to a loftier level, promising in return for the visit missed, not one day, but the speaker's entire life.

Instance (line 2) means an earnest urging, solicitation, plea, or entreaty; an insistent argument; insistence. The term also has juridical overtones, referring to a legal request or proceeding, or a degree of jurisdiction.

87. This combination of qualities is associated with the figure of the beloved male poet in many poems of the *Rymes*. (For example, see above, n80 for poem 17.) The speaker tells us elsewhere that the beloved's learning and eloquence attract her; she specifies here that those virtues have enchanted her thoughts, i.e., her mind. The rapport between the body's physical desires and "perfect" love—associated with the mind/spirit/intellect—is a central motif of the *Rymes*. The language Du Guillet uses to represent the coexistence of these two types of love echoes Leone Ebreo's elaborations of Neoplatonic theory. (See the Introduction for further discussion of Ebreo's influence on the *Rymes*.) In the first of Ebreo's dialogues on love, Philo attributes to Sophia the qualities of virtue, intelligence, and grace (an honest and gracious disposition). Sophia has asked Philo to explain the type of love he bears for her and its origins. Philo assures Sophia that his love for her is of the true and perfect variety, which is born of reason and subsequently engenders desire—and not vice versa. Guided by reason, he appreciates and has been attracted to her for her virtue, intelligence and grace; that spiritual and intellectual attraction has given birth to a desire, not necessarily governed by reason, to be joined as one with her in both soul and body. See *Philosophy of Love*, 57; see also *Dialogues*, 70–71.

POEM 20

88. Like the previous epigram, poem 20 opens in a conversational tone. There is nothing particularly philosophical or lyrical about her question: "I desired to see you—do you know why?" The speaker's answer to her own query, however, immediately draws her readers—and her interlocutor—to a cosmic level of discourse with an explanation that is both spiritual and mythological, recalling the first two epigrams of the collection.

89. The maker—Nature or a Creator God—never finished the work of creating the speaker. Her description of this unfinished process evokes a tenuous, half-formed state of existence, much like what preceded the appearance of "that divinity" ("celle divinité") in the first epigram. The happiness promised by the stars at her birth went unfulfilled until the appearance of her Day, who enlightened her world, as we learn in epigram 2, and as this poem reiterates. Finch was careful to choose language that echoes the original poem in avoiding any determination of the gender of that maker/creator, referred to as "l'ouvrier" (the maker or worker) in line 2 and "Nature" in line 5.

90. Here the speaker clarifies the basis for her highest hope—that she will come to know her beloved's mind ("esprit"), which astonishes the entire world. The concluding line of poem 20 echoes the language but reverses the values of the opening line of Scève's *dizain* 7: "Celle beaulté, qui embellit le Monde" (That beauty, which embellishes the World) (*Délie*, 7). Délie's divine light awakens the lover, but with the only result that he is more aware of the darkness of the abyss of suffering where he finds himself. In Scève's poem, it is the beloved's

beauty that adorns or embellishes ("embellit") the world, in contrast with Du Guillet's epigram, where the beloved's mind astonishes ("esbahit") the world.

POEM 21

91. In the tradition of *amour courtois*, the *service* of the courtly lover warrants his lady's recompense or reward.

92. Leone Ebreo's dialogues on love open with a discussion of the differences between love and desire. Philo explains to Sophia that "we always desire what we have not" (*Philosophy of Love*, 8; *Dialogues*, 38), and that "the object of desire is what is not" (*Philosophy of Love*, 12; *Dialogues*, 41). To obtain what one desires, then, puts an end to that desire.

93. The poet anticipates the surprise of her readers, unaccustomed to reading thoughts focused on extending pleasure, penned by a female poet. Finch's translation, "though thought untoward," echoes the awareness of the risk of censure evident elsewhere in the *Rymes* and in Du Moulin's preface.

POEM 22

94. Millery is a village located 15 km to the southwest of Lyon, in a region where viticulture remains an important part of the economy today, as it was in the sixteenth century. The first two lines of the epigram imply either that the grain harvest was late or that the grape harvest (*vendange*) was early, or both.

95. Cotgrave's dictionary tells us that "verd" means not only "green" (i.e., fresh and youthful) but also "rawly tart, or sharpe, as unripe fruit, or wine."

96. Du Guillet's epigram revolves around a Latin proverb—well known by Renaissance writers and Northern European Mannerist painters—that appears in the Roman dramatist Terence's play, *Eunuchus* (*The Eunuch*), in Act 4, Scene 5, line 7: "Without Ceres [goddess of grain] and Libero [god of wine], Venus [goddess of love] grows cold" (*Sine Cerere et Libero friget Venus*). To view the proverb in the English translation of Terence's play by Henry Thomas Riley (New York: Harper Bros., 1874), see the Perseus online database of classical works: http://www.perseus.tufts.edu/cgi-bin/ptext?lookup=Ter.+Eu.+726. Rabelais uses this verse in his *Tiers Livre*, chap. 31, in which the doctor Rondibilis counsels Panurge regarding marriage. The doctor explains that, although excessive consumption of wine hinders the "act of generation," a temperate consumption of wine benefits the lover: "L'antique proverbe nous le designe, on quel est dict: que Venus se morfond sans la compaignie de Ceres & Bacchus" (The ancient proverb tells us this: that Venus catches cold without the company of Ceres and Bacchus). Rabelais, *Œuvres complètes*, vol. 1, ed. Pierre Jourda (Paris: Garnier, 1962), 533.

For interesting comments regarding the prediction of two cold winters, see the notes by Barataud and Trudeau for this poem (*Rymes*, 70). Rajchenbach points out that the mention of "Venus froide" (cold Venus) in this epigram calls to mind the Venus of "Conde Claros de Adonis" (poem 64), who behaves in a more rational manner than does the goddess in Mellin de Saint-Gelais's poem on the same theme (*Rymes*, 132). Saulnier suggests that Du Guillet was inspired by Marot's use of the proverb in his epigram about a statue of Venus given to the king, "La mesme Venus de marbre dict en vers alexandrins" (cited in *Etude*, 32). Marot's epigram, written in alexandrine verse (twelve-syllable lines) like Du Guillet's, ends with the line, "Sans Ceres, & Bacchus tousjours Venus est froyde" (*Œuvres poétiques*, vol. 2, 216–17). This is the only poem in the *Rymes* based entirely on alexandrine verse, still a relatively rare form of French versification in the first half of the sixteenth century. Poem 40 reflects experimentation with mixed versification; each five-line stanza uses alexandrines in lines 1, 2, 3, and 5, with a hexasyllabic (six-syllable) fourth line.

POEM 23

97. This is the first poem in the *Rymes* in which the speaker addresses her beloved as "vous." Prior to poem 23, she either talks about the beloved in the third person or addresses him as "tu." Throughout the collection, the female lyric voice addresses her beloved using either "tu" or "vous," without a clear reason for the choice in each poem. It may be that the poems were written at different points in the young poet's life, for different occasions, and even perhaps with different interlocutors in mind. This line in the original, "Que dessus vous je m'osasse avancer," is somewhat ambiguous, suggesting that she would presume to equal him *or* that she would presume to outdo him. The manner of this audacious overtaking or advancing is left to our imagination. Given the speaking subject's self-conscious comparisons with the beloved's eloquence and the references to her work as writer in the opening poems of the *Rymes* (particularly 1, 2, 5, 6, and 7), Finch's decision to translate this transgressive movement into the arena of work (i.e., writing) is logical in the context of the poem and of the collection as a whole.

98. With the mention of what is "due" her, the female speaker of poem 23 introduces a legalistic argument that occurs again, and more prominently, in poems 24 and 27. See the Introduction for more about the medieval tradition of the courts of love and their debates and judgments, made popular in the fifteenth and sixteenth centuries by Martial d'Auvergne's *Arrêts d'Amour.*

99. In line 8 the speaker acknowledges the reactions of others (ranging from jealousy to censure) to her attempts to obtain what she believes is hers by right.

100. The speaker reminds her beloved of a truth fundamental to Neoplatonic theory—that the lover, in loving, gives himself to the beloved, who will in turn cherish him as a possession. See the Introduction for more on this point. See also poem 70, "Solace."

POEM 24

101. These questions regarding obligation reflect both legal and philosophical discourse, evoking the medieval tradition of debates and judgments of the courts of love, known in the sixteenth century through numerous reprintings of the fifteenth-century *Arrêts d'Amour.* The language of this epigram also recalls a passage from Ebreo's dialogues on love, in which

Philo assures Sophia that "just as the lover is prior to love, so is the beloved; for if there were not a first lovable person or object, it would be impossible to love, and there would be no love" (*Philosophy of Love*, 268; *Dialogues d'amour*, 197). In other words, love cannot exist without the lover, who in turn cannot be a lover without the prior existence of the beloved and loveable person.

102. The lover owes his heart to Love (Cupid); to the Lady he owes his soul.

POEM 25

103. The first two lines convey the speaker's uncertainty and agitation; her question of whether one person can in fact engender two loves may refer to the prospect of the beloved causing two women to admire him, or to the possibility that he inspires two types of love in her—physical desire and spiritual affection. Either way, in lines 3 through 7, the speaker wonders how any heart, however large, can possibly pursue both (either the love of two different ladies or the two different types of love) satisfactorily.

104. Without resolving the question she explored in the first seven lines, the speaker switches focus in the last five lines, affirming that the duality of love applies differently to the lady. Just as affection leads to increased desire, a point recognized by the Italian Neoplatonists, the lady's attraction to her lover may be doubled. Her tremendous obligation to virtue, however, determines the real source of her "double passion." The beloved's noble and virtuous "qualité" doubles *his* merit as well as *her* passion.

POEM 26

105. The gender of the speaker appears to shift within the French poem. The adjective "deceue" (deceived, disappointed) of line 2 indicates a female speaker in the opening stanza. Jeanne de Marnef, editor of the 1546–47 edition published in Paris, made this adjective masculine, but Jean de Tournes maintains the feminine form in his subsequent 1552 edition.

106. The general observations in the second stanza may be attributed to a speaker of either gender. This speaker, male or female, observes the contradictory experiences of lovers—some deliriously happy, others in deep pain—and perceives that both passions reign within him/herself, a typical condition for the Petrarchan lover.

107. In the third stanza, the speaker fears that another ("*un* autre")—a male rival—may be gaining the upper hand. We presume a male speaker, based on the collection's backdrop of heterosexual love, but there are several passages such as this where the original ambiguity leaves room for a broader interpretation encompassing the experience of all lovers. The disconnect between seeing and believing (lines 17–18) is also the topic of poem 45.

108. In the final stanza, the speaker expresses hope that "cil" (he /that one) will avenge the wrong and pain he has caused the speaker. If we presume a female speaker here, it may be the same voice as in the first stanza—one who hopes that the unfaithful male lover will see

the light and transform the suffering he has caused into the good that she currently holds as a dear illusion. It is the guilty party (the one who caused the speaker's pains) who will offer recompense, or carry out this vengeance, a notion that is not inconsistent with the idea of free will and choice in human actions that appears in poem 68, "The Night." Barataud and Trudeau suggest alternatively that "cil" (line 22) may designate Cupid (*Amour*) himself, who might finally reach the wayward lover with his arrows, repairing the harm caused to the lady (*Rymes*, 78).

109. This poem, like many in the *Rymes*, concludes with the notion that suffering will ultimately be transformed into the good ("bien") of reciprocal affection. That is the hope expressed by the speaker of the final stanza, but the last line ends with the recognition that, for the moment, such good persists only as an illusion. The awaited resolution of suffering remains strictly hypothetical. The speaker continues to hope—with no reassurance from the beloved—that things will turn around, that this faith will eventually be rewarded by the beloved's change of heart, recalling Marot's *chanson*, "Long temps y a, que je vys en espoir," which treats the same theme. *Œuvres poétiques*, vol. 1, 191.

Because the 1545 edition makes no use of the accent mark to distinguish between the conjunction, *ou* ("or"), and the relative pronoun, *où* ("where"), we are left to ponder which role the *ou* in this final line was intended to play. We have chosen the relative pronoun, which focuses the final line on the speaker's current doubts as she waits and hopes for the good ending that she acknowledges may never come. Either way, the conclusion conveys the speaker's awareness that the long-awaited good, still hypothetical, may never be realized.

Regarding the gender of the speakers, Rajchenbach suggests that the two central stanzas may represent a quotation, a "staging of the masculine complaint"—as in poem 69, "Despair"—that would explain the floating gender of the poetic subject (*Rymes*, 135). Alternately, we might imagine each stanza recited or sung by a different voice, male or female as appropriate, or by two voices, one female and one male. The "Mummery: Five Posts of Love" provides a model of a longer poem with a different speaking voice in each stanza, although all are male. Poem 69, "Despair," conveys a male voice, whereas the gender of the speaker who provides the response in poem 70, "Solace," is never made clear. That unidentified speaker addresses the lover and defends the lady. Clearly Pernette du Guillet did not confine herself solely to a female lyric voice. The English version of this poem imposes no resolution regarding the gender of the speaker(s).

POEM 27

110. The opening line evokes an epigram by Marot that begins in a similar way: "Prenons le cas, Cahors, que tu me doibves / Aultant, que doibt à son Maro Mantue" (Let us present the case, Cahors, that you owe me / As much as Mantua does to its Maro[t]). The "lady" Marot's poem addresses is his native city of Cahors, however, whom he entreats to welcome the king and queen on their visit (*Œuvres*, vol. 2, 279). Line 2 of poem 27 echoes the end of poem 23, which concludes that, "if the power of giving you / Belongs to Love and Faith, you are all mine." Both of Du Guillet's poems envision an ideal of reciprocity and equality that nevertheless remains hypothetical.

111. The common good that ensures the lovers' reciprocal rights and duties is an essential element of the Neoplatonic ideal of pure love. Poem 27 addresses the issue in a legalistic discourse that echoes the popular medieval tradition of debates argued and judged in the courts of love, ruled by ladies. See the Introduction for further discussion of this tradition. The focus on the common good due in mutual affection differs from the lover's suffering represented in many of the medieval debates, but the conventions of the tradition provide a uniquely appropriate framework in which to present this particular case.

POEM 28

112. Like the preceding poem, this epigram also evokes the debates about the nature and laws of love in the medieval courts of love and the judgments handed down by the ladies that presided over them, as recorded by Martial d'Auvergne. Here, the debate reflects another issue central to Neoplatonic theory—the relative strengths of affection and desire. By presenting "L'affection" and "le desir" as performing the debate themselves, Du Guillet also recalls the medieval allegorical traditions that remained popular in the Renaissance.

113. As in poem 18, this "you" ("vous") may represent the beloved or another individual, but also addresses a wider audience of readers who may be interested in the question and how to resolve it. The speaker in poem 28 highlights the truth of the resolution ("sans fiction") explained in the final two lines.

114. Du Guillet's conclusion reflects the ideal of perfect love described in Neoplatonic philosophy. In Ebreo's dialogues, Sophia asks Philo to clarify the confusing relationship between love, desire, and pleasure. Philo explains that a less worthy type of love is born of desire and sensual appetite. This imperfect love dies with pleasure (i.e., when desire is satisfied). Perfect love, however, *gives birth* to desire. The force of this worthy sort of love causes the lover to desire both spiritual and corporeal union with the beloved, as Philo elaborates: "the other love itself generates desire of the beloved, instead of being generated by that desire or appetite: in fact we first love perfectly, and then the strength of that love makes us desire spiritual and bodily union with the beloved" (*Philosophy of Love*, 56; *Dialogues d'amour*, 70). Physical pleasure ("jouyssance") does not kill this love. Even when desire and sensual appetite cease, pure love (*parfaict amour, parfaicte affection*) continues.

POEM 29

115. Saulnier notes that this *chanson* was published anonymously in the 1547 edition of the *Œuvres* of Saint-Gelais (Lyon: Pierre de Tours) and again in two songbooks: the *Second et tiers livre de toutes belles chansons nouvelles* (Paris: Veuve N. Buffet, 1559) and the *Recueil et eslite de plusieurs belles chansons* (Antwerp: Jean Waesberge, 1576) (*Etude*, 15). Regarding other poems on the same theme also published anonymously in Saint-Gelais's *Œuvres* (1547), see Barataud and Trudeau, *Rymes*, 137. This *chanson* and Du Guillet's poem 73 ("A un sot rimeur") have been set to music and sung by Chantal Grimm, as recorded on *Les poétesses de la Renaissance.*

116. The speaker emphasizes the discrete and chaste quality of her love. Her "spark" ("estincelle") of chaste love that flares anew each day recalls the sparks of light that the second Venus passes on to the world in Neoplatonic theory. According to the Neoplatonists, the first of the two Venuses shines with divine light, which she transmits to the second Venus, who passes on the sparks of that light in the matter of the world (Ficino, *Commentaire,* 154). See the discussion of this topic in the Introduction. Although the lyric subject of the *Rymes* frequently refers to her beloved as her Day ("Jour") in terms that evoke dawn's light, here the speaker calls attention to the sparks that are lit every day under her own care. In the French (line 2), the spark is tended "soubz mon esselle," meaning, literally, under my arm, and used in this context to indicate that the modest flame that flares each day is protected close to the speaker's body and near her heart.

117. The refrain represents a gentle reproach to the beloved. Finch has wisely chosen the English equivalent, "Will you not say you'll love me one day?" for the refrain of all stanzas, despite the shift from the present tense to the future in lines 16 and 20 of the original. Any attempt to translate the slight shift in tense—involving only the addition of the "r" in the French verb form—would detract from the consistency and gentle insistence of the refrain in English. Moreover, Finch's refrain includes a rhyme at the *caesura*, as does the original French, "Ne me debv(r)ez vous bien aymer?"

118. Here, and in the previous stanza, the speaker describes her hidden despair and reluctance to incite any quarrel against or with her beloved, whose affections appear to have strayed "for one less fair" ("pour moins belle"). Elsewhere in the *Rymes*, however, we encounter a voice that boldly reproaches the beloved for these same reasons, as in poems 35 and 36. Here, despite her claim that she seeks no quarrel, the speaker does betray her own desire by claiming her beloved as her own ("pour mien vous veulx reclamer"). Barataud and Trudeau call attention to the feudal associations of the verb "reclamer," used to pursue, claim, and call back serfs who have left their lord's lands without permission (*Rymes*, 81).

119. By emphasizing again that she does not wish to complain, followed by the reproachful nudge of the refrain, the speaker surely registers her point with her beloved. The word "plaincte," as Cotgrave's dictionary indicates, means complaint and lamentation, but also accusation, recalling the legalistic framework and vocabulary used in poem 27. The theme of the "plainte" recurs in poem 46.

120. As in poem 19, in which the speaker, to make amends for missing a social visit, offers her entire life ("toute ma vie") to her beloved, here the lyric subject highlights her fidelity and the enduring nature of her love, as time will affirm. Poem 30, which follows, concludes similarly, with the speaker reminding her beloved that she will remain his all her life ("toute ma vie"). Likewise, the ring in poem 10 serves as a reminder of the lady's enduring devotion.

POEM 30

121. Time may confirm the speaker's fidelity and the force of her love, as in the previous poem, but time also has brought experience and life lessons.

122. The speaker tells her beloved, whose vast eloquence and learning she admires in other epigrams, that he will not win her over by treating her rudely, as a master (or master teacher) might. "Gaigner le pris" conveys both the general sense of "winning over" someone, along with the notion of the prize or recompense that the courtly lover strives to deserve and to win from his lady. The allusion to courtly tradition strengthens the lady's admonition to the lover, who is required to live up to and follow his lady's standards. In the medieval courtly tradition, the lover seeking to merit his lady's favor will not act in a rude and dominating manner.

123. Beginning with "And yet" ("Et toutesfois"), the second *quatrain* shifts the focus away from the lessons of time and the rules of courtly behavior with the speaker's observation that her beloved is continually drawn to her. The reward or prize ("prys") of line 4 is replaced at the rhyme by "pris," the past participle of the verb "prendre" ("to take"), describing the beloved's attraction to the speaker. His concern displays the opposite of rude, domineering behavior; it shows her the "noble good" ("ce hault bien") that captivates her and compels her to remain his all her days ("toute ma vie"). See also poems 10, 19, and 29 for a similar assertion of the enduring nature of her affection for her beloved.

POEM 31

124. The meaning of lines 5–6 is difficult to pin down with precision, but from the context of the entire poem it seems clear that the speaker is filled with both chagrin and ire from hearing "clamors of disdain" against the "bien"—against the good that her beloved embodies and that she holds dear.

125. The speaker's suffering is the result of ugly rumors and gossip regarding her esteem and affection for her beloved. The need to defend herself against such "calomnies" is the topic of poem 42, and Du Moulin addresses the same concern in his preface to the Ladies of Lyon.

POEM 32

126. *doulx amer*: sweet bitterness, the only remedy available to the lover in the Petrarchan tradition. The following stanza shows that the speaker has experienced—and continues to hope for—something more.

127. In a wonderful example of the rich ambiguity that permeates the *Rymes*, the terms used in the original French in these two lines blur the distinctions between the vocabulary of physical pleasure ("jouyssance") and that of spiritual love ("le bien"); one can know and enjoy either or both. For the speaker, this knowledge came from her beloved. The lines that follow emphasize the pure quality of their affection in Neoplatonic terms.

128. Lines 9 and 10 embody the ideal of reciprocity and equality in love held by the Neoplatonists who, following Plato, believed that the human individual was originally a four-legged being encompassing two different but equal parts. Punished by Zeus, the complex beings were cut in two, with each half destined to seek out its other half for true love. In Plato's *Symposium*, Aristophanes explains, "Each of us then is but the token of a

human being, sliced like a flatfish, two from one; each then ever seeks his matching token" (*The Dialogues of Plato*, vol. 2, 132). In his commentary on the *Symposium*, Ficino explains that "each human half seeks its own half.[...] And so the desire and longing for the whole to be restored receives the name of love" (*Commentary*, 72). See also poem 38.

129. Enjoying her beloved's virtues and the reciprocal affection they share, at this particular moment the speaker finds their love more sweet than bitter.

130. The triumph of the sweet over the bitter is short lived. In the absence of her beloved "amy," artful Love (Cupid) divests her of that confidence, disarming her and leaving her once again vulnerable to the "mal d'aymer" ("love's dark duress"). Barataud and Trudeau observe that this *chanson*, unlike many in the collection, moves from a positive perspective and sentiments to a more pessimistic conclusion, with a reliance on a "vocabulary of defeat" in the final stanza (*Rymes*, 86).

POEM 33

131. The first epigram of the *Rymes* attributes to the "lofty power from the Stars" ("hault pouvoir des Astres") the providential arrival of the speaker's beloved Day. In this poem, however, the Sky ("le Ciel," representing the heavens) is ruled by envious Fortune, who is happy to see the sun set and day disappear, anticipating that the night sky's influence will overturn the positive effects of the day's light.

132. The speaker rejects astrological divination as a source of understanding the course of her own life, preferring a different source or discourse ("autre discours"). The sight of her Day continues to give her life, as it did for the first time in poem 2.

133. This stanza echoes the concerns voiced at the end of the previous poem, where the absence of the beloved entails a loss of confidence in the strength and nature of his love for her. Note that the verb form, "trouves," in line 13 of the French, represents either the second-person singular or the second-person plural of the verb in the spelling norms of the mid-sixteenth century. From the context of the poem—and the second-person plural verb form used in line 50—the speaker appears to address her reflections here to a collective "vous" (you, plural). Fortunately, the English poem does not require any resolution of that ambiguity.

134. The notion that, from her birth, the speaker and her beloved were destined for each other by the gods recalls the first poem of the collection.

135. This "valued friendship" ("amytié bien prise") encompasses friendship, chaste affection, and virtuous love—the elements of the ideal "parfaicte amytié" discussed in the Introduction and in the notes to poem 39.

136. Echoing a belief in free will that surfaces elsewhere in the *Rymes* (68, "The Night," and 69, "Despair," for example), the speaker remarks that she has *chosen* this "amytié," in

addition to undergoing the effects of the will of the gods and the noble power of the stars that brought her beloved Day to her.

137. The glimpse of her Day that fills her with pleasure recalls the second poem of the *Rymes*. In this stanza and the following, the speaker refers to *my* fortune twice ("*ma* fortune" and "*mon* heur") to indicate her particular "happy Fate" ("heureuse destinee"). She distinguishes her own good fortune from the more general figure of "envious Fortune" of the first stanza.

138. Calling this her "happy Fate," the speaker pronounces that she knows no woman alive who could resist having half of such a "noble amytié," nor who could resist a half-share of her beloved's charms.

139. Elsewhere in the *Rymes* the speaker expresses concern that the beloved is admired and sought by other women, her rivals. This line, however, provides an unusual reference to the female speaker's own admirers, although she emphasizes that she has no interest in those suitors because her beloved's virtues have captured her heart.

140. The humble stance of the speaker recalls poem 43, as well as poems 3 and 6.

141. Her "fermeté"—steadfast love in the face of her critics—echoes the last stanza of poem 29, where the speaker indicates that time will affirm her love and loyalty. Her faithful, enduring love is the final reason given by the speaker of poem 29 as to why her beloved should return her affection. Here, the speaker concludes with the assertion that her "fermeté" (her "refusal to relent" to those who would wish to part them) will bring contentment to her beloved.

POEM 34

142. Lines 3 and 4 capture a fascinating ambiguity that leads to two different yet not contradictory interpretations of the poem. The two readings are based on possible meanings of the verb "rendre" in line 3: to render/make or to express/transmit/represent. Finch's translation of these lines is based on the first option, which implies that the speaker's will ("voulenté")—associated with rational choice and the workings of the *esprit*—seeks to render her desire so pure, according to the ideal of "parfaicte amytié," that the desire and the will shall seek the same end. In that case, the will would no longer need to control wayward desire and would therefore be superfluous. The speaker does not wish to eliminate desire, but she envisions an ideal wherein the will and the desire would act as one, sharing the same goal. A variant interpretation reads line 3 as saying that the speaker's will cannot *express* her perfect desire. This reading makes line 4 more difficult to interpret, but Barataud and Trudeau suggest that the speaker's will cannot represent or express her desire without seeming unreasonable or excessive in relation to it (*Rymes*, 92).

143. Throughout the poem, "it" refers to the speaker's will ("voulenté"); in line 6, however, "its" could refer either to the will or to the desire.

144. For now, at least, the will has retreated and renounced its effort to control desire. In the alternate reading described above, the will gives up its attempt to express desire. This ambiguity leading to two parallel interpretations is a characteristic quality of Du Guillet's poetry.

POEM 35

145. "Celle" (her, that woman) is the rival. The speaker cannot believe the beloved's words when he tells her that he wishes her as much good as he appears to direct to the other woman.

146. The meaning of this line is not entirely clear in the French. It appears to suggest that the beloved, in his displays of affection toward another woman, has been neglecting what he should be doing for himself—implying that he should have been paying his attentions to the speaker, who is more worthy of his affections and therefore better for him.

147. The speaker asks her beloved which lady is more worthy of his esteem—she who trembles with a full heart and dares not say what he would like to hear (perhaps words of flattery or assent to his desires) *or* she who says those things to him under false pretense. The following epigram presents the same juxtaposition of the worthy, yet underappreciated, Lady with a rival who all too easily gives the beloved what she thinks he wants, leading to another pointed question regarding which lady he will choose.

POEM 36

148. Like the preceding poem, this epigram draws a contrast between one lady (presumably the speaker, but presented initially in the third person) who is not sure that her true and pure love will be well received, and the other woman—a rival—who does everything in her power to please the beloved. The notion of duty ("debvoir") is used ironically, or at least only in reference to a more worldly or courtly framework, indicating the lady may feel an obligation to reward the devoted lover with her favors.

149. The question addressed here by the speaker to her beloved echoes that of the second *quatrain* in the preceding poem.

150. The rival sheds her "best" ("de son bien se devest"), implying both the loss of her greatest asset—i.e., her chastity—and the shedding of clothing that would entail.

POEM 37

151. The speaker, presumably female, addresses an unidentified interlocutor ("vous")—her beloved, perhaps, or anyone whose good opinion is important to her. She defends herself with regard to malicious gossip and lies spread about her by another man. He who tells the lies may *appear* to speak simply, but his hidden, harmful meanings are evident to the speaker. With its use of "rhyme équivoque"—"amplement" and "ample ment," "d'ire" and "dire"—Du Guillet's own poem offers an example of a meaning hidden in plain sight. Finch

has captured the play of meaning and form, typical of the *Rhétoriqueur* tradition, in the concluding rhyme of the English poem.

POEM 38

152. "To trifle with the feelings": Finch's line in English seizes the essence behind a problematic line in the original, "que l'amour appetisse." The verb *appetisser*, according to Huguet, Cotgrave, and other historical dictionaries, meant either "to diminish, to lesson" or "to desire, to seek with an appetite." In the latter case, the verb *appetisser* is related to *appeter*. Given that the two meanings are contradictory, it is difficult to know whether love is diminished when divided between two hearts (i.e., when a lover promises his love to two different hearts), or whether love increases (appetite grows) between two hearts promised to one another. Either way, however, it is clear that Love (Cupid) is trifling with the hearts involved, provoking a rejoinder from the female speaker.

153. Barataud and Trudeau suggest that the paradox represented by the rhymes in lines 5 and 6 indicates that "la légereté sera érigée en loi par usage ou application universelle" (frivolity will become law by use or universal practice) (97).

154. They are not contributing their half of the ideal "parfaicte amytié." The element of reciprocity in Neoplatonic theories of pure love stems in large part from Plato's *Symposium* and the speech of Aristophanes, who explains how Zeus, to punish the original humans for their presumption, cut the round, four-legged beings in two, from which point on, individuals have been born with the urge to love and seek the missing half of their being. (See above, n128, for poem 32.) Along with the other Renaissance Neoplatonists, Ficino expounded on this concept, explaining that because of the division of the original humans, "a reciprocal love is innate in men [...] each human half seeks its own half. [...] And so the desire and longing for the whole to be restored receives the name of love" (*Commentary*, 72). Because of the original soul's division, the lover for a time plunges into "the abyss of the body," pursuing physical pleasure alone, but with maturity the natural light within shines forth and urges the soul to recover the divine light: "this instigation and appetite is true love, under the guidance of which one half of the man desires the other half of the same man, because the natural light, which is one half of the soul, tries to kindle again in the soul that divine light, which is called the other half of the same soul, formerly neglected" (76–77).

155. Here, as in poems 24 and 27, the poet uses legal vocabulary in defense of the ladies, their actions and their expectations. See above, nn98 and 111, and the Introduction for more on the medieval tradition of the courts and judgments of love.

156. The speaker recognizes that she has unwittingly—by not knowing how to hide her emotions in a courtly fashion—fanned the flames of her admirer's passion.

157. In other words, women have learned this from men and their behavior. By evoking the infinite choice of lovers ("infinité d'amis") in this stanza, the speaker playfully observes that it is from men that women learn the transformative effects of desire, which can lead

to many—perhaps countless—admirers and lovers. The same phrase, "infinité d'amis" appears in line 292 of Bertrand de la Borderie's *L'Amye de court*, published by Dolet in Lyon in 1542: "Pour durer belle il m'est doncques permis / De recouvrer infinité d'amys" (In order to remain beautiful, I am therefore permitted / to procure an infinite number of lovers.) The female "amye" in La Borderie's text is a courtly lady who manipulates social rules and her admirers to her advantage. She knows the language of the Petrarchist poets and the Neoplatonists fluently, but acts according to her own mercenary interests, not hiding her intention to protect her own heart and to find a rich husband whom she can then govern. See *L'amie de court* (1542), ed. D. Trudeau (Paris: Honoré Champion, 1997). To view these lines in a sixteenth-century edition of works representing the *querelle des amyes*, view the digital facsimile of the *Opuscules d'amour, par Heroet, La Borderie, et autres divins poëtes* (Lyon: Jean de Tournes, 1547) online at "The Renaissance in Print" at the University of Virginia: http://iris.lib.virginia.edu/rmds/gordon/gordonimages/Gordon1547_O68/, p. 122.

158. Despite the cynical observations in the preceding stanzas and a less-than-flattering depiction of men who claim to love women but are ruled by desire, the final stanza of the poem rehabilitates the lovers and love itself. The ladies' honest passions will allow Love to avenge them, and the men will be captivated by the faith and devotion of the ladies.

POEM 39 ("PERFECT LOVE")

159. The title alludes to Antoine Héroët's influential poem, *La parfaicte amye*, published by Dolet in Lyon in 1542 and central to the Renaissance *querelle des amyes*. For more on the *querelle*, see the Introductions to this volume and to the series.

160. The idea that love is but a dream, and that dreams are lies, echoes opening observations in Héroët's *La parfaicte amye*, where the female speaker says her book will *not* reflect such fables and lies: "Perfection d'amour sera mon livre / Intitulé: pour lequel accomplir / Il n'est besoing de fables le remplir; / D'inventions poëtiques je n'en use" (The perfection of love will my book be entitled: To accomplish this there is no need to fill it with fables; I use no poetic inventions). *La parfaicte amye*, ed. Christine Hill (Exeter: University of Exeter, 1981), 3. If the preceding poem alludes to La Borderie's *L'Amye de court*, whose "heroine" explains the reason for her many suitors, Du Guillet's *Parfaicte amytié* echoes Héroët's response to La Borderie. Both texts were published by Dolet in Lyon in the same year, 1542, three years before the publication of the *Rymes*.

The first two lines of this elegy also recall the beginning of the medieval allegorical poem, *The Romance of the Rose*, begun by Guillaume de Lorris and completed by Jean de Meun, a text which remained popular in the first half of the sixteenth century. The opening lines of the *Rose* allegory explain that the art of love is enclosed in the work, adding that "Maintes gens vont disant que songes / Ne sont que fables et mensonges" (Many people say that dreams are but fables and lies). The narrator of the *Rose* points out, however, that some dreams don't lie, as in the case of the allegorical dream narrative to follow.

Another popular text combining a dream and an allegorical tale of love is the curious narrative work originally entitled *Hypnerotomachia Poliphili* (Rome: Aldus Manutius, 1499), translated into French as the *Discours du songe de Poliphile, Deduisant comme Amour le combat a l'occasion de Polia* (Paris: Jacques Kerver, 1546) and partially translated into

English as *The Strife of Love in a Dreame* in 1592. The *Hypnerotomachia* recounts the dream journey of a young lover named Poliphile through a fantastical landscape of classical ruins and fanciful gardens and edifices in search of his beloved Polia. For the modern English translation of this book, including reproductions of the original woodcut illustrations, see Francesco Colonna, *Hypnerotomachia Poliphili: the strife of love in a dream*, ed. and trans. Joscelyn Godwin (London: Thames & Hudson, 1999).

161. The characterization of Love as crafty and prone to ruse and deceit appears elsewhere, and notably in poem 32.

162. *Portant tousjours l'amour en sa devise*: The "devise" refers to both a motto associated with an individual *and* to the figure or emblematic image that may appear in association with that motto—in the tradition of the coat of arms, yet unique to the individual, rather than representing an entire family. Finch's choice of "code" encompasses both a verbal and a visual "devise."

163. For the Neoplatonists, the pure heart, retaining a spark of its divine origins, is naturally attracted to the good.

164. As in the first epigram, the speaker interprets her beloved's "amytié" as a heaven-sent gift. In poem 11, the speaker explains how, despite this divine intervention, she did not for a time truly see or understand this gift.

165. False Appearance and Danger are allegorical figures in the *Romance of the Rose*. (See above, n160.) Du Guillet has added the figure of Alteration ("Changement") as a source of "infection," in keeping with her insistence throughout the collection on the constancy of true love, or "parfaicte amytié."

166. The reciprocal contentment brought about by virtue is held up as an ideal throughout the *Rymes*, albeit with the recognition that lovers often fall short of the goal. In this elegy, the speaker presents the "parfaicte amytié" she shares with her beloved as an example to all lovers.

POEM 40

167. This opening evokes the lyric tradition of the moment of *innamoramento* when the young lover—wandering aimlessly and happily in youth—is struck suddenly by love's wounding arrows. The speaker of this *chanson* tells us that in the spring of her life she had no knowledge yet of love. She had not yet uttered a single sigh ("aucun souspir"), recalling the "sospire" (sighs) that the first sonnet of Petrarch's *canzoniere* tells readers they will hear in his rhymes, now that he is a different man from what he was in his "youthful error":

> You who hear in scattered rhymes the sound
> of those sighs with which I nourished my heart
> during my first youthful error,
> when I was in part another man from what I am now… [line breaks added]

Voi ch'ascoltate in rime sparse in suono
di quel sospire ond'io dudriva 'l core
in sul mio primo giovenile errore,
quand'era in parte altr' uom da quel ch' i' sono"...

Petrarch's Lyric Poems, 36–37.

Scève's *dizain* 6 depicts the young man, free in his youth—"Libre vivois en l'Avril de mon aage" (I lived free in the April of my age)—who is suddenly captivated by love (*Délie*, VI, 7). The word "liberté" (line 3) meant both "freedom" and "free choice" or "free will" in the sixteenth century. See also line 172 of poem 68, "The Night," where the speaker laments the effects of a monstrous imagination on the working of free will.

168. In the Petrarchan and Neoplatonic traditions, eyes are the source of darts, sometimes poisonous, that enter the eye of the victim to wound his or her heart. Pure and spiritual love also begins with sight—with the image of the beloved entering the body through the eyes in order to touch the lover's soul. See Ficino, *Commentary*, 119 and 160. In the third sonnet of Petrarch's *canzoniere*, the speaker describes how, stunned by his lady's beautiful eyes, he was left off guard: "Trovommi Amor del tutto disarmato, / et aperta la via per gli occhi al core / che di lagrime son fatti uscio et varco" ("Love found me altogether disarmed, and the way open through my eyes to my heart, my eyes which are now the portal and passageway of tears"). *Petrarch's Lyric Poems*, 38–39. Similarly for Scève, the suffering lover in *dizains* 5 and 6 of the *Délie* is struck through the eyes—not by arrows, but by the eyes of the Lady, depicted as an archer. From that moment on, as *dizain* 6 tells us in the concluding line, "En sa beaulté gist ma mort, et ma vie" (In her beauty lies/rests my death, and my life). *Délie*, VI, 7. On Chariteo's Petrarchan poetry as a source for this *chanson*, see Rajchenbach, *Rymes*, 149.

169. The speaker of Du Guillet's poem is only finally wounded when Cupid consults the "Archers of Virtue." The love she experiences transports her, allowing her to taste the "good" that corresponds to the Neoplatonic ideal of contemplation associated with intellectual and spiritual love, unlike the wound that causes continuous suffering for the Petrarchan lover.

170. As in poem 11, the speaker describes herself, entering into the experience of love, as one who is blindfolded. As elsewhere, her beloved's identity is tied to his writing, his "fine and noble words" ("ses escriptz divins") and to his virtue. Here she also offers a hint of a reproach to him for being, as his name suggests, too severe ("comme de nom, severe"), alluding to the Latin word, *severus*, meaning severe, which the poet suggests as the etymology of her beloved's name. In the first edition of 1545, the word "nom" in line 34 is printed as "mon." The obvious error was corrected in the 1552 edition. The first line of the following poem (41) makes the same link between the beloved's name and his behavior.

171. The suggestion of a reproach in line 34 is developed in this final stanza. The speaker claims to understand why other ladies are drawn to her virtuous and eloquent beloved, and to excuse him for striving to do his duty toward them—with "right" here corresponding to the attention required by courtly and polite society, rather than with the idea of duty owed through reciprocal love. The final phrase, "je l'excuse," however, keeps the focus on the notion that the beloved *needs* to be forgiven, simultaneously reinforcing and softening the speaker's reproach.

POEM 41

172. As in the previous poem (40), the speaker reproaches her beloved, associating his name (Scève) with his behavior (severe) toward her. His perceived severity, however, inspires her to "persevere" in her art and learning.

173. In order for the original line ("Ne t'esbahis si point je persevere") to make sense, we must assume *either* that "si" and "point" were inadvertently reversed, perhaps by the compositor (typesetter) in the print shop, with "point" completing the negative particle "ne", *or* that "point" was intended to accompany the verb "persevere." Under the first assumption, the line means, "Don't be very surprised if I persevere…." Under the second, "point" reflects a usage carried over from medieval French into the sixteenth century, in which the adverb is used positively to mean a very small amount or quantity. The line would then be translated literally as "Don't be very surprised if I persevere a bit (a little)…," creating a poetic understatement that does not contradict the first reading. See also Barataud and Trudeau, 107, for their careful analysis of this line.

174. Unlike the preceding poem, in which the speaker resolves to excuse her beloved's behavior and his inclination to frequent the company of other female admirers, here she tells him that she will try, through art and learning ("par art, et par sçavoir") to inspire his restraint. Despite the speaker's claim in lines 6–7 that she doesn't wish to complain or constrain her beloved's freedom, we understand that is precisely what she intends.

175. In the sixteenth century, the adjective "sainct" meant "excellent" in a secular context, as well as "holy," in religious terms. In this context it serves to highlight the divine, spiritual, and intellectual nature of the beloved's words and his eloquence—what she calls "ses escriptz divins" ("his fine and noble words") in poem 40.

176. The verb "empraindre" (line 9) encompasses a rich range of meaning, from "ingrain" and "impress" to "imprint," "print," and "stamp," and includes both the idea of "inspirer" (to inspire) and "féconder" (to impregnate, make fertile). See the Introduction for more on the Neoplatonic metaphor of the image of beauty imprinted or engraved upon the soul. The "golden words" ("motz dorez") evoke the golden rain with which the god Jupiter impregnated Danae, a mythological allusion that appears again at the beginning of the following poem. In addition, Renaissance readers would have recognized in the expression "motz dorez" a reference to a popular French translation of Cato's *Distichs*, entitled, *Les mots dorez du Caton en Latin et en francoys: avec plusieurs bons et tres utiles enseignemens, proverbes, adages, authoritez et dictz moraulx des sages*…, published in Paris, Troyes, and Lyon in the 1530s. The beloved's golden rain and wise, eloquent words will only truly be fruitful when imprinted/ingrained in her own heart, which belongs to him. The final clause reinforces the Neoplatonic goal of pure love, in which each lover belongs to the other.

POEM 42

177. The figure described in this stanza is Danae, rather than Daphne, although it is not known whether Pernette du Guillet introduced this confusion of the two mythological figures or whether it was the result of a typographical error. Danae, locked in a tower, was visited and impregnated by the god Zeus, who came to her in the form of a golden rain. (See above, n176.) Here, the substitution of Daphne for Danae—no matter who was responsible for the switch—results in an interesting slippage between the mythological tales of two women at the mercy of male gods and their passions. Daphne flees from and escapes Apollo's amorous pursuit only by being transformed into a laurel tree, whose leaves henceforth represent and glorify Apollo and his talents. Danae, imprisoned by her father in an attempt to escape the prophecy that indicates her son will kill her father, is nevertheless ravished and impregnated by Zeus.

178. The first four stanzas address a series of slanderous charges, or "calomnies," that appear to have been made against the speaker by malicious gossips. She closes each of the four "accusation" stanzas with the refrain, "Worse than that I do not know" ("Je ne sçay rien moins, que celà"). The French refrain means, literally, "I know nothing less than that," or "I don't know anything less than that," encompassing the idea that the speaker knows nothing at all about such things (that she would never dream of doing anything of the sort), and that she knows nothing worse than those accusations (that she can't imagine anything worse). The refrain shifts in the last two quatrains to "Je ne sçay rien mieulx, que celà" (literally, "I know nothing better than that"). With "mieulx" easily translated as "better," it made sense to translate "moins" as "worse" in the first four quatrains, to echo the parallelism of the two refrains in French, and to emphasize the speaker's awareness of the gravity of the slanderous charges against her.

179. Following her rejection of the charges made against her, the speaker outlines what it is that she *does* know best, evoking a perfect and ideal love, inspired by virtue and governed by honor.

POEM 43

180. This elegy may be the best known of Pernette du Guillet's poetry. Its fantasy of seduction, unique use of Ovidian myth, and thought-provoking conclusion have inspired much commentary and continue to engage readers. A first translation of this elegy by Ann Rosalind Jones appeared in Katharina Wilson's anthology, *Women Writers of the Reformation* (University of Georgia Press, 1987). Critical studies that comment in detail on this elegy (poem 43) include: Françoise Charpentier, "Projet poétique, travail poétique dans les *Rymes* de Pernette du Guillet: Autour de trois quatrains," in *Poétique et Narration: Mélanges offerts à Guy Demerson*, ed. François Marotin and Jacques Philippe Saint-Gérand (Paris: Champion, 1993), 143–55; JoAnn DellaNeva, "Mutare/Mutatus: Pernette Du Guillet's Actaeon Myth and the Silencing of the Poetic Voice," in *Women in French Literature*, ed. Michel Guggenheim (Saratoga, Calif.: Anma Libri, 1988), 47–55; Lance K. Donaldson-Evans, "The Taming of the Muse: The Female Poetic Voice in Pernette du Guillet's *Rymes*," in *Pre-Pléïade Poetry*, ed. Jerry C. Nash (Lexington: French Forum Publishers, 1985), 84–96; Philip Ford, "A propos des

'élégies' de Pernette Du Guillet," in *L'émergence littéraire des femmes à Lyon à la Renaissance, 1520–1560*, ed. Michèle Clément and Janine Incardona (Saint-Etienne: Publications de l'Université de Saint-Etienne, 2008), 165–76; Karen Simroth James, "On veult responce avoir: Pernette du Guillet's Dialogic Poetics," in *A Dialogue of Voices: Feminist Literary Theory and Bakhtin*, ed. K. Hohne and H. Wussow (Minneapolis: University of Minnesota Press, 1994), 171–97, and "Pernette du Guillet: Spiritual Union and Poetic Distance," in *Feminism*, ed. A. Maynor Hardee and Freeman G. Henry, *French Literature Series* 16 (1989), 27–37; Ann Rosalind Jones, *The Currency of Eros: Women's Love Lyric in Europe, 1540–1620* (Bloomington: Indiana University Press, 1990), chap. 3, and "Surprising Fame: Renaissance Gender Ideologies and Women's Lyric," in *The Poetics of Gender*, ed. Nancy K. Miller (New York: Columbia University Press, 1986), 74–95; Lawrence D. Kritzman, "Pernette du Guillet and a Voice of One's Own," in *The Rhetoric of Sexuality* (Cambridge: Cambridge University Press, 1991), 11–28; Pierre Martin, "De Maurice Scève à Pernette du Guillet, ou le jeu d'Actéon," in *Le mythe de Diane en France au XVIe siècle*, ed. Jean-Raymond Fanlo and Marie-Dominique Legrand, Albinea 14, Cahiers d'Aubigné (Niort; Paris: Librairie Honoré Champion, 2002), 39–55; Gisèle Mathieu-Castellani, "Parole d'Echo? Pernette au miroir des *Rymes*," in *Esprit Créateur* 30:4 (Winter 1990), 61–71; Stephen Murphy, "The Death of Actaeon as Petrarchist topos," in *Comparative Literature Studies* 28: 2 (1991), 137–55; T. A. Perry, "Pernette du Guillet's Poetry of Love and Desire," in *Bibliothèque d'Humanisme et Renaissance* 35 (1973), 259–71; Kirk D. Read, "Poolside Transformations: Diana and Actaeon Revisited by French Renaissance Women Lyricists," in *Renaissance Women Writers: French Texts / American Contexts*, ed. Anne R. Larsen and Colette Winn (Detroit: Wayne State University Press, 1994), 38–54; Josiane Rieu, "Pernette du Guillet: Poétique et réflexivité dans les *Rymes* (1545)," in *Dans les miroirs de l'écriture: La Réflexivité chez les femmes écrivains d'Ancien Régime*, ed. Jean-Philippe Beaulieu and Diane Desrosiers-Bonin, *Paragraphes* 17 (Montreal: Université de Montréal, 1998), 33–47; Colette Winn, "Le procès du même et de l'autre: Pernette du Guillet et le mythe ovidien de Diane et Actéon," in *Les représentations de l'Autre du Moyen Age au XVIIe siècle*, ed. Evelyne Berriot-Salvadore (Saint-Etienne: Publications de l'Universtité de Saint-Etienne, 1995), 263–71; Cathy Yandell, "Carpe Diem, Poetic Immortality, and the Gendered Ideology of Time," in *Renaissance Women Writers*, 115–29.

181. The references to the clear fountain pool ("la clere fontaine") in line 3 and to the clear water from the spring ("la pure eau de la clere fontaine") in line 26 conjure up two different mythological pools of water. The speaker envisions herself strolling alongside a pool that resembles the Castalian spring, fountain of the muses and source of poetic inspiration associated with the god Apollo. The "clere fontaine" also recalls the forest pool in which Diana bathed in the Ovidian tale of Actaeon, the wandering hunter in Greek myth who inadvertently spies the goddess bathing nude, leading to his fatal metamorphosis—an allusion that forms the basis of the speaker's fantasy in the first part of this elegy.

182. The speaker would be unaccompanied. Cotgrave translates "mesnie" ("maignie") as "A meynie, familie, household company, or servants." "Sans aucune maignie" means "without the company of any of my family or household members," without a chaperone—in other words, "on my own."

183. Here, as elsewhere, the beloved ("cil" or "celuy") is described as well versed in philosophy, aligned with Apollo and the Muses, and filled with a virtue that encompasses both moral qualities and a devotion to noble works.

184. See the Introduction for a discussion of the association of lute playing with the poet's art as well as with feminine sensuality. For more on this association in the works of Du Guillet, Scève, Labé, and others, see Zecher, *Sounding Objects*, 139; 149–52. See also Tetel, "Le luth et la lyre de l'Ecole Lyonnaise," 949–62.

185. In the Ovidian recounting of the myth, Actaeon inadvertently spies the goddess Diana bathing nude in a pool with her nymphs. As punishment, Diana throws water into Actaeon's face, causing his transformation into a stag who is then chased and eaten by his own hunting dogs. A similar "clere et heureuse fontaine" is used by Scève in *dizain* 235 of the *Délie*, and the emblematic illustration preceding *dizain* 168 depicts Actaeon transformed and chased by his hounds. (See the Introduction for a discussion of the intersection between these poems by Du Guillet and Scève.) Du Guillet's language is closer to that of Petrarch in poem 23 of the *Rime sparse*, which evokes this mythological tale, although her conclusion diverges radically from his. Petrarch's use of the Diana/Actaeon myth ends with the suffering lover (the speaker) transformed into the stag, fleeing his hounds—an image that translates the perpetual silence and suffering of the lover/poet in the *Rime sparse* and in Scève's *Délie*. Du Guillet's speaker uses wordplay to explain that the water of the fountain will transform the transgressing lover not into a stag ("cerf"), but into a devoted servant ("serf," "serviteur"), with her terms connoting not only service to a master in feudal society, but—more importantly—the service and devotion required of the lover in the courtly tradition, the "service d'amour."

With regard to this elegy, Philip Ford notes a similar association of the *locus amœnus* with poetic inspiration in two odes by the neo-Latin poet Jean Salmon Macrin, whose works were well known in the literary circles of Lyon in the first half of the sixteenth century ("A propos des 'élégies' de Pernette Du Guillet," 170–71).

186. In a moment of elation (lines 34–39), the speaker imagines herself a goddess, with such power that Diana would feel displaced and envy her. (Her vision of seduction and power would silence the other poet.) Reconsidering her fantasy, however, the speaker wonders if, in thus following her desire, she would truly wish to displease Apollo and the Muses, depriving them of one—her beloved—who is supremely capable of serving and bringing them honor through his poetry. Ford points out that the feminine plural ending of the past participles in line 42 ("privees, et confuses") emphasizes the important role of the Muses, leaving Apollo out of the picture, or at least momentarily highlighting the "rapports féminins" ("A propos des 'élégies' de Pernette Du Guillet," 173).

187. The tone of humility here reflects a rhetorical stance adopted by many Renaissance poets and which appears frequently in the works of women poets, in particular, whose virtue was exposed to censure as a result of the publication of their work. In the end, the speaker refuses to keep her lover captive, as servant or slave, which would prevent him from writing poetry and therefore of serving Apollo and the Muses, to the benefit of all readers. Elsewhere (in poems 23 and 28, for example), the *Rymes* evoke the ideal of the lovers' mutual and reciprocal attachment, an essential component of Neoplatonic theories

of love. Here the speaker rejects a possession that would not be reciprocal—that would bring *her* glory, but render the beloved subservient and silent.

188. *déïté*: a mythological divinity, including the concept of divine anger or furor. Here the speaker imagines that her silencing of the beloved male poet could unleash Apollo's divine power—and possibly his fury—causing the god to incite the world and its readers against her for having deprived them of the beloved's poetry ("ses escriptz"). The relationship between Apollo and the beloved here recalls the conclusion of poem 61, the first of the two Italian epigrams, where Apollo says of the man standing in the spring, bearing garlands of laurel leaves, "*This one, if he's inclined, shall bring me praise*" ("questo sara l'honor mio gran se vuole").

In addition to recognizing the pleasure that the world will derive from her beloved's poetry, the speaker also draws attention to the contentment she herself will gain from his work. This mutual contentment that comes from a reciprocal exchange of learning and knowledge is a *leitmotiv* of the *Rymes*. The rhetorical stance of humility vis-à-vis the beloved and the god Apollo does not negate the evidence here of the poet's own erudition and skill, including her ability to project, consider, and reject a captivating vision of power and control. The speaker's conclusion brings the entire imagined tableau of power—greater than Diana's and sufficient to anger Apollo—to a close, focusing in the end on the work of both poets. Even as the rhetorical mask of humility is raised, we learn that the words of one poet do not require or rely on the silence of the other, which in the end represents a powerful stance in the face of poetic tradition.

POEM 44

189. Although we don't know to what degree this epigram may be autobiographical, it does clearly establish a troubling dilemma for the speaker; she loves the one she should hate—her beloved—and hates the one she should love—presumably her husband, based on the mention of legal rights to follow.

190. The speaker's esteem for her beloved's good ("le bien") comes as no surprise. If he flees from her because she is unlike him ("sa non semblable"), it may be due to the difference in their learning and accomplishments—a humble self-assessment by the speaker that is repeated elsewhere in the *Rymes*.

191. The other's "pernicious" pleasure may refer to the physical union of husband and wife, which—although lacking the qualities of a spiritual, Neoplatonic union—is protected by law. Line 8 seems to indicate that her husband's pleasure ("trop damnable"), upheld by law, takes away the speaker's right to decide whom she loves and to control her own sexuality. The speaker of Antoine Héroët's *La parfaicte amye* struggles with the same dilemma. In lines 339–40, the "amye" wonders which one is harmed more by her love: "Ou à celuy qui de mon heur abuse, / Ou à celluy que maulgré moy reffuse?" (the one who abuses my happiness, or the one whom I refuse despite myself?). For more comments on Héroët's work in relation to this poem, see Rajchenbach's notes in *Rymes*, 157.

192. Despite the laws that govern marriage, the speaker explains that she feels a greater obligation to the one who is not legally bound to her, separating the right and reason of her emotions from her civil and social status.

POEM 45

193. The topic of jealousy—its causes and effects—reappears throughout the *Rymes*, including poems 29, 35, 41, 46, 49.

194. After acknowledging the negative effects of jealousy, the final six lines of the epigram emphasize that the speaker's feelings stem from what she has seen and judged with her own eyes. She doubts therefore that anyone could possess arguments capable of convincing her that she is wrong—that she is mistaken in her reasoned understanding of the situation—although she would welcome such consolation. In this example of the poet's irony, it is clear that the only one who could indeed convince the speaker that she is mistaken, and bring her true consolation, would be her beloved, her Day.

POEM 46

195. Poem 46 presents a conversational scenario in which the speaker addresses her concerns to an unidentified person who may be unhappy or offended by her complaints and doubts regarding her beloved's fidelity. Finch's English version maintains the ambiguity surrounding the gender and identity of the addressee in the original. The speaker appears to regret putting a mutual friend in a position that will mean the end of an otherwise good friendship between that person and the speaker's beloved. The friend, troubled by the infidelity he observes and loyal to the speaker, may sever his ties of friendship with the speaker's beloved, an unfortunate consequence in the speaker's view. Finch suggests the possibility that the interlocutor may even be the poet's husband, and that the husband—a friend of the master poet—may have encouraged the mentor relationship; if the beloved poet were to turn his attentions to a less talented protégé, that would cause a breakup of the friendship between the two men. It is also possible that the poem is an address to the rival herself, with the speaker making an ironic claim that she doesn't wish to annoy the other woman by complaining, but implying that the "friendship" ("amytié") between the other woman and the beloved separates the speaker from him, concluding with a verbal insult that leaves no doubt as to the speaker's opinion of her rival. The verb "desjoindre" in line 8 has no direct object, keeping us from knowing for sure whose friendship is at risk of being dissolved.

196. As in poem 41, the speaker's careful denial—her insistence that she does not complain about or blame her beloved for paying his attentions elsewhere—implies the contrary. The last line of the poem confirms that her rival is "a lesser one" ("une moindre").

POEM 47

197. As in the conclusion of the preceding epigram, which identifies the rival as a less worthy woman, the speaker of poem 47, having now seen her rival, finds her to be "no more fair than good" (i.e., nothing special).

198. What upsets her is not the mediocrity of the other woman, but that her beloved's reputation may have suffered from the affair.

199. This line seems to reflect the speaker's realization that the "eclipse" that has befallen her beloved may turn out to be a benefit to her. As the final two lines of the poem suggest, this situation allows her to understand what her beloved's previous actions would have revealed to her if she had not been so blindly trusting.

POEM 48

200. The Day is compared to the sun in other poems in the *Rymes*, but the image here of the sun traveling in the sky—ascending and descending—not only suggests the great influence and glory of the beloved's light, but also his fickleness. The sun takes his light here and there, to various places, recalling the wandering attentions and affections for which the speaker reproaches her beloved elsewhere in the collection, particularly in the three preceding poems (45, 46, and 47).

201. In line 5, the feminine plural pronoun, "toutes," refers literally to the regions ("places") illuminated by the sun. The French pronoun also suggests the speaker's rivals, those who receive her beloved's illuminating attentions. The speaker acknowledges that others—other women, that is—will be attracted by her beloved's light. The association of night with ignorance recurs in poems 2, 63, and 68.

202. Huguet's dictionary cites examples of the rhyme of "lumiere" with "fumiere" from Jean Lemaire de Belges, Joachim du Bellay, and Pierre de Ronsard.

203. The firelight that appears brightest next to the darkest smoke seems to represent the beloved's intellect and eloquence, shining all the more brightly in contrast to the ignorance of those around him, including the women implied by the pronoun "toutes" in line 5. (See above, n201.) The meaning of the last line remains ambiguous, however. The speaker may be drawing attention to her own dark night of ignorance (recalling poems 1 and 2) and telling her beloved that he should stick by her because his light shines brightest in her company. Such a stance would echo poem 41, where the speaker tells her beloved that his golden words will yield the most fruitful results when they are engraved and implanted in her. The concluding line of this poem, however, may also serve as an ironic reminder to the beloved that, although he may seem to shine more brightly when in the company of other women, that is only because they are more ignorant than herself. Finch's translation captures the proverbial quality of the last two lines while also maintaining the ambiguity

that calls for the reader to consider the possible interpretations and decide what the poem is telling us about fire and smoke, light and darkness, learning and ignorance.

POEM 49

204. *Traictz à la Gregeoise*: arrows or darts lit with fire, like those that Byzantine soldiers and sailors used in the crusades, according to the *Dictionnaire historique de la langue française*. According to Cotgrave's dictionary, "feu gregois" meant "wild-fire, or the best kind thereof; such as will burn within the water." Clearly the speaker wants us to know that Cupid's arrows were of the most dangerous type.

205. The expression "la Bourgeoise" at the rhyme of line 7 in the original simply indicates that the potential rival was an inhabitant of the town or city. Victor Graham read this as a possible allusion to Clémence de Bourges, to whom Louise Labé's *Œuvres* are dedicated (*Rymes*, 66; 68). As others have pointed out, however, Clémence de Bourges would have been only about twelve years old in 1544, making her an unlikely rival. (See Barataud and Trudeau, *Rymes*, 124, and Rajchenbach, *Rymes*, 160.)

206. *Callimera*: Greek for "bonjour." The blithe greeting in Greek is the humorous counterpart of the fiery "Greek" arrow.

207. To the speaker, the greeting in Greek, "callimera," sounded suspiciously like the French, 'qu'il l'aymera" (literally, "that he will love her," or, "may he love her"). The pun demonstrates that the speaker recognizes the humor in the jealousy that also causes her great pain. Finch's English version maintains the similarities of meaning and sound between the two phrases in order to echo the wordplay in the original.

POEM 50

208. This poem is a follow-up to the previous epigram. There, suspicion and jealousy overwhelm the speaker; here, she comes around to a more positive interpretation of what she oversaw and overheard.

209. *Imera*: Greek for "day."

210. In the previous epigram, the speaker fears that Cupid has proclaimed, "qu'il l'aymera" ("Captivate *her*"), but here she returns to a more comforting interpretation, "qu'il m'aymera" ("he will love and captivate *me*").

211. The referent of the demonstrative pronoun "cil" (the one, that one) may well be Cupid, who held the flaming arrows in the previous poem. The speaker here envisions her beloved Day inflamed or filled with ardor, just as Love set her own heart aflame with love. (In poem 40, Cupid finally succeeded in capturing the young woman's heart with the aid of the "Archers of Virtue.") The pronoun "cil" could also possibly refer to the beloved Day himself, in which

case the poem implies that the man who first inflamed the speaker's heart had changed and perhaps wandered astray, but that now he too will find his heart filled with ardor.

POEM 51

212. Poem 51 juxtaposes the long-lasting and slow-growing ardor founded on virtue with the violent but short-lived flames of physical passions.

213. According to Graham, the noun "clemence" may be a reference to Clémence de Bourges, the dedicatee of Louise Labé's *Œuvres* (*Rymes*, 68). As subsequent editors have pointed out, Clémence de Bourges would still have been quite young in 1544. (See above, n205.) Here, "clemence" denotes the clemency and indulgence of each lover toward his/her beloved, as well as the quality of meekness, mildness, and moderation—rather than the violence of uncontrolled passion—that strengthens and nourishes true love. In this era, the word "clemence" also denotes mercy, leniency, or compassion in a religious or legal context, hence Finch's choice of the word "indulgence," in English. This epigram highlights the unusual nature of true love—vigorous in its clemency, slow-growing and eternal.

POEM 52

214. An earlier version of this poem was set to music and published in the *Second livre contenant XXVII chansons nouvelles à quatre parties en ung volume*, by Pierre Attaingnant and Hubert Jullet (Paris, 1540) and published also in 1540 in the *Parangon des chansons, sixiesme livre contenant XXV chansons*, by Jacques Moderne in Lyon. For details of the publication history and an analysis of this poem with regard to its model, also printed in the same songbooks, see Joyce Miller, "In the Margins," 354–57. Miller has shown that the early (1540) version of Du Guillet's poem responds to an epigram appearing in Attaingnant's 1538 songbook, the *Second livre contenant XXVII chansons*, printed in Paris.

215. As Miller explains, this epigram is an example of the poetic *rebours*, in which one poem "responds" to another, using the last line of the model as the first line of the new poem, the first line of the model as the last line of the new response poem, and borrowing some of the other rhyming words ("In the Margins," 358). Du Guillet's poem specifies that the contentment and unbelievable sweetness of love—evoked in the model poem—is the result of this "lasting good" ("ce bien durable"), with "high learning" ("le sçavoir estimable") as evidence of this happiness.

216. Pernette du Guillet takes advantage of the *rebours* tradition to end her poem on a note of certainty. The model begins with the juxtaposition of what is difficult to believe and yet known with assurance, but ends with a comparison of the lover's sweet contentment to a dream that the speaker dares not think is real. Du Guillet's epigram, reversing the first and last lines of the model and adding the focus on "le bien durable" and "le sçavoir estimable," moves from doubt and uncertainty over the reality of the sweet feelings of contentment to an assurance of the truth this good represents. Miller makes the important point that the

association here of the "'contentement' of virtuous love with the perception of knowledge of the 'good,'" is central to the *Rymes* (357).

POEM 53

217. Like the previous poem, this epigram was set to music and published in the *Second livre contenant XXVII chansons nouvelles à quatre parties en ung volume*, by Pierre Attaingnant and Hubert Jullet (Paris, 1540) and published also in 1540 in the *Parangon des chansons, sixiesme livre contenant XXV chansons* by Jacques Moderne in Lyon. For details of the publication history and an analysis of this *rebours* poem with regard to its model, which has been attributed to François Ier, see Joyce Miller, "In the Margins," 357–59. See also H. H. Kalweis, "The *Responce* Genre in Early Modern French Renaissance Poetry," in *Bibliothèque d'Humanisme et Renaissance* 65 (1983), 77–86.

218. As Miller reports, the gender of the lyric speaker of this epigram changes from male in the early version appearing in the 1540 songbook to female in the version published in the *Rymes* in 1545. The change involves two variants, in line 2 and 4. The speaker in the model poem by François Ier is female, a woman who says she will suffer in silence, so as not to give satisfaction to her ungrateful lover ("l'ingrat"). Du Guillet's epigram for the songbooks follows the "practice of replying in a male voice to a piece spoken or sung in a female voice and vice versa" (Miller, 358). In the 1540 version, line 2 of Du Guillet's poem is "Je veulx tout seul tourment supporter," and the rhyming words for lines 2 and 4 are reversed (Miller, 359). Appearing in the *Rymes*, without its model, the epigram has been changed to convey the voice of a female speaker.

219. Miller observes that Du Guillet's epigram moderates the tone of despair in François Ier's model, but also that it projects a voice quite different from the rest in the *Rymes*, remaining in the "courtly tradition of regret and lamentation," rather than moving from regret and suffering to any affirmation of pure love or spiritual contentment (358–59).

POEM 54

220. This remains one of the most fascinating and enigmatic poems in the collection. Du Guillet uses mathematical metaphors from a variety of poetic traditions to compose her epigram about both love and the lyric traditions that inform her poem. The preceding epigram highlights the sad separation of the two lovers who were—at least for a time—joined as one, sharing one love between them. In addition to believing that two lovers joined in spiritual union become one, Ebreo and the other Neoplatonists also theorized that in love each individual becomes two—each one is both lover and beloved—and then that combining those two pairs makes four. See Ebreo, *Dialogues*, 193, and *Philosophy of Love*, 259–60. The opening of this epigram may allude to this Neoplatonic mathematical theory of love, but the rest of the poem moves beyond it. Regarding this epigram, see also Saulnier, *Etude*, 56; Gisèle Mathieu-Castellani, "La Parole chétive," 54–60, and *La Quenuoille et la Lyre* (Paris: J. Corti, 1998), 152–68; Miller, "In the Margins," 367; *Rymes*, ed. Rajchenbach (Droz, 2006), 72–73, 162–63; *Rymes*, ed. Barataud and Trudeau (Champion, 2006), 132–33.

221. The "one" that she hates (line 1) may refer to the figure of *Amour* (Cupid), responsible for the lovers' suffering in other poems. In any case, the love the speaker describes here is harmful and linked with blind youth, bitterness, and distress. There is an initial suggestion that the inner turmoil caused by youthful love—characterized by "sweet bitterness" in the Petrarchan tradition—is in fact more bitter than sweet in the speaker's experience. (In stanza 2 of poem 32, the speaker—inspired by her beloved's virtue and "bien"—finds the opposite: that her love is more sweet than bitter, "plus doulx, qu'amer").

222. Ebreo's Neoplatonist theory does not explain why or how the "fourth" would be associated with an injustice or wrong committed with regard to the speaker, and does not directly account for "the three" ("les trois") from whom she flees—or who flee from her—in line 9. Saulnier, noting the popularity of this type of play on numbers in the poetry of the period, cites a poem first attributed to François Ier and written in the style of Marot that begins, "D'en aymer trois ce m'est force et contrainte" (I am compelled to love three of them) (56). Entitled "Comment Amour navra de trois dardz le plus perfaict des vrays amans" (How Cupid wounded with three darts the most perfect of true lovers) in the 1534 *Les Fleurs de Poesie Françoyse*, the poem projects the voice of a speaker lamenting his distress at being compelled by Cupid to love three different women. Gérard Defaux attributes the poem not to the king, but to Claude Chappuys, another poet in Marot's circle. See *Les Fleurs de Poesie Françoise*, 198–99. Gisèle Mathieu-Castellani reads Du Guillet's epigram as a rewriting of the poem by the king or Chappuys, arguing that poem 54 of the *Rymes* may well describe the plight of a woman with too many lovers or suitors, and that Du Guillet's poem reveals two contradictory intertexts (one Neoplatonic, the other libertine), with a resulting ambiguity that requires the reader's careful engagement ("La parole chétive," 55–60). The reference in the model poem to being held by *Amour* (Cupid) in "ses destroictz" (his narrows, his jurisdiction; also, a difficult or dangerous situation) is reflected in the "amorous agony" ("amoureuse destresse") in line 4 of Du Guillet's epigram.

223. The desire to acquit oneself of a wrong and pay a debt owed to a beloved is the topic of poem 19. Here it is not evident why the speaker wishes to acquit herself in the eyes of one or multiple lovers.

224. Including herself in the various equations, the female speaker implies that she might lose her own sense of identity in the distress caused by love, a risk not covered by Neoplatonist theory.

225. Although the reasons are not divulged, nor the math explained, it is clear that the speaker feels she must—for her own good—leave behind all lovers or aspects of love, even the fourth, perhaps a privileged or more highly admired suitor.

226. Quartan fever is a type of malarial fever that recurs in what is considered a four-day cycle; the fever strikes on the first day, then the patient is symptom-free for two days, and the fever returns again on the fourth day (actually the first day of the next cycle). Miller notes that "'fièvre quarte' was a common topic of satirical verse in antiquity and in the Renaissance," proposing that the conclusion of Du Guillet's epigram represents a "facetious allusion to Ficino's description of the disease of love as 'la fièvre tierce' (tertian fever)"

(367). Rajchenbach refers to a poetic tradition associating "fièvre quarte" with love, citing Marot's "Epistre à son amy, en abhorrant folle amour," which compares a lover's pain to quartan fever (*Rymes*, 163). See Marot, *Œuvres poétiques*, vol. 2, 155. Susan Silver's study of the impact of quartan fever on Ronsard and his poem, "la Salade," indicates that Ficino also suffered from this type of fever, which the Italian Neoplatonist physician attributed to excessive melancholy—to which men of letters were believed to be particularly vulnerable. See "'La Salade' and Ronsard's Writing Cure," in *Romanic Review* 89:1 (Jan. 1998), 21–36. Barataud and Trudeau propose that Du Guillet's poem presents the endless cycle of the "erreur amoureuse" perpetuated by the courtly love tradition, and that the speaker at the center of this cycle wishes to break away from "ce mécanisme qui lui donne la 'fièvre' et ressaisir la totalité de son être" (this mechanism that gives her the fever and to recover the totality of her being), 133.

It appears that the notion of the quartan fever itself—long associated with love poetry and suffering lovers—serves ingeniously as the organizing principle of Du Guillet's epigram. Without negating the importance of the multiple literary traditions evoked, the fever itself suggests an explanation of the "jeu numérique" that is otherwise difficult to resolve: the "one I loathe who dictates I love two" might represent the first day and the onset of the fever, meaning that the victim will then have two "likeable" fever-free days. The first three days lead inevitably to the fourth, when the fever recurs, explaining why the speaker would view "the fourth" as committing a wrong or injustice in her regard and wish to flee all four in order to rid herself of the fever and regain her health. Quartan fever as organizing concept allows the poet to combine popular Neoplatonic theories of the math of love with the Petrarchan tradition of suffering in love in a fascinating blend that undoubtedly appealed to Renaissance readers familiar with the textual sources, with the genre of the poetic enigma (which asks readers to solve a puzzle whose answer lies hidden in the verse), as well as with quartan fever as medical ailment and literary conceit.

POEM 55

227. Leone Ebreo presents a debate about theory and practice in the context of love in his *Dialogues d'amour*. Sophia tells Philo, "you cannot deny that knowledge of the theory should always precede application in practice, as it is reason which rules Man's actions" (*Philosophy of Love*, 233; *Dialogues*, 178). Like Sophia's observation, Du Guillet's conclusion here, that love (i.e., theory) precedes the lover (i.e. practice, or the practitioner), appears to contradict Philo's assertion later in the *Dialogues* that the beloved person or thing precedes the lover, who precedes love. In that case, love is the practice applied and experienced by the lover, rather than a theory he knows in advance. The sequence described by Philo is the basis for Du Guillet's poem 24. (See above, n101.)

228. In Ancient Greece, the sophists were wise men, teachers of philosophy and rhetoric. Under the criticism of Plato and Aristotle, the term sophist came to mean one who uses cunning and specious arguments. For the verb "sophistiquer" in the sixteenth century, Cotgrave's dictionary gives, "to sophisticate, falsifie, counterfeit, adulterate, corrupt; also, to play the sophister, dispute subtily, argue cunningly, to deceive." Du Guillet introduces the Sophists and their reasoning into her "debate" with humor: even a "Sophistique" would concede the point in his sleep—that art is formed from what is known.

229. Cotgrave's dictionary indicates that a "replique" (line 7) is not only a reply or "second answer," but also a "new confirmation of former assertions." The verb "répliquer," according to Huguet's dictionary, means "répéter." The speaker's conclusion confirms what "some have said," as reported in the opening lines of the poem: Theory comes before Practice, and Love comes first, before the Lover.

POEM 56

230. Du Guillet's *chanson* was set to music and recorded by Véronique Pestel in *L'appeau des mots* (Toulouse: Scalen distribution, 1998). While working on the translation of this poem, Finch noticed that the French stanzas without longer lines can be sung to the tune of the traditional folk song, "Au clair de la lune."

231. The opening stanza associates happiness with suffering for honorable and virtuous love, a topos that appears early in the collection, in poem 13, in which the speaker asks the blind god of love to grant "long-lasting satisfaction of the mind" ("en noz espritz contentement durable") to those who know this "worthy suffering" ("du bien le mal en effect honnorable"). That suffering for something so praiseworthy is a source of great contentment is the speaker's point of departure in poem 18.

232. The second and third stanzas describe what the speaker in poem 39, "Perfect Love," calls "pleasures found in uncontrolled affection" ("le plaisir de folle affection"); such base pleasures do not lead to contentment and are associated with the carnal knowledge of all creatures. These stanzas also call to mind the "ardeur commune" that gossips attribute to the speaker and against which she defends herself in poem 42. In poem 63, the speaker explains that shameful thrills play no role in the "amytié" shared with her beloved, which is grounded equitably in virtue.

233. As in poem 51, where the violence of physical love that quickly burns itself out is contrasted with the slow-growing, enduring flame of virtuous love, here the toil of the lover who seeks the "common vice" goes up in smoke when reason appears on the scene—reason that accompanies each noble and virtuous heart and triumphs over physical pleasure.

234. Poems 3 and 4 link the beloved's virtue with learning and eloquence, which inspire the speaker's love and her pursuit of the good through him. Here, stanzas six and seven evoke love united with virtue—presumably the beloved's—which engenders a desire on the part of the speaker for "all good" and for the knowledge that will ensue.

235. Lines 35 and 36 recall poem 40 and Cupid's vain efforts to wound the speaker until he finally obtained the aid of the "Archers of Virtue," allowing him to reach her heart. In poem 12, the speaker explains that giving up or moving beyond the delights of physical pleasure that form the base of Cupid's power will cause the god of love to be struck and pinned by his own arrows, bringing new life to the lovers.

236. The focus here on the strength and resoluteness of her love ("mon cueur ferme, & fort") echoes the conclusion of poem 33, where the speaker expresses her hope that her firm refusal to relent (to those who would attempt to dissuade her from her love) will bring contentment to her beloved. In the concluding lines of poem 39, "Perfect Love," the speaker displays a similar trust in the effects of her fidelity: "With him thus certain of my confidence, / I'm free, myself, from fear and ignorance" ("Parquoy, luy seur de ma ferme asseurance, / M'asseureray de craincte, et ignorance.") Mutual assurance, freedom from ignorance, virtue linked with learning—these are the qualities of perfect, pure love in Pernette du Guillet's *Rymes*. On the influence of Marot's use of the concept of "ferme amour," see Gérard Defaux, "Marot et 'Ferme Amour': essai de mise au point," in *Anteros*, ed. Ullrich Langer and Jean Miernowski (Orléans: Paradigme, 1994), 137–67. Defaux includes Pernette du Guillet in the group of poets who, in Marot's wake, depict the struggle or quarrel of "ferme" and "folle amour" in their works. See *Œuvres poétiques complètes*, vol. 2, 935–36.

237. The words "travaillant" and "immortel soucy" leave room for different—though not contradictory—interpretations of this stanza. The verb "travailler" in Middle French meant "to toil" or "to labor," both in the sense of working hard and in the sense of suffering for something. The path of "immortel soucy" (immortal concern or care) may refer to the eternal nature of the love and devotion she holds as an ideal, as well as to the poet's concern for immortality through poetry. The image of the "dure impression" being engraved in poem 1 signals at the beginning of the collection a recognition of the work involved in writing and printing that recurs in subtle ways throughout the volume. See also poem 63, where night is filled with ignorance, and daylight—the light of her Day—brings "labor that well suits us" ("le travail qui nous duit").

238. The concluding stanza offers a reminder that pure love and desire also bring pleasure—different from the delights of physical attraction governed by *Amour* (Cupid), but powerful nevertheless, and beneficial for both lovers. As poems 12, 13, and 14 also indicate, the death of base desire and the birth of love for a higher good bring new life to the lovers.

POEM 57

239. Graham and subsequent editors have noted that this poem was set to music by Maillard in a volume published after the poet's death, entitled the *Quart livre de chansons nouvellement composé en musique à quatre parties* (Paris: A. Le Roy and R. Ballard, 1561). See Rajchenbach's additional notes about this songbook in *Rymes*, 167.

240. The first eight lines enumerate the causes of a lover's pain and suffering in order from the least severe (not daring or knowing to whom to complain about an offense) to the most tragic (to love passionately with no hope of relief), emphasizing the recurrent nature of this pain by the repetition of the phrase, "It's terrible" ("C'est un grand mal") at the beginning of lines 1, 3, 5, and 7. Miller has shown how this epigram provides a lyric *responce* to a poem by Pontus de Tyard in *Les Erreurs amoureuses I*, entitled, "Ce m'est un mal que je n'eusse pensé." In this type of response poem, explains Miller, the text parallels the model poem, with variations, introducing something new in the conclusion, or final "pointe" ("In the Margins," 361–64).

241. The last three lines of Tyard's poem focus on the suffering that increases the lover's passion, even as he realizes that the more he desires to serve his lady, the less her affection toward him grows. Du Guillet's epigram concludes with a correction that appears to go so far as to scold the lover, reminding him that the sweet languor he ultimately feels is a vindication and a reward, a "grand bien" rather than a "grand mal."

POEM 58

242. The use of the word "maistre" (master or teacher) recalls poem 30, in which the female speaker tells her beloved that he will never win her over by treating her rudely or harshly, "comme maistre." Here, the speaker appears to acknowledge her beloved's role as superior and teacher, reflecting the admiration she expresses in many poems for his noble learning and eloquence. Nevertheless, her recognition of the beloved's innate superiority and the humility she says must characterize her attitude toward him are presented with a rhetorical twist and a healthy dose of irony. Insisting repeatedly that she does not want to swell with pride herself or to constrain or govern her beloved suggests quite the opposite. Graham and subsequent editors of the *Rymes* have observed that lines 9–10 of Scève's *dizain* 202 convey a similar attitude on the part of the lover who does not wish to deprive the beloved of her "naifve et libre intention" (naïve and free intention). *Rymes* (Droz, 1968), 77. Du Guillet's entire epigram, however, is built on the expansion of this denial, repeating it anaphorically with strong rhetorical impact.

243. Rather than to have one heart be subservient to or control the other, the speaker wishes for a reciprocity that will align the beloved's desire with her own.

POEM 59

244. Graham makes note of a poem by Charles de Sainte-Marthe, "Qui dit Amour estre plein de langœur" in *Poesie Françoise* (Lyon, 1540), that addresses a similar topic, telling those who blame *Amour* (Cupid) for love's "langœur" that in reality the blame lies with our own intemperance (*Rymes*, 78).

245. Contrary to the entire Petrarchan tradition, the speaker tells us that *Amour* (Cupid) has no form or substance with which to hold sway over us. As the final six lines indicate, we have only our own "folle plaisance" to blame—the mad pleasures that rule frivolous and fickle hearts. This poem refutes in the most direct manner the literary and philosophical traditions that perpetuate the image of the blind god of love and his powers. Other poems in the collection depict *Amour* and his influence in humorous terms (49 and 50, for example) or describe Cupid's defeat when confronted with virtue and honor (12, 13, 40) or when compared in importance to the Lady herself (24). Poem 59, however, bluntly reveals a truth that applies to all, including the speaker, encompassed by a universal "nous." A similar observation about human nature surfaces at the end of the extended allegorical poem 68, "The Night," when the speaker recognizes that the monstrous beings in her nightmare, who in fact have no essence, become—through dangerous imagination—our true science/knowledge ("nostre vraye science").

POEM 60

246 The debate between friends over the relative merits of Italian and French is reminiscent of the *Concorde des deux langaiges* by Jean Lemaire de Belges, first published in 1511. Saulnier notes that Du Guillet was inspired not only by the topic of the relative merits of the two languages, of great interest in the early and mid-sixteenth century, but also by the framework of Lemaire's debate—between friends, with one noting that French is genteel, sufficient, worthy, and elegant, and the other noting that Italian, a language spoken with "greater emotion" ("plus grande affection") allows one to express one's intention more fully in love and other matters. (See *Etude*, 30.) For Pernette du Guillet, liveliness is a "Tuscan attribute" ("le Thuscan a plus d'affection") and "Precision renders French speech more delightful" ("le François parle plus proprement"). For the relevant passages in the Concorde, see Lemaire, *Œuvres*, vol. 3, ed. Stecher (Louvain, 1885), 98–99, or *Concorde des deux langages*, 3–5.

247. Cotgrave, Huguet, and other historical dictionaries tell us that "depeindre" (or "despeindre") had two different meanings in the sixteenth century. The verb meant either to depict/describe *or* to pale/fade/take away color. If we opt for the first meaning here, the conclusion presents an even-handed judgment, recognizing the merits of each language. In that case, Finch proposes the following variant ending to this epigram in English:

For fine descriptions, each one qualifies;
Or, to offer a judgment more insightful:
One depicts what the other one implies.

Such a conclusion, echoing Jean Lemaire de Belges, would not be uncharacteristic for Du Guillet, whose poems often resolve debates in ways that avoid giving either party the upper hand. Barataud and Trudeau opt for interpreting the conclusion in this manner, finding that "il faut donner à *dépeindre* sa pleine valeur picturale," and that for Du Guillet, Italian has an evocative, painterly quality, compared to the more rational expression of the French language (147).

If the second meaning of the verb applies here, however, then the conclusion presents a judgment resolutely in favor of the merits of French over Italian: "Tuscan" conveys but a pale version of that which French expresses. Such a confirmation of the value of the French language may well reflect the shift in attitudes and confidence of French writers in their own language by the 1540s. Finch has based her translation on this meaning of the verb "despeindre," as has Norman Shapiro in the concluding line of his English version of the epigram: "Tuscan makes pale what French can best express" (*French Women Poets*, 123). Both meanings of the verb coexisted in the sixteenth century, and the two different interpretations they lend to this poem's conclusion are entirely logical in the context of the *Rymes* and the period in which Du Guillet was writing. As with other ambiguous lexical choices or syntactical twists in the *Rymes*, poem 60 leaves us to weigh alternative meanings and to make our own judgment of the friendly dispute.

POEM 61

248. Both of the recently published French critical editions provide a modern French translation of this epigram. See *Rymes*, ed. Rajchenbach (Droz, 2006), 224, and *Rymes*, ed. Barataud and Trudeau (Champion, 2006), 148.

249. In ancient Greece and in classical mythology, Mount Parnassus and the Castalian spring were sacred to Apollo and the Muses and associated with poetic inspiration.

250. It is not clear to whom the pronoun "colei" ("celle," "she") refers in line 2. It may indicate a muse who inspires the poet, or it could refer to the Delphic Oracle, the ancient prophetess of Apollo in his temple at Delphi, located below the Castalian Spring on Mount Parnassus. The "sponde" (banks, shore) of the spring are sacred, consecrated to Apollo and poetry. The "one" who emerges from or stands in the waters of the pool might first be mistaken for the god Apollo himself, but the following lines of the poem make it clear that this individual serves the god of poetry, by whom he is favored.

251. The man standing in or emerging from the sacred waters bears "tre ghirlande assonte"—either three simple "crowns" that one could wear together or three garlands wound together—made from young branches and leaves of a laurel tree that shades the spring. In the Italian, the figure standing in the water *has* three garlands/crowns, but it is not specified whether he holds them in his hand or is wearing them on his head. Interestingly, Alciato's popular illustrated emblem collection includes a poem and woodcut depicting "Love of Virtue" ("Amour de Vertu"), in which naked Cupid kneels by a stream, wearing one "crown"—clearly a garland—and holding three more in his hand. The accompanying verse explains that this Cupid is he who inspires noble, virtuous love, and has nothing to do with the "common Venus" of physical pleasure. According to Alciato's text, the four garlands represent the four cardinal virtues—wisdom, temperance, courage, and justice—and because the crown of wisdom ("sapience") is the most important, that is the one that the noble Cupid wears on his head. It is likely that Du Guillet knew this iconographical and philosophical tradition, conveyed by Alciato's emblem and its woodcut illustration, which raises the question of what might have happened to the fourth crown, presumably that of wisdom. To view a facsimile of this emblem in Alciato's book, see the online resources of "The Renaissance in Print" at the University of Virginia Library: http://iris.lib.virginia.edu/rmds/gordon/gordonimages/Gordon1548_A54_n1_2/ (file numbers 0308_pg133.tif and 0309_pg134.tif).

The laurel tree and its branches represent Apollo and evoke the myth of Daphne. Being pursued by ardent Apollo, Daphne asks the river god Peneus for help, which he grants, allowing her to be transformed into a laurel tree on the banks of the river just as Apollo reaches her and stretches out his arms to embrace her. In his grief, Apollo makes the laurel his sacred tree and thereafter wears a wreath made from its leaves. The association of the laurel wreath with Apollo was a commonplace in the Renaissance, but the myth of Daphne and Apollo may have held particular interest for Du Guillet, as the tale of a young woman pursued by, effectively silenced by and then made famous through the words of a great poet. As Barataud and Trudeau note, there is a resemblance between the elements of this epigram and that of poem 43 (elegy 2), including the spring, Apollo and the muses. The female speaker of the elegy, however, is the one standing in the water, while the poet favored by Apollo remains on the shore (*Rymes*, 148).

252. Apollo's words clarify that the "one" in the water is most favored by the god himself. This poet who shall bring Apollo honor and praise is apparently the same one who, according to poem 43, so brilliantly serves Apollo and all the muses.

POEM 62

253. See *Rymes* (Droz, 2006), 224–25, and *Rymes* (Champion, 2006), 149, for modern French translations of this epigram. Saulnier identifies this poem as a close variant of a *strambotta,* entitled "In colpa donna amor se troppo volsi," by the Italian Petrarchist poet, Serafino Aquilano (*Opere,*Venegia, 1548). *Etude*, 41. Because Du Guillet's epigram is very close to the original, it is likely she had transcribed one of the variants of Serafino's poems circulating in manuscript or print, and that her transcription was then included in the *Rymes* by the editor and printer of the posthumous collection.

254. The speaker (whose gender is not indicated) gives in to—or at least contemplates giving in to—the sweet and overwhelming passion of love's first kiss, longing for the pleasurable death that accompanies the surrender to physical desire. That this poem was a transcription of the Italian rather than a variant or response by Du Guillet herself is further corroborated by its topic, although the poems of the *Rymes* do not deny the powerful attraction of physical desire evoked by this Italian epigram. (Here the speaker blames *Amour*, contrary to the advice of poem 59.)

POEM 63

255. The opening lines of this *chanson* convey a central metaphor of the *Rymes.* Finch's translation captures the relationship between the "Jour" and the "Journée" on an etymological level (the "Journée" being that which is born from the "Jour") and as keywords representing the relationship between the speaking woman and her beloved. The choice of the feminine "journée" to correspond to the masculine "jour" further underscores their unique relationship. Frequently in Du Guillet's poetry, the speaker identifies her beloved as the Day. She attributes her spiritual and intellectual birth to his rays in poem 2, for example, and asks for a share of his knowledge and eloquence in order to praise him in turn (to reflect his light) in poem 6. The difference between the two nouns in French is difficult to define, but, in contrast to the "jour" (day itself, and daylight), "journée" is used to refer to the duration of an individual day and the activity taking place in that time ("journée de travail, journée de repos"—day of work, day of rest, etc.).

256. The association of night with sin, villainy, and frightful visions developed in this poem is also explored at length in poem 68, "The Night." In both poems, the beloved Day brings the relief of light, goodness, and virtue.

257. Poem 39, "Perfect Love," juxtaposes the pleasures derived from uncontrolled affection (by others) with the love that the speaker shares with her beloved: "toward honor so completely driven" ("amytié ... à l'honneur toute tant adonnée").

258. As Jones observes, "'équité' is the crucial word here, a term meaning 'equality' as well as fairness and instinctive justice" (*Currency of Eros*, 95). In translating this *chanson*, Finch noticed that, after the word "équité" appears in the middle stanza of the poem (line 24), the keywords "jour" and "nuict" are no longer capitalized in the remainder of the poem. Although we do not know how this poem appeared in Du Guillet's manuscript, nor who was responsible for the capitalization in the original 1545 edition, the change within the poem in the printed version is noteworthy, coinciding as it does with a shift in focus from the evils of the night to the joys of day's illumination and the work and happiness that daylight fosters. For this reason, Barataud and Trudeau argue for reintroducing the capital "J" for "[J] our" in the final stanza (line 42) of the poem (*Rymes*, 153). After the middle stanza—where *équité* is featured—there is also a shift from "vous" to "tu" forms in the speaker's address to the beloved. "Our" ("nostre") appears once in the fourth stanza, referring to "nostre amytié," and the indirect pronoun "us" ("nous") appears in the seventh stanza, in reference to the beneficial effects of daylight and work on the speaker and her beloved, but also for all readers.

259. Idleness was often associated with the risk of evil and vice in the Renaissance. (The same association is reflected in the modern English saying that "Idle hands are the devil's tools," or "Idle hands do the devil's work.") Du Guillet associates both idleness and vice with nighttime and darkness, whereas daylight brings activity that instructs and suits us and forms us into more worthy beings. In line 32, the 3rd person singular form of the verb "nuire"—"nuit"— homophonically links the ill effects with the night that promotes them.

260. The speaker addresses the "day" and refers to herself in the third person. "She" ("Celle") is the one who has been illuminated and rescued from the dangers of darkness.

261. An "s" is missing in line 40 of the first edition—the required agreement of the past participle "escarté[s]" with the direct object ("ceulx") that precedes it in line 39. We have chosen to follow the example of the other modern editions of the *Rymes* by leaving the error uncorrected in the French.

262. The speaker returns to the first person. She is, after all, the "Journée," the Day's reflection. The light of her Day has rescued her from the risk of a "time of dejection" or unpleasantness ("fascheux sejour") in line 4 and assured her of a "plaisant sejour" in line 44. The expression "pleasant stay" ("plaisant sejour"), while perhaps not immediately evoking a spiritual or intellectual experience, provides the necessary conditions—rest, tranquility, leisure, a stopping point and place—for the beneficial work mentioned above. Just as the French word, "sejour," derives from "jour," the day governs the length and nature of her stay in this state of illumination and happy, virtuous activity.

POEM 64 ("BALLAD FOR ADONIS")

263. See the Introduction for a brief discussion of the poetic models for this poem and the rapport between Du Guillet's "Conde Claros" and Mellin de Saint-Gelais's "Deploration sur la mort d'Adonis," with which it was frequently published in sixteenth-century anthologies. For a thorough and illuminating analysis of this *chanson* and the tradition that inspired it, see Perrine Galand-Hallyn, "Le latin à la rescousse du français. Trois humanistes autour de Vénus éplorée," in *Lyon et l'illustration de la langue française à la Renaissance*, ed. Gérard Defaux, with the collaboration of Bernard Colombat (Lyon: ENS Editions, 2003), 308–43. In the appendices to her study, Galand-Hallyn includes the full text of Saint-Gelais's and Du Guillet's poems, as well as that of the neo-Latin poet, Jean Salmon Macrin, who wrote a Latin ode on the same mythological topic. See also C. Martinez, "Conde Claros de Adonis," in *Il Rinascimento a Lione*, ed. Antonio Possenti and Giulia Mastrangelo (Rome: Edizioni dell'Ateneo, 1988), 683–97.

264. "Conde Claros" is the name of a Spanish ballad about the Count Claros of Montalban that circulated widely in Europe in the fifteenth and early sixteenth centuries, and the term also refers to the tune to which the Spanish "romance" was sung. The romance and its accompanying melody were well known in France in the sixteenth century. Other poems of a similar type were often sung to the familiar tune—"sur l'air de Conde Claros." See Saulnier, "Mellin de Saint-Gelais, Pernette du Guillet et l'air 'Conde Claros,'" 525. For the musical notation of the "Conde Claros / Conteclare" tune and its variants, see Pascale Boquet and Gérard Rebours, *50 Standards, Renaissance & Baroque*, 46. For comments on the "profil mélodique" of Du Guillet's poem, see *Rymes*, ed. Rajchenbach, 80. Although Du Guillet's poem does not represent French *ballade* form, the term is appropriate with regard to both the Spanish legend and Finch's English poem and conveys the musical nature of the text to readers of the translation. For more on the use of ballad meter in the English, see the Translator's Note.

Venus's lament at the death of Adonis was the topic of Hellenistic odes that inspired both Mellin de Saint-Gelais and Pernette du Guillet. In most versions of the mythological tale, Adonis dies from being pierced by the tusks of a wild boar sent by Diana (Artemis) in retaliation for Venus's instigation of the death of Hippolytus, beloved by the goddess of the hunt. Venus hears Adonis's cry from afar and comes quickly, but cannot save him.

265. The poem opens with the depiction of two mythological figures, Cupid and Psyche, in a surprisingly domestic scene. In line 38, we learn that Psyche is the spouse ("espouse") of Cupid, but the dramatic events leading up to their marriage in mythology have no part in the cozy tableau presented here.

266. In addition to a long association with tragic song, the swan is linked to both Apollo and Venus. In particular, swans draw Venus's chariot, so it is not surprising that Cupid identifies the lament of the swan as a cry "from my mother's emissary" and a sign of "ill portent."

267. Again, the poet juxtaposes a domestic detail—husband and wife rushing to the window—with an element of mythological and epic narrative, the foreboding cry of the swan below.

268. The goddess invoked by the swan is either Diana or Juno. The "too-subtle scheme" and the mention in the next stanza of the jealous gaze that ended Adonis's life seem to point clearly to Diana. The swan, however, qualifies the goddess as the one who reigns in the "ciel Empirée" (the Empyrean, or highest heaven), and Juno was the queen of the heavens in classical mythology. It may be that in Du Guillet's telling of the tale, Diana's act of vengeance and jealousy and the ensuing tragedy set her up as a divine force to be reckoned with on a level with the queen of the heavens. Barataud and Trudeau also point out that, although Juno plays no role in the original myth of Adonis, in Saint-Gelais's "Déploration," Venus calls out to Juno. Here the address to Juno represents not only an allusion to Saint-Gelais's poem, but also "un déplacement de voix, puisque ce n'est pas Vénus qui invoque Junon, mais le cygne, animal doté de parole, comme le sanglier" (a displacement of voice, because it isn't Venus who invokes Juno, but the swan, an animal endowed with speech, like the boar). *Rymes*, 157.

269. I.e., Venus (the swan's mistress).

270. Huguet's dictionary explains that green was the color of joy and cites contemporary examples, including *dizain* 254 of Scève's *Délie*: "Si le blanc pur est foy immaculée / Et le vert gay est joyeuse esperance…" (If pure white is immaculate faith / And gay green is joyous hope…). Ronsard writes of "le verd-gay que Venus aime tant" (the bright, gay green that Venus so loves) (*Mascarades* [III, 494]), cited by Huguet. The opening lines of Mellin de Saint-Gelais's "Déploration de Vénus, sur la mort du bel Adonis" address the goddess, telling her she will have to put aside the green she loves in her new grief and pain. See Perrine Galand-Hallyn in "Le latin à la rescousse du français," 332.

271. In this stanza, too, we find the juxtaposition of a domestic detail—the departing husband embracing his wife—with a description of Cupid in terms that evoke his traditional depiction in mythology. He is called "l'Enfant," a reminder of his relationship to Venus, and the poet describes how he spreads his wings and takes off in flight, emphasizing his role as the winged god of love.

272. Some mythological accounts of Cupid indicate that he had at least two brothers, Anteros and Himerus. The Graces are probably present here for several reasons. Usually considered the daughters of Zeus and Eurynome, some tales identify them as the offspring of Dionysus/Bacchus and Aphrodite/Venus. In that case, the Graces would be present as daughters of Venus and half-sisters of Cupid. The exact nature of the relationships between the various mythological figures is much less important here than the general sense that this is a family matter, and that all present are united in their sadness and in their commitment to seek vengeance on the "violent beast."

273. Pernette du Guillet's poem focuses on the trial of the boar, his confession, and punishment, rather than on Venus's suffering and lament. Barataud and Trudeau argue that "Vénus esplouree"—the classical elegaic tradition of Venus's lament of Adonis's death—is reduced here to two lines (*Rymes*, 161).

274. Unlike Mellin de Saint-Gelais's emotional Venus, Du Guillet's goddess quickly channels her grief into a controlled and reasoned search for justice. Galand-Hallyn compares Pernette du Guillet's Venus poem with those of Mellin de Saint-Gelais and their Greek models in this and other respects. In particular, see the comments regarding "La Vénus froide de Pernette," in "Le latin à la rescousse du français," 315–19. Venus gathers the assembly under a thick tree ("soubz un arbre espais") for the boar's trial. Finch's decision to call this old tree "an ancient oak" suggests the tradition of justice dispensed at a gathering under a tree—typically an oak—dating back to the Middle Ages. The legendary tales of Saint Louis, for example, tell of his court of justice under an oak tree in Vincennes.

275. *Jeune enfant*: The adjective "jeune" in the original calls attention to Adonis's youth and the fact that he was cut down in his prime. Referring to him as "child" or "youth" (though he was a young man at this point) emphasizes his innocence and reminds us that Aphrodite/Venus and Persephone/Proserpina fought over the beautiful child from his birth.

276. Cotgrave links the color scarlet with an apple by the same name, hence Finch's translation, which evokes both Christian and pagan traditions associating the fruit with temptation. The boar's description of the young man's physical beauty reflects the terms conventionally used in the lover's account of his lady's attractions in the courtly and Petrarchan poetic traditions (delicate white skin, scarlet lips). The zeal ("ardeur") that surprises him echoes the *innamoramento* of Petrarchan tradition—the moment when love is born and the lover is unexpectedly overcome by passion. Traditionally, this occurs as the young man is wandering about with no particular aim, as was the boar in the woods. Barataud and Trudeau point out that Pernette du Guillet's decision to represent the boar as victim of this sort of "erreur amoureuse" is significant, indicating the poet's resistance to the prestige of Petrarchan love that Cupid represents (*Rymes*, 163).

277. Cupid, his brothers, and the three Graces. All are moved by the boar's contrition and intervene on his behalf with Venus.

278. Pernette du Guillet uses the mythological context to invent an explanation for the attraction of these animals to mud.

279. Du Guillet's version of the fable also offers a mythological explanation for the cleft hooves of pigs. Henceforth they will serve as a reminder of the wrong done to Venus in the death of her beloved Adonis. Early Christians associated the cleft—or cloven—hoof with the Devil; the boar is not depicted here as evil, however, but as a contrite sinner who gave way to unreasonable passions. He demonstrates the depth of his sorrow and repentance in the last two stanzas by willingly accepting his penance, thanking those in attendance at the execution of his sentence, and abiding by the decree that he would never more make his home in the woods.

POEM 65

280. Saulnier notes the influence of Plato's *Lysis* here and suggests that Du Guillet may have been inspired by Des Périer's translation of the Platonic dialogue, published in Lyon in 1544

(*Etude*, 19). In Plato's dialogue, Socrates cites the words of the great poets and wise men, who wrote that like is always attracted to like. Du Guillet's epigram echoes this Platonic theory as it is explained by the female narrator of Héroët's *La parfaicte amye*:

> Consider that love comes from likeness
> as much of minds as of temperaments.
> If I have brought faithful, strong affection
> to my beloved, because I resemble him,
> he must have (or at least it seems thus to me)
> some resemblance himself to me
> which compels his good will toward me.
>
> Pensez qu'amour vient de similitude
> tant d'esprits que de complexions.
> Si j'ay porté fermes affections
> À mon amy, pource que luy ressemble,
> Il fault qu'il ayt (au moyns il le me semble)
> Luy ressemblant à moy quelcque semblance
> Qui le contraigne à une bienveillance. (1642–1648)

At the conclusion of Héroët's long poem, the speaker assures other women that true love has always been and always will be reciprocal:

> Ladies, I promise you,
> That it will never happen, and it has never happened,
> That true love *not* be reciprocal.
>
> Dames, je vous promets
> Qu'il n'adviendra, et il n'advint jamais,
> Que vraye amour n'ayt esté reciproque. (1653–55)

Du Guillet emphasizes that very point in the second *quatrain* of poem 65; like attracts like, and—because a noble heart always seeks another noble heart, recognizing and seeking the spark of light and perfection that reflects the divinity in the other—true and virtuous love will therefore be reciprocal, ultimately bringing contentment to the souls who may feel pain in the process of seeking the ideal good. Antoine du Moulin refers to the Platonic notion of like souls that attract one another in the opening lines of his preface to the *Rymes*, where he predicts that the virtuous ladies of Lyon will be drawn instinctively to the works of this noble, virtuous young poet.

281. Following Plato's theory (see the preceding note), the second *quatrain* reminds us that it takes a noble heart ("cueur hault") to recognize another such worthy heart, to see and recognize the perfection that each person of virtuous heart and mind inevitably seeks. In many of the poems of the collection, a female speaker validates her admiration of the learned and eloquent beloved in these terms. Her own noble heart and mind allow her to recognize her beloved's virtue, and he in turn should recognize hers. Another important element of this "perfect" or "pure" love is that pain suffered for such a worthy and virtuous love must in the end bring contentment to the lovers. This good ("bien") will be the return or profit ("usure") on the lover's investment of pain and toil.

POEM 66

282. This epigram presents another example of the rich ambiguity that characterizes Du Guillet's poetry, allowing for two different yet complementary readings. On one level, the entire epigram evokes the illumination brought and protection given to the speaker against Love's arrows and errors by "this light that moves—no darkness yet to render" ("celle clarté mouvante sans umbrage"). The speaker subsequently passes from the physical delights and dangerous vision associated with the eyes of the body to chaste desire, new life, and purer sight through the eyes of the mind and soul. In this way, the poem echoes earlier epigrams in the collection that link the light of the Day with the speaker's birth, and her passage from physical pleasure to desire of the virtuous good that her beloved embodies. (See poems 1, 2, 8, 12, 14, 33, 56, 68.)

Reading the epigram from another perspective, Barataud and Trudeau suggest that it conveys the voice of the young poet at the end of her life, suffering from the illness that eventually caused her death. They interpret lines 2, 4, and 9 as direct allusions to the effects of illness on the body and on the spirit of the dying poet. The autobiographical interpretation is based in particular on a reading of line 8 as a reference to the poet's impending death, and of line 9 as alluding to a disease affecting her eyes and eyesight, such that she can no longer see her beloved or enjoy the pleasure of reading his works. Whether or not these lines are in fact autobiographical is less important than recognizing this type of rich ambiguity that permeates the collection and allows for multiple, often complementary, readings of the poems.

283. This mystical light moves—like the sun—yet casts no shadow. In line 2, the speaker qualifies as dark and gloomy her days before the arrival of this light.

284. The masculine singular form of the past participle, "consommé," represents either a typographical error—a missing "e" that would confirm the female gender of the speaker, logical in the context of the *Rymes*—or an indication that the speaker of this poem is, and was intended to be, male. Certainly the feelings and experience described could apply to any lover, male or female, in a similar situation. The uncertainty stemming from the form of the past participle in the first edition reminds us to be careful in assigning autobiographical interpretations to the poems. See the Introduction for more discussion of the issues related to autobiographical approaches to the collection.

285. The bright light blinds the errant, "inconstant" one (i.e., Cupid), preventing him from seeing the speaker and therefore protecting the speaker from Love's stray, error-inducing arrows. (In poem 40, Cupid was unable to find and strike the female speaker, who successfully hid from his eyes and arrows until he obtained the help of the "Archers of Virtue").

286. The mind, following chaste desire, gains new life instead of the death associated with surrender to physical passions. Lines 7 and 8 echo stanza 12 of poem 56, where the speaker calls on "longings so chaste" ("une chaste envie") to bolster her hope of vanquishing Love and Death. See also poems 12 and 14.

287. The last two lines suggest the progression up the Neoplatonic ladder in the experience of love, which entails leaving behind physical desire—the death associated with carnal passion—and the eyes that mislead us when focused on outward beauty. Progressing from the eyes of the body, through which much harm reaches us, to the eyes of the mind means leaving behind the charmed memories of physical pleasures known. Poem 8 also makes the point that the "esprit" (mind/spirit), when illuminated by the beloved Day's constant rays, can perceive that which the eyes themselves could never see. Poem 11 demonstrates what happens when the body doesn't allow the mind to see ("le corps ne permect point de veoir, / a son esprit"). In that case, the more the speaker "saw" her beloved—without the mind's nobler vision—the less she was able to recognize him. She wore the blindfold of ignorance over her eyes before a more virtuous and pure desire took hold and allowed her to recognize such good ("si hault bien"). Poem 16 emphasizes the importance of the soul and the mind for being able to discern the good. In poem 56, love united with virtue conceives a new sort of noble desire in the heart, engendering a passion for seeing ("une ardeur de veoir") and for acquiring learning of a higher order ("quelque hault sçavoir").

The eyes are also associated here with the speaker's physical suffering. Tears flowing from the eyes drain the body of its water, which inspired Finch to use the term "blight" (a sickness that dries out and kills plants) to translate the drying out of the suffering body in the original ("dont le corps souffrant seche").

POEM 67 ("COCK-AND-BULL STORY")

288. This particular type of poem, the *coq à l'âne*, was invented and made popular by Clément Marot. The phrase, "sauter du coq à l'âne" (to jump from the rooster to the ass) describes the way the poem jumps from topic to topic, without evident logic or coherence. This apparent incoherence, however, veils criticisms of current events and societal mores. Given the nature of the genre, it can be difficult to pinpoint precise meanings, but Du Guillet's "Cock-and-Bull Story" (*Coq à l'asne*) projects the voice of a male speaker who focuses on the moral lassitude of women and their obsession with making themselves appear more beautiful, along with the related theme of the fool, or "fleeced pigeon."

289. The dangers of idleness and the theme of the fool who triumphs over the wise man are common topics in moral proverbs of the day.

290. The "handsome donor" ("beau donneur") evokes the figure of the wealthy courtier, buying the favors of ladies who are more interested in his money and gifts than in true love. Poem 69 ("Despair") includes a related observation (lines 63–66) of how the truest lover is often passed over for one less worthy.

291. *une estrangere*: Davis explains the ambivalence felt by the native inhabitants of Lyon vis-à-vis the many foreigners among them, particularly during the fairs. Foreigners represented exciting new ideas and exotic additions to the culture of the city, and their commerce was crucial to its economic prosperity. Nevertheless, those same foreigners also strained the social fabric of the city: "people feared that this opulence, this freedom of exchange, would burst the dams controlling the human appetites" (*The Sacred and the Body Social*, 44–45).

292. The female narrator of Héroët's *La parfaicte amye* receives conflicting advice regarding love and lovers, including the worldly, cynical counsel that she should change lovers as one changes clothing or attire, "Faisant d'amour, comme d'accoustrement / Qui se reprend et se laisse aysément" [Treating love like clothing, that is put on and left off with ease] (lines 375–76). The "estrangere" ("female you haven't met") of Du Guillet's *coq à l'âne* seems to embody this outlook.

293. *pigeon*: In French and in English, a naïve person, easily fooled, cheated, or duped. *Tourterelles*: literally, turtledoves; the precise meaning is not clear, but the turtledoves may well suggest the flighty young women of loose morals (foreigners among them), the same who love a "handsome donor" and who are concerned with their complexion in the lines that follow.

294. Lines 29–30 evoke the "querelles" of the Greeks with the Trojans, that is, the Trojan War.

295. The "moyens" in line 30 can signify ways or means of doing something, financial resources, or mediators. Finch has chosen "techniques" to convey the range of possible interpretations of the original line. Barataud and Trudeau make the interesting point that the legal allusions in the last part of the poem may favor the latter of the possible meanings, which would make the techniques in question those of moderators seeking to arbitrate the "querelles."

296. *tabourin* (also spelled *tambourin*): a small drum—sometimes described as being tall and narrow—associated with war, and carried by foot soldiers.

297. The city of Lyon is situated at the confluence of two rivers, the Rhône and the Saône. For additional interesting remarks on the juxtaposition of the natural element and the ladies' artifice, see Barataud and Trudeau, *Rymes*, 177.

298. Cotgrave gives the proverb, "Ceux qui nous doibvent nous demandent," meaning "Our debtors are as bold with us as if they were our creditors [... referring to] those that having received great favours, are not satisfied, but either impudently demand more, or ungratefully complaine they have not had enough."

299. A dress "faicte a l'antique" could indicate a garment in the style of the ancients (of classical antiquity) or, more generally, in an outdated style. Either way, a dress not made in the current style would likely have a looser fit than was the fashion for aristocratic women in the sixteenth century.

300. *ethique*: either of a moral/ethical nature or extremely thin. The latter meaning comes from "etique," or "hectique," indicating a type of fever—the "fievre hectique"—which left its victims emaciated.

301. The exact nature of the dress in question is not clear, but it obviously is not up to the standards of the fashionable Renaissance courtesan. "Courtisaner" means to play the courtier, to adopt the manners and fashions of the court and its society. Huguet's dictionary cites this example from Pernette du Guillet's *coq à l'âne* in the entry for "courtisaner" and for "à la buste," which is defined as "à la mode nouvelle" (in the new fashion). Maurice Dumoulin explains that prior to the Renaissance the woman's bust was not constrained by her clothing. During the sixteenth century, a small waist became fashionable, and a type of corset was developed to narrow the waist and enhance the bust. During the sixteenth and into the seventeenth century, what was first a simple band of fabric laced around the middle became a shell imprisoning the body, ornately decorated, particularly at the "busque" or "buste"—often covered with gold and damask and decorated with emblems, ornaments and allegorical designs. See "Ce qu'elles faisaient pour être belles," in *Revue de la Renaissance* 9 (Geneva: Slatkine Reprints, 1968), 230–31. See also Elizabeth Ewing, *Underwear: A History* (New York: Theatre Arts Books, 1972), 20–23, for an account of the development of the corset and its role in fashion. Ewing points out that the early forms of what we call a corset appeared in the sixteenth century, intended to emphasize the bust and narrow the waist.

302. The pronoun "elle" in this line refers to the feminine noun "journee" in the previous line, but Finch has chosen to maintain the nuance inherent in the French pronoun, which also suggests that "she"—the woman doing the cheating a few lines above, as well as the day itself—has tarried too long.

303. Cotgrave's dictionary gives the proverb, "Cela cornoit prise," meaning "That finished the cha[s]e, that made a full end of the matter."

304. This line is a variant on a popular proverb, "Tant va la cruche à l'eau qu'à la fin elle se brise," found in the thirteenth-century *Roman de Renart* and in a later ballad by Villon. Literally, it means that the jug goes to water so often that it breaks. Figuratively, it conveys the universal observation that things break with repeated use, and that people eventually succumb to dangers when repeatedly exposed to them. For more thoughts on the possible meaning of the proverb's use in this poem, see Barataud and Trudeau, *Rymes*, 179.

305. Mestier: trade, or occupation; also (as here) need/necessity/want. The online *Dictionnaire du moyen français*—DMF2009 (ATILF)—defines the expression "faire mestier" as "être nécessaire (à qqn)," to be necessary or needed (by someone). Once the pot is broken, it becomes all the more necessary to us.

POEM 68 ("THE NIGHT")

306. "The Night" is written in *terza rima*, the form first used by Dante in his *Divine Comedy*, in which three-line stanzas—tercets—are woven together with an interlocking rhyme scheme (aba bcb cdc, etc.). In addition to its poetic form, the dark vision of the prologue to Dante's *Inferno* doubtless served as a model for Du Guillet's elegy. Petrarch adopted the *terza rima* in his *Trionfi* (*Triumphs*), an influential work encompassing a long, six-part series of pageants or processions involving allegorical, mythological, and biblical figures. Accompanied by his guide, the speaker in the *Trionfi* observes and questions the characters

in the processions on the subjects of love, fame, and immortality. Jean Lemaire de Belges introduced the *terza rima* into French in his description of the Temple of Venus, part of his *Traité de la concorde des deux langages*, first published in 1511. As Lemaire's narrator seeks the Temple of Venus, he suffers restless, dream-filled nights: "Ie quis sommeil cuydant prendre repos, / Mais le songer infesta mon dormir" (I sought sleep, thinking to take my rest, / But dreams infested my sleep). *Œuvres*, 103. *Terza rima* was not widely adopted by the French poets of the Renaissance, although it was used in several long poems by Mellin de Saint-Gelais and Marguerite de Navarre.

Du Guillet's dream-like vision also recalls both the allegorical dream vision of the *Hypnerotomachie, ou discours du songe de Poliphile* and Clément Marot's "Déploration sur le trespas de Messire Florimond Robertet." Marot's poem includes three female allegorical figures—"La Mort hideuse" (hideous Death), a great lady (The Roman Catholic Church), and another lady (the French Republic)—who are part of a procession to lament the death of Florimond Robertet (*Œuvres poétiques*, vol. 1, 207–23). Du Guillet's poem differs from these models in numerous ways, but the textual evidence indicates that she was familiar with them and drew from the poetic and allegorical traditions they represent. For more on the links between the *Rymes* and Marot's poetry, see Gisèle Mathieu-Castellani, "Les enfants de Marot," in *Clément Marot, «prince des poëtes françois,» 1496–1996,* Actes du colloque international de Cahors en Quercy, 1996 (Paris: Honoré Champion, 1997), 713–35.

307. The juxtaposition of night (the darkness associated with ignorance) and day (bringing illumination and contentment) is a central metaphor of the collection. See, for example, poems 2, 8, and 63.

308. Barataud and Trudeau suggest that these lines furnish both a biographical detail (the speaker's insomnia and subsequent dreamlike trance) and an allusion to the insomnia experienced by the narrator of Lemaire's "Temple de Vénus" (*Rymes*, 182).

309. In a state between sleep and wakefulness, the speaker enters into a "contemplation" in which her imagination has free reign.

310. At first, the space of her dream seems idyllic, but a sudden and unsettling silence dispels her sense of ease. Note the shift from a feeling of "aise" (ease), in line 14, to "malaise" (discomfort, anxiety, ease dispelled), in line 18.

311. Finch's choice of "intolerance" in English conveys the intensity of the "impatience" that these monsters exhibit. Barataud and Trudeau point out that this impatience (in the strongest sense of the word) characterizes the crowd of figures pressing in around the great Lady and the Queen later in the poem (*Rymes*, 184).

312. The Great Queen corresponds allegorically to Ambition, who serves and controls the Lady, Vainglory. This correspondence is sometimes blurred, however, as in a dream, when characters and roles merge or switch places.

313. The precise meaning of the original line in French is somewhat obscure, but implies the idea of rumors circulating behind the Queen's back, whether in praise of her or against her.

Finch's translation expresses the cunning and the constant efforts of the gossips to position themselves to advantage in the court of Ambition and Vainglory.

314. I.e., the Queen's oppression. (The Queen advances the cause of those she favors and forsakes the others.)

315. "Les plus loings" in the original encompasses both the "the Kings" ("les Roys") mentioned below in line 69—whose power she envisions usurping and who therefore fear her wrath—and the individuals, fearful of the Queen's power and pride, who nonetheless strive to reach her and the Lady, yet find themselves at the back of the crowd.

316. "Elle" (she) in this line could refer either to the Great Lady or to the Queen. Because of the rapport between the Queen and the Lady, it seems likely that the pronoun here refers to the Lady. She (thanks to the Queen's manipulations) believes herself to be omnipotent. Reading the pronoun as referring to the Queen would shift the meaning slightly, implying that the Queen led the Lady to believe that she—the Queen—was all-powerful. It is the Queen who holds the reigns of power, but the Lady's vanity prevents her from thinking about anything but her own glory.

317. Lines 79–81: Again, the pronoun references in the French are unclear. In keeping with the unfolding scenario of the Queen who manages and governs the actions and affairs of the Lady, these lines appear to indicate that the Queen is quickly able to set the Lady up as supreme sovereign—a figurehead whom she (the Queen) controls. The Great Lady's beautiful face has a seductive power that makes it easy for the Queen to put her into power as a figurehead—the allegorical translation of the expression, "Never trust a pretty face." An alternate reading of the pronoun "la" in line 81 as referring to the Queen herself does not entirely contradict the first reading; it would shift the focus directly onto the Queen's power, bypassing the Lady's titular role.

318. The "Crone," or hideous old woman ("Vieille hideuse"), may recall the figure of hideous Death ("la Mort hideuse") in Marot's "Déploration sur le trespas de Messire Florimond Robertet," but this Crone serves the Queen. Barataud and Trudeau propose that the "Vieille," in her service to the Queen (Ambition), may represent either Greed or Envy, both qualities that compel Ambition to pull the strings of Vainglory (*Rymes*, 187).

319. The "other Lady" is the fourth allegorical figure in the poem, associated with the well born and characterized by gentility and reticence. She is "eloquent of speech" and "discreet in deed," separating herself from the "the villainous and shameful crowd" ("gent infame"). The redness of her face is a sign of modesty and chastity, according to Barataud and Trudeau, who call this fourth lady "Honte" (*Rymes*, 188). The term "honte" is problematic for translation into English, however, because its sixteenth-century use encompasses both the positive value of modesty/bashfulness and the negative value of shame/dishonor.

In line 98, we learn that the "other Lady's" face is covered by a mask, which Barataud and Trudeau interpret as a sign of duplicity and false humility, particularly in the context of courtly society (*Rymes*, 188). The terms describing her here, however, are overwhelmingly positive, and we learn that those who love what is right and flee from the false are her followers (lines 103–105). In this dream-like and nightmarish vision (as in courtly society), things are not always what they seem, so we cannot be sure what factors motivate the Lady behind the mask.

320. The Great Lady welcomes her admirers and followers, unlike the discriminating, ambitious Queen, who manipulates the flow of those trying to reach the Lady and controls their access to her. In the lines that follow, the ambitious join with the envious against the followers—identified as "the good" ("les bons")—of the "Masked Lady."

321. At the approach of the "Masked Lady" ("dame Honteuse") in line 131, the ambitious and envious withdraw in confusion and rage, and the Crone tears her hair in distress to see her followers overshadowed. In the sixteenth century, "honteuse" meant *either* timid/bashful/chaste/demure *or* shameful/dishonest/dishonorable. The fact that both meanings—necessarily translated with different terms in English—coexisted in the same French word in the Renaissance, combined with the uncertainty regarding the true nature of this figure in the dream world of the elegy (discreet protector of the righteous, or masked player in courtly maneuvers?), led to the decision to translate "la dame Honteuse" as "the Masked Lady," in order to maintain the rich ambiguity of the original.

322. The speaker's feelings and voice resurface at this point in the account, expressing her wariness, disgust, and amazement at the monstrous nature of the Great Lady's attendants.

323. As in Dante's *Divine Comedy* and Petrarch's *Triumphs*, the speaker questions the characters she encounters in the dream crowd.

324. The follower of the beautiful "Princesse" (the Great Lady) explains that he and the others have been blinded by the light shining from her eyes. Those followers reflect to an excessive degree the ideals of courtly love and the Petrarchan poetic tradition; their endless labor and torment provide their only rest and joy. Although they have never had any recompense from her (nor even seen her), they strive to do all they can to please their Lady.

325. The behavior of the Great Lady's followers at first strikes the speaker as ridiculous, even impossible to believe, but as she contemplates the depth of their confusion, she becomes angry and begins to curse the monsters who represent the vanity and viciousness of the court of the Great Lady and the Queen.

326. In lines 169–180, the speaker explains that these monsters invade our minds. Although they may be "mere shadows" and lacking any real "essence," they represent the vain, envious, and malicious urges that feed our "longings and follies." By the rash workings of our imagination, the monsters and what they represent form the basis of what we know about the world, "our one true science." (The French word, "science," in this time period meant learning and knowledge in a general sense, rather than a particular discipline or branch of knowledge.) The explanation includes remarkably astute psychological observations, as well as theological overtones in the poet's reference to the free will ("libre arbitre") that is obstructed by these monstrous desires.

327. With echoes of classical philosophy and Christian theology, the speaker decries the miserable human condition, in which she includes herself ("nous humains"). By giving rein to monstrous and vain desires—allowing them to obstruct our free will—we "invent" our own ruin. The term "perdition," meaning destruction and complete ruin, inevitably also alludes to the Christian concept of the separation of souls from Christ through sin. Finch has combined the notion of humanity "inventing" or forging its own ruin with the idea that false, monstrous desires and follies become "nostre vraye science" in her English version of line 179. Humanity is "always eager, through myth or allegory" to "invent our own perdition." The monsters in our minds are but allegorical or invented figures, yet they acquire a destructive force because we do not or cannot control them.

328. The arrival of dawn's light brings release from the vices of ignorance, as in poems 2 and 8. The "noisome" rabble of Vainglory, Ambition, and Shame disappear from view. These three allegorical figures correspond loosely to the Great Lady, the Queen, and the Masked Lady. (See above, n 321, regarding the meanings of "honte" and "honteux" in the sixteenth century.) The Crone may represent Envy, in the service of Ambition. From another perspective, however, we might view the Crone and the Masked Lady as two sides of "Honte"—shame *and* modesty. The Crone exhibits shameful behavior and is indeed shameless in her actions to promote the ambitious. The Masked Lady exhibits modesty, reserve, and "shamefaced" behavior. Exactly how we might associate the four allegorical ladies in the body of the elegy with the three figures named at the end is less important than the fact that, as Barataud and Trudeau aptly conclude, "elles résument cependant l'arrivisme qui tourmente les humains" (they nevertheless represent the ambitiousness that torments human beings). *Rymes*, 193.

329. As elsewhere, it is her beloved, her Day ("Jour"), who brings light and relief from the unpleasant night, filled with its visions of vice. Clark-Evans explains that the beloved's arrival transforms the night into day, allowing the lovers to attain the knowledge of self and intellectual revelation that makes art and poetry possible ("L'art et l'amour," 170–71).

330. The appearance of her Day's light allows the female speaker to see and know her beloved *and* herself, according to the Neoplatonic ideal of pure or "perfect love," which holds that the self is attracted to a like soul, and that the two become one and the same being in spiritual union. To know the beloved other is to know oneself. The final line of Du Guillet's elegy, "It is enough—one's self to comprehend" ("Comme il se faict assez de soy congnoistre") echoes a passage in the third and final part of Antoine Héroët's *La parfaicte amye*. This part of Héroët's poem describes the importance of knowing oneself and explains that she who knows her "semblable" (one who is like her) knows herself, because of their resemblance. After getting to know her beloved, she will seek and find herself in him, which is enough to allow her to know herself:

> When she seeks in him and sees how
> She sometimes finds herself entirely in him;
> When she is better off in him than she can be in herself;
> Isn't that enough to know herself?
>
> Quand dedans luy cherche et voit de maniere
> Qu'elle se trouve aulcunesfoys entiere;

Quand en luy est myeulx qu'en soy ne peult estre;
N'est-ce bien assez pour se congnoistre? (1333–1336)

La parfaicte amye, 36.

Du Guillet echoes this same thought: the Day/dawn's appearance is *enough* for her to comprehend him, and therefore herself. His light, as we see in poems 2 and 8, initially awakened her to life and continues to sustain her and chase away ignorance. Here, the light of her beloved Day also permits her to know herself ("soy congnoistre").

POEM 69 ("DESPAIR")

331. Saulnier cites François Ier's prose "Paragon translaté d'ytalien en francoys par le Roy" as Du Guillet's model, but Graham argues that both French writers probably imitated the same unidentified Italian source. Saulnier transcribed the king's manuscript in his *Etude* (42–45), with some modernization of the text and added punctuation. Rajchenbach's recent edition of the *Rymes* includes a transcription of François Ier's text that reproduces the original punctuation of the manuscript (238–41). Barataud and Trudeau offer interesting insights regarding Du Guillet's choice of the elegy form for her poem, compared with the epistolary genre used by François Ier (*Rymes*, 195).

332. Maurice Scève apparently knew the same model text, beginning his *dizain* 60 with the nearly identical lines: "Si c'est Amour, pourquoy m'occit il doncques, / Qui tant aymay, & onq ne sceuz hair?" (*Délie*, 31). Scève's *dizain*, like Du Guillet's "Despair," uses the Petrarchan antithesis of living and dying in love's suffering to evoke the contradictory emotions caused by *Amour* (Cupid). All four writers—the unidentified Italian source, both French poets, and François Ier—echo Petrarch's *Rime sparse*, 132:

If it is not love, what then is it that I feel?
But if it is love, before God, what kind of thing is it?
If it is good, whence comes this bitter mortal effect?
If it is evil, why is each torment so sweet? [line breaks added]

S'amor non è, che dunque è quel ch'io sento?
ma s'egli è amor, per Dio, che cosa e quale?
Se bona, ond'è l'effetto aspro mortale?
se ria, ond'è si dolce ogni tormento?... (1–4)

Petrarch's Lyric Poems, 271.

333. This topic and the overtly Petrarchan orientation here might seem out of place in the *Rymes* without the elegy that follows it.

334. The voices coming from the depths of the suffering lover's soul cannot be heard by the lady he loves, for she remains distant and far above him.

335. The lady cannot see the ardor of the passion that burns deep down in his heart, and her own eyes shine so brightly with her beauty that she puts the sun to shame.

336. *Travaulx*: suffering—so great here that the speaker would prefer death, although even death will not provide the relief that the lover seeks.

337. The term "chetif" derives etymologically from the word for "captive," or "prisoner," an appropriate association for the suffering lover, imprisoned by love in line 16.

338. The precise meaning of this remark is not clear. Coming between a realization (lines 56–60) that the lover's ardor might possibly meet with "compensation that may prove unkind," and the observation that often the least worthy is best rewarded (lines 63–66), lines 61–62 appear to highlight the unfortunate truth that Lovers may serve well, hoping for due compensation, but that the force of their love may go unrewarded, and their sharp pain therefore unappeased.

339. Marot's *chanson*, "Puis que de vous je n'ay aultre visage," expresses similar sentiments. The lyric speaker bids his beloved lady goodbye, because he has had no response from her, and imagines that a lesser suitor—one who loves her less—will have more success: "Ung moins aymant aura, peult estre, mieulx." *Œuvres poétiques*, vol. 1, 196.

340. In a world like that of the court, where vice is rewarded as if it were virtue and unworthy lovers often receive the best recompense, true virtue in effect resembles a vice in that it dooms the virtuous lover to suffering. Loyalty and service lose their worth.

341. "My will also—toward anguish preordained" ("Et mon arbitre en mal predestine"): Both recent critical editions note the Calvinist influence in this line, not apparent in François Ier's prose version. The lover's death by suicide would indeed prove him to be "preordained" to anguish, even if he acted of his own free will. Barataud and Trudeau observe that extreme despair, accompanied nevertheless by choice and free will, echoes a perspective evident elsewhere in the collection, "que l'homme fait son propre malheur" (that man makes his own unhappiness). *Rymes*, 204. Poem 68, "The Night," makes the same point regarding the monsters that we allow to invade our thoughts and rule our desires.

342. The final six lines syntactically compose one long sentence, whose many clauses accumulate wounds and suffering alongside hope and desire, all of which lead inevitably to death, the only escape from the painful deceits of Love.

POEM 70 ("SOLACE")

343. If "despair" seems an uncharacteristic topic for the author of the *Rymes*, the response provided in "Solace" answers any questions as to how the lover's pain must be addressed and represents a logical selection to conclude the original edition, no matter who made that editorial decision. With great finesse, poem 70 provides consolation to the suffering lover and—more importantly—an apology for the lady who does not reward him in the way he wishes. A third person—identity and gender unknown—speaks in this elegy, offering advice to the despairing lover, defending and explaining the lady's dilemma, thoughts, and actions in terms that echo other poems in the collection.

344. The poem opens with reflections on the nature of patient, virtuous love, which remains true, even when suffering pain and insult. Constant lovers remain immune to Fortune's authority *except* when wrongful love ("l'injuste Amour"), acting without recourse to reason, intervenes. We can imagine these remarks based on time-tested wisdom delivered by a third party (a mutual friend of the despairing lover and his lady, perhaps the persona of the poet herself) or even spoken by the suffering lover to himself in an internal dialogue.

345. Here, the speaker suddenly focuses on his/her particular interlocutor, the same suffering lover who speaks of his despair in the preceding elegy. The speaker's wise and omniscient voice addresses the lover and talks to him about his lady.

346. The vocabulary evoking legal discourse recalls the medieval tradition of the courts and judgments of love. See also poems 23, 24, 27, and 28.

347. Lines 19–20, including the verb "blasonner" in the original, remind us of the sometimes harsh or cruel ways in which male poets depicted and objectified women in the popular *blason* and *contreblason* poems, a genre initiated by Marot. (See above, n61.) Scève contributed two *blasons* to a popular collection of these poems, although his were written in praise of the lady's eyebrow and a tear falling from her eye, unlike the poems of a cruder sort about female body parts written by some of his contemporaries.

348. Barataud and Trudeau identify this focus on virtue and its sweet odor as a "glose pernettienne," a departure from the prose model (*Rymes*, 207). Huguet's dictionary cites this line by Pernette du Guillet as an example of the verb "odorer." In the same entry, Huguet also cites the concluding lines of Scève's *dizain* 4, which display the same figurative use of the transitive verb: "quand je vien a odorer les fleurs / de tous tes faictz, certes, quoy que tu faces, / Je me dissoulz en joyes et en pleurs." (The lover smells the sweet "flowers" of his lady's deeds, and dissolves into tears of joy.) In translating line 22 of Du Guillet's elegy ("en ton cueur sa vertu odorer"), Finch thought of the odor of sanctity, the Catholic concept of a sweet odor long believed to emanate from the body of saints at their death. The lady here is very much alive, but the speaker links her virtues to saintly qualities and, in line 84, describes the regret those who never knew this lady will feel "throughout the centuries left till Kingdom Come" ("Tous Siecles Sainctz, qui apres toy viendront").

349. The attempt to confine that liberates and the untying that eternally binds extend the series of antithetical motivations and actions introduced in the previous lines, where the lover acquits his lady by accusing her and honors her by blaming her. Finch "unravels" these puzzling lines through the image of the knotted ribbons on ornate dresses of the period, which had to be straightened out before they could be tied anew.

350. Lines 31–34 begin the defense of the lady, revealing the emotions and motivations behind her reactions. The speaker explains that the lady must appear *not* to care for love or for the lover because of fear that her desire will be misconstrued—a danger recognized elsewhere in the *Rymes*, particularly in poem 42.

351. The lover's desire and his charms are met not with disdain, but with a love that is hidden by discretion and restricted by the bounds of reason and propriety.

352. The speaker portrays the lady's plight with great sympathy. Moved ("stirred up"), the lady would be inclined to enjoy mutual, reciprocal affection if it weren't for the restrictions placed on her by "honte" (meaning not simply "shame," but also "modesty" and "chastity"). See the notes for poem 68, "La Nuict," for further discussion of the words "honte" and "honteux" in the context of the *Rymes*.

353. The speaker reiterates that the lady, too, feels the charms of desire, but abides by reason's rule. See poem 18 for another example of the role of "meur entendement" (mature understanding; wisdom) and of reason in overcoming physical desires and the pains they may cause the suffering lover.

354. The lover, in loving, must experience these contradictory emotions, expansions of the Petrarchan antithesis of "doux" and "amer" (sweet and bitter). In line 49, the verb "choisir" underlines again the notion that the lover *chooses* his fate, as was the case in the closing lines of the preceding elegy, echoing also the references to free will in poem 68, "The Night." The lines that follow encourage the lover to take comfort, to demonstrate his strength against *Amour* (Cupid), and not to allow despair to get the upper hand.

355. Lines 65–72 depict an exchange of written words. The lady reads the lover's laments, selects words, and sets them down with her own hand to show her affection to the lover. This is not done lightly; the speaker explains that these are things never before accorded to another or recorded.

356. See the Introduction for a discussion of the association of the lady with the moon in Scève's *Délie* and the allusions in the *Rymes* to the moon's role in the cosmos. For more about cosmic imagery in the *Délie*, see Kathryn Banks, *Cosmos and Image in the Renaissance: French Love Lyric and Natural-Philosophical Poetry* (London: MHRA, 2008). Of particular interest is ch. 3, "Illumination and Darkness: The Lunar, Solar, and Divine Lady," 120–50.

357. The implication is that if the lover truly loves his lady, he will not wish upon her the shame that would ensue if he were to be successful in gaining his desired reward from her.

358. Along with her "holy renown" ("saincte renommee"), the lady's "immortal words" (line 103) will touch the lover, bringing him comfort that is eternal—as opposed to physical desires, which are short-lived. This will be the recompense for his toil and suffering, bringing him "cool relief" (line 110). The references to "immortal words" and "toil," or "labor," serve also as a reminder that this very experience is what allows the lover to write beautiful poetry. Relief and contentedness must come from thoughts and words of immortality, rather than from more immediate gratification. In the Petrarchan lyric tradition, immortal words also provide the only outlet for love that goes unreturned, but with a focus on the suffering that informs those words, rather than on the comfort or spiritual contentment they may provide.

359. Torment that leads to "contentement" is the topic of poem 15.

360. As discussed above in relation to poem 23, the Neoplatonists based their ideal of reciprocity in love on the theory that the lover, in loving, gives himself to the beloved, who will in turn cherish him as a possession. This type of reciprocity appears in lines 119–20. Barataud and Trudeau highlight the providential nature of the Lady, depicted in line 122 as a divinity whom the lover must trust to know what is best for him (*Rymes*, 216).

361. The lover's submission to the lady brings benefits for both. Barataud and Trudeau describe the "feudal" nature of the relationship depicted here, emphasized by the rhyming of "cure" and "procure," "perdition" and "possession" (*Rymes*, 216). Du Guillet's blend of theological allusions, courtly tradition, and elements of Neoplatonic discourse serves to communicate an essential point—that the two lovers belong to each other and that they can find contentment (and perhaps glory) in virtuous reciprocity, which includes the exchange of reason and knowledge. This ideal is a recurring theme of the *Rymes*, but this last elegy, expressed in the voice of a third person, uniquely develops the lady's point of view—her understanding, her sentiments, her own suffering, and yet her unwavering adherence to the highest ideals, her care for the lover, and her nearly divine capacity to know what is right for him as well as for both of them.

The poems by Pernette du Guillet ended here in the 1545 edition of the *Rymes*, followed by the *épitaphes*. Because there is general agreement as to the authenticity of the three poems added in Jean de Tournes's 1552 edition, we have inserted them here, before the epitaphs, for logical reasons.

POEM 71 ("MUMMERY: THE FIVE POSTS OF LOVE")

362. For the three poems added to the work in the 1552 edition, we have used the French text from Victor Graham's edition of the *Rymes* (Droz, 1968), with the adoption of two minor variants for the "Mommerie" that appear in both of the recent French critical editions. In line 3 of the Second Post, where Graham's edition gives "Vous allez deux petits mots dire," the recent Droz and Champion editions both display the corrected line, "Vous aller deux petits mots dire." In line 7 of the Third Post, Graham's edition shows "veoir," rather than "voir"; we have adopted the correction made in the two recent French editions. See *Rymes*, ed. Rajchenbach, 207–208; *Rymes*, ed. Barataud and Trudeau, 217–19.

363. Greimas and Keane, in the *Dictionnaire du moyen français*, define the *mommerie* as a "mascarade, divertissement dansé, comédie" (mascarade, entertainment presented with dance, comedy). Following Saulnier, Graham describes the *mommerie* as a celebration or fantasy in dialogue, performed or recited in costume (*Rymes*, 116). Marot provided two models of the genre, the "Epistre presentée à la Royne de Navarre par Madame Ysabeau et deux autres damoyselles habillées en Amazones en une mommerie" and the "Mommerie de quatre jeunes damoyselles, faicte de Madame de Rohan à Alençon" (*Œuvres poétiques*, vol. 2, 75–76 and 313–15). In Du Guillet's *mommerie*, each stanza conveys the voice of one "post" (courier) sent by Cupid to the gentlewomen of the court. Rajchenbach suggests that Pernette du Guillet's *mommerie* might have been composed for the festivities marking one of the royal entries into the city of Lyon (*Rymes*, 204).

Du Guillet's five "posts" represent four different forms of versification. The first and the fourth are both *huitains* (eight-line poems) of decasyllabic verse. The second is an octosyllabic *dizain* (ten-line poem) in rhyming couplets. The third is an octosyllabic *dizain* with a unique rhyme scheme, ending with a couplet. The fifth is an octosyllabic *huitain* that follows a rhyme scheme used throughout the collection.

364. These words are sent by Cupid, informing the ladies that they should trust this "poste"—his messenger—just as they would trust him. The last two lines tell us who sends the message: the one ("celuy," i.e., Cupid) who harbors the hearts of maidens and gentlewomen under his wings.

365. In dictionary entries for the expression "ranger sous" (translated here as "harboring under"), the object of the preposition "sous" is often "la loi" or "ses lois" (the law/his laws), implying an act of ordering and controlling by force of law—consistent with the idea of Cupid as a god who controls the hearts of women and men. The act of placing or taking someone under one's wing ("sous les ailes"), however, suggests a protective gesture, as in several biblical passages (including Ruth 2:12 and Psalms 17:8, 36:8, 57:2) that contain the image of God harboring his children or followers under his wings. The concluding lines of the Second Post evoke a benevolent divinity protecting his followers (in this case, the gentlewomen), but also suggest a harsher account of the god of love, capturing and lining up the hearts of young women under his wings. The message carried by Cupid's courier is ambiguous, leaving open the question of whether the god of Love is *protecting* or *controlling* the hearts of the "damoiselles."

Cotgrave's dictionary indicates that a "Damoiselle" is "a Gentlewoman; any one, under the degree of a Ladie, that wears, or may weare, a Velvet hood." Greimas and Keane's *Dictionnaire du Moyen français* defines "damoiselle" as the title reserved for women of nobility and lesser nobility ("la petite noblesse"); the young wife of a gentleman; an intermediate rank between that of noble lady and of "dames bourgeoises," corresponding to the rank of the husband.

366. The fourth courrier serves as Cupid's "fourrier," or harbinger, the person sent in advance of troops or a party of traveling royalty to secure lodgings.

367. Regarding the term, "Damoiselle," see above, n65, for the Second Post.

368. Like the third messenger, who—because of Cupid's praise of the ladies—expects to be succored by them after his difficult horseback ride over muddy roads to reach them, the fifth courier also nourishes sparks of hope that whoever serves such beautiful ladies will be rewarded for his suffering. He may have set out on a mission for Cupid, but he appears to transfer his allegiance to the beautiful ladies with tender hearts, for whom he declares himself willing to endure hardship.

POEM 72 ("ANATOMY LESSON")

369. This epigram reflects the widely held philosophical view in the Renaissance of man as a microcosm of the universe, the topic of Scève's *Microcosme*. The image of man as a "petit

monde," or microcosm, appears in a *rondeau* by Mellin de Saint-Gelais, "Pour m'acquitter de l'obligation," in which the speaker tells his beloved that although he cannot give her the world ("la grand fabrique ronde") as she merits, he can give her instead the "petit monde" that he himself encompasses:

And let's have as resolution
That each man is alone a little world,
This world that rests in me alone
I present to you with affection
To discharge my debt.

Et que l'on tient pour resolution
Que chacun homme est seul un petit monde,
Ce monde-cy qui en moy seul se fonde
Je vous presente avec l'affection
Pour m'acquitter. (lines 11–15; *Œuvres poétiques*, vol. 1, 261)

Barataud and Trudeau interpret Du Guillet's epigram as an inscription written for a book of human anatomy (*Rymes*, 220). Whether for a book or not, the poem does suggest a lesson ("If one would know... Let him view...") ("Qui bien voudra contempler... Vienne voir..."), hence Finch's title for the English poem.

370. Finch wasn't sure the slightly archaic use of "confine" worked here, so re-wrote the line; she was encouraged to leave it, however, after rereading Shakespeare's Sonnet 84: "... that you alone are you, / *In whose confine* immurèd is the store..." (lines 2–3, emphasis added). *The Sonnets*, ed. G. Blakemore Evans (Cambridge: Cambridge University Press, 1996).

371. The "round Machine" is the earth. Greimas and Keane's *Dictionnaire du Moyen français* defines the "machine ronde" as "le globe terrestre" (the terrestrial globe).

372. "He"—God the Creator, who understands *and* encompasses all—has included the entire universe in this, his "small world" ("ce sien petit monde"), i.e., man.

POEM 73 ("TO A FOOLISH RHYMER")

373. Inspired by Clément Marot's "Petite epistre au Roy," Du Guillet's poem is built around similar wordplay based on the words "rime" and "rimeur." The term "rimeur" became a pejorative one in the 1540s, with Thomas Sébillet making the distinction between "writers of rhyme" and "poets" in his 1548 *Art poétique français*. Pernette du Guillet's title includes the puzzling element of the verb "aymer." The poem itself does not deal with the topic of love. Instead, the speaker (presumably female) defends her decision not to pursue this type of rhyming endeavor. Barataud and Trudeau suggest that the editor of the 1552 edition (where this poem appears for the first time) mistakenly read "d'aymer" for "de rymer" in the title on the manuscript. The speaker of the *épître* does, in fact, respond to one who has urged her to rhyme ("rymer"), rather than to love (*Rymes*, 221). Or, the verb "aymer" may simply suggest an association between the traditions of love poetry and the type of "rhyming" that Du Guillet's lyric speaker ultimately rejects.

374. The implication here is that there was a time when the speaker was content to write rhymes, although they brought her little return. Line 4, "Que d'avoir biens sans rime assez," echoes line 6 of Marot's épître, "Des biens avez, et de la rime assez," but Du Guillet's speaker makes a point that is contrary to Marot's. She explains in the lines that follow that those who spend their time "rhyming" end up with nothing, while Marot's speaker says his rhyming has kept him fed: "Et m'est advis, que si je ne rimoys / Mon pauvre corps ne seroit nourry moys, / Ne demy jour...." (And it's my opinion that if I didn't rhyme / My poor body would not be nourished for a month, / nor for half a day...). *Œuvres poétiques*, vol. 1, 87. Finch has moved a small step away from the French ("rien à mascher") to the alliterative "no room for rumination" in the English version.

375. Marot's poem concludes with a supplication to the king to allow the young "rimeur" to achieve happiness, as well as fame and glory, through his rhyming. Du Guillet's *épître*—the last poem in the 1552 edition—reverses Marot's model, dismissing the "maistre rimeur" and the illusory praise and honors of "all such rhymers" ("tous telz rimonneurs"). Rieu notes that whereas Marot's poem justifies his poetic vocation, Du Guillet's denounces literary artifice and the search for "vaine gloire" (42).

"EPITAPHS"

376. Maurice Scève. Thomas Hunkeler points out similarities between Scève's lyric epitaphs for Pernette du Guillet and two epigraphs written earlier, upon the premature death of the *dauphin* François in 1536 (*Le vif du sens*, 146–51).

377. *estuy*: in sixteenth-century usage, either a casket or a case, sometimes ornate, which held small personal items such as scissors, a pen-knife, or a bodkin (a needle-like object used for making holes in fabric or leather or pulling ribbon through loops or hems; also, a long hairpin). These two meanings enrich the language of grief in Scève's lyric epitaph; the "riche estuy" evokes the image of the casket holding the beloved lady's body, as well as of a beautiful box holding the objects that represent metonymically the everyday life of a gentlewoman. By extension, the body itself serves as a sort of "estuy," a beautiful shell or casing that enclosed a virtuous and noble soul.

378. *One poem or two?* In the 1545 edition of the *Rymes*, the first four lines appear at the bottom of one page, with the title, "Other" ("Aultre"). The next eight lines appear on the following page, with the same title appearing again at the top of the page. This division was maintained in the subsequent sixteenth-century editions, but the editors of the nineteenth-century editions joined the two parts on the assumption that they were meant to be one twelve-line *épitaphe*, resulting in two lyric epitaphs of the same length by Scève. The two parts are presented as one poem in Graham's 1968 edition and in Barataud and Trudeau's 2006 (Champion) edition. Rajchenbach's 2006 (Droz) edition maintains the distinction of the *quatrain* followed by the *huitain*, contending that the rhyme schemes make more sense as two poems (*Rymes*, 201).

There are good arguments for both arrangements. On the one hand, the two parts can certainly stand alone in meaning and form. The *quatrain* presents a beautiful, brief epitaph that contrasts the death of physical beauty with the enduring nature of virtue that lives on in this world just as the "esprit" (mind, spirit) lives on in heaven. The *huitain* that follows focuses on the young woman's "esprit." Putting the two parts together creates one longer poem, with twelve lines addressing the topic of the eternal life of the "esprit," contrasted with the immortal praise ("immortel los") of her name that the poet left behind on earth. We have chosen to maintain a visual division between the two parts to reflect the break between them in the first edition, whether intended to be read as one poem or two. By presenting the *quatrain* and the *huitain* on the same page, and in translation, we hope to facilitate an evaluation of these twelve lines, whether as one epitaph or two, or perhaps as both.

379. Finch has chosen to translate the verb "souspirer" (literally, to sigh) into the very breath of life, rendered useless in the face of "thieving Death." Hunkeler identifies the first line of this epitaph as the French translation of line 15 of an Italian sonnet attributed to Petrarch and presented as having been discovered by Scève (along with the tomb of Petrarch's Laura) in Jean de Tournes's preface to his edition of Petrarch's poems (Lyon, 1545). See *Le vif du sens*, 50.

380. The initials stand for the *devise*, or motto, of Jean de Vauzelles: "D'un Vray Zèle" (with true zeal). He was part of the network of intellectuals associated with the printer, Jean de Tournes, in Lyon, and his brother married Maurice Scève's sister. He may have been part of the same literary and social circle as Pernette du Guillet, although we have no documentary evidence that they knew each other.

381. The first line includes a pun on the poet's name: "Perle nette" for "Pernette." Similar wordplay appears in the second line.

382. The epitaph attributes the same virtue, learning, and eloquence to the poet as she did to her beloved throughout the *Rymes*, and specifically alludes to her musical achievements and to the extensive learning which she acquired in her short life, bringing us full circle to the comments in Du Moulin's prefatory letter.

383. Jean de Vauzelles (author of the previous lyric epitaph).

384. The first line includes another play on the poet's name: "per nette" (pair nette) for Pernette. We do not know precisely why she is called "cousin" here (and in the title to the "epitaphes"), as well as "sister." The historical dictionaries tell us that, beyond expressing a familial tie, the term "cousin(e)" was used to convey affection and a close relationship, as within a family. Whether indicating an actual familial relationship or bonds of friendship, referring to the poet in these terms would undoubtedly help to counter any critics who might misinterpret the emotions and motives behind her poems, a concern that surfaces in the *Rymes* and in the editor's preface.

385. The epitaph confirms that the young poet followed the "sure path" to the highest and noblest good, the same ideal upheld in many of her poems. Among the "Bourgeoises" (citizenry, inhabitants of the city) of Lyon, she was an esteemed model of virtue and

learning. This final epitaph echoes the assessment of the poet's life offered by Antoine du Moulin in his prefatory letter addressed to the Ladies of Lyon.

386. After describing the final moments of the young poet's life in spiritual and even mystical terms that recall the lives of saints, the last lines conclude in a manner similar to Scève's second *épitaphe*: just as the soul has a new life and lives on in heaven, so the poet's name lives on earth through her reputation and through her poetry.

387. *Requiescat in pace* (Latin for "May she rest in peace").

(aux) abboys (64): barking, baying
absouldre (25): to absolve or pardon; to discharge or deliver from danger
abuser (38, 58): to abuse; to deceive, to mislead
accoller (64): to embrace
accoustrement (67): clothing, garment
(faire) accroire (45): to convince of something that isn't true
adumbrer (69): to shadow, overcast, overshadow
advis m'est/estoit;
il me fut advis (41, 64, 68): it seems/seemed to me
advouer (6, 7, 70): to attribute; to recognize, to accept (as one's own)
affole(e) (40): wounded, bruised; undone, ruined; besotted
aigu (69, 70): sharp, pointed, penetrating
ains (43, 64, 68): but, rather
allegeance (57, 64): a lightening (of cares or grief), comfort
alteration (70): thirst, drought
amande (19, 64, 67): penalty, fine
amas (preface): heap, pile, bundle
amuser (59): to delay or hold someone with words or discourse; also, to amuse, or cause to wonder
amytié ("To the reader from the printer", 17, 32, 33, 38, 39, 40, 46, 59, 60, 63): pure, chaste love; affection; friendship
appeau (67): appeal; also, a lure (specifically, a type of whistle used to lure birds to a trap)
appetisser (38): to diminish, lessen; also, to desire, to seek with an appetite (as a form of *appeter/appetir*)
appoint (63): fit for, corresponding to
appointement (60): agreement, reconciliation
asseurance (26, 32, 39, 47): trust, confidence, assurance
asseuré(e) (preface, 39, 56, 63, 64): confident, secure; firm, certain; bold, fearless
asseurer (32, 38, 39): to assure, confirm; to affirm; to protect, safeguard

assez (4, 68, 70, 73): enough, sufficiently; also, very well, very
attente (32, 39, 56): expectation, hope
attoucher (68): to come in contact with, briefly or slightly; to reach
au fort (68): after all, finally; at most, at worst
augure (50): divination, sign, forewarning
avanture (preface, 50, 64): chance, luck, fortune
(s') avanturer (34): to try, to venture, to try one's luck at something

bailler (56): to give, to confer
basté (71): saddled with a packsaddle (i.e. in the saddle)
besoing (8, 53, 68): indigence, need
blasonner (70): to reprove, revile; also, to praise, proclaim the virtues of
bout (21, 33): end; head, top, extreme or utmost part
bouter (64): to thrust, move forward
brouillars (preface): drafts
(à la) buste (67): in the new, or latest, fashion

caducque (56, epitaph 2): frail, feeble
cault(z) (32, 63): cunning, crafty
cautelle (29): ruse, maneuver
ceindre (ceinct) (56): to enclose, encompass, gird
celer (preface, 29, 42, 69): to hide
cerf (43): stag
(chaloir) Plus ne m'en chault (47): It doesn't matter to me
cheoir (70): to fall; **cheut** (64): fell
chetif(z) (69): wretched, miserable, forlorn; also, captive
comme ainsi soit que (preface): just as, even as; it being so that…
complaincte (64): a lament or complaint
complaire (complaisant) (preface, 19, 36, 68): to please, delight (to serve)
complexion (preface): disposition, nature, temperament
confit (70): steeped, imbued with
confus (43, 68, 69): confused, disordered; also, troubled, dismayed

consommer,
consumer (preface, 12, 29, 51, 66): to consume, destroy, cause to perish; also, to accomplish, finish, perfect, consummate
consummation (preface): achievement, perfection
convier, convyer (1, 24, 30, 70): to urge, push, incite; to invite
corner (67): to sound (a horn); **corner la prise**: to finish the chase, bring the matter to a close
coulpe (70): fault, offense, transgression
courroucer (68): to anger, offend
courtisaner (67): to play the courtier, to adopt the manners and fashions of the court and its courtesans.
creance (71): trust, confidence; belief
cure (63, 70): care, protection, heed
cuyder (17, 43): think, suppose, believe, presume

damoiselle (preface, 67, 71): gentlewoman
debvoir (6, 13, 23, 36, 40, 43, 70): duty, obligation, service
deduire (68): to develop a discourse about, to discuss in detail
delaisser (46, 68): to leave, abandon, forsake
delecter
(delectoit) (68): to delight, give joy to
delivre (69): free (adj.)
delivrer (69): to free, release, liberate
demener
complaincte (64): to express a lament or complaint with great agitation or passion
demeurance (64): abode, dwelling, residence
depescher (71): to dispatch
descharger (45, 70): to disburden, unload, deliver from
desjoindre (46): to divide, separate, part
deslier, deslyer (64, 70): to unloose, untie, unbind, free
despartir (53): to share, distribute
desplaisance (46, 64): grief, anguish, unhappiness
desplier (10, 64): lay open to view, display; also, to unfold, deploy (64)
despourveu (45): deprived, defective
dessaisir (32): to steal away, to divest someone of something

dessirer (deschirer)	(69): to tear, rend (in two, or in pieces)
destraindre	(70): to unloose, untie; also to wring, to restrain
(se) desvestir de	(36): to give up, give over, forego something; to divest oneself of something
desvier	(69): to mislead; also, to die
devaller	(48): to descend, go down
devis	(69, epitaph 4): words, speech, discourse
devise	(39): emblem, motto, device
(à) dextre	(58): on the right; on the right hand
dict	(70): (noun) saying, speech, word(s)
diffame	(70): infamy, dishonor, disgrace
dissention	(60): debate, variance, dissention
docilité	(preface): aptitude for learning, quickness of apprehension
docte	(65): learned
dolent(e)	(preface, 64): grieving, suffering
dont	(1, 9, 13, 56, 64, 68): (adverbial use) whereby, whereupon, whence
douleance	(26): lament, expression of suffering
(se) douloir	(31, 33, 64): to suffer; to lament
dresser	(63): to lift up, to raise up
duire	(63): to teach, instruct, lead; to profit, be useful to; to suit
duisant	(69): pleasant, agreeable, fitting

effect	(13, 34): act, action, accomplishment
(faire) effort	(45): to do violence, to wrong
(à l') emblee	(68): in secret, secretly
embridez	(68): restrained, held back; bridled
(ciel) Empiree	(64): the Empyrean, or highest heaven
empraindre	("To the reader from the printer," 41): to imprint, engrave, ingrain, stamp; to inspire; to make fertile, impregnate
enclos(e)	(42, 72, epitaph 2): enclosed, contained; imprisoned
encombre	(68): obstacle, obstruction, trouble
engin	(preface, 64, 68): understanding, wit, intelligence
ennui, ennuy	(9, 46): vexation, distress, anguish
(s') enquerir	(68): to inform oneself

entendement (preface, 18, 43, 70): understanding, intelligence, judgment

entente (9): intention, purpose

entonner (43): to tune, sound, sing, chant; to begin or give a tune (in singing)

envie (preface, "To the reader from the printer," 64, 68, 69, epitaph 1–2): desire; envy

équité (63): equity, equality; also, moderation, uprightness, clemency

errer (5, 7): to err; to stray, to wander

erreur (5, 7, 11, 66): error; ignorance; a wandering or straying

es (39, 40): in the (equivalent of *dans les* or *aux*)

(s') esbahir, esbayr (preface, 20, 38, 41, 44, 47, 68): to marvel, be astonished, be amazed, wonder at

escarlate (64): bright red color; scarlet

escarmoucher (40): to assail, assault, attack

(s') escarter (43, 54): to move away; to lose oneself (from *escarter*: to scatter, disperse, discard)

eschetz (64): chess

esclarcir (66, 67, 68): to clarify, light up, illuminate

esgard (46): consideration, regard, heed

esguillon (preface): a spur, goad; a provocation; dart

esguilloner (64): to poke, prod; to urge forward

esles (64): wings

eslire (70): to choose, elect

esmoy (23, 64, 71): chagrin, trouble

esplo(u)re(e) (64): full of tears

esprit (preface, 3, 4, 8, 11, 13, 14, 16, 18, 20, 43, 66, 68, 70, epitaph 2–4): mind, wit, spirit, soul,

(soubs mon) esselle (29): under my arm, close to my body

estable (10): stable, steadfast

estincelle (29, 71): spark

estinceller (42): to spark, kindle

estuy (epitaph 1): case, small sheath, or box for items such as scissors or penknife; casket

ethique (67): of a moral/ethical nature; *or* extremely thin

exploict (70): action, achievement; also, execution of a judgment (legal)

extraict(e) (preface): extracted, drawn from; issuing from; taken from; written or copied out from

faconde (4, 17, epitaph 3): eloquence

facture (preface): the making or fabrication of something; workmanship

faillir (failly, faillant) (23, 66): to err, go astray; to be mistaken; to lack; to deceive or disappoint

(il) failloit (38): one must (variant spelling of *il falloit*, from *falloir*); **comme il falloit aymer**: how one must love

faintise (39): ruse, trickery, dissembling

fallace (40): deception, wile

fanges (71): mud, mire

fantasie (45): imagination, vision

fascherie (69): vexation, grief

fault (8, 56 [line 20], 69 [line 39]; 70 [line 106]): 3rd person singular form of the verb *faillir*, to lack, to be missing; also, to deceive

fendre (64): to cleave, divide

fiancé (68): confidence, trust

fluant(e) (4): flowing, fluid

(se) fonder (20): to place one's reliance on; to base one's hope or assurance on

forclos (epitaph 2): excluded, expelled; dismissed from

fors (1, 6, 40, 69): except

(au) fort (68): enough, after all

fouler (42): to disgrace, to dishonor, discredit

fourree (42): covered, sheathed

fourrier (71): forward scout, or person who secures lodging in advance for troops or for nobility/royalty; harbinger

frequentation (preface): company, time spent in a person's company

frequenter (65, 68): to frequent, spend time with, keep company with

fumiere (48): smoke (variant of *fumée*)

(chemin) gasté (71): a road in very bad condition (from *gaster*: to waste, ruin)
gecter (40, 43, 64): to throw; to emit (40); to direct (64)
gent (43): (adj.) noble
gent(z) (42, 68): (noun) people; also, nation(s)
gentil(le) (preface, epitaph 1): gentle, mild, gracious; tender; gallant, noble
grace (preface, 3, 17, 70, 71): grace, favor, good will; also, a good disposition, an inclination to goodness
gré (43, 57): will, willingness; consent, accord
grever (epitaph 4): to aggrieve, trouble, oppress
grief (47): grievous, troublesome
guerdon (70): recompense, reward
guerdonner (16): to reward, give recompense

hacher (73): to hack, chop in pieces
hanter (65): to spend time with; to be with
heur (preface, 13, 16, 18, 33, 52, 73): luck, fortune, good fortune
honte (68, 69, 70): shame; also, timidity, bashfulness, chaste reserve
honteux (64, 68, 70, epitaph 1): shameful, dishonorable; also, timid, bashful, shy
hure (64): the head of a wild beast

importun(s) (68): insistent, troublesome
importuner (42, 73): to urge, press insistently
impression (1): imprint, impression, printed book or page, printing
incensé, incense(e) (57, 64): unreasonable; mad, outside the bounds of reason
indiscret(te) (23): imprudent, rash
infame (68): infamous, shameful, ignominious
injure (70): wrong, harm, injustice
instance (19): insistence
instant(es) (preface): urgent, insistent
intentif (70): attentive

jouyssance	(3, 26, 28, 32, 46, 63): enjoyment of, possession; delight, pleasure
justement	(34): impartially; fully; precisely
lairra, lairrois	(41, 43), future and present conditional (old forms) of the verb *laisser*: to stop, leave off, relinquish (41); to let, allow (43)
lasche	(67): languishing, weak, slack
(à la) legere	(67): (fig.) without reflection; related expressions: *être armé/vêtu à la légère*, to be lightly armed/dressed
legereté	(38, 59): lightness; inconstancy, fickleness
loysir, loisir	(preface, 68, 71): ease, leisure; free time
loz, los	(preface, 7, 24, 70, 73, epitaph 2, epitaph 4): praise, laud, commendation
machiner (machinantz)	(68): to conspire, plot (against)
maignie	(43): family members, household company, or servants; chaperone
maille	(73): a half-penny, or something of very little value; **n'avoir maille**: to have nothing, or next-to-nothing
malefice	(64, 68): evil, offense
marestz	(64): marshes, swamps
marrie(e)	(preface, 73) : sad, aggrieved, afflicted
marrir (marrissoit)	(2): to grieve or feel sorrow for, to be sad or vexed at
maulgré	("To the reader from the printer," 23, 68): despite
meffaire (meffeit)	(64): to offend, to wrong, cause harm
meffaict	(64): (noun) fault, offense, wrong
mescheut	(64): misfortune befell (him) (past tense of *mescheoir*)
meslé	(3): diverse, multiple
mesme que	(50): although
mesmement	(preface): namely, especially, chiefly
(faire) mestier	(67): to be necessary
moleste	(70): troublesome, offensive, disagreeable
muer	(5): to change, transform

net(te) (epitaph 3, epitaph 4): pure, spotless
nonchalloir (70): heedlessness, indifference
nonobstant que (68, 71): although, notwithstanding
noyse (49): strife, discord, trouble
nuire (8, 63): to hurt, harm, offend
nuisant(e) (68): hurtful, harmful, offensive
nuysance (3): harm, offence, wrong

occire (occist) (69): to kill, slay
odorer (70): to smell, to perceive a scent
offence (64): attack, harm
offencer (27, 69): to wound, harm; **offensé**, **offencee** (57, 64): wounded, harmed
office (5, 38, 68): duty, function, job, service
onc, oncques (preface, 8, 34, 40, 42, 67, 68, 69, epitaph 3, epitaph 4): never
ordonnance (20): arrangement, ordering; order, decree
ordonner (16): to order, put in order; command
oster (43, 58): to remove, put off, take away
oultrage (preface, 40, 64): injury, wrong, abuse
oultrageux (preface, 64): injurious; unreasonable
oultré (64): pierced, harmed
oultre (preface, 57, 69): beyond; still (69); **en oultre** (70): moreover, besides
oultrecuydez (68): presumptuous
ouyr (31, 64, 68): to hear; **ouy**, **ouyes** (64, 69): heard (past participle of *ouyr*, to hear)
oysiveté (67): idleness, sloth

(se) paistre de (39, 68): to nourish oneself with, to be nourished by
pallier (69): to mitigate, palliate; to cloak, cover up; to shadow, to color
pardurable (10): enduring, lasting, permanent
parvenir (9, 67, 68): achieve, attain, arrive, reach
pensement (70): dressing, care of a wound or wounded person; also, thought, meditation
per (epitaph 3, epitaph 4): peer, match (alt. spelling of *pair*)
pipperie (67): deceit, ruse
plaisance (59, 64): pleasure, delight

plumer (67): to pluck; to fleece, to rob

poindre (poinct) (56): to prick, sting

pourchasser (33, 56, 64): to pursue, to seek

(se) pourmaine (se pourmener) (43, 70): to walk (equivalent of modern French, *se promener*)

pourveoir (70): to provide for, to furnish; **pourveu** (45, epitaph 4): furnished, equipped

pretendre (26, 39, 53, 56): to aspire (to), aim (for), seek; to claim (26)

prise (67): (noun) the death or fall of a hunted animal; catch

priser (preface): to esteem, value; **prisez** (68): valued, esteemed

promptitude (preface, 3): aptitude, readiness

propice (36): favorable

propos (45, 49, 70, epitaph 3, epitaph 4): words, discourse, speech

(à) propos (preface): aptly, fitly; also, opportunely, to the purpose

(à tous) propos (68): at each instant, on each occasion

prys (4, 30, 64): reward, prize, honor

qualité (1, 25): quality; goodness, nobility, excellence; calling

quant et quant (43): at the same time; also, by and by

racheptable (10): redeemable

ravir (preface, 12, 14, 19, 40, 43, 66, epitaph 1, 2, 4): transported, delighted, enchanted; stolen away

rechiner (68): to frown, be surly, look grim or sullen; **rechiner des dents**: to grin like a dog (expression cited in Cotgrave)

recorder (70): to record, report; also, to testify, relate

recreer (preface): to delight, please; to give solace, revive

redevable (44): indebted, beholden

rediger (24): to direct, draft, drive

reduire (63): to bring back; to reclaim

refrigeration (70): refreshing comfort

regraver (1): to engrave (anew)
regrecter (40, 53): to desire, long for; to grieve, lament for
reluire (48, 69): to shine, to glow
renger (38, 71): to order, array, arrange
repaistre (58): to nourish
reprise (38): blamed, accused, reprehended
requis(e) (33): sought, solicited; esteemed, appreciated
retraire (69): to withdraw
revocquer (70): to recall, countermand
roguement (68): arrogantly, presumptuously
royne (68): queen (equivalent of modern French, *reine*)
rudement (30): rudely, churlishly, roughly, harshly
rys (26): [line 9] laughs, laughter; **rys** [line 13]: first person singular form of the verb *rire*, to laugh

sainct ("To the reader from the printer," 41, 42, 43, 56, 67, 68, 70, epigraph 3, epigraph 4): holy, sacred, pure, perfect
science (68): learning, knowledge, understanding
sejour (19, 33, 63, 66): a stay, a visit, a rest; time of leisure or rest
sejourner (67): to stay, remain
(à) (main) senestre (58, 68): on the left; on the left hand
sens (16, 45, 70): wit, understanding, reason; sense
serf (43, 69): slave, serf
service (5, 24, 56, 69): service, attendance, duty
simplesse (67): ignorance, folly
soulas (9): solace, comfort
souldre (soult) (70): to undo, loosen, resolve
souloir (il souloit, etc.) (30, 53, 64): to be accustomed to, wont to, used to
souspeçon (49): suspicion, jealousy, doubt
spirituel(le) (preface, epigraph 1): spiritual (focused on matters of the soul or spirit); witty (quality of the mind or intellect, showing quick thinking and lively humor)
suicte (64): pursuit
supplier (64): to petition, entreat
survenu (47): happened, befallen
susciter (43): to incite, stir up; also, to awaken, raise

tabourin (67): drum; (often referring to a small drum)
tailler (taillé) (10): cut, engrave
tant soit… (18, 43, 68, 70, 71): no matter how… , however…
tascher (5, 23, 40, 65, 68): to attempt, try, endeavor
taster (71): to touch, strike; grope for
tourbe (68): rabble, crowd, throng
tourterelle (68): turtledove
toutesfois (24, 25, 26, 30, 34, 43, 56, 64, 68, 69, 70): yet, nevertheless
(de) tout en tout (34): completely
traictz (12, 40, 49): arrows, darts
train (71): retinue, followers
transmuer (5): change, alter, transform
travail (56, 63, 68, 70, 71): trouble, care, fatigue; toil, labor
travailler (56, 68): to toil, labor; to trouble
tromperies (69): wiles, deceits, tricks
trousse (64): quiver
(donner la) trousse (64): to trap, catch in a trap
umbrage (66): shadow
usure (65): interest (on an investment)

vague (40): wandering
vain (40, 68, 69): empty, idle, vain
(se) veaultrer (64): to wallow
veine (4): vein (a vein in the body, but also a style of writing)
voire (preface, 57, 59, 70): indeed, truly, surely
volage (38, 66): erratic, flighty, fickle
(à la) volee (40): rashly; at random; precipitously
vulgaire(s) (preface): vernacular (languages)

ysser (yssoit) (68): to issue, come forth

Concordance

Indicating the correspondence of the poem numbers (using continuous numbering) with the names/numbers used in Victor Graham's edition (Droz, 1968). See the Introduction for more information on the naming and numbering conventions applied to the *Rymes*.

Chanson I	26	Epigramme XXIII	23
Chanson II	29	Epigramme XXIV	24
Chanson III	32	Epigramme XXV	25
Chanson IV	33	Epigramme XXVI	27
Chanson V	38	Epigramme XXVII	28
Chanson VI	40	Epigramme XXVIII	30
Chanson VII	42	Epigramme XXIX	31
Chanson VIII	56	Epigramme XXX	34
Chanson IX	63	Epigramme XXXI	35
Chanson X	64	Epigramme XXXII	36
Elegie I	39	Epigramme XXXIII	37
Elegie II	43	Epigramme XXXIV	41
Elegie III	68	Epigramme XXXV	44
Elegie IV	69	Epigramme XXXVI	45
Elegie V	70	Epigramme XXXVII	46
Epigramme I	1	Epigramme XXXVIII	47
Epigramme II	2	Epigramme XXXIX	48
Epigramme III	3	Epigramme XL	49
Epigramme IV	4	Epigramme XLI	50
Epigramme V	5	Epigramme XLII	51
Epigramme VI	6	Epigramme XLIII	52
Epigramme VII	7	Epigramme XLIV	53
Epigramme VIII	8	Epigramme XLV	54
Epigramme IX	9	Epigramme XLVI	55
Epigramme X	10	Epigramme XLVII	57
Epigramme XI	11	Epigramme XLVIII	58
Epigramme XII	12	Epigramme XLIX	59
Epigramme XIII	13	Epigramme L	60
Epigramme XIV	14	Epigramme LI	61
Epigramme XV	15	Epigramme LII	62
Epigramme XVI	16	Epigramme LIII	65
Epigramme XVII	17	Epigramme LIV	66
Epigramme XVIII	18	Epigrammes LV-LIX	71
Epigramme XIX	19	Epigramme LX	72
Epigramme XX	20	Epitre I	67
Epigramme XXI	21	Epitre II	73
Epigramme XXII	22	Mommerie (Cinq postes)	71

Index of First Lines and Titles

Editor's Bibliography

PRINCIPAL EDITIONS OF THE *RYMES*

SIXTEENTH CENTURY

Du Guillet, Pernette. *Rymes de gentile et vertueuse dame D. Pernette du Guillet, Lyonnoise.* Lyon: Jean de Tournes, 1545.

_____. *Les rithmes et poésies de gentile et vertueuse dame D. Pernette du Guillet, Lyonnoise. Avecq' le triomphe des Muses sur Amour et autres nouvelles composicions.* Paris: Jeanne de Marnef, 1546.

_____. *Les rithmes et poesies de gentile et vertueuse Dame D. Pernette du Guillet, Lyonnoise. Avecq' le triumphe des Muses sur Amour et autres nouvelles composicions.* Paris: Jeanne de Marnef, 1547.

_____. *Rymes de D. Pernette du Guillet, Lyonnoize. De nouueau augmentées.* Lyon: Jean de Tournes, 1552.

NINETEENTH CENTURY

_____. *Poésies de Pernette du Guillet.* Edited by Coste and Péricaud. Lyon: Louis Perrin, 1830.

_____. *Rymes de gentile et vertueuse dame D. Pernette du Guillet.* Edited by J.-B. Monfalcon. Lyon: Louis Perrin, 1856.

_____. *Rymes de gentile et vertueuse dame D. Pernette du Guillet.* Edited by Nicolas Scheuring. Lyon: Louis Perrin, 1864.

TWENTIETH AND TWENTY-FIRST CENTURIES

_____. *Rymes de gentile et vertueuse dame D. Pernette du Guillet Lyonnoise.* In *Poètes du XVIe siècle,* 227–268. Edited by Albert-Marie Schmidt. Bibliothèque de la Pléiade. Paris: Gallimard, 1953. [Includes all poems by Du Guillet in the 1545 edition except the two Italian epigrams. Does not include Antoine du Moulin's preface, Jean de Tournes's liminary poem, the lyric epitaphs, or the three poems by Du Guillet added to the 1552 edition of the *Rymes.*]

_____. *Rymes.* Edited by Victor E. Graham. Geneva: Droz, 1968.

_____. *Rymes.* Facsimile reprint of the 1830 (L. Perrin) edition. Geneva: Slatkine, 1970.

_____. *Rymes*. In Louise Labé, *Œuvres poétiques, précédées des Rymes de Pernette du Guillet avec un choix de Blasons du Corps féminin*, edited by Françoise Charpentier. Paris: Gallimard, 1983. [Includes all poems by Du Guillet from the 1545 and the 1552 editions; does not include Du Moulin's preface, Tournes's liminary poem, or the lyric epitaphs.]

_____. *Rymes*. Edited by Christian Barataud and Danielle Trudeau. Paris: Champion, 2006.

_____. *Rymes* (1545). Edited by Elise Rajchenbach. Geneva: Droz, 2006.

OTHER PRIMARY SOURCES

Les fleurs de poesie françoyse; Hécatomphile. Edited by Gérard Defaux. Paris: Société des Textes Français Modernes (STFM), 2002.

Opuscules d'amour par Héroet, La Borderie & autres divins poëtes. Lyon: Jean de Tournes, 1547. Facsimile reprint. Edited by M. A. Screech. [East Ardsley] S. R. Publishers; [New York] Johnson Reprint Corp., 1970.

Alciati, Andrea. *A Book of Emblems: The Emblematum Liber in Latin and English*. Edited and translated by John F. Moffitt. Jefferson, NC: McFarland, 2004.

Castiglione, Baldesar. *The Book of the Courtier*. Translated by Charles Singleton. New York: Anchor Books, 1959.

Colonna, Francesco. *Hypnerotomachia Poliphili: the strife of love in a dream*. Edited and translated by Joscelyn Godwin. London: Thames & Hudson, 1999.

Ebreo, Leone. *Dialogues d'amour. Translated by Pontus de Tyard*. Edited by T. Anthony Perry. Chapel Hill: University of North Carolina Press, 1974.

_____. *The Philosophy of Love (Dialoghi d'Amore) by Leone Ebreo*. Translated by F. Friedeberg-Seeley and Jean H. Barnes. London: The Soncino Press, 1937.

Ficino, Marsilio. *Commentaire sur le Banquet de Platon*. Edited and translated by Raymond Marcel. Paris: Les Belles Lettres, 1956.

_____. *Commentary on Plato's Symposium on Love*. Translated by Sears Jayne. Woodstock, CT: Spring Publications, 1985.

______. *Three Books on Life.* Edited and translated by Carol V. Kaske and John R. Clark. Tempe, AZ: Medieval and Renaissance Texts and Studies (in conjunction with The Renaissance Society of America), 1998.

Héroët, Antoine. *La parfaicte amye.* Edited by Christine M. Hill. Exeter: University of Exeter, 1981.

La Borderie, Bertrand de. *L'amie de court (1542).* Edited by D. Trudeau. Paris: Honoré Champion, 1997.

Labé, Louise. *Complete Poetry and Prose: A Bilingual Edition.* Edited with prose translations by Deborah Lesko Baker. Poetry translations by Annie Finch. Other Voice in Early Modern Europe. Chicago: University of Chicago Press, 2006.

______. *Œuvres complètes.* Edited by François Rigolot. Paris: Garnier-Flammarion, 1986.

Lemaire de Belges, Jean. *Concorde des deux langages.* Edited by Jean Frappier. Paris: Droz, 1947.

______. *Œuvres.* 3 vols. Edited by Auguste Jean Stecher. Louvain: J. Lefever, 1882–1885. Reprint. Geneva: Slatkine Reprints, 1969.

Marot, Clément. *Œuvres poétiques de Clément Marot.* 2 vols. Edited by Gérard Defaux. Classiques Garnier. Paris: Bordas, 1990, 1993.

Martial d'Auvergne. *Les arrêts d'amour.* Paris: A. & J. Picard, 1951.

Ovid. *Metamorphoses.* Translated by A. D. Melville, with introduction and notes by E. J. Kenney. Oxford; New York: Oxford University Press, 1998.

Petrarca, Francesco. *Petrarch's Lyric Poems: The Rime Sparse and Other Lyrics.* Edited and translated by Robert Durling. Cambridge, MA: Harvard University Press, 1976.

Plato. *The Dialogues of Plato*, vol. 2, *The Symposium.* Translated by R. E. Allen. New Haven: Yale University Press, 1991.

______. *The Portable Plato.* Translated by Benjamin Jowett. Edited by Scott Buchanan. New York: Penguin Books, 1977.

Saint-Gelais, Mellin de. *Œuvres poétiques françaises.* 2 vols. Edited by Donald Stone, Jr. Paris: Société des Textes Français Modernes, 1993, 1995.

Scève, Maurice. *Délie, object de plus haulte vertu.* 2 vols. Edited by Gérard Defaux. Geneva: Droz, 2004.

______. *The entry of Henri II into Lyon: september 1548.* Edited by Richard Cooper. Tempe, Arizona: Medieval & Renaissance Texts and Studies, 1997.

_____. *Sixty Poems of Scève*. Translated by Wallace Fowlie. New York: The Swallow Press, 1949.

Sébillet, Thomas. *Art poétique français* (1548). In *Traités de poétique et de rhétorique de la Renaissance*, edited by Francis Goyet, 37–183. Paris: Livre de Poche, 1990.

Shakespeare, William. *The Sonnets.* Edited by G. Blakemore Evans. Cambridge: Cambridge University Press, 1996.

Vives, Juan Luis. *The Education of a Christian Woman.* Edited and translated by Charles Fantazzi. The Other Voice in Early Modern Europe. Chicago: University of Chicago Press, 2000.

DICTIONARIES

Cotgrave, Randle. *A Dictionarie of the French and English Tongues.* London: Adam Islip, 1611. Reprint. Columbia: University of South Carolina Press, 1950. A searchable version created by Greg Lindahl from scans in the Bibliothèque nationale is available online at http://www.pbm.com/~Elindahl/cotgrave/.

Dictionnaire de l'Académie française. 1st edition. Paris: Veuve de Jean Baptiste Coignard, 1694. Search the full-text version of this dictionary on the ARTFL Project website, http://dictionnaires.atilf.fr/dictionnaires/ACADEMIE/PREMIERE/search.fulltext.form.html.

DMF: Dictionnaire du moyen français (1330–1500). 2009 version. ATILF - Nancy Université & CNRS. Search the online database at http://www.atilf.fr/dmf.

Godefroy, Frédéric. *Dictionnaire de l'ancienne langue française, et de tous ses dialectes du IXe au XVe siècle.* 10 vols. Paris: F. Vieweg, 1881–1902.

Grandsaignes d'Hauterive, R. *Dictionnaire d'ancien francais: Moyen Age et Renaissance.* Paris: Librairie Larousse, 1947.

Greimas, Algirdas Julien and Teresa Mary Keane. *Dictionnaire du moyen français: la Renaissance.* Paris: Larousse, 1992.

Huguet, Edmond. *Dictionnaire de la langue française du seizième siècle.* 7 vols. Paris: Didier, 1925–1973.

Nicot, Jean. *Thresor de la langue françoyse.* Paris: David Douceur, 1606. Search the full-text version of this dictionary on the ARTFL Project website, http://dictionnaires.atilf.fr/dictionnaires/TLF-NICOT/search.fulltext.form.html.

Rey, Alain. *Dictionnaire historique de la langue française*. 2 vols. Paris: Editions Le Robert, 2006.

SECONDARY SOURCES

Ardouin, Paul. *Maurice Scève, Pernette du Guillet, Louise Labé: L'amour à Lyon au temps de la Renaissance*. Paris: A. G. Nizet, 1981.

______. *Pernette du Guillet, l'heureuse Renaissante: Miracle de l'amour, de la lumière et de la poésie*. Paris: A. G. Nizet, 1991.

Aynard, Joseph. *Les poëtes lyonnais, précurseurs de la Pléiade*. Paris: Bossard, 1924.

Balsamo, Jean. "L'italianisme lyonnais et l'illustration de la langue française." In *Lyon et l'illustration de la langue française à la Renaissance*, edited by Gérard Defaux, with the collaboration of Bernard Colombat, 211–29. Lyon: ENS Editions, 2003.

______. "Marot et les origines du pétrarquisme français (1530–1540)." In *Clément Marot, «prince des poëtes françois,» 1496–1996*, Actes du colloque international de Cahors en Quercy, 1996, edited by Gérard Defaux and Michel Simenon, 323–37. Paris: Honoré Champion, 1997.

______. *Les poètes français de la Renaissance et Pétrarque*. Geneva: Droz, 2004.

Banks, Kathryn. *Cosmos and Image in the Renaissance: French Love Lyric and Natural-Philosophical Poetry*. London: MHRA, 2008.

Baur, Albert. *Maurice Scève et la Renaissance lyonnaise*. Paris: Champion, 1906.

Bauschatz, Cathleen. "To Chose Ink and Pen: French Renaissance Women's Writing," In *A History of Women's Writing in France*, edited by Sonya Stephens, 41–63. Cambridge: Cambridge University Press, 2000.

Berriot-Salvadore, Evelyne. *Les femmes dans la société française de la Renaissance*. Geneva: Droz, 1990.

Bloom, Harold, ed. *Petrarch: Modern Critical Views*. New York: Chelsea House, 1989.

Boney, Jan. "'Ardeur de veoir': Reading Knowledge in Pernette du Guillet's *Rymes*." *Esprit Créateur* 30 (Winter 1990): 49–60.

Boquet, Pascale, and Gérard Rebours. *50 Standards, Renaissance & Baroque, avec variantes, exemples, & conseils pour jouer & improviser*. Courlay: Editions Fuzeau, 2006.

Bots, W. J. A. "Maurice Scève, Pernette du Guillet, ou la victoire de deux voix sur les escarpements de la syntaxe." *L'information littéraire* 39:3 (1987), 102–106.

Boucher, Jacqueline. *Présence italienne à Lyon à la Renaissance, du milieu du XVe siècle à la fin du XVIe siècle.* Lyon: Editions LUGD, 1994.

Bourgeois, Louis. *Quand la cour de France vivait à Lyon, 1494–1551.* Paris: Fayard, 1980.

Braden, Gordon. *Petrarchan Love and the Continental Renaissance.* New Haven: Yale University Press, 1999.

Brésard, Marc. *Les foires de Lyon aux xve et xvie siècles.* Paris: A. Picard, 1914.

Bright, Francis T. "Language as Object: Gift-Giving and Dialogue in Scève and Pernette du Guillet." *MIFLC Review* 1 (Oct. 1991), 48–57.

Buche, Joseph. "Pernette du Guillet et la <<Délie>> de Maurice Scève." In *Mélanges de Philologie offerts à Ferdinand Brunot*, 33–39. Paris, 1904. Geneva: Slatkine Reprints, 1972.

Caron, Elisabeth. "Les femmes et la politique du Néo-Platonisme: Les enjeux à la Renaissance d'un baiser de Platon." *Etudes littéraires* 27:2 (1994), 97–109.

Caron, Philippe. *Des <<belles lettres>> à la <<littérature>>, une archéologie des signes du savoir profane en langue française (1680–1760).* Louvain: Diffusion Peeters, 1992.

Carron, Jean-Claude. "Imitation and Intertextuality in the Renaissance." *New Literary History* 19:3 (Spring 1988), 565–79.

Cartier, Alfred. *Bibliographie des éditions des de Tournes*, 2 vols. Paris: Bibliothèques Nationales de France, 1937.

_____, and Adolphe Chenevière. "Antoine Du Moulin, Valet de chambre de la Reine de Navarre." *Revue d'histoire littéraire de la France* 2 (1895), 469–90.

Chang, Leah. "The Gender of the Book: Jeanne de Marnef Edits Pernette du Guillet." In *Early Modern Women and Transnational Communities of Letters*, edited by Julie D. Campbell and Anne R. Larsen, 97–120. Aldershot: Ashgate, 2009.

_____. *Into Print: The Production of Female Authorship in Early Modern France.* Newark: University of Delaware Press, 2009.

Charpentier, Françoise. "Diane Lyonnaise." In *Le mythe de Diane en France au XVIe siècle*, edited by Jean-Raymond Fanlo and Marie-Dominique Legrand, 25–38. Cahiers D'Aubigné; Albineana 14. Niort; Paris: Librairie Honoré Champion, 2002.

______. "Projet poétique, travail poétique dans les *Rymes* de Pernette du Guillet: Autour de trois quatrains." In *Poétique et Narration: Mélanges offerts à Guy Demerson*, edited by François Marotin and Jacques-Phillippe Saint-Gérand, 143–55. Paris: Champion, 1993.

Clark-Evans, Christine. "L'art et l'amour dans *Les Rymes* (1545) de Pernette du Guillet." *Le Moyen Francais* 35–36 (1996), 161–73.

______. "The Brain and the Nervous System in Two French Renaissance 'Scientific' Poets: Pernette du Guillet and Guillaume du Bartas." *Bibliothèque d'Humanisme et Renaissance* 65 (2003), 289–303.

______. "On the Communion of Women: Reading and Writing in the Poetry of Pernette du Guillet and Louise Labé." *Proceedings of the PMR Conference: Annual Publication of the International Patristic, Mediaeval and Renaissance Conference* 12–13 (1987–88), 67–80.

Clément, Michèle, and Janine Incardona, eds. *L'émergence littéraire des femmes à Lyon à la Renaissance, 1520–1560*. Saint-Etienne: Publications de l'Université de Saint-Etienne, 2008.

Cottrell, Robert. "Pernette du Guillet's *Rymes*: An Adventure in Ideal Love." *Bibliothèque d'Humanisme et Renaissance* 31 (1969), 553–71.

Cox, Virginia. *The Renaissance Dialogue: Literary Dialogue in Its Social and Political Contexts, Castiglione to Galileo*. Cambridge: Cambridge University Press, 1992.

______. "Seen But Not Heard: The Role of Women Speakers in Cinquecento Literary Dialogue." In *Women in Italian Renaissance Culture and Society*, edited by Letizia Panizza, 385–400. Oxford: European Humanities Research Centre, 2000.

Davis, Natalie Zemon. "Le monde de l'imprimerie humaniste: Lyon." In *Histoire de l'édition française*, vol. 1, *Le livre conquérant*, edited by Henri-Jean Martin and Roger Chartier, 255–77. Paris: Promodis, 1983.

______. "The Sacred and the Body Social in Sixteenth-Century Lyon." *Past and Present* 90 (February 1981), 41–70.

______. *Society and Culture in Early Modern France*. Stanford: Stanford University Press, 1975.

Defaux, Gérard, ed. *La génération Marot: Poètes français et néo-latins, 1515–1550*. Actes du colloque de Baltimore, 5–7 décembre 1996. Paris: Honoré Champion, 1997.

_____, ed. *Lyon et l'illustration de la langue française à la Renaissance*. Paris: ENS, 2003.

_____. "Marot et 'Ferme Amour': Essai de mise au point." In *Anteros*, edited by Ullrich Langer and Jean Miernowski, 137–67. Orléans: Paradigme, 1994.

Delaney, Susan. "Lyric Dialogue in the 'Ring' Poems of Pernette du Guillet and Maurice Scève." *French Review* 68:5 (April 1995), 822–29.

DellaNeva, Joann. "'Mutare / Mutatus': Pernette du Guillet's Actaeon Myth and the Silencing of the Poetic Voice." In *Women in French Literature: A collection of Essays*, edited by Michel Guggenheim, 47–55. Stanford French and Italian Studies 58. Saratoga, CA: Anma Libri, 1988.

_____. *Song and Counter-Song: Scève's "Délie" and Petrarch's "Rime."* Lexington, KY: French Forum, 1983.

Dobbins, Frank. "Lyons: Commercial and Cultural Metropolis." In *The Renaissance: From the 1470s to the end of the 16th century*, edited by Iain Fenlon, 197–215. Man and Music. Englewood Cliffs, NJ: Prentice Hall, 1989.

_____. *Music in Renaissance Lyon*. Oxford: Clarendon Press; New York: Oxford University Press, 1992.

_____. "Recueils collectifs de musique et de poésie." In *Le poète et son œuvre: De la composition à la publication*, edited by Jean-Eudes Girot, 147–71. Geneva: Droz, 2004.

Donaldson-Evans, Lance K. *Love's Fatal Glance: A Study of Eye Imagery in the Poets of the "Ecole lyonnaise."* University, MS: Romance Monographs, Inc., 1980.

_____. "The Taming of the Muse: The Female Poetic Voice in Pernette du Guillet's *Rymes*." In *Pre-Pléïade Poetry*, edited by Jerry C. Nash, 84–96. Lexington: French Forum Publishers, 1985.

Dumoulin, Maurice. "Ce qu'elles faisaient pour être belles." *Revue de la Renaissance* 9 (Geneva: Slatkine Reprints, 1968), 230–31.

Easthope, Antony. *Poetry as Discourse*. London: Methuen, 1983.

Eisenbichler, Konrad, and Olga Zorzi Pugliese, eds. *Ficino and Renaissance Neoplatonism*. Ottawa: Dovehouse Editions, 1986.

Festugière, Jean. *La philosophie de l'amour de Marsile Ficin et son influence française au XVIe siècle.* Etudes de philosophie médiévale 31. Paris: Librairie philosophique Vrin, 1941.

Fineman, Joel. *Shakespeare's Perjured Eye: The Invention of Poetic Subjectivity in the Sonnets.* Berkeley: University of California Press, 1986.

Finucci, Valeria. *The Lady Vanishes: Subjectivity and Representation in Castiglione and Ariosto.* Stanford: Stanford University Press, 1992.

Ford, Philip. "A propos des 'élégies' de Pernette Du Guillet." In *L'émergence littéraire des femmes à Lyon à la Renaissance, 1520–1560,* edited by Michèle Clément and Janine Incardona, 165–76. Saint-Etienne: Publications de l'Université de Saint-Etienne, 2008.

_____, and Gilian Jondorf. *Intellectual Life in Renaissance Lyon.* Proceedings of the Cambridge Lyon Colloquium, 14–16 April 1991. Cambridge: Cambridge French Colloquia, 1993.

Foucault, Michel. "What is an Author?" Translated by James Venit. *Partisan Review* 4 (1975), 603–14.

Galand-Hallyn, Perrine. "Le latin à la rescousse du français: Trois humanistes autour de Vénus éplorée." In *Lyon et l'illustration de la langue française à la Renaissance,* edited by Gérard Defaux, with the collaboration of Bernard Colombat, 308–43. Lyon: ENS Editions, 2003.

_____, and Fernand Hallyn. "'Recueillir des brouillars': Ethique de la silve et poétique du manuscrit trouvé." In *Le poète et son œuvre: De la composition à la publication,* edited by Jean-Eudes Girot, 9–34. Geneva: Droz, 2004.

Gascon, Richard. *Grand commerce et vie urbaine au XVIe siècle, Lyon et ses marchands.* Vol. 1. Paris: Ecole Pratique des Hautes Etudes and Mouton, 1971.

Genette, Gérard. *Paratexts: Thresholds of Interpretation.* Translated by Jane E. Lewin. Cambridge: Cambridge University Press, 1997.

_____. *Seuils.* Paris: Seuil, 1987.

Gerig, L. "Le Collège de la Trinité à Lyon avant 1540." *Revue de la Renaissance* 9 (1968), 73–94.

Girot, Jean-Eudes, ed. *Le poète et son œuvre: De la composition à la publication.* Geneva: Droz, 2004.

Goodrich, Peter. "Law in the Courts of Love: Andreas Capellanus and the Judgments of Love." *Stanford Law Review* 48:3 (February 1996), 633–75.

Gray, Floyd. *Gender, Rhetoric, and Print Culture in French Renaissance Writing*. Cambridge: Cambridge University Press, 2000.

Greene, Thomas M. *The Light in Troy: Imitation and Discovery in Renaissance Poetry*. New Haven: Yale University Press, 1982.

Griffin, Robert. "Pernette du Guillet's Response to Scève: A Case for Abstract Love." *Esprit Créateur* 5 (1965), 110–16.

Haahr, Joan G. "Justifying Love: The Classical Recusatio in Medieval Love Literature." In *Desiring Discourse: The Literature of Love, Ovid Through Chaucer*, edited by James J. Paxson and Cynthia Gravlee, 39–61. Selinsgrove, PA: Susquehanna University Press, 1998.

Heninger, S. K., Jr. *Touches of Sweet Harmony: Pythagorean Cosmology and Renaissance Poetics*. San Marino, CA: The Huntington Library, 1974.

Holmes, Olivia. *Assembling the Lyric Self: Authorship from Troubadour Song to Italian Poetry Book*. Minneapolis: University of Minnesota Press, 2000.

Huchon, Mireille. *Louise Labé, une créature de papier*. Geneva: Droz, 2006.

Hunkeler, Thomas. *Le vif du sens: Corps et poésie selon Maurice Scève*. Geneva: Droz, 2003.

Izzi, Liliane. "Lecture d'un dizain de Pernette du Guillet." *Courrier du Centre international d'études poétiques* 200 (1993), 15–41.

James, Karen Simroth. "On veult responce avoir: Pernette du Guillet's Dialogic Poetics." In *A Dialogue of Voices: Feminist Theory and Bakhtin*, edited by Karen Hohne and Helen Wussow, 171–97. Minneapolis: University of Minnesota Press, 1994.

______. "Pernette du Guillet: Spiritual Union and Poetic Distance." In *Feminism*, edited by A. Maynor Hardee and Freeman G. Henry, 27–37. French Literature Series 16. Columbia, SC: University of South Carolina, 1989.

______."Pernette du Guillet." In *Renaissance and Reformation, 1500-1620: A Biographical Dictionary*, edited by Jo Eldridge Carney, 121–22. Westport, CT: Greenwood Press, 2001.

Jondorf, Gillian. "Petrarchan Variations in Pernette du Guillet and Louise Labé." *Modern Language Review* 71:4 (October 1976), 766–78.

Jones, Ann Rosalind. "Assimilation with a Difference: Renaissance Women Poets and Literary Influence." *Yale French Studies* 62 (1981), 135–53.

_____. *The Currency of Eros: Women's Love Lyric in Europe, 1540–1620.* Bloomington: Indiana University Press, 1990.

_____. "Pernette du Guillet: The Lyonnais Neoplatonist." In *Women Writers of the Renaissance and Reformation*, edited by Katharina M. Wilson, 219–31. Athens: University of Georgia Press, 1987.

_____. "Surprising Fame: Renaissance Gender Ideologies and Women's Lyric." In *The Poetics of Gender*, edited by Nancy K. Miller, 75–95. New York: Columbia University Press, 1986.

Jordan, Constance. *Renaissance Feminism: Literary Texts and Political Models.* Ithaca: Cornell University Press, 1990.

Kalweis, H. H. "The *Responce* Genre in Early Modern French Renaissance Poetry." *Bibliothèque d'Humanisme et Renaissance* 65 (1983), 77–86.

Kelso, Ruth. *Doctrine for the Lady of the Renaissance.* Urbana: University of Illinois Press, 1978.

Kennedy, William J. *Authorizing Petrarch.* Ithaca, NY: Cornell University Press, 1994.

Kritzman, Lawrence. "Pernette du Guillet and a Voice of One's Own," chap. 1 in *The Rhetoric of Sexuality and the Literature of the French Renaissance.* Cambridge: Cambridge University Press, 1991.

Kushner, Eva. *Le dialogue à la Renaissance: Histoire et poétique.* Cahiers d'Humanisme et Renaissance 67. Geneva: Droz, 2004.

_____. "The Dialogue of Dialogues." In *The Dialogue in Early Modern France, 1547–1630: Art and Argument*, edited by Colette H. Winn, 259–83. Washington, DC: Catholic University of America Press, 1995.

La Garanderie, Marie-Madeleine de. *Christianisme & lettres profanes: Essai sur l'Humanisme français (1515–1535) et sur la pensée de Guillaume Budé.* Paris: Honoré Champion, 1995.

Larsen, Anne R., ed. and trans. *From Mother and Daughter: Poems, Dialogues, and Letters of Les Dames des Roches, The Other Voice in Early Modern Europe.* Chicago: University of Chicago Press, 2006.

_____. "'Un honneste passetems': Strategies of Legitimation in French Renaissance Women's Prefaces." *L'Esprit Créateur* 30:4 (1990), 11–22.

_____, and Colette H. Winn, eds. *Renaissance Women Writers: French Texts/American Contexts.* Detroit: Wayne State University Press, 1994.

Lesko Baker, Deborah. *The Subject of Desire: Petrarchan Poetics and the Female Voice in Louise Labé*. West Lafayette, IN: Purdue University Press, 1996.

Lloyd-Jones, Kenneth. "Writing the Language of Love: Lyonnais Poetry and the Portrayal of Passion." *Romance Languages Annual* 7 (1995), 112–19.

Maclean, Ian. *The Renaissance Notion of Woman: A Study in the Fortunes of Scholasticism and Medical Science in European Intellectual Life*. Cambridge: Cambridge University Press, 1980.

Martin, Henri-Jean. "Les imprimeurs et l'humanisme." In *Lyon, l'humaniste*, edited by Claude Royon, 67–74. Paris: Editions Autrement, 2004.

Martin, Pierre. "De Maurice Scève à Pernette du Guillet, ou le jeu d'Actéon." In *Le mythe de Diane en France au XVIe siècle*, edited by Jean-Raymond Fanlo and Marie-Dominique Legrand, 39–55. Cahiers D'Aubigné; Albineana 14. Niort; Paris: Librairie Honoré Champion, 2002.

Martinez, C. "Conde Claros de Adonis." In *Il Rinascimento a Lione*, edited by Antonio Possenti and Giulia Mastrangelo, 683–97. Rome: Edizioni dell'Ateneo, 1988.

Mathieu-Castellani, Gisèle. "Les enfants de Marot." In *Clément Marot, «prince des poëtes françois», 1496–1996*, Actes du colloque international de Cahors en Quercy, 1996, edited by Gérard Defaux and Michel Simenon, 713–35. Paris: Honoré Champion, 1997.

_____. "La parole chétive: Les *Rymes* de Pernette du Guillet." *Littérature* 73 (February 1989), 50–51.

_____. "Parole d'Echo? Pernette au miroir des *Rymes*." *L'Esprit Créateur* 30:4 (1990), 61–71.

_____. *La quenouille et la lyre*. Paris: José Corti, 1998.

Mazzotta, Giuseppe. "The Canzoniere and the Language of the Self." *Studies in Philology* 75 (1978), 271–96.

Merrill, Robert. *Platonism in French Renaissance Poetry*. New York University Press, 1957.

Miller, Joyce. "In the Margins of Amatory Discourse: The *Responces* of Pernette du Guillet." *Sixteenth-Century Journal* 24:2 (Summer 1993), 351–68.

Murphy, Stephen. "The Death of Actaeon as Petrarchist Topos." *Comparative Literature Studies* 28:2 (1991), 137–55.

Nardone, Jean-Luc. *Pétrarque et le pétrarquisme.* Paris: Presses Universitaires de France, 1998.

Panizza, Letizia, ed. *Women in Italian Renaissance Culture and Society.* Oxford: European Humanities Research Center, 2000.

Perry, T. A. "Pernette du Guillet's Poetry of Love and Desire." *Bibliothèque d'Humanisme et Renaissance* 35 (1973), 259–71.

Planté, Christine. "Tout.e écrivain.e est 'de papier.'" In *L'émergence littéraire des femmes à Lyon à la Renaissance, 1520–1560,* edited by Michèle Clément and Janine Incardona, 257–72. Saint-Etienne: Publications de l'Université de Saint-Etienne, 2008.

Raffini, Christine. *Marsilio Ficino, Pietro Bembo, Baldassare Castiglione: Philosophical, Aesthetic, and Political Approaches in Renaissance Platonism.* New York: Peter Lang, 1998.

Rajchenbach, Elise. "'Tu le pourras clerement icy veoir': les *Rymes* de Pernette Du Guillet, publication vertueuse ou stratégie éditoriale?" In *L'émergence littéraire des femmes à Lyon à la Renaissance, 1520–1560,* edited by Michèle Clément and Janine Incardona, 123–64. Saint-Etienne: Publications de l'Université de Saint-Etienne, 2008.

Read, Kirk. "Poolside Transformations: Diana and Actaeon Revisited by French Renaissance Women Lyricists." In *Renaissance Women Writers: French Texts / American Contexts,* edited by Anne R. Larsen and Colette Winn, 38–54. Detroit: Wayne State University Press, 1994.

______, and François Rigolot. "Discours liminaire et identité littéraire: Remarques sur la préface féminine au XVIe siècle." *Versants* 15 (1989), 75–98.

Rieu, Josiane. "Pernette du Guillet: Poétique et réflexivité dans les Rymes (1545)." In *Dans les miroirs de l'écriture: La réflexivité chez les femmes écrivains d'Ancien Régime,* edited by Jean-Philippe Beaulieu and Diane Desrosiers-Bonin, 33–47. Montreal: Département d'Etudes Françaises, Université de Montréal, 1998.

Rigolot, François. *L'erreur de la Renaissance: Perspectives littéraires.* Paris: Honoré Champion, 2002.

______. *Louise Labé Lyonnaise, ou la Renaissance au féminin.* Paris: Honoré Champion, 1997.

Risset, Jacqueline. *L'anagramme du désir: Essai sur la Délie de Maurice Scève.* Rome: Mario Bulzoni Editore, 1971.

Romier, Lucien. "Lyons and Cosmopolitanism at the Beginning of the French Renaissance." In *French Humanism, 1470–1600*, edited by Werner L. Gundersheimer, 90–109. London: Macmillan, 1969.

Rothstein, Marian. "Pernette du Guillet." In *French Women Writers: A Bio-bibliographical Source Book*, edited by Eva Martin Sartori and Dorothy Wynne Zimmerman, 143–52. New York: Greenwood Press, 1991.

Roussel, Brigitte. "Pernette du Guillet." In *Encyclopedia of Woman in the Renaissance: Italy, France, and England*, edited by Diana Robin, Anne R. Larsen, and Carole Levine, 176–79. Santa Barbara, CA: ABC-CLIO, 2007.

Sankovitch, Tilde. *French Women Writers and the Book: Myths of Access and Desire*. Syracuse, NY: Syracuse University Press, 1988.

_____. "Inventing Authority of Origin: The Difficult Enterprise." In *Women in the Middle Ages and the Renaissance: Literary and Historical Perspectives*, edited by Mary Beth Rose, 227–43. Syracuse: Syracuse University Press, 1986.

Saulnier, V-L. "Etude sur Pernette du Guillet et ses *Rymes*." *Bibliothèque d'Humanisme et Renaissance* 4 (1944), 7–119.

_____. "Mellin de Saint-Gelais, Pernette du Guillet et l'air 'Conde Claros.'" *Bibliothèque d'Humanisme et Renaissance* 32:3 (1970), 525–37.

Shapiro, Norman, ed. and trans. "Pernette du Guillet." In *French Women Poets of Nine Centuries: The Distaff and the Pen*, 120–33. Baltimore: The Johns Hopkins University Press, 2008.

Skenazi, Cynthia. *Le poète architecte en France: Constructions d'un imaginaire monarchique*. Paris: Honoré Champion, 2003.

Smarr, Janet Levarie. *Joining the Conversation: Dialogues by Renaissance Women*. Ann Arbor: University of Michigan Press, 2005.

Stallybrass, Peter. "Patriarchal Territories: The Body Enclosed." In *Rewriting the Renaissance: The Discourses of Sexual Difference in Early Modern Europe*, edited by Margaret W. Ferguson, Maureen Quilligan, and Nancy J. Vickers, 123–42. Chicago: University of Chicago Press, 1986.

Sturm-Maddox, Sara. *Petrarch's Metamorphoses: Text and Subtext in the Rime Sparse*. Columbia: University of Missouri Press, 1985.

Tetel, Marcel. "Le luth et la lyre de l'Ecole Lyonnaise." In *Il Rinascimento a Lione*, edited by Antonio Possenti and Giulia Mastrangelo, 949–62. Rome: Edizioni dell'Ateneo, 1988.

Vianey, Joseph. *Le pétrarquisme en France au XVIe siècle*. Montpellier: Coulet et fils,1909. Geneva: Slatkine Reprints, 1969.

Vickers, Nancy. "Diana Described: Scattered Woman and Scattered Rhyme." *Critical Inquiry* 8 (1981), 265–79.

Wiesner, Merry E. *Women and Gender in Early Modern France*. Cambridge: Cambridge University Press, 1993.

Wilson, Katharina M., ed. *Women Writers of the Renaissance and Reformation*. Athens: University of Georgia Press, 1987.

Winn, Colette H. "Le chant de la nouvelle née: Les *Rymes* de Pernette du Guillet." *Poétique* 78 (April 1989), 207–17.

_____, ed. *The Dialogue in Early Modern France, 1547–1630: Art and Argument*. Washington, DC: Catholic University of America Press, 1993.

_____. "La femme écrivain au XVIe siècle: Ecriture et transgression." *Poétique* 84 (1990), 435–52.

_____. "Mirrors of the Subject: Women Poets of the Renaissance." In *Understanding French Poetry: Essays for a New Millennium*, edited by Stamos Metzidakis, 121–38. Birmingham, AL: Summa Publications, 1994.

_____. "Le procès du même et de l'autre: Pernette du Guillet et le mythe ovidien de Diane et Actéon." In *Les représentations de l'Autre du Moyen Age au XVIIe siècle*, edited by Evelyne Berriot-Salvadore, 263–71. Saint-Etienne: Publications de l'Université de Saint-Etienne, 1995.

_____, and Anne R. Larsen, eds. *Renaissance Women Writers: French Texts / American Contexts*. Detroit: Wayne State University Press, 1994.

Yandell, Cathy. *Carpe Corpus: Time and Gender in Early Modern France*. Newark: University of Delaware Press, 2000.

_____. "Carpe Diem, Poetic Immortality, and the Gendered Ideology of Time." In *Renaissance Women Writers: French Texts / American Contexts*, edited by Anne R. Larsen and Colette Winn, 115–29. Detroit: Wayne State University Press, 1994.

Zecher, Carla. *Sounding Objects: Musical Instruments, Poetry, and Art in Renaissance France*. Toronto: University of Toronto Press, 2007.

Zegura, Elizabeth Chesney, ed. *The Rabelais Encyclopedia*. Westport, CT: Greenwood Press, 2004.

Index